DISCRETION IN CRIMINAL JUSTICE

SUNY Series in New Directions in Criminal Justice Studies
Austin T. Turk, Editor

DISCRETION IN CRIMINAL JUSTICE

The Tension Between Individualization and Uniformity

edited by

LLOYD E. OHLIN
and
FRANK J. REMINGTON

State University
of New York
Press

Published by
State University of New York Press, Albany

Production by Susan Geraghty
Marketing by Dana Yanulavich

Printed in the United States of America

For information, address State University of New York
Press, State University Plaza, Albany, N.Y. 12246

Library of Congress Cataloging-in-Publication Data

Discretion in criminal justice : the tension between
    individualization and uniformity / edited by Lloyd E. Ohlin and
    Frank J. Remington.
        p.   cm. — (SUNY series in new directions of crime and justice
    studies)
    Includes bibliographical references and index.
    ISBN 0-7914-1563-5. — ISBN 0-7914-1564-3 (pbk.)
    1. Criminal justice, Administration of—United States—Decision
making. 2. Police discretion—United States. 3. Judicial
discretion—United States. I. Ohlin, Lloyd E. II. Remington,
Frank J., 1922– . III. Series.
HV9950.D6   1993
364.973—dc20   92–30233
                                                                      CIP

10 9 8 7 6 5 4 3 2 1

CONTENTS

Acknowledgments   *xi*

Foreword by Michael Tonry   *xiii*

Chapter 1   Surveying Discretion by Criminal Justice
Decision Makers   1
Lloyd E. Ohlin

    The American Bar Foundation Survey   5
        The Survey Origins   5
        Research Methodology   7
        Major Observations of the Survey 9
    The Pilot Project Reports and the Survey Books   12
    The Impact of Ideology on Practice and Research   14
    Policy Choices   16

Chapter 2   Confronting the Complexity of the
Policing Function   23
Herman Goldstein

    Introduction   23
    The State of Knowledge Before the ABF Survey   24
    The American Bar Foundation Survey   28
        Methodology   29
        Substantive Findings   30
    Developments Since the ABF Survey   39
        The Varied Nature of the Police Function 40
        The Infinite Variety of Situations Police
            Are Called on to Handle 44
        The Varied Uses of Arrest   47
        The Prevalence of Discretion in Policing 52
        The Police Decision Not to Arrest 56
        The Criminal Justice System as a System 58
    Conclusion   60

Chapter 3   The Decision to Charge,
    the Decision to Convict on a Plea of Guilty,
    and the Impact of Sentence Structure
    on Prosecution Practices   73
    Frank J. Remington

        Introduction   73
        The Charging and Guilty Plea Decisions
                as Seen in the Pre-ABF Research   77
            The Charging Decision   78
            The Guilty Plea Decision   80
            Summary   85
        The Charging and Guilty Plea Decisions
                in the ABF Research   85
            The Charging Decision   86
            The Guilty Plea Decision   91
            Lessons Learned in the ABF Research
                on Charging and Guilty Plea Decisions   92
        Post-ABF Developments   96
            The Charging Decision   96
            The Guilty Plea Decision   100
            The Changing Roles of Trial Judge,
                Prosecutor, Defense Counsel, and
                Victim in the Charging and
                Guilty Plea Decisions   106
        Conclusion   109

Chapter 4   Sentencing, Parole,
    and Community Supervision   135
    Walter J. Dickey

        Introduction   135
        Pre-ABF Research and Developments   136
            Classical and Positivist Theories   136
            Implementation of Rehabilitative Theory
                in American Practices   138
            Ideological Framework of the
                Pre-ABF Research   139
            Pre-ABF Research Findings   140
            Sentencing Discretion in Pre-ABF Research   143
            Conclusions on Pre-ABF Research   144
        The American Bar Foundation Research   146

Trial Judge Sentencing in Wisconsin
 as Described by the ABF Research 147
Parole Release in Wisconsin 148
Probation and Parole Supervision in Wisconsin 149
Significance of the ABF Research 150
Post-ABF Research and Developments 151
The Experience in Wisconsin
 After the ABF Survey—
 Sentencing and Parole Release 159
Conclusion: Discretion in Sentencing
 and Corrections on the National Scene 164

Chapter 5 Criminal Justice Responses
to Domestic Violence 175
Raymond I. Parnas

The ABF Survey's Contribution
 to Domestic Violence Issues 176
Related Developments on Domestic Violence Issues 180
Influences on the Development of
 Full Enforcement Policies 185
Research Findings on Full Enforcement 189
The Future: From Low Visibility to
 High Visibility; From Adjustment
 to Arrest; So What? 193

Chapter 6 Police Rule Making and the
Fourth Amendment: The Role of the Courts 211
Wayne R. LaFave

Police Rule Making and the Fourth Amendment 214
Impoundments and Inventories: The *Bertine*
 "Standardized Procedure" Requirement 218
Inspections: The *Camara* "Reasonable...
 Administrative Standards" Requirement 226
Stops: By "Plan" or By "Profile" 231
Arrests: Police Limits on Force and Custody 240
The Role of the Courts to Date 248
Remaining Problem Areas 256
Denouement 268

Chapter 7   The American Bar Foundation Survey and the
Development of Criminal Justice Higher Education   279
Donald J. Newman

Criminal Justice Education   280
    Development of Educational Materials   281
    Summer Seminars for Legal and
        Social Science Scholars   282
    Law Student Summer Field Placements
        in Criminal Justice Agencies   283
    Problems with Teaching and Researching
        Criminal Justice in Law School Settings   284
    Creation of the State University of New York
        and the First School of Criminal Justice   286
    Governor Nelson Rockefeller and
        the State University of New York   286
    Origins of the School of Criminal Justice
        at Albany   288
    The Role of Eliot Lumbard   288
    Meeting the Personnel Needs of
        Criminal Justice Agencies   290
    Early Consultants to the Albany School   292
    The Planning Year: Creation of
        the Albany Model   294
    Criminal Justice Education Defined   295
    Graduate Curriculum in Criminal Justice:
        The Albany Model   297
    Structure of the School:
        Faculty and Student Criteria   299
    The Albany School After Twenty Years   300
The Spread of Criminal Justice Higher Education   301
    The Federal Office of Manpower and Training   302
    Criminal Justice Education Proselytizers   304
    The Creation of the Academy of
        Criminal Justice Sciences   306
    Survival After the Demise of LEAA   306
    Location and Identity in Universities
        and Colleges   308
    Location on New and Secondary Campuses   309
    Why Survival and Growth?   310

The American Bar Foundation Survey and
    Criminal Justice Education Today 311
Major Contributions of the ABF Survey
    to Criminal Justice Higher Education 313
Contrary Developments and Unanticipated
    Consequences in the Academic Field of
    Criminal Justice 315
The Future of Criminal Justice Education 333
    Solidifying the Field 333
    Location on Prestigious Campuses 334
    New Student Populations 334
    Curriculum Standardization 336
    Research Trends 337
    Increased Professionalism of On-Line Personnel 340
Conclusion 341

Appendix A   *About the Authors* 351

Appendix B   *Project Participants* 355

Index 357

ACKNOWLEDGMENTS

The authors express appreciation to the Ford Foundation and particularly to President Franklin Thomas and Vice-President Susan Beresford for their assistance, without which this book would not have been written.

Francis A. Allen; Huber C. Hurst, eminent scholar and professor at the University of Florida; Sanford H. Kadish, Morrison Professor at the University of California, Berkeley; Jack Ladinsky, professor of sociology, University of Wisconsin; and Victor G. Rosenblum, Nathaniel L. Nathanson Professor at Northwestern; participated in a three-day conference and shared with us their insight and views about the history of efforts to deal with the difficult problems that have confronted the criminal justice system. The opportunity to benefit from their experience was of great value to us.

Sue Center and the staff of the Criminal Justice Reference and Information Center at the University of Wisconsin Law School provided helpful bibliographic assistance.

Lucille Hamre had responsibility for the editorial clarity and accuracy of the text and citations.

And Diane Roessler furnished much of the basic secretarial service.

We acknowledge, with appreciation, the permission to quote from the following materials:

Albert W. Alschuler, The Failure of Sentencing Guidelines: A Plea for Less Aggregation, 58 U. Chi. L. Rev. 901 (1991).

Frank J. Remington, Book Review, Fair and Certain Punishment, 29 Vand. L. Rev. 1309 (1976).

Anthony G. Amsterdam, Perspectives on the Fourth Amendment, 58 Minn. L. Rev. 349 (1974).

Study Finds No Way For Police to Predict Domestic Homicides, 21 Crim. Just. Newsl. 3 (1990).

Silas J. Wasserstrom and Louis Michael Seidman, The Fourth Amendment as Constitutional Theory, 77 Geo. L.J. 19 (1988).

Herman Goldstein, Trial Judges and the Police, 14 Crime & Delinq. 14 (1968) (Sage Publications).

Joseph Goldstein, Police Discretion Not to Invoke the Criminal Process: Low-Visibility Decisions in the Administration of Justice, 69 Yale L.J. 543 (1960); and Steve Y. Koh, Reestablishing the Federal Judge's Role in Sentencing, 101 Yale L.J. 1109 (1992)(Yale Law Journal and Fred B. Rothman & Co.).

Samuel H. Pillsbury, Understanding Penal Reform: The Dynamic of Change, 80 J. Crim. L. & Criminology 726 (1989).

Herbert L. Packer, The Model Penal Code and Beyond, 63 Colum. L. Rev. 594 (1963).

Frank J. Remington, The Limits and Possibilities of the Criminal Law, 43 Notre Dame Lawyer 865 (1968).

Lynn M. Mather, Comments on the History of Plea Bargaining, 13 Law & Soc'y Rev. 281 (1979); and Malcolm M. Feeley, Perspectives on Plea Bargaining, 13 Law & Soc'y Rev. 199 (1979).

The Bureau of National Affairs, Inc., 4 BNA Criminal Practice Manual 568 (1990).

Charles L. Becton, The Drug Courier Profile: "All Seems Infected That Th' Infected Spy, As All Looks Yellow to the Jaundic'd Eye," 65 N.C. L. Rev. 417 (1987).

Steven L. Winter, *Tennessee v. Garner* and the Democratic Practice of Judicial Review, 14 N.Y.U. Rev. L. & Soc. Change 679 (1986).

Carl McGowan, Rule-Making and the Police, 70 Mich. L. Rev. 659 (1972).

Gerald M. Caplan, The Case for Rulemaking by Law Enforcement Agencies, 36 Law & Contemp. Probs. 500 (1971); Jerry V. Wilson and Geoffrey M. Alprin, Controlling Police Conduct: Alternatives to the Exclusionary Rule, 36 Law & Contemp. Probs. 488 (1971); and H. Richard Uviller, The Unworthy Victim: Police Discretion in the Credibility Call, 47 Law & Contemp. Probs. 15 (1984) (Duke University Law School).

FOREWORD

Michael Tonry

If only policymakers today had learned the lessons of the "American Bar Foundation Survey of Criminal Justice" in the 1950s, many blunders could have been avoided. It becomes ever more apparent that many policy initiatives of the 1970s and 1980s were misconceived and ineffective. Every state and the federal government enacted mandatory penalty laws; many jurisdictions adopted sentencing guidelines of varying degrees of rigidity; some abolished parole release; some banned plea bargaining. Some of these changes were misconceived in that they ignored the complexity of the criminal justice system and the near certainty that efforts to eliminate discretion will move it someplace else. Many of the changes were ineffective in that they failed to deter crime or reduce disparities, their ostensible rationales. Often they were circumvented by lawyers, judges, and corrections officials, too often they treated defendants unjustly, and nearly always there were unintended, undesired consequences.

The ABF survey, an intensive examination of criminal justice processes from defendants' first contacts with the police through processing by prosecutors and courts to probation and parole supervision and revocation, was the most extensive and, probably in constant dollars, most expensive empirical investigation of the criminal justice system ever undertaken. In *Discretion in Criminal Justice*, Lloyd Ohlin and Frank Remington and their colleagues describe the survey, its findings, the base of knowledge on which it stood, and subsequent developments concerning the issues and practices it identified.

Discretion in Criminal Justice may be more timely in the 1990s than in the 1950s, when the survey was conducted, or in the 1960s, when five books reported its findings. In the 1950s and 1960s indeterminate sentencing was little challenged; it was taken for granted that rehabilitation was a primary goal and that judges and correctional officials needed ample discretion to tailor sentences to offenders' needs and prospects. Today, by contrast, few see rehabilitation as a primary goal of sentencing, and official discretion is widely distrusted—from the right, from concern for the chimera of "undue leniency"; from the left, from concern that discretion will be exercised invidiously or capriciously. Because exercise and control of discretion are central modern policy issues, the survey's evidence on how discretionary systems operate is especially salient.

The survey's findings punctured myths and illuminated insights. Among the demolished myths were belief in the desirability or the existence of full enforcement of the law by the police, the belief that it is possible to eliminate discretion within the system, the belief that the primary police role is law enforcement, and the belief that attrition of cases after arrest implies inefficiency, corruption, or both.

The key findings documented the distance between the law in action and the law in books. First, most of the important discretionary decisions are made at the bottoms, not the tops, of bureaucracies—the cop on the street, the assistant district attorney, and the line probation officer decide when not to take action and often what action to take. The concerns and perceptions of low-level officials are at least as important to understanding how decisions are made as are the ostensibly governing laws and policies. Second, the survey demonstrated the interconnecting complexity of the criminal justice system, the myriad ways that multiple actors make or shape decisions, and the even more complex patterns of interactions among different officials. Third, the survey revealed the practical and normative problems in balancing the competing calls for unstinting application of legal rules and sensitive appreciation of situational and human needs—whether posed by plea bargaining or by police arrests in cases in which individualized probable cause cannot be shown. Fourth, the survey documented the systems quality of the criminal justice system, the "hydraulic" nature of discretion, the certainty that efforts to limit the discretion of some officials nearly inexorably lead to shifts of discretion to other officials. Fifth, the survey demonstrated how court "work groups," with their own sets of patterned relations and norms, importantly shape how the system works overall and in individual cases.

In the years since Maine in 1975 abolished parole and became the first determinate sentencing jurisdiction, followed by countless innovations elsewhere intended to structure, confine, limit, or abolish discretion, stacks of research reports have confirmed the ABF survey's findings and documented foreseeable, undesirable consequences that could have been avoided. Mandatory penalty laws have produced widespread circumvention, cynical manipulation, and gross injustices and have undermined the system's credibility. Harsh and mechanical sentencing guidelines have encountered comparable resistance, circumvention, and hypocrisy. Plea bargaining bans have seldom done more than trigger compensating changes in other processes. Parole abolition has removed the institutional capacity to reduce aberrantly long sentences and to ameliorate prison crowding. As the 1990s unfold, policymakers are again beginning to understand that quick fixes do not solve complex problems, that the interacting discretions of the criminal justice system make mechanistic solutions unrealistic.

The great value of this book is not in the memorialization of a path-breaking research project and the tracing of its influence but in its lessons for the here and now. The survey is at least as relevant to our time as to its own, and if this book redirects the attention of researchers and policymakers to the original survey's findings, it will have accomplished a great deal.

It is curious that the survey is less well known than its originality, size, and enduring relevance might make one expect. Although most of the published reports deal with court processes, the survey's clearest influence has been on police research and policy. A spate of publications on police discretion based on the survey appeared long before the books that reported the survey's findings. By the mid-1960s, social scientists interested in the police had followed the survey's then-innovative practice of putting researchers into police cars to observe how police do their jobs, giving rise to the most important case studies of policing in modern times—by Egon Bittner, Albert J. Reiss, Jr., Jerome Skolnick, James Q. Wilson, and others. A path leads to the police policy experiments of the 1970s and 1980s and to the policy prescriptions of problem-oriented and community-based policing in the 1980s and 1990s.

Influence on prosecution, sentencing, probation, and parole is less apparent. It is bewildering that policy debaters in the 1970s and 1980s argued over whether restraints on judicial discretion would shift power to the prosecutor, rather than over what the survey showed to be the real questions: how much power would be shifted, in what circumstances, and with what effect. Similarly, social science research in the 1970s and 1980s on prosecutorial and judicial discretion, on court work groups, and on the effects of policy innovations reveals little awareness of the ABF survey, often to the detriment of the more recent work. Empirical investigations of the effects of changes in sentencing policy, for example, often look only at disposition of cases once they result in formal charges or indictments and blithely ignore the possibility—entirely predictable from the survey—that policy changes may alter prosecutors' decisions about charges or indictments or cause shifts in the locus of plea bargaining from post- to preindictment, making comparisons of case dispositions postindictment inherently misleading.

Why the survey did not have more influence on social science research is unclear. One possible explanation may be that the survey's origins lay in the legal community and its execution largely in the hands of lawyers. A second may be that the volumes, when they appeared, were published by Little, Brown, a publishing house familiar to lawyers and legal scholars, but less familiar to social scientists. A third is that the five reports were published ten to fifteen years after the data were collected, and inferences about timeliness and topicality may have become confused. Whatever the explanation, both the quality of social science research and the wisdom of criminal justice policy have suffered.

The survey had substantial indirect influence on criminal justice policy and research through the careers of the scholars who shaped it and were shaped by it. In a fascinating story that is probably until now known only by insiders, Donald Newman tells of the origins of the School of Criminal Justice at Albany, which became the model for criminal justice education in the United States and had its roots in the survey. The primary and most influential advisor to the State University of New York in creating the school was Frank Remington, director of field research for the survey. Newman himself, then working in Wisconsin on survey data, was invited to become the school's first dean and became its second. The initial teaching materials at Albany focused on the survey's methods and findings and led to a delineation between "criminology," the subdiscipline of sociology interested in the origins and manifestations of deviance, and "criminal justice," in which Albany specialized, focusing on the operations and effects of the criminal justice system. Within the law schools, for many years the only textbooks in use for teaching criminal justice administration were developed by lawyers and social scientists who had worked on the survey. Finally, the survey created a cadre of influential policy-concerned scholars whose careers placed them in positions of great influence. Some of this is briefly noted in appendix A.

The survey's findings, especially as reported and revivified in the essays in this book, are as fresh and timely today as they were forty years ago. I hope that this time the research and policy communities will read and heed and avoid in the 1990s the avoidable mistakes of the 1970s and 1980s.

CHAPTER 1

Surveying Discretion by Criminal Justice Decision Makers

Lloyd E. Ohlin

Current efforts to curb crime and drug use are creating a massive overload on the criminal justice system. This is especially true of the correctional system. Legislatures have enacted longer minimum and maximum sentences, more mandatory penalties, less discretion and more punitive guidelines for judges, and more repressive measures for drug use and sale; eliminated or curtailed parole; and tremendously increased appropriations to build, staff, and operate new prisons and jails. The increase in the United States of confined persons under correctional supervision, especially since 1985, has been awesome. On December 31, 1985, 488,000 persons were in federal and state prisons; by 1990, the number reached 745,000, an increase of 53 percent. From the end of June 1985 to 1990, the number of persons in jails grew from 255,000 to 403,000, an increase of 58 percent. The number under probationary and parole supervision in the community grew by 41 percent from year end 1985 to 1990, or from 2,269,000 to 3,202,000 persons. Thus the approximate daily count of persons under correctional supervision totaled 4,350,000 in 1990.[1]

What accounts for these developments? Undoubtedly the public fear of crime fed by increases in criminal violence, struggles for control of the drug trade, and increasing evidence of public disorder, especially in the urban centers, has generated a mood that evokes support for more punitive measures. In addi-

1

tion to the newly confined drug offenders, new networks for discovering the physical and sexual abuse of women and children has added large numbers of offenders to jail and prison populations. Changes in the attitudes toward drinking drivers have also increased jail populations. Officials responding to public concern have urged greater police efforts, not just to reduce drug use and sale, but to dip deeper into the pool of criminal law violators and to forward these offenders to an increased number of prosecutors and judges. The perception that imprisonment is the only meaningful weapon to repress crime has also led to longer mandated sentences and in general a significant increase in legislated restrictions on discretion throughout the criminal justice system.

Members of the academic community concerned with criminal justice issues have also provided major support for these developments. During the 1970s and 1980s a voluminous literature was created debating the merits of different philosophies and strategies of punishment and crime control.[2] Should the guiding principles of sentencing be based on a retributive philosophy of "just deserts" that seeks the equalization of punishment based on the nature of the current offense? Or should sentences primarily reflect a more utilitarian objective such as the deterrence of future crimes by offenders and others like them? Is it best to pursue a policy of prolonged incapacitation by imprisonment of those perceived as most dangerous, most violent, or most likely to commit more crimes? Or should the rehabilitation and reintegration of offenders be our ultimate objective?

The greatest impact on current sentencing policies has been achieved by those academics and allied interest groups who have argued for either retribution, deterrence, or incapacitation as the primary objective. In each case the aim is to distribute punishments uniformly to achieve equality and predictability in the sentences imposed on similarly situated offenders who meet specified criteria. These criteria, of course, differ among these three objectives. The test for retribution is the heinousness of the crime, the amount of harm done in the instant offense. The tests for deterrence are judgments about the ability of the sentence to deter the offender and others from criminal acts in the future. The test for incapacitation is the prediction of dangerousness. In practice these tests are applied singly or in combination.

The important point, however, is that separately or together these objectives and their criteria tend to increase the use of incarceration as the only meaningful punishment, especially in criminal justice systems where probation or imprisonment are the only viable options. Furthermore, the stress on uniformity to maximize predictability and equality in the imposition of punishments leads inevitably to constraints on the ability to take account of many significant individual differences among offenders and the circumstances of their offenses. If uniformity is the central concern, curtailment of the discretion of decision makers becomes inevitable. In practice it leads to the specification of a small number of factors that must be taken into account in sentencing. The current popularity of guidelines for sentencing and parole decisions is testimony to this outcome.[3] Grids that specify sentencing actions to be taken based on offense and criminal record are common, though sometimes harm to the victim and use of a weapon are added criteria. Constraints are greater when the range between the minimum and maximum sentence is narrow and limitations on the ability to take account of mitigating or aggravating circumstances are strict. The problem is that individualization to take into consideration in sentencing the complex interaction of offender, victim, offense, and situation becomes impossible under these conditions.

It should not be assumed that the attack on the allocation and use of discretion is confined to sentencing decisions alone. Parole boards are being eliminated or their discretion curtailed by legislated mandatory sentences or judicial use of split sentence provisions in which part of the sentence must be served in confinement and part under community supervision. Attempts have also been made to limit the freedom of prosecutors to engage in charge or plea bargaining. The police use of discretion has also been challenged, most notably in the mandatory use of arrest in responding to domestic violence complaints. All of these efforts to limit discretion by frontline practitioners are discussed more fully in the chapters that follow. Underlying some efforts is the assumption that discretion is too easily abused, that it produces disparity in processing similarly situated offenders, that it leads either to excessive leniency or punitiveness, and that it must be controlled by legislative mandates. The current metaphor of a "war" on crime and drug trafficking lends ideological support because it calls for highly punitive measures in situations where the discretion to employ different types of crime control measures may constitute a more desirable and effective response.

In all of these relatively recent efforts to cope with the crime problem, therefore, the most vexing problem has involved the allocation, use, and control of discretion. As noted above, the resolution of these matters varies with the dominant objectives in criminal justice and the ideological commitments of the times. Always evident is a tension between the individualization of decision making and the desire for uniformity and predictability. In effect we want responsiveness to individual differences in persons and events and also fairness and equity in distributing penalties or benefits. How are we to achieve a proper balance? Uncertain about what to do, policies vacillate between dependence on the integrity, professionalism, and problem-solving capacity of criminal justice practitioners and rigid mandates and controls over discretion.

This allocation, use, and control of discretion is the central theme explored in this book. Our intent is to examine the current trends to curtail the discretion of criminal justice decision makers and to explore the cost this policy imposes on the capacity of the system to respond effectively to crime problems. To gain perspective on the relevant issues today, we make use in the following chapters of the results of the "American Bar Foundation Survey of Criminal Justice in the United States." This survey provided a well-grounded benchmark for assessing the state of knowledge about discretion in criminal justice. It examined the nature of the problems encountered by frontline practitioners in criminal justice agencies and the appropriate role of discretion in responding to them. Though the field work phase of the survey was conducted in three states—Wisconsin, Kansas, and Michigan—in 1955 through 1957, the research methodology generated a set of data that is still unique and highly relevant to our exploration of the role of discretion in criminal justice today. One reason is that it employed an ethnographic approach by sending field observers to report the problems encountered, the actions taken, and the considerations involved in making the decisions. Another reason is that observations were made at the same time on the uses of discretion by the police, prosecutors, courts, and probation and parole personnel in the same criminal justice system. It also provided comparable data on different state systems. Finally, it took place at a time when most states operated under an indeterminate sentencing system that provided a very large measure of freedom in making decisions, in contrast to the more prevalent determinate sentence systems today.

A review of the major insights and observations about decision making in the criminal justice system that were generated offer relevant cautions about the effect of current policy trends. They offer a clear reminder that the distrust of official discretion and the consequent attempts to legislate uniformity in decision making produce a rigid equality that cloaks much injustice. Similarly the assumption that greater use of incarceration and longer sentences is the only effective sanction for controlling crime is creating chaos in corrections and in state budgets. It neglects the utility and cost-benefit of intermediate punishments between prison and probation of community-based custody, surveillance, and treatment programs.[4] It neglects a range of dispositional alternatives that should be built into the options available to police, prosecutors, judges, and correctional administrators.

THE AMERICAN BAR FOUNDATION SURVEY

Our primary objective in this book is not to provide a historical account of the findings of the ABF survey, for that is already available in various published sources.[5] Instead, in the following chapters we use these findings where appropriate to highlight problems we now face in allocating discretion in criminal justice. To provide background for this inquiry, however, we provide here a brief account of the organization, methodology, and products of the survey. This leads to a discussion of the impact of ideology on practice and research and, finally, a consideration of policy choices.

The Survey Origins

In the early 1950s, the American Bar Association decided it was once again time to analyze criminal justice in the United States.[6] A survey by the Wickersham Commission,[7] for example, conducted in the early 1930s was out of date. A grant was received from the Ford Foundation, and planning was begun on what was intended as a pilot study of the three states. It was hoped that, eventually, other states would be included, but this was not to be. The information gathered from the three pilot states was so extensive that the survey ended, many years later, with publication of five books based on the initial data.

The first chairman of the American Bar Foundation's Advisory Committee on this study was Robert H. Jackson, associate justice of the Supreme Court. After his death General William J. Donovan and then Harold A. Smith were named chairman. Each of these outstanding leaders strongly supported the research effort. Justice Jackson urged an open-ended inquiry by the Bar Foundation survey to discover how criminal justice actually works and what its problems are.[8]

Arthur Sherry, professor of law at the University of California, was appointed as the overall project director. The on-site leader of the project was Frank J. Remington, professor of law at the University of Wisconsin, who was both director of field research and the editor of the series of books that was eventually published based on the field studies. Lloyd Ohlin, a sociologist with a research appointment at the University of Chicago, was the chief consultant on the field work of the survey.[9]

Remington decided from the outset that the ABF survey would be different from earlier studies, much less concerned with official summary statistics and more concerned with the analysis of the criminal justice system in daily operation. He and Lloyd Ohlin met with the other consultants, all experts in some aspect of crime control, to develop a general approach to the field work. Various focuses were considered. One approach would call for looking at specific problems ranging from one- or two-man squad cars to the police use of force on the street. A second approach would look at official roles; for example: Who are the police? How are they recruited and trained? Who are prosecutors? What are the duties and functions of judges? System corruption and brutality could well have been a theme. All of these were rejected in favor of an approach that concentrated on decision making. What do the police, prosecutors, judges, and probation and parole officers actually do in everyday practice? What decisions do they make? How do they go about making them? What alternative decisions are possible, and why is one alternative chosen in a given situation? It was to be an attempt to look at what the police and other official actors actually do, rather than what statutes, cases, or public expectations say they should do. It was to be a study of law in action rather than of the law on the books. It was to be an attempt to understand the everyday world of criminal justice agencies engaged in the processing of offenders, including the issues and circumstances surrounding each major decision point.

Research Methodology

The basic research technique was qualitative and ethnographic. It involved field observation of daily practices—the types of situations encountered and the actions taken. As in many classic sociological and anthropological studies, the major aim was understanding rather than measurement. The focus was on discovering how official actors defined the situation, the criteria used to make decisions, and the choice of alternative actions: Do police arrest persons with no intention to prosecute? Why? What situations are involved?

Observational research has fallen on hard times in this computer era, but even back then some advisors, mostly sociologists, wanted "hard data" collected. Remington pointed out, quite correctly, that until we know the right questions to ask and are aware of the range and complexity of the problems, attempting to measure anything is futile.

Field teams of observers were sent into the cities and rural areas of the three states that had been selected. They rode in police cars on all shifts with all units. They observed station house behavior. They watched prosecutors review cases and charge defendants. They sat in courtrooms, talked to judges, and watched arraignments and sentencing. They spent time with probation officers, read presentence investigation reports, and observed supervision. They sat with parole boards and came to understand the release and revocation decisions. They wrote their observations in "field reports," which were collected and roughly classified and coded. Because the field observers had such a broad mandate ("observe actions, probe decision, and write it down"), the field reports filled many file cabinets.[10]

The survey methodology employed was not without its roots in prior efforts both in its intellectual orientation and in its research approach. It would be important to recognize the work of the progressives in the early decades of this century and subsequent interest in a sociological jurisprudence. The empirical work on the criminal justice surveys of the 1920s and 1930s was heavily influenced by Roscoe Pound's advocacy of the importance of studying the law in action. In 1920 Pound, dean of the Harvard Law School, was widely recognized as a vocal crusader for law reform and court reorganization in America. He endorsed the idea of a sociological jurisprudence and was in touch with prominent sociologists of the day, Albion Small and E. A. Ross. Pound agreed to direct the Cleveland Crime Survey and devoted over half of the final report in 1921 to an exposition of his views on sociological jurisprudence and "legal realism."[11] Nevertheless it was his advocacy in behalf of criminal law reform and his interest in the facts about law in action that set the pattern for subsequent work and, in particular, the influential Missouri Crime Survey in 1926 and the Illinois Crime Survey in 1929.[12]

The Cleveland, Missouri, and Illinois surveys concentrated on gathering official data on the flow of cases through the criminal justice system. When cases were diverted from full enforcement, for whatever reason, they were regarded as evidence of case mortality and a failure of the process. Such failures were attributed to incompetence or corruption. They were regarded as evidence of the need for reforms to make the criminal justice system a more effective instrument for coping with crime and halting the publicly perceived epidemic of lawlessness. But these surveys did not develop data on what was happening subsequent to arrest in criminal justice as a system of case processing.

Another important strand contributed to the research design of the American Bar Foundation project. This came from the research orientation of the sociologists at the University of Chicago. Under the early influence of Robert Park and Ernest Burgess, great stress was placed on the importance of field observation to advance understanding of whatever social phenomena were being studied. The city was an urban laboratory to be explored firsthand in the field. In addition, Professor Everett Hughes and his students at Chicago were undertaking pioneering work on the use of participant observation in the study of organizational structure and operations. They demonstrated the feasibility of studying organizations through the use of field observers, a research technique equally applicable to the study of criminal justice agencies. Ohlin had recently received his doctoral degree in sociology at the University of Chicago and collaborated with Frank Remington to build this research approach into the survey.

What was especially unique about the ABF survey in contrast to the earlier efforts was the focus on gathering information on decision making in the various agencies of criminal justice and the simultaneous conduct of field work on the system as a whole. Since then many useful studies of decision-making processes, cited in the following chapters, have been conducted in the individual agencies of criminal justice from police to probation and parole. However, the ABF survey stands alone in its systemic approach to studying criminal justice in action and in its ability to assess the importance of discretion in responding to the complexity of cases at each major decision point. As the field work progressed in Wisconsin, Kansas, and Michigan, the focus on observing decision making and probing for the underlying reasons became the central task of the field work.

Major Observations of the Survey

The ABF survey research focused, for the first time, on *low-visibility* decisions of all participants in the criminal justice system. "Low-visibility" referred to crime investigation and case processing not commonly litigated, not ordinarily mentioned in codes or standards, and not known by persons outside the system. The revelation of low-visibility decisions and the universality of discretion in applying the criminal law was a major contribution of the Bar Foundation research. And high visibility decisions— arrest, formal charges, adjudication, and imposition of sentence—were highlighted, too. Indeed the relationship of low visibility to more commonly exposed decision points was a major thrust of the research. An important result was increased visibility of formerly sub rosa practices, a number of which were a focus of the earlier crime surveys as well, especially the effect of prosecutorial practices on the mortality of cases. Police stopping and questioning suspicious persons, prosecutors reducing charges or promising lenient sentences in exchange for guilty pleas, judges sentencing defendants on the basis of individualized consequences rather than the conviction label alone, and parole release decisions for reasons other than risk of reviolation—all these processes and more were still not widely known or understood, were rarely reflected in formal criminal justice literature, and almost never appeared in appellate court decisions. And yet this was the way the criminal justice process daily went about its business. It involved choices, judgments, and the sensible exercise of discretion in tailoring formal criminal law and procedures to the myriad variety of persons and circumstances of cases caught in the enforcement net.

In addition to showing the universal exercise of discretion and reasons for it, beyond making visible a nearly invisible process of law enforcement, a major contribution of the Bar Foundation research was to demonstrate the *complexity* of the criminal justice process. The circumstances requiring judgments by law enforcement and correctional personnel were often extremely complicated, not easily categorized or controlled. Fitting possible sanctions to the multiplicity of problems falling under criminal statutes and dealing with persons and circumstances of almost endless variations in culpability and cultural background were delicate matters calling for imaginative and sensible judgments on the part of system personnel. Choices necessarily lead to consequences, and of course the likely consequences (Will crime stop? Will persons be helped?) affected the choices in the first place.

Yet the system itself was in relative homeostatic balance. The various parts of the system were so interdependent, the resources allocated in such a fashion that attempts to change any one part, to control any one decision point, affected the others. Discretion denied to sentencing judges by legislatively mandated prison terms simply pushed sentencing choice and variations back to the prosecutors in their bargaining capacity. Early parole release of chronic offenders affected police practices in the communities to which they were returned. In short, the Bar Foundation showed a system of complex individualization of justice, adaptively balanced, not easily controlled, and certainly not inevitably improved by attempts to mandate choices, remove discretion, or impose well-meaning but simplistic panaceas on such a highly complex process.

The Bar Foundation research revealed a system much like that described in the assembly-line, crime-control model in Packer's two systems.[13] All major agencies and most major decision points were the focus of the ABF research. It also explored the reciprocal links between decisions made at different points.

This emphasis on the functioning of the total system was a contribution of the project that had particular significance for the later development of criminal justice as an academic field.

The total system overview provided an essential integrating concept for organizing the research and analyzing the interactive effects of the constituent agencies. But when this concept is overextended, it leads to the neglect of the subsystems operating within these agencies. In daily activity involving the processing of individual cases, the police, for instance, rarely concern themselves with how their practice impacts on the system. This seems too esoteric, too far down the line. In general, the police respond the best they can to a problem that falls within their bailiwick (often because there is no other agency to deal with it) and attempt to work out sensible solutions. The question rarely asked is how increased arrests of child molesters, drunk drivers, wife batterers, and the like would affect the correctional system. Instead the police deal with such problems as very much their own, except in aggravated cases that are forwarded to the prosecutor to invoke the full criminal process. In short, the police in particular have their own little systems of justice, with intake and output, in which moving on to further stages is an exception. In a way the ABF survey stress on the total system from investigation to parole lent itself occasionally to abuse and oversimplification in failing to focus sufficiently on other criminal justice responses short of full involvement of the decision network.

In Packer's model, the production units move cases along from intake labeling, court processing, and final correctional packaging without diversion or much loss. But the criminal justice process reduces the cases processed from its broadest net of police intervention to final incarceration in jail or prison. Certainly, the cases that go all the way demonstrate the system as a system. But absent rigid legislative mandates or other external controls on discretion, most persons caught in the net, most criminal cases, are not subject to maximum processing. So although full enforcement does exist as a total system, other more abbreviated systems exist within it to respond to the different problems and the infinite variety of persons dealt with by enforcement officials. The Bar Foundation emphasis on discretion, on low-visibility decisions, on the interlocking stages of the system, and on the astounding complexity of our crime control response was a major contribution to the understanding of criminal justice in our society.

THE PILOT PROJECT REPORTS AND THE SURVEY BOOKS

After the field teams finished, the seven-volume "Pilot Project Reports"[14] were prepared in which the field reports were ordered by area and roughly summarized. The reports focused primarily on data collected in the urban areas—Wichita, Milwaukee, and Detroit—where the types and volume of crime created the most pressure on the processes of criminal justice. The first volume dealt with the organization of the research effort, its history, staff organization, and methodology, its system for classifying the field reports and consultant commentaries, and information on budgetary allocations. The next five volumes focused on the way in which major decision points were dealt with in the cities, as did the subsequent books on crime detection, arrest, prosecution, conviction, and sentencing. The final volume assembled commentaries by the project director and also by the four consultants on police, prosecution and defense, courts and sentencing, probation and parole.

These "Pilot Project Reports" were used to conduct summer seminars at the University of Wisconsin Law School in 1958, 1960, and 1963. Interested scholars from a number of disciplines, such as sociology, social work, law, and political science, were invited to attend the seminars in 1958 and 1960, and young criminal law teachers were invited for the 1963 session. These seminars captured the different interests of the participants and led to a number of articles published in law reviews and social science journals.[15] Several of these publications focused scholarly attention and stimulated a burgeoning literature: an article in 1960 by Prof. Joseph Goldstein of the Yale Law School on the discretion of the police not to invoke the criminal process in low-visibility decisions;[16] an article in 1962 by Prof. Sanford Kadish examining the tension between legal norms and discretion in police and sentencing policies;[17] and articles by Herman Goldstein, Frank Remington, Wayne LaFave, and Donald Newman that are reflected in the chapters they have written for this book. What is important to note is that work continued at a steady pace to absorb, analyze, and disseminate the results of the

ABF research. An important monograph by Donald M. McIntyre, Jr., for the American Bar Foundation disseminated the contents of the field and pilot project reports from the observations in Detroit, Michigan.[18]

Eventually, under the editorship of Frank Remington, five books based on the survey were published. These books covered most of the major decision stages in the criminal justice process. All published by Little, Brown and Co., they are:

Detection of Crime: Stopping and Questioning, Search and Seizure, Encouragement and Entrapment by Lawrence P. Tiffany, Donald M. McIntyre, Jr., and Daniel Rotenberg; ed. Frank J. Remington (1967);

Arrest: The Decision to Take a Suspect into Custody by Wayne R. LaFave; ed. Frank J. Remington (1965);

Prosecution: The Decision to Charge a Suspect with a Crime by Frank W. Miller; ed. Frank J. Remington (1969);

Conviction: The Determination of Guilt or Innocence without Trial by Donald J. Newman; ed. Frank J. Remington (1966); and

Sentencing: The Decision as to Type, Length, and Conditions of Sentence by Robert O. Dawson; ed. Frank J. Remington (1969).

Notice the long time involved from the start of the field project to the final product. Planning began in about 1953, field teams were out in 1955, 1956, and 1957, and the final volume in the series was published in 1969. A total of some sixteen years! Was it worth it? I think there is no doubt that it was. The delay in producing the preliminary reports and the final books was unavoidable. During the field work, to facilitate open access to frontline actors at work, confidentiality was promised. Assurances were also given that the survey was interested not in exposes of malpractice but in the way in which problems were defined and resolved. To protect this guarantee, the pilot project reports were made available in a limited distribution to those who required access for scholarly purposes and who pledged to respect confidentiality in the use of the material. As noted above, they were used effectively in the summer sessions at the University of Wisconsin Law School. (For a fuller description of these seminars, see the chapter by Donald J. Newman.) Out of these sessions emerged the plan for the five books. Ordering, analyzing, and digesting the voluminous data in the field reports took time and dedication by the authors and the constant oversight of Frank Remington.

THE IMPACT OF IDEOLOGY ON
PRACTICE AND RESEARCH

In theory, empirical research carefully conducted and executed should be unaffected by the popular ideology of the time. In reality, ideology has an important effect on the selection of issues for study and on the acceptability of conclusions reached by the research.

Over the past seven decades, the principal ideological alternatives have been belief in the importance of dramatizing the seriousness of criminal behavior (for example, by imposing punishment measured to reflect the seriousness of the harm caused) versus a belief in the ability to devise a criminal justice response that will achieve more diverse and individualized objectives (for example, rehabilitation of the offender).

The prevalence of one belief over another has varied. In the 1920s and 1930s and, again, in the 1970s and 1980s, the dominant ideological commitment was to full enforcement (arrest, prosecution, conviction, and prisons) at least against those who engage in serious crime. In contrast, in the 1940s, 1950s, and 1960s the commitment was to more varied objectives like the reduction of crime by dealing with causes of crime, such as poverty, and the rehabilitation of those who engage in criminal conduct. These latter themes are examined in the chapter by Walter Dickey.

The impact of the popular ideology on the empirical research of the time is plainly evident. During the decades when the emphasis was on dramatizing the seriousness of criminal conduct, research was concerned with the failure to arrest and prosecute persons who commit offenses; with the dismissal of cases in which prosecution had previously been commenced; with accepting a plea of guilty to a lesser offense or to less than the original number of offenses that had been charged; and with sentences believed to be overly lenient or disparate. The obvious research assumption was that less than full arrest, charging, conviction, and punishment detracts from the ability of the criminal justice system to deal effectively with the conduct involved. A principal illustration is in research on the guilty plea, a topic more fully developed in the chapter by Frank Remington. At times when the ideological emphasis was on dramatizing the seriousness of the criminal conduct, the guilty plea, at least the negotiated plea, was seen in the early surveys as the cause of undesirable case mortality. The assumption was that the "law" defined the desirable outcome of the case and failure to fully enforce the law was seen as a weakness in the system. This explains why the early surveys gave much less attention to the work of police. If the function of police was merely to enforce the written law, police obviously did not make important decisions like the prosecutor's decision to charge or accept a guilty plea to a lesser offense or the trial judge's choice of sentence.

The current ideology not only influences the focus of empirical research but also affects the attention given to the research findings. At a time when severity and full enforcement are the ideological commitment, there is a greater willingness to accept the validity of research critical of plea bargaining, research supportive of mandatory arrest and prosecution in domestic violence cases, and research on sentence guidelines designed to restrict judicial discretion to a sentence calculated to reflect the seriousness of the conduct involved. (For a fuller discussion of mandatory arrest policies in domestic violence disputes, see the chapter by Raymond Parnas.)

In the forties, fifties, and sixties, the dominant ideology reflected faith in the possibility of bringing about social change and rehabilitation of the individual offender. The ABF research afforded the opportunity to learn about the practices, decisions, and experiences of frontline practitioners and factors they considered in identifying objectives and socially desirable and effective responses to the problems they confronted. This approach maintained that attention has to be focused on those who deal directly with the problems on a day-to-day basis, because understanding and evaluating the objectives of current criminal justice responses can be understood adequately only if one knows in detail what methods are in fact being used and with what results. In addition, observing criminal justice practices at the level at which they take place forces confrontation with the complexity of the problems and the improbability of simple solutions.

Undoubtedly, periodic swings in popularity from uniformity and severity of punishment, on the one hand, to individualization and treatment of offenders, on the other, will continue. We are already seeing such a change as skepticism about the utility of tough law enforcement as a response to the drug problem is being reflected in increased calls for treatment of drug abusers as a preferable response.[19]

POLICY CHOICES

The important question is whether the empirical research of the past affords a firm basis on which to develop criminal justice policies to respond adequately to the complexity of the problems encountered. In our view, the ABF research demonstrates that in research studies it is helpful, indeed essential, that the experiences, practices, and views of those at the bottom, those who confront the problems on a day-to-day basis, be given prominence in deciding what criminal justice policies are workable and, within that context, assist greatly in deciding what practices and policies are desirable. For example, the ABF survey and subsequent research demonstrate quite clearly that a policy of full enforcement as a uniform objective is probably undesirable, but is unattainable in any event. No system has yet been created that can prevent the exercise of discretion at some stage of the process. The desire to individualize the treatment of offenders by frontline practitioners is very strong. In addition, evidence is increasing that the public is more willing to support the exercise of discretion by practitioners to individualize the treatment of offenders than is ordinarily assumed.[20]

Difficulty occurs where empirical reality and ideological commitment conflict, as is the case when the dominant ideology favors uniform and severe punishment of all offenders. One way to deal with this conflict between ideology and reality is to create a system committed to the myth, but not to the reality, of full enforcement. This is a politically attractive alternative because it seems as if one can "eat one's cake and have it, too." This has been common in the past when the visibility of many criminal justice decisions, particularly by the police, meant that the conflict between reality and ideology was hidden from view. The difficulty lies in the loss of control over the use of discretion and the loss of knowledge about significant differences in offenses and offenders and the impact of varied responses. The result is a lack of accountability and an inability to evaluate the methods being used. Recognizing the complexity of the task seems clearly preferable.

Also preferable is recognizing the necessity of making decisions about individuals, the need to exercise judgment and discretion, and the need to structure the system so that all of this can be done in an open, responsible manner. It would then be possible to evaluate the work of police and the criminal justice system by the extent to which the decisions that are made effectively respond to the problems being confronted. This approach focuses attention on frontline decision makers. It deemphasizes the formalities of procedure and doctrine and instead focuses attention on how these procedures and doctrines are implemented in practice. It highlights the importance of understanding the wide variety of problems being dealt with, especially by the police. And it makes clear that overly simple, if ideologically popular, responses will not work.

The authors of the chapters in this book were involved in the field research of the American Bar Foundation survey or prepared articles, books, or teaching materials utilizing the results of that survey. Shades of difference exist among them in reactions to the tensions between individualization and uniformity—for example, with respect to the use of mandates, guidelines, or rules to achieve equity and predictability. Some would place much greater emphasis on the need to individualize responses through greater flexibility in decision making and on the development of accountability through mechanisms other than mandates, quantitative guidelines, and rules. Others would prefer a system that uses these measures, such as written policies or rules, in varying ways, depending on the behavior of concern.

There would, however, be agreement that the current assault on discretion by criminal justice officials may be producing a system that is too rigid in application and likely to be unresponsive to the need to temper criminal justice with social justice. Most of the authors would endorse a position stated as follows:

> Complexity is a fundamental attribute of the variety of problems officials encounter at all major points of decision in

the system of criminal justice. Responses to criminal offenders must address this fact if they are to be sufficiently flexible to take account of individual differences. A prevalent response at present is to try to simplify this complexity through the use of mandatory guidelines. Though these have a role to play, the tendency is to apply them too rigidly. They then fail to allow for adequate consideration of the detailed facts of individual cases. The best resource for decision making is a responsible official adequately trained, properly guided, well motivated, and fully accountable.

Much of the effort in recent decades has been to create ways to deal with the incompetent, poorly trained, improperly motivated decision maker, an obviously important objective. But the substitution of rigid rules and quantitative criteria for the exercise of intelligent judgment has limited the ability of the competent practitioner to deal with the complex problems being confronted. Rewarding excellence is much more likely to make a significant contribution than is attempting to prevent incompetence by removing flexibility and the exercise of judgment from decision making.

Charting a middle course that neither ignores nor oversimplifies the appropriate response is possible. It stresses the need to support and encourage the exercise of thoughtful discretion by police, prosecutors, trial judges, and correctional personnel, which is where the frontline responsibility for dealing with crime and criminals resides. It requires training in decision making that is guided by the basic values of a democratic society and professional norms of conduct. It also requires constructive use of supervision, review procedures, and policy development involving frontline decision makers. It calls for rules that do not take the form of mandated action but require attention to the criteria that should guide action and inform sensible judgments. The challenge is to devise controls that preserve and nurture that kind of discretion.

NOTES

I am indebted to Frank Remington and Herman Goldstein for many useful notes and suggestions that I have incorporated in this chapter. I especially wish to acknowledge my indebtedness to Don Newman for his description of the ABF study organization, process, and products, which appears here in edited form. Jack Ladinsky, in notes and conversation, gave me a much richer appreciation for the intellectual roots of the survey approach we employed.

1. Department of Justice, Bureau of Justice Statistics, Bulletin: *Probation and Parole 1990* (Washington, D.C.: Department of Justice, Bureau of Justice Statistics, Nov. 1991), table 4. Numbers in the text are rounded to the nearest thousand.

2. It is not possible here to cite that literature in detail. Numerous citations are contained in the notes to the chapter by Walter Dickey. A recent reexamination of the philosophies and the issues they raise may be found in Edgardo Rotman, *Beyond Punishment: A New View on the Rehabilitation of Criminal Offenders* (New York: Greenwood Press, 1990).

3. Michael Tonry, "Structuring Sentencing," in *Crime and Justice: A Review of Research*, vol. 10, ed. Michael Tonry and Norval Morris (Chicago: University of Chicago Press, 1988), 267.

4. Michael Tonry and Norval Morris, *Between Prison and Probation: Intermediate Punishments in a Rational Sentencing System* (New York: Oxford University Press, 1990).

5. References to these may be found in note 15 below.

6. An initial product of the ABA decision to initiate a survey was a detailed plan that also describes an organization and early sponsorship. Arthur H. Sherry, *The Administration of Criminal Justice in the United States: Plan for a Survey to Be Conducted Under the Auspices of the American Bar Foundation* (Chicago: American Bar Foundation, 1955).

7. *Report of National Commission on Law Observance and Enforcement* (Wickersham Commission), 14 vols. (Washington, D.C.: U.S. Government Printing Office, 1931; Montclair, N.J.: Patterson Smith, 1968).

8. Robert H. Jackson, "Criminal Justice: The Vital Problems of the Future," *American Bar Association Journal* 39 (Aug. 1953):743.

9. For a list of the project participants, see appendix B.

10. "American Bar Foundation Survey of Criminal Justice: Field Reports" (1956; on file with the Criminal Justice Reference and Information Center, University of Wisconsin–Madison, Law School).

11. Roscoe Pound and Felix Frankfurter, *Criminal Justice in Cleveland: Report of the Cleveland Foundation Survey of the Adminis-*

tration of Criminal Justice in Cleveland, Ohio (Cleveland: Cleveland Foundation, 1922).

12. See The Missouri Association for Criminal Justice, *Missouri Crime Survey* (New York: Macmillan, 1926); Illinois Association for Criminal Justice, *The Illinois Crime Survey,* ed. John H. Wigmore (Chicago: Illinois Association for Criminal Justice in cooperation with the Chicago Crime Commission, 1929).

13. Herbert L. Packer, *The Limits of the Criminal Sanction* (Stanford, Calif.: Stanford University Press, 1968).

14. "American Bar Foundation Survey of Criminal Justice: Pilot Project Reports," 7 vols. (Dec. 1957, Mimeo.: on file with the Criminal Justice Reference and Information Center, University of Wisconsin-Madison, Law School).

15. Following is a list of publications to 1965 that preceded the publication of the five books:
Glenn M. Abernathy, "Police Discretion and Equal Protection," *South Carolina Law Quarterly* 14, no. 4 (1962):472–86;
Francis A. Allen, "Federalism and the Fourth Amendment: A Requiem for Wolf," in *The Supreme Court Review*, ed. Philip B. Kurland (Chicago: University of Chicago Press, 1961), 75;
Edward L. Barrett, Jr., "Police Practices and the Law—From Arrest to Release or Charge," *California Law Review* 50, no. 1 (1962):11–55;
Robert O. Dawson, "The Decision to Grant or Deny Parole: A Study of Parole Criteria in Law and Practice," *Washington University Law Quarterly* 1966:243;
Herman Goldstein, "Full Enforcement vs. Police Discretion Not to Invoke the Criminal Process," May 22, 1963 (paper presented at the National Institute of Police and Community Relations, Michigan State University);
Herman Goldstein, "Police Discretion: The Ideal Versus the Real," *Public Administration Review* 23 (1963):140;
Joseph Goldstein, "Police Discretion Not to Invoke the Criminal Process: Low-Visibility Decisions in the Administration of Justice," *Yale Law Journal* 69, no. 4 (1960):543–94;
Sanford H. Kadish, "Legal Norm and Discretion in the Police and Sentencing Processes," *Harvard Law Review* 75, no. 5 (1962):904–31;
Sanford H. Kadish, "The Advocate and the Expert—Counsel in the Peno-Correctional Process," *Minnesota Law Review* 45 (1961): 803–41;
Wayne R. LaFave, "Detention for Investigation by the Police: An Analysis of Current Practices," *Washington University Law Quarterly* 1962, no. 3:331–99;

Wayne R. LaFave, "The Police and Nonenforcement of the Law—Part I," *Wisconsin Law Review* 1962, no. 1:104–37;

Wayne R. LaFave, "The Police and Nonenforcement of the Law—Part II, *Wisconsin Law Review* 1962, no. 2:179–239;

Wayne R. LaFave and Frank J. Remington, "Controlling the Police: The Judge's Role in Making and Reviewing Law Enforcement Decisions," *Michigan Law Review* 63, no. 6 (1965):987–1012;

Frank W. Miller and Robert O. Dawson, "Non-Use of the Preliminary Examination: A Study of Current Practices," *Wisconsin Law Review* 1964, no. 2:252–77;

Frank W. Miller and Frank J. Remington, "Procedures Before Trial," *Annals* 339 (1962):111–24;

Frank W. Miller and Lawrence P. Tiffany, "Prosecutor Dominance of the Warrant Decision: A Study of Current Practices," *Washington University Law Quarterly* 1964:1–123;

Donald J. Newman, "The Effect of Accommodations in Justice Administration on Criminal Statistics," *Sociology and Social Research* 46 (1962):144;

Donald J. Newman, chap. 12 in *Applied Sociology: Opportunities and Problems,* ed. Alvin W. Gouldner and S. M. Miller (New York: Free Press, 1965);

Lloyd E. Ohlin and Frank J. Remington, "Sentencing Structure: Its Effect upon Systems for the Administration of Criminal Justice," *Law and Contemporary Problems* 23, no. 3 (1958):495–507;

Frank J. Remington, "Criminal Justice Research," *Journal of Criminal Law, Criminology and Police Science* 51, no. 1 (1960):7–18;

Frank J. Remington, "The Law Relating to 'On the Street' Detention, Questioning and Frisking of Suspected Persons and Police Arrest Privileges in General," *Journal of Criminal Law, Criminology and Police Science* 51, no. 4 (1960):386–94;

Frank J. Remington, "Social Change, the Law and the Common Good," (paper presented at the Tenth Annual National Institute on Police and Community Relations, East Lansing, Mich., 1964);

Frank J. Remington and Victor G. Rosenblum, "The Criminal Law and the Legislative Process," *University of Illinois Law Forum* 1960, no. 4:481–99;

Cyril D. Robinson, "A Proposed Study of Chicago Police Department Arrest Procedures to Determine the Proper Use of Summons and Notice to Appear," *Chicago Bar Record* 45, no. 9 (1964):434–42;

Daniel L. Rotenberg, "The Police Detection Practice of Encouragement," *Virginia Law Review* 49, no. 5 (1963):871–903.

16. J. Goldstein, "Police Discretion Not to Invoke," 543.

17. Kadish, "Advocate and the Expert," 803.

18. Donald M. McIntyre, Jr., *Law Enforcement in the Metropolis* (Chicago: American Bar Foundation, 1967).

19. M. Douglas Anglin and Yih-Ing Hser, "Treatment of Drug Abuse," in *Drugs and Crime,* ed. Michael Tonry and James Q. Wilson (Chicago: University of Chicago Press, 1990), 393.

20. John Doble, "Survey Shows Alabamians Support Alternatives," *Overcrowded Times* 2, no. 1 (1991):2.

CHAPTER 2

Confronting the Complexity of the Policing Function

Herman Goldstein

INTRODUCTION

The police constitute one of the most important institutions of government. The quality of our lives, especially in congested urban areas, is heavily dependent on them. But important as they are, the police, until recently, have not been the subject of studied attention. Little effort has been devoted to gaining an in-depth understanding of their function, their relationship to the law, their capabilities, and their effectiveness. Contributing to this neglect has been the strongly held popular view that the police are engaged in a relatively simple, straightforward job of enforcing the criminal law in an aggressive fashion—an essentially unambiguous function that demands physical strength, integrity, and determination more than knowledge, sensitivity, and thought.

Against this background, the ambitious "American Bar Foundation Survey of Criminal Justice" in the late 1950s was an important milestone in the history of policing in this country. It reversed the long pattern of neglect by opening a window, through its unique research methodology, into the world of policing. By accompanying police officers as they went about their day-to-day activities—in squad cars, on the streets, in private homes, and at their headquarters—the survey's field observers made visible the wide range of incidents that the police are expected to handle and the way in which they respond to them.

This new visibility, in turn, documented some of the complexities of policing. It raised difficult questions about, for example, the proper role of the police, the use of authority conferred on the police by the criminal law, the discretion exercised by individual police officers, and the relationship of policing to the rest of the criminal justice system.

Since the ABF survey, many studies have been completed that have added substantially to our understanding of policing. As a consequence, significant advances have been made in the quality of policing, especially in the past decade, due mainly to the increased awareness of the intricate nature of the police task. But efforts to recognize and confront the complexity of the police task constantly compete with the overwhelming, magnetic attraction of the simplistic model. Enormous pressures are constantly exerted on the police to conform their activities to the traditional, nondiscretionary, full-enforcement conception of what the police should do and how they should do it. These pressures grow more acute when problems for which the police are thought to be responsible, such as drugs, become more aggravated. When this occurs, little patience exists for using knowledge already acquired about the complexity of the police function and for confronting the perplexing issues that this new knowledge raises. And there is even less patience and support for new research.

This chapter is concerned with the growth in our understanding of the complexity of the police function over the past thirty-five years. It looks at the development of methods used to gain such understanding. And it looks at our ability to act on that understanding in an atmosphere in which there is constant tension between the need to face complexity and the pressures for simple responses. Since this volume takes the findings of the ABF survey as a point of reference, this chapter samples the larger picture of developments in policing by focusing on the experience and results of that survey and on the degree to which the police, legislatures, and others subsequently have addressed the issues initially identified by the survey.

THE STATE OF KNOWLEDGE BEFORE THE ABF SURVEY

In an effort to establish what was then known about the police, the planners of the ABF survey, which was launched in 1955, turned quite naturally to the literature on policing. The results of that search produced a surprisingly meager number of relevant works, occupying no more than a few feet on a library shelf, that included relatively little evidence of serious scholarship and research. The major works fell into several distinct categories: (1) reports on investigations of specific police agencies, (2) treatises on the organization and staffing of the police, (3) autobiographical reflections on policing by several especially thoughtful police administrators, (4) reports on police performance that were part of the wave of crime surveys in the 1920s, and (5) two in-depth observational studies.

Most of the material fell into the first category, consisting of reports on investigations into alleged wrongdoing and corruption or into the circumstances that led to major crises, such as the Boston police strike in 1919[1] or the police handling of the Chicago steel strike in 1937.[2] These reports tended to focus on organizational deficiencies and the need for police to maintain a neutral position regarding the social problems of the day. This was exemplified by the best known study, conducted by the National Commission on Law Observance and Enforcement (commonly known as the "Wickersham Commission"),[3] which examined the breakdown of law and order throughout the country after the failure of prohibition. It focused on, as the most serious problems, the use of the third degree and the structural defects in police administration, highlighting such matters as incompetent leadership, insecure executive tenure, and the lack of competent, efficient police officers.

The leading treatises reflected this same concern with the weaknesses in the police structure. Raymond Fosdick, Bruce Smith, and O. W. Wilson dwelt on the organization, staffing, and equipping of police agencies; on the need for insulation from political pressures; and on the development of a more professional form of management.[4] Wilson's text, *Police Administration*, in particular, was heavily prescriptive. The standards he established for a quality police agency gained wide acceptance and set the model for "professional" policing. The combined work of Fosdick, Smith, and Wilson shaped police organizations and service for several decades. As the experts in the field, their concentration on the management of police agencies and the absence of alternative perspectives had an enormous influence in defining those matters considered most important and deserving of the highest priority.

Three books, reflecting the views and experiences of two practitioners, were more thoughtful about the complexity and diversity of policing. Arthur Woods, the police commissioner of New York City from 1914 to 1918, first wrote *Crime Prevention*[5] in which, departing from the traditional views of the time, he explored crime control as a problem of prevention—discussing poverty, mental illness, alcoholism, drugs, and public cooperation relating to crime and policing. Subsequently, in a series of lectures at Yale published in *Policeman and Public*,[6] Woods examined the role of the police in society, the public conception of the police officer, and the policeman as judge and advocate of public interests against private intrusion.

August Vollmer, the chief of police of Berkeley, California, from 1905 to 1932, was the mentor of a whole generation of police administrators, including O. W. Wilson; and much of his contribution to policing is reflected in the work of others, like Wilson, and in reports such as that of the Wickersham Commission, of which he was a principal author. Vollmer, however, was by no means as narrowly oriented as is the professional model currently described as his legacy. In his major publication, *The Police and Modern Society*,[7] written after his appointment to the faculty of the University of California, he identifies and openly struggles with many of the complexities in policing: the conflicts within the police role and the sensitive nature of that role, the uses and limitations of the criminal law, the interdependence of the police and the community, and how best to deal with the wide range of behaviors the police are expected to handle. Most important, he complains repeatedly about the widespread ignorance of the complex nature of the police job and the failure of the public to learn about the problems the police confront. In this regard, he takes the police to task, arguing that, based on their firsthand knowledge, they ought to do more to educate the community and to advocate for needed changes.

The writings of Woods and Vollmer were exceptions and apparently did little to stimulate further inquiry about the issues they raised. And provocative as they were, they did not raise questions about the police role in deciding whether to conduct an investigation, whether to arrest, and whom to arrest. They said little about how police set their priorities, the role of the police in initiating a criminal prosecution, or the role of the police vis-à-vis that of the prosecutor, the trial judge, and those engaged in operating jails and prisons or in supervising those who were on probation or parole. More significantly, none of the above works described day-to-day police operations (except for Vollmer's accounts of some of his street experiences) or reported in a systematic way what police officers on the streets did and how they did it.

The crime surveys of the 1920s contained the first efforts of independent observers to collect hard data about police operations. The three most famous surveys, conducted in Cleveland, Missouri, and Illinois, were heralded for being scientific.[8] "They have provided for serious students of criminal law administration a body of information which it is possible to use in comparative studies and thus to remove from discussion of crime and its treatment some of the prejudices with which it is so full."[9] Because the focus of these studies was on the total response to the crime problem, they looked at the police function within what has since come to be referred to as the "criminal justice system," analyzing thousands of criminal cases. But the inquiries were devoted almost exclusively to collecting data for the application of newly developed methods of statistical analysis. They attached great significance to the number of arrests made and especially the number that were not prosecuted. Because they did not explore in depth the explanations for why arrests did not always result in a successful prosecution, the disparity was seen as indicative of sloppiness or corruption of the process. The surveys then moved quickly to exploring remedial measures, which took the form of recommendations regarding the organization and operation of police departments—recommendations not unlike those contained in the reports and treatises that had been written without benefit of such field research.

In examining the publications gathered prior to the start of the ABF survey, two works were discovered that seemed especially relevant. The first was very modest—an unusual inquiry by Samuel Bass Warner, a Harvard law professor who set out to study the law of arrest in an effort to ascertain whether the police could operate within its limitations and, if not, what changes were necessary to make it both a practical standard of police conduct and a safeguard of personal liberty.[10] He arranged to accompany police officers as they went about their job and subsequently summarized his findings in what may have been the first reported empirical study of police operations as they occur on the street. His observations led him to conclude, in sharp contrast with the other types of surveys, that the elimination of improper practices might best be achieved by refinements in the law of arrest that recognized the complexity of the situations police were called on to handle.

The second was a study by William Westley, a doctoral student in sociology at the University of Chicago. Depending heavily on interviews of police in Gary, Indiana, Westley acquired much previously unavailable information about the day-to-day operations of police officers—about the informal procedures used, the factors that influenced decision making, and the development of a subculture that separates the police from the community they serve. Completed in 1951, Westley's thesis got little attention for twenty years and was not published until 1970, when interest in police operations dramatically increased.[11] Along with the short Warner piece, it stands out in the skimpy literature then available on the police for its value as a description of what the police actually do—a description that challenged the prevailing image of the police and thus was a beginning in documenting the complexities of policing.

In summary, the literature on the police available prior to the ABF survey reflected a preoccupation with the organization of police agencies, the qualifications of officers, and various other factors that were thought to contribute to corruption and the abuse of authority. It reflected little knowledge or insight regarding the decisions that police made in their day-to-day operations.

THE AMERICAN BAR FOUNDATION SURVEY

If the ABF survey had followed its original plan for that portion of its inquiry relating to the police, it would not have added much to the sparse knowledge then available. Like the police field itself, the plan was heavily influenced by the prevailing perception of what was important in policing—the technical and administrative aspects of running a police agency. The detailed agenda for inquiry identified fifteen different categories of information that were to be systematically acquired, with all but two categories relating to the organization, administration, staffing, and equipping of a police agency.[12] The product would have been an inventory of the degree to which the police agencies conformed with the then-prevalent standards for managing a police agency. The two exceptions in the outline for study were the last categories that called for inquiries about "miscellaneous considerations" and areas of activity where civil liberties might be jeopardized. These categories apparently were tacked on as a concession to staff members who viewed them as more central to the study than any of the preceding thirteen categories.

Methodology

The decisions made about research methodology, at the beginning of field work, turned the study around and ultimately accounted for its successes. The methodology that was adopted called for field observers knowledgeable about policing to accompany police officers as they went about their regular business, absorbing all that they could. Emphasis was placed on getting a picture of the work of officers at the lowest level of the organization, in contact with citizens on the streets and in their homes. The field staff was encouraged to "hang around"; to ask and subsequently observe what was "hot"; to identify "critical incidents" and follow the handling of those incidents. They were instructed to report their observations in a nonjudgmental manner. Practices, issues, and problems that surfaced from these open-ended observations were then used to shape subsequent observations. Thus the observations, rather than a set of questions that reflected a prejudgment of what was important, steered the inquiry.

The resulting reports dictated by the field observers are, to this day, remarkable documents. With sometimes overwhelming detail, the observers clinically recorded what they saw while accompanying officers who were patrolling in squad cars, responding to citizens' calls for help, ferreting out criminal conduct, seeking to identify those responsible for committing crimes, conducting interrogations, arresting and jailing suspects, presenting cases to prosecutors, and testifying in court. No one previously had obtained such free access to a police agency and such graphic, candid accounts of the day-to-day operations of the police. This was all the more notable given the strong commitment to secrecy that Westley had discovered in his work.

Because of the richness of the original reports, using the detailed accounts requires a substantial investment of time. That is why those who have drawn on the results of the ABF survey have depended heavily on the two levels of analysis of the original data: the intermediate "Pilot Project Reports," in which an effort was made to make maximum use of the original reports to compile a composite picture of how the criminal justice system operated in each of the three major urban areas in which field observations were conducted (with some coverage of state systems where that was relevant); and the series of five published volumes whose authors, at a more abstract and generalized level of analysis, used the survey data to describe how critical decisions in the criminal process were made and how the survey data related to the exploration of issues then current.[13] Helpful as these publications have been, it is important to recognize that for the pure product of the ABF project, one must turn to the original reports of the field observers. Important, too, is the realization that the process of analysis and publication, which stretched over ten years, left much data "on the cutting room floor." Fortunately, the substantial number of individuals who were involved in the ABF project have drawn on the residue in various ways to help in addressing policy questions that were not the subject of coverage in the published volumes.

Substantive Findings

No single document presents in crystallized form the findings of the ABF survey. That realization emphasizes the unique character of the survey, for the primary objective was to produce a mass of data descriptive of the operations of the criminal justice agencies in the jurisdictions studied. Analysts in the latter stages of the study and others interested in the reported observations were left to mine the data from their unique perspective and for differing policy implications.

Now, however, one can retrospectively highlight the principal findings or themes relating to the police that were given greater visibility by the survey and thereby contributed to the gradual increase in awareness of the complexity of police operations. This is made possible by the passage of time, the publication of numerous works that drew directly on the ABF data, and many citations to the study and its progeny. Such retrospective attribution would obviously be subject to criticism if one were to claim the survey as the exclusive source of the findings, since there is no way to trace, with any precision, the development of such knowledge. But that is not my objective. Rather it is to use, as a starting point, a selection of the findings of the ABF survey and, acknowledging that these findings may have been duplicated, developed, and more widely disseminated by subsequent studies, reflect on the aggregate response to them since they were first identified.

The Police Do Many Things Besides Investigate Crime and Arrest Offenders   Given the initial impetus for the ABF survey and its focus on the increase in "crime," field observers were initially troubled that the research method that committed observers to accompanying police officers resulted in so much time being spent observing activities that, at the time, seemed peripheral to the interests of the survey. The application of the prevailing standards used to evaluate police operations would have used this experience to confirm the belief that police were overly burdened with miscellaneous tasks; that they were unable to concentrate on serious crime and should therefore be freed of many of these responsibilities. With the survey's unique research methodology, however, all the activities were faithfully recorded; their full significance was recognized in subsequent years.

What were police found to be doing? They were, for example, taking intoxicated persons into protective custody, clearing the streets of prostitutes, responding to a wide range of disputes, directing traffic and enforcing parking limits, checking alleged trespassers, investigating accidents, censoring movies and books, finding missing persons, checking suspicious circumstances, handling stray animals, providing first aid, and collecting overdue library books and the assessed fines. Aggregate data that the staff collected from sources like annual reports further confirmed the volume of such activities and their variety. The manner in which these incidents were categorized, frequently as "miscellaneous," reflected the police attitudes toward handling them.

All of the police departments studied viewed these miscellaneous activities as a drain on their resources, as the "garbage of policing." Special units within a department had a hierarchy of priorities that discounted the importance of categories of incidents, leaving them for regular patrol officers to handle. But, as will be noted in the subsequent discussion of nonenforcement, even patrol officers at the bottom of the status hierarchy defined many routine matters that came to police attention, such as domestic disputes, as not really part of the central police task and therefore dealt with them perfunctorily.

The ABF data make it clear this somewhat cavalier setting of priorities, consistent with a more simplistic notion of policing, concealed important decisions that, on exposure, drew attention to the complexity of the police function in the context of public expectations. The observations of day-to-day operations identified numerous factors that influenced the police response. It was apparent, for example, that the public expected the police to handle the incredibly wide range of problems without regard to how the police perceived the problems and without regard to whether the police had the authority, resources, or training to handle them. The public continued to turn to the police despite the police attitude and the questionable value of their response, probably because they had no one else to whom to turn.

From the police perspective, the significance of the interrelationship between different aspects of their operations was not clear, but it was generally recognized that some relationships existed. The full dimensions of what initially appeared to be a minor incident, for example, were not always apparent until after an investigation was made. Contact with intoxicated persons, vagrants, and prostitutes was often used by the police to develop information and gain cooperation relating to the investigation of more serious offenses. The substantial police involvement in an activity like traffic control, through the arrests made and the searches conducted, was used in various ways to control serious crime. On the other hand, some problems the police routinely handled had no relationship to serious crime but, nevertheless, demanded high priority because they affected community order and the level of fear felt by the community. Most important, in the ABF observations, was the realization that the police, through their mere presence, brought authority—however ambiguous that authority—to bear on unpredictable, critical, but difficult-to-categorize situations that required *some* form of authority. In summary, not only did the field observations document police involvement in many matters unrelated to serious crime but they also documented a perplexing entanglement of public expectations, pressures, limited definitions of authority, an interdependence of functions, and the realization that the police had to improvise their way through many situations. To assume that the criminal law alone defined the police function was clearly naive.

Even Within Conduct Labeled Criminal, the Incidents the Police Are Called on to Handle Are Infinite and Unpredictable, Requiring Flexibility in Responding to Them   The ABF observations drew attention to the loose manner in which, in the interests of simplicity, *crime* and *criminal* are used both by the public and by those operating within the criminal justice system. The attraction in using these terms apparently stems from some assumptions about what will automatically follow: for example, that the behavior will be condemned, that the police will be responsible for handling the behavior, and that the police have the necessary authority to take action by making an arrest.

"Crime" obviously included homicide, burglary, and robbery. But it also included trespass, drunkenness, truancy, and the showing of movies containing nudity, because these forms of behavior were also clearly proscribed as criminal. And although "crime" was always used to describe the conduct on which the police were supposed to focus, the ABF research disclosed that police were in fact responsible for responding to a wide variety of community problems that, if they could be labeled criminal at all, came— often with some stretching—under such statutes as vagrancy and disorderly conduct. Authority to deal with this wide range of community problems was frequently conferred by making the conduct a violation of county or city ordinances, which, at least in Wisconsin, made such conduct, from the legal perspective, a civil forfeiture violation. Thus, problems commonly perceived by the community as criminal often involved behavior that was outside the conduct prohibited by the criminal law.

Because the ABF reports described in great detail the specific incidents that the police handled, they drew attention to the broad range of conduct commonly lumped under the umbrella of crime. Within categories of specific crime labels (like assault, burglary, and certainly disorderly conduct), they illustrated with unusual clarity the endless number of unpredictable variables that distinguished one incident that the police handled from another (e.g., the presence of mental illness, the involvement of alcohol, the relationship between the victim and the offender, the age of the alleged offender, the prior record of the individuals involved). The police were pressured to ignore these distinctions; to fit the incidents into categories for disposition that masked these important differences.

Despite these pressures, however, the ABF survey found that individual police officers, in many of the cases they handled, did distinguish between incidents. They often improvised in their responses to take note of the variables, using criteria that, depending on who reviewed them, might be praised or condemned and with results that were equally mixed. The varied responses, viewed neutrally, carried a strong message. They illustrated the need for flexibility in handling the infinite variety of situations that are brought to police attention. The distinctions that the police were crudely making in the handling of police business were clear indications of the complexity of the police job. And this complexity was compounded because there were so many pressures to ignore it. If officers responded to unique factors in an incident, as they often did, they were usually compelled to act in an informal, sub rosa manner.

Public outrage about specific incidents, about categories of behavior, and about crime rates, plus concern about lack of fairness in police decision making, frequently results in administrative controls and legislation that value uniform rather than more individualized responses. The ABF survey's microscopic description of police business and of the improvised responses to so much of the police workload identified one of the most fundamental dilemmas in policing: how to respond categorically to incidents that often require individualized treatment if one's concern is fairness and effectiveness.

The Police Use Their Authority to Arrest to Achieve Many Objectives Other Than the Initiation of a Criminal Prosecution

It is widely assumed that the primary—some would even argue the exclusive—purpose of arrest is to initiate a criminal prosecution. That assumption was strong at the time of the ABF survey. (It had been reinforced by the "mortality tables" of the 1920 crime surveys, which characterized as failures arrests that did not result in a prosecution and conviction.) The assumption remains strong today, buoyed by the additional argument that arrests made without the intent to prosecute constitute a misuse of the power and a possible violation of civil rights.

The ABF survey gave visibility to the wholesale practice of using arrest to achieve a wide range of objectives other than the initiation of a criminal prosecution.[14] It found that persons were routinely taken into custody to conduct further investigations; for harassment, as a means of controlling a problem; to preserve testimony; and for safekeeping. For some categories of offenses, the arrests made for these purposes in Detroit far exceeded the number of arrests made with the limited objective of pursuing a prosecution.

The exposure of this practice—the routine manner in which arrests were carried out, the explanations candidly stated, and the absence of any pretense that prosecution was a goal—was the direct result of field observations. Statistical summaries of the arrests would have made no distinctions as to the purpose of the arrests had reliance been placed on them.

In some cases, the police had sufficient evidence of the offense for which the arrest was made (although their objective may have been to get at another offense) and therefore had the option of prosecuting if they chose to do so. But in the vast percentage of these cases, the practice was so wholesale that no effort was made to acquire the evidence to support an arrest and prosecution. And since the cases did not go forward in the system, the police decision to arrest was not subject to any review.

Avoiding a judgment regarding the legality and propriety of such arrests, the ABF survey's clinical documentation of them led to the exploration of a wide range of complex questions that had not previously been raised. How common was the practice in other police agencies? What needs were being met by this previously invisible practice? How strong were the arguments in support of the expressed needs? Should some of these needs, such as the down-and-out alcoholic's need for safekeeping, be met by a limited grant of authority to intervene and detain without prosecution? And if so, how can that be accomplished in a way that is both fair and effective? What were the consequences for the individuals subject to such practices? Were they abused? helped? Or were the detentions mutually accommodating for both the police and those arrested? What were the consequences for the community? How were the practices viewed? Were they seen as offensive to specific neighborhoods or groups of citizens and contributing to negative, hostile attitudes toward the police? Or were they seen as helpful and responsive? And finally, what was the relationship between such practices and the broader role of the police in dealing with more serious crime, in maintaining order, and in creating a sense of security in a community?

The Police—and Especially Individual Police Officers—Exercise Enormous Discretion   The ABF observations painted a picture of police operations in which the discretion of individual officers was pervasive. In sharp contrast with widespread expectations and the image the police themselves sought to project, the survey recorded incident after incident in which officers at the lowest level in the organization were making extremely important decisions with little, if any, guidance. Police officers regularly decided, for example, whether to stop and question, whether to initiate an investigation, whether to use undercover methods, whether to arrest, whether an arrestee was to be physically detained, and what charges, if any, were to be included in the police report.

Documentation of this vast sea of discretion, found from the top to the bottom of a police agency, raised profound questions about fairness, accountability, and control. It created havoc with the professional image that reformers sought to give to the police, built as that image was on a foundation of neutrality to be maintained without "fear or favor." It also created havoc in legal circles, with commentators appalled that the "rule of law" had been replaced by a police officer's predilections, that such important decisions, assumed to be reserved for legislatures, elected officials, or judges—to be made in state capitols, city halls, or in courthouses—were in fact being made by police officers on the streets. The immediate reaction, in some quarters, was to press for arrangements that would require the police to adhere strictly to legislative mandates. Others, however, concluded that, despite the sensitive nature of their function, police inevitably exercise discretion, that this was the natural consequence of the police being called on to handle such a wide variety of situations, each characterized by different, unpredictable circumstances. They argued that the presence of discretion was symptomatic of the complexities in policing and in the use of the criminal justice process, that the challenge was in attempting to structure it in ways that made the police more accountable for its use. If this was indeed the challenge, how was it to be met? Who was to provide the guidance: the legislature, courts, local elected officials, or police administrators? What engagement, if any, was there to be with the community most directly affected? And what were the implications for defining the job of the police officer and for the supervision, training, and recruitment of police officers?

Although Evidence of a Crime May Be Present, the Police Often Decide Not to Arrest   The discretion that police were found to exercise in deciding whether to arrest emerged as being of special import. In the traditional view of the police function, it was assumed that the police were mandated to make an arrest when evidence of a crime came to their attention. Much support existed for this assumption in state statutes, municipal ordinances, and police manuals.[15] The view was reinforced by the professional movement within policing that, to avoid allegations of bias and corruption, placed a high value on full, objective application of the law.

The picture acquired by the ABF of police operations was in sharp contrast with this stated ideal and with the prevailing understanding of what was then police practice. In many situations, there was overwhelming evidence that a crime had been committed and no question as to who committed it, but arrests nevertheless were not made. This was especially common in cases involving an assault in which the victim and offender had some prior relationship and in all domestic situations.

Was this further evidence of inefficiency, corruption, and the negation by the police of legislative intent? Or was nonenforcement of some offenses a crude indicator of other problems and needs, such as limited police resources, the lack of clarity in statutory language, or the desire to be more discriminating in the treatment of individual incidents? Was the criminal law more like an arsenal that authorized the police to act when they needed to act than a mandate to the police? These were among the questions on which analysts with earliest access to the ABF data focused.[16] These works, in turn, led to proposals for controlling the selective use of the criminal law,[17] followed by a spirited debate regarding the legality of selective enforcement and nonenforcement.[18] The exploration of these issues has added a whole new dimension to understanding the complexities of policing.

The Police Are a Part of the Criminal Justice System; Their Actions Heavily Influence Other Agencies in the System Whose

Actions, in Turn, Strongly Influence the Police   The ABF project's design reflected an awareness of the systemic nature of the criminal process. That is why observers were sent into police departments, probation and parole agencies, prosecutors' offices, and the courts. And that is why the commitment, from the outset, was to understand what happened to cases as they proceeded through the different agencies. Whether those who planned the project anticipated the extent to which the actions of one agency affected another is not clear. The magnitude of the influence, however, and the degree to which it was institutionalized were among the most significant observations made in the ABF survey.

It was found, for example, that a large police department would shift its enforcement priorities on the last day of the month in anticipation of a new judge taking the bench in the court handling initial appearances. Police officers would make decisions about arrests or about conducting searches based on what they interpreted as a judge's personal biases, rather than on the basis of relevant statutes and case law. And in like fashion, in adjudicating and sentencing, judges would take into consideration certain assumptions about the police practices that resulted in prosecution. The anticipation of being affected by policies attributed to prosecutors or judges resulted in the development of accommodations that terminated or modified the processing of cases at an earlier stage in the process or that resulted in the police developing an alternative response that did not involve prosecution.

These observations led quickly to the conclusion that it was imperative to view all operations by agencies in the criminal justice process as part of an intricate, albeit unmanaged, system. And from that point on, the personnel of the project incorporated "system" into the daily vocabulary of the study. This was to be one of the main legacies of the survey. The police could no longer be viewed in isolation; they did not operate in a vacuum. They were an integral part of the criminal justice system. Their effectiveness was heavily dependent on the operations of the rest of the system.

The concept of a system was helpful in analyzing the critical decision-making points. Analogizing to the flow of a river, the systemic concept created a greater awareness of the limitations of the system, most notably that narrowing the flow at any point, through more rigorous standards and restricting discretion, thereby building a "dam," absent other measures, would create a backup and ultimately an overflow in the form of a new stream or accommodation. Such changes might shift the primary locus of decision making from one agency to another; for example, from the police to the prosecutor or from the prosecutor to the police. Yet the agency to which the shift occurred may not have been as well equipped to handle the processing as the agency from which the shift was made. The police, as the first agency in the system, responsible for intake, were making decisions that were critical—for their effect both on the system and on the individuals involved.

Widespread adoption of the criminal justice system as the framework for viewing the police and other agencies opened many vistas. It provided a vehicle for reflecting more intelligently on the impact of proposed changes in public policy relating to crime. It provided the unifying scheme for academic programs committed to education and research relating to crime. And it stimulated ideas about how better coordination could be achieved by local and state governments of the various agencies involved in the criminal process. But it also had some confining effects. It reinforced the notion that the primary function of the police was to deal with crime and that the primary means the police had for dealing with everything—both crime and noncriminal matters—was the process of arrest, prosecution, trial, and punishment.

DEVELOPMENTS SINCE THE ABF SURVEY

In contrast with the neglect of the pre-ABF era, a plethora of studies relating to the police have been conducted in the years since the ABF study, and policing itself has undergone major change. Both the studies and the actions taken have been stimulated in large measure by increased recognition of the important role that the police have been called on to play in dealing with racial tensions, urban riots, political conflict, increased personal violence, increases in other types of serious crime, disorder on our streets, and—as a parallel problem—the fear generated by all of these conditions.

From among all that has occurred, my limited goal here is to reflect on how the points previously identified as having been given visibility by the ABF survey have fared, with the ultimate objective—in summation—of assessing, through this sampling, the degree to which the complexity of the police function is being recognized and understood and how this, in turn, is influencing the shaping of police operations.

The Varied Nature of the Police Function

When crime became a major domestic issue in the mid 1960s, President Johnson, echoing many of the concerns expressed by Justice Robert Jackson that led to the ABF survey, created his Commission on Law Enforcement and Administration of Justice. The commission funded much new research, including extensive observations of police activity,[19] but mainly depended on a pulling together of then-available knowledge as a basis for informing public policy decisions and developing a consensus on an agenda for action. It drew heavily on the ABF survey.[20]

In its efforts to present a coherent picture of the operations and needs of the police, the commission acknowledged repeatedly the varied character of the police function and that the police spent much of their time dealing with matters other than serious crime. It recognized the complexity of the issues these functions raise, examining the pros and cons of police continuing to be responsible for what it characterized as nonenforcement tasks. But it concluded that, on balance, "the performance of many of the nonenforcement duties by the police helps them to control crime, and that radically changing the traditional police role would create more problems than it would solve."[21] In addition to the focus on crime, the commission was also concerned with the need to improve relations with young people and minorities. The combination of these concerns led them to propose a three-step staffing concept for police departments, with the lowest level being a community service officer whose primary responsibilities would include performing nonenforcement duties and improving relationships with the community.[22] Thus, by justifying involvement in nonenforcement duties based on the contribution this made to dealing with crime and by relieving police officers of such duties so that they could concentrate on crime, the commission lent support to the concept of the police as primarily crime fighters. But at the same time, it reversed the earlier movement to divest the police entirely of all nonenforcement tasks.

Bittner's ethnographic work on the role of the police on skid row[23] and on handling the mentally ill,[24] among the best observational studies of the police, led him to highlight the inseparable nature of many of the functions performed by the police.[25] He concluded that the potential, unpredictable need for force was the dominant factor that resulted in police involvement. The studies of police workloads and activities by Cumming, Skolnick, Wilson, Livermore, Rubinstein, and Muir[26] added to a more comprehensive understanding of what the police did and to the realization that the capacity of the police to deal with crime depended, in some measure, on their involvement in many other activities and, in turn, that their ability to handle these other activities derived, in some measure, from their coercive authority to deal with crime. Reflecting on these and other studies, Punch, heralding the new visibility given to the "largely undocumented and thereby partly submerged aspect of policemen's work," observed that the studies had opened a Pandora's box.[27] But he argued that because police work was so important, yet so diverse and diffused, it deserved much more study as a multifaceted social control agency serving multiple ends and various audiences.

By 1973, the thought given to the nature of the police function had developed to the point that the American Bar Association, with the endorsement of the International Association of Chiefs of Police, made this observation in its promulgation of standards relating to the urban police function:

> To achieve optimum police effectiveness, the police should be recognized as having complex and multiple tasks to perform in addition to identifying and apprehending persons committing serious criminal offenses. Such other police tasks include protection of certain rights such as to speak and to assemble, participation either directly or in conjunction with other public and social agencies in the prevention of criminal and delinquent behavior, maintenance of order and control of pedestrian and vehicular traffic, resolution of conflict, and assistance to citizens in need of help such as the person who is mentally ill, the chronic alcoholic, or the drug addict.[28]

The widespread "hunch" that police services outside traditional law enforcement have positive value gained support, in a roundabout way, from the controlled experiments conducted in the 1970s and 1980s. They questioned the value of traditional methods of policing by testing specifically the value of motorized patrol, foot patrol, response time, and fear reduction strategies.[29]

The studies documented the limited capacity of the police, using these methods, to control crime. They questioned the value of investing so heavily in reacting to citizen mobilizations. They surfaced the problem of fear as a concern separable from that of crime. And they gave further exposure to the activities in which the police were involved that did not fall into the category of "serious crime." Thus, collectively, the experiments made a major contribution toward stimulating more serious thought about the relative importance of the various tasks in which the police were involved.

Equally significant were the contributions that the controlled experiments made to the development of research methodology designed to better understand the complexities of policing. Whereas the ABF survey had moved freely across wider issues, these studies focused on specific police strategies. The ABF survey had opened the police to observation. The first of the controlled studies, the Kansas City Patrol Experiment,[30] opened a police agency not only to observation, but also to manipulation of its operating practices so as to maintain experimental conditions subject to measurement. Of special importance was the involvement in the research of police officers and management. The partial ownership of the project by the police—especially rank-and-file officers—and the "scientific" character of the studies gave added weight to the results and marked an important advance in the meaning of professional policing.

On realizing (at a time of great concern about crime, fear, and hostility directed at the police) that the principal methods on which they had depended for dealing with crime were of questionable value, progressive police administrators began searching for new, more effective practices. The programs that emerged reflected several different emphases: (1) improving relationships with the young and minorities, with the primary objective to reduce tensions and with the secondary objective to increase the police capacity to deal with crime; (2) being more proactive rather than reactive as, for example, in setting up sting operations with the primary objective to more aggressively identify criminal conduct and acquire evidence; (3) enlisting the help of the community in preventing crime; (4) making more arrests for "quality of life" offenses, with the primary objective to reduce fear; and (5) responding more effectively to a broad range of common calls to the police in the hope that doing so would improve relations with the public, reduce fear, and indirectly improve the capacity of the police to deal with crime. The latter was strongly reinforced by the widely cited article "Broken Windows,"[31] which developed the nexus between the physical deterioration of an area, disorderliness, the police response to disorderliness, and crime.

These varied movements, in many jurisdictions, have merged and are now characterized under the single umbrella of community policing, fleshed out by supportive changes in organization, staffing, and operations. They have given rise to a whole new approach to providing police services that places heavy emphasis on the importance of ties between individual officers and the community to which they are assigned, engaging the community in working with the police, and a proactive commitment on the part of the officer. Emerging as a central feature of this approach to police work is a strong commitment to deal effectively with those varied matters that were formerly thought to have the lowest priority in policing and to expand the police role to encompass additional concerns not previously within the police ambit.

With greater acceptance of the multiple functions of the police and an awareness of the limited value of depending on criminal prosecutions, the focus shifts, not simply to identifying more effective ways in which to deal with crime, but to identifying more effective ways in which to carry out all aspects of the broader police function. The concept of 'problem-oriented policing'[32] builds on what has been achieved under the community policing label by going one step further: by proposing a radical new perspective of the police function in which the police are committed, first and foremost, to respond to a wide array of community problems. In this scheme, decisions about police practices, including the choice of enforcing the criminal law and engaging the community, are made with a primary concern for what is likely to be most effective and fair in responding to a specific problem. The approach elevates the specific problems police are called on to handle to a preeminent position around which all other organizing concepts revolve. To achieve this objective, the concept calls for a commitment to identifying each problem; to analyzing it in depth with the objective of understanding contributing factors and the manner in which it is manifested; and to searching broadly and without traditional limits for means by which it can be eliminated or reduced, reaching far beyond the use of the criminal law.

Thus, in a major departure from the prevailing concepts at the time of the ABF survey in the 1950s, when it was assumed that the criminal process (as the prime means by which the police operated) fully defined the police function and when all but serious crime was thought to be unimportant, a forthright identification of all the problems police are expected to handle collectively defines the police function, with a commitment to thoughtful analysis of each problem in determining what constitutes the best response from among many responses. In this type of analysis, a high value is placed on working preventively to avoid or reduce problems and on the involvement of rank-and-file police officers in the thought processes and supportive research. A high value is also placed on candor, forthrightness, and honesty in confronting the need for appropriate resources and authority, in the uses made of the criminal law and in acknowledging the discretion police are required to exercise—thereby reducing the need to improvise or to squeeze everything into the mold of a criminal prosecution. The change in orientation attributes much more responsibility, latitude, and discretion to a police officer than is implied by the common practice of referring to the police as "law enforcement officers."

In summary, the greater visibility given to the various functions of the police, starting with the ABF survey, has revealed the enormous complexity of the police function—in sharp contrast with the simplistic notions of the past. Recognition of these complexities has led to some dramatic reconceptualizations of the role of the police. More important, substantial action has been taken in implementing these new concepts. Although many questions remain and most jurisdictions are still unaffected by these advances, and although there are occasional calls for "back to basics," the momentum of the changes that have occurred, propelled by some very pragmatic considerations, now appears irreversible. A strong commitment currently exists to both further action and the acquisition of additional knowledge.

The Infinite Variety of Situations Police Are Called on to Handle

When President Johnson issued his charge to his newly appointed Commission on Law Enforcement and Administration of Justice, he stated "we have taken a pledge not only to reduce crime but to banish it."[33] It is significant that, two years later, at the very outset of its report to the president, the commission observed:

> A skid-row drunk lying in a gutter is crime. So is the killing of an unfaithful wife. A Cosa Nostra conspiracy to bribe public officials is crime. So is a strong-arm robbery by a 15-year-old boy. The embezzlement of a corporation's funds by an executive is crime. So is the possession of marijuana cigarettes by a student. These crimes can no more be lumped together for purposes of analysis than can measles and schizophrenia, or lung cancer and a broken ankle. As with disease, so with crime: if causes are to be understood, if risks are to be evaluated, and if preventive or remedial actions are to be taken, each kind must be looked at separately. Thinking of "crime" as a whole is futile.[34]

The advice of that commission still is not taken seriously, as political leaders and various interest groups, acting out of understandable frustration, continue to exhort the police and the public to war on "crime." All that has been learned compels a more discrete, systematic approach to the specific problems police handle and, within these problems, to giving appropriate consideration to the variables that surface in specific incidents.

In the 1970s, the pressure for a generic response was manifested most clearly in the demands for "law and order," which translated into a demand for "toughness" in dealing with everything from serious crime to political protest. Yet, amidst that climate were the beginnings of some significant experiments, hatched by the follow-up to the president's commission studies, that singled out specific aspects of police business for attention. Most notable was Morton Bard's initiative in bringing a new response to domestic violence.[35]

More recently, the pressure for categorical responses has been reflected in the desire to alter public attitudes regarding subcategories of offensive behavior. For example, the strong desire that the public take more seriously all forms of sexually motivated attacks on women resulted in the enactment of statutes that placed a wide range of conduct, previously defined separately, under the new, single umbrella of sexual assault. One of the prime objectives was to convince the police themselves to view such conduct as more serious. But for those police whose attitudes are now changed, or who did not need convincing, the development of a rational program for preventing and responding to sexual assault requires that they think in terms of the different variables that distinguish one sexual assault from another. A sensible response to the sexual abuse of children obviously requires a different approach than a carefully thought through response to date rape or to an unidentified rapist who has attacked several women in a single neighborhood.

Problem-oriented policing stresses the need to disaggregate problems as a preliminary step in analyzing them. It criticizes, in particular, the tendency to use criminal law labels (like arson) to mask important distinctions that exist among various types of behavior—distinctions that have major implications in attempting to think through what constitutes the most effective response.[36] At the same time, it rejects the notion that each incident the police handle is unlike any other incident. To the contrary, one of the major thrusts of problem-oriented policing is to elevate police thinking so that the police do not spend all their time responding to incidents but seek instead to collect incidents into clusters that make them more amenable to being analyzed and, subsequently, to being dealt with more effectively by the police.[37]

In the resulting search for an appropriate level of categorization, the more advanced police efforts, as part of the process of analyzing specific problems, have identified important variables that ought to influence, though not dictate, their response. Thus, for example, building on Bard's work relating to domestic violence, police agencies, with a commitment to being both fair and effective, identified factors (like age, the presence of mental illness, and the relative aggressiveness of the parties) that should be considered in determining the police action.[38] This appeared to result in programs that succeeded in identifying abusers and in subjecting them to appropriate treatment within the criminal justice system. In some jurisdictions, however, reflecting impatience with police responses thought to be inadequate, legislatures have acted to mandate police arrest if probable cause exists to believe that a battery was committed.[39] Forced to ignore all variables, police are now making large numbers of arrests. With available resources overwhelmed, prosecutors and their staffs must seek to filter out cases based on the same factors that the police previously were instructed to consider. It seems likely that the most awkward results of mandated arrests will ultimately lead to a further refinement in which some discretion will be returned to the police to enable them to deal differently with those situations in which prosecution appears to do more harm than good, both for the individuals involved and for getting a credible message out regarding the seriousness of domestic violence.

Absent legislative action of the type taken regarding domestic violence, the police have enormous opportunities to improve the quality of their responses by thinking through the various problems they handle and, within each, the factors that ought to be considered in deciding on an appropriate response. They have the opportunity, also, to work at instilling a set of values that gives officers residual guidance on which they can draw in dealing with unpredictable situations to which no amount of prethought can speak. From the experience of the past several decades, it appears that the degree to which outside forces will impose categorical responses on problems, without regard to the variety of situations that compose these problems, will depend in large measure on the degree to which the police proactively take the initiative in refining their operations. But for this to be possible requires public and legislative support that recognizes the futility of pressing the police to view their responsibilities as dealing with a monolithic category of conduct, subject to a single, simplistic response.

The Varied Uses of Arrest

If the job of the police is seen simply as defined by the criminal law, it is understandable why so much dependence is placed on arrest in getting the job done. It is also understandable why, given what is expected of the police, arrest is adapted to meet so many other needs. With recognition of the multifaceted nature of the police function, the complexities that grow out of the varied uses of arrest become apparent. This has resulted in facing up to the need for forms of authority other than arrest.

In their standards for the Urban Police Function, the American Bar Association, with the approval of the International Association of Chiefs of Police, asserted:

> The assumption that the use of an arrest and the criminal process is the primary or even the exclusive method available to police should be recognized as causing unnecessary distortion of both the criminal law and the system of criminal justice.

There should be clarification of the authority of police to use methods other than arrest and prosecution to deal with the variety of behavioral and social problems which they confront.[40]

The most significant advance in this regard has occurred regarding the use made of arrest for safekeeping of intoxicated persons, which once accounted for the greatest volume of arrests.[41] The courts, in the 1960s, appeared to be moving in the direction of prohibiting the use of arrest and the criminal process as the primary means for responding to the person incapacitated by alcohol. But the United States Supreme Court reversed that trend, expressing reluctance to deny the police this traditional method for dealing with the "down and out drunk" in the absence of a clear indication that another alternative, less disruptive of the intoxicated person's rights, was both available and effective.[42] In response to concerns about civil rights, the criminal justice system, and the plight of homeless alcoholics, some states on their own then moved to grant the police specific authority to take an incapacitated person into custody for transport to a detoxification center, creating an elaborate system for review, release, or, if need be, commitment for treatment.[43] It was made explicit that being intoxicated in public was not criminal; that custody was not to be considered an arrest. Twenty-two states have now adopted some form of this authority,[44] thereby creating an alternative to arrest for a category of behavior that accounted for 40 percent of all nontraffic arrests made in the nation in 1965.[45] In the latest national report on arrests, for 1988, only 17 percent of all nontraffic arrests were made for public drunkenness.[46]

As the first breakthrough in authorizing the police to take a person into custody without arresting that person for a crime, the provisions, when initially proposed, met some skepticism, as one would expect for so radical a change, but no strong opposition. The lack of any significant challenge and the rapid adoption of the proposal appear due to several factors: the urging of those concerned about the ravages of alcohol and the attraction of what seemed like a more humane response; the desire of the criminal justice agencies (especially the courts and jails) to rid themselves, to the extent they could, of the burden of handling intoxicated persons; the powerlessness of those most directly affected—the chronic inebriates—if they did have some concerns; and the recognized absence of substantial resources for detoxification and treatment, which made it unlikely that the new system would pressure intoxicated persons to do more than they were previously coerced into doing. (The change actually brought on a new issue—the propriety of continuing to use the criminal justice process, despite the legislative resolve, for lack of adequate resources to support the new alternative.)

More than a decade since enactment, many questions remain about the effectiveness of the new process as a response to alcoholism. But few, if any, questions have been raised regarding what is perhaps the most novel aspect of the process—the use made by the police of their new authority to take incapacitated persons into custody without having to arrest them and charge them with a crime.

In a parallel development, as part of the overall revision of the laws relating to the mentally ill, the police were given explicit authority in many jurisdictions to make an emergency detention of a mentally ill person until a hearing could be held to determine if a commitment was warranted.[47] This replaced the need to utilize the criminal process, which, in reference to this behavior, was generally considered especially inappropriate. But the new grant of authority was narrowly circumscribed, requiring, among other criteria, evidence of dangerousness. The test was thus much more rigid and more subjective than that prescribed for the person incapacitated by alcohol. The grant of authority is nevertheless unique, but its significance has been overshadowed by the enormous increase in street problems associated with the mentally ill. For substantial segments of the public, the limits on the authority newly conveyed to the police and the curtailment in the use of the criminal law have created the impression that the police are powerless, negligent, or both. But for those who are better informed, the fact that specific authority was carved out for the police and was so narrowly limited has helped to convey the complexity of trying to deal with one form of street disorder while protecting the rights of the mentally ill—a result that is preferable to the old practice of not facing the problem by simply stretching the use of the criminal law to deal with it.

Much less progress has been made in forthrightly working through the issues raised by the use of arrest to maintain street order (candidly labeled "harassment" in the ABF survey) involving behavior caused by other than alcohol or mental illness. When given visibility, the practice of harassing prostitutes, for example, was widely condemned in the courts and in the public forum. This condemnation was sometimes based on traditional grounds reminiscent of the crime surveys of the 1920s. Pointing to the large number of arrests that were dropped short of prosecution, critiques of the criminal justice system called on the prosecutor to account for the failure to prosecute or on the police to explain the absence of adequate grounds to support a prosecution. More often, however, the condemnation alleged violations of civil liberties. The practice of arresting specific categories of persons engaged in offensive behavior had become so wholesale in some jurisdictions that no effort was made to acquire probable cause before an arrest was made. The acknowledged objective was simply to harass those arrested. Persons caught in the net successfully challenged the practice in the courts. In one of the most publicized challenges, Chicago police were forced to stop their practice of arresting gang members as a primary means of controlling street gangs, when it was clearly established that the arresting officers had no intention to prosecute the cases; the obvious intention in jailing the arrestees was to disrupt their activities and administer a form of summary punishment.[48]

When the use of arrest in this manner to control street prostitution was challenged, initiatives were taken to deal more forthrightly with the problem of concern by the enactment of statutes and ordinances that established loitering for purposes of prostitution as an offense.[49] This was an effort to define specifically the behavior that was of concern, thereby increasing the potential that the police could acquire sufficient evidence to justify an arrest, as compared with the difficulty in acquiring the evidence needed to support a charge of solicitation. More ambitiously, moving in a different direction, several analysts explored the feasibility of authorizing the police to intervene in a broad range of street order problems without becoming committed to a criminal prosecution.[50] These inquiries, however, were not pursued to the point that they resulted in legislative proposals, let alone enactments.

The use of arrest to control and harass, suppressed for some years under challenge, has reemerged in the past several years because of the intensified problems of street sale of drugs and the violence of youth gangs. Faced with enormous pressures to "take back the streets," the police have reinstituted the practice of conducting street "sweeps," making hundreds of arrests that are not subsequently prosecuted.[51] Continued uncertainty exists regarding the legal basis for the arrests. But it is clearly now much easier to create a legal floor for such arrests with the recent line of court decisions that approve the use of an objective standard for determining legality when it is alleged that an arrest was made on a pretext.[52] Thus, even if an officer really wanted to check out a driver for possession of drugs, the officer's contention that the driver was initially stopped for speeding will be accepted as justification for the stop and for whatever subsequent actions are taken. Another significant factor behind current practices is that they often have the enthusiastic endorsement of the same communities that severely criticized them when used in a different context in the past.

If it were possible to analyze all arrests made in some large urban areas, based on the intent of the arresting officer, it is likely, given the wholesale use now being made of "street sweeps," that more arrests are made for this purpose than are made with the intention of initiating a criminal prosecution. Among the costs of this practice are the commitment it reflects to a form of summary punishment, the enormous potential for arbitrariness and abuse, the negative impact on those arrested and detained, and the degree to which the practice contributes to a rise in racial tensions. And yet the need for some form of authority and intervention appears to grow greater, as urban areas attempt to deal with the dramatic increase in the volume of street order problems involving not only drug sales and gang activities, but also the conflicts that arise from the use of the streets by the homeless, the intoxicated, the mentally ill, and the addicted.

Thus, the need is more critical today than it has ever been to confront the complexities in maintaining street order. And with the recognition of this set of complexities comes these questions. What is the specific nature of the need? Are alternative ways to maintain order available that do not require physical intervention? And if some form of physical intervention is required, is it possible to fashion an appropriate form of limited authority that would enable the police, for example, to remove individuals from a specific location without committing themselves to jailing and prosecuting those who are removed? Can a person be "unarrested" once the immediate need that led to taking the person into custody has been met? And if such authority can be spelled out, how can its use be subjected to review? The current tendency to avoid facing these questions attaches a positive value to improvising by the police and to their having to be less than honest in the majority of cases in which they make use of their awesome arrest power. This return to simplicity is at great cost to the credibility of police operations, to those who may be arrested and detained without adequate grounds or opportunity for review, and to the integrity of the criminal justice process.

The Prevalence of Discretion in Policing

Accounts of the discretion exercised by the police were among the first publications emanating from the ABF survey.[53] They focused, for the most part, on the discretion used in determining whether to invoke the criminal process. The prevailing image of the police as a ministerial agency was so deeply imbedded, these accounts and especially the contention that discretion was inevitable were initially somewhat shocking to the police field. And yet police tended to accept the picture that was portrayed and to engage openly in discussion of police discretion. It was almost as if it were cathartic to talk about something that had been kept sub rosa for so long.

Although the term *police discretion* is now in common use, it carries many different meanings—primarily because there are so many different forms of discretion. The varied uses made of arrest (discussed above) is one such category. For some commentators, the primary category of concern is the decision not to arrest or, if arrests are to be made, the decision as to who from among a larger number of violators is to be arrested (discussed below).[54] These categories of discretion receive special attention because they relate to what traditionally has been viewed as the most important decision-making aspect of policing—the making of an arrest—and because they pose some especially difficult questions. But many of the same questions are posed by other forms of discretion exercised by the police—in deciding, for example, on the priority to be given each function from among their many functions; whether to take the initiative in launching investigations or wait for complaints to be filed, and on the use made of different forms of investigation (e.g., informants, surveillance, undercover operations).

The documentation of these various forms of discretion, initially given visibility in the ABF survey, has vastly increased, stimulated largely by major controversies over police operations that have arisen in the past several decades. Challenges to police practices as violations of civil rights, as producing tensions in minority communities, or as wrongful responses to political protest and demonstrations all tended to focus on what were essentially discretionary decisions. A police decision in a given situation (e.g., to use force, to use an undercover operative, to conduct a surveillance, or to disperse a crowd) on review commonly raised difficult questions. Was a conscious decision made to take the action that was taken? By what standards? By what authority? And subject to what review? Who made the decision? An elected official to whom the police were responsible? The police chief? Or a police officer? Was it considered appropriate by superiors? Such questions could no longer be brushed aside or answered with the contention that the police had no discretion in the matter. The police could not resist open discussion of the tough policy questions that were raised. With these questions and a commitment to increased openness by police agencies came a recognition of the complexity and responsibility that the acknowledgment of discretion entailed.

Absent any agreement as to the best means for addressing the varied policy questions raised, there has been a flurry of activity. Legislatures have enacted statutes that curtail, clarify, guide, or mandate police actions (e.g., regarding stopping and questioning, strip searches, use of force). City councils have used their budgetary and legislative powers to set police priorities (e.g., marijuana enforcement, the decision to prosecute drug cases under federal law) and to control investigations (e.g., surveillance of political groups). The citizenry, through initiatives and referenda, have sought to provide more specific guidance to their police on issues of local concern (e.g., marijuana enforcement, use of force). Prosecutors have been more assertive in making policy decisions affecting police practices regarding matters that are subsequently of concern to them.

The most significant and sustained effort to guide police discretion has been made by the police themselves. This movement was given impetus by the president's commission, which, echoing the ABF survey's findings regarding discretion, gave great emphasis at an especially critical time to their recommendation that police agencies develop guidelines for all forms of police action.[55] Their recommendation was supported by a detailed proposal for doing so, drawing heavily on adapting procedures commonly employed by government agencies in using administrative rule making to structure their discretion.[56] The more advanced police departments responded enthusiastically to these urgings. Confronted with criticism or controversy or the desire to avoid it, these agencies turned to the articulation of their policies as one of the primary means for responding to concern about their operations in sensitive areas. The movement was endorsed by the American Bar Association in their standards relating to the police function, which received the approval of the International Association of Chiefs of Police.[57] The desirability of articulating policies is now so firmly established that it is required regarding many sensitive aspects of operations by the standards for accrediting police agencies.[58]

The response of the courts to this whole movement is more complex, especially with regard to police operations involving fourth amendment issues, as reflected in the detailed treatment of their position in the chapter by Wayne LaFave that appears in this book.[59] The United States Supreme Court case that restricted the police use of deadly force against fleeing felons[60] is often cited as the ultimate example of judicial endorsement of administrative policymaking in that the initiatives of police agencies, brought to the attention of the Court by the police, were commended and used by the Court to support the position it adopted.

This substantial effort to address the issues raised upon acknowledging the discretion exercised by the police stands out as one of the stronger examples of progress having been made in responding to complications inherent in the nature of policing. That is not to say, by any means, that the full dimensions of the complexity that was uncovered have been recognized, let alone addressed. As reflected in the chapters by LaFave and Parnas in this book, it is not yet at all settled who, among the various decision makers, can best make the important policy decisions that must be made in guiding the exercise of police discretion—the legislature, municipal officials, the courts, the prosecutor, or the police. Generally, police have been recognized as properly adopting policies that set down standards regarding their practices in investigating conduct defined as criminal and in the processing of alleged offenders.[61] Greater difficulty continues to be experienced in determining if the police should set the standards for deciding if a criminal statute should be enforced at all and, if so, if it should be enforced in only some of the situations it covers (see below).

Among continuing concerns is the status that should be given to written police policies. Are they to be viewed as controlling for establishing responsibility in disciplinary actions, in judging liability, or in deciding on the admissibility of evidence? The intent, on the part of the original proponents, was to view the development of policy as a way to encourage responsible thought about a difficult issue and to view the end product as a conclusion of this process—as a statement of the way in which a given police agency thinks about a problem—which can then serve as guidance for its personnel. The tendency in practice, however, is to treat anything that is written down as rules, which then are interpreted as edicts. When this occurs, the desired flexibility is lost, and any necessary diversion from the rules to meet the variety of situations the police confront returns the police to acting in a sub rosa manner.

Equally troubling is the tendency on the part of legislatures, courts, and the police to take comfort in the fact that a policy exists—that an agency has provided guidance in a discretionary area—without appropriate concern about its content. This may be based on an assumption that the willingness of an agency itself to articulate its stance achieves accountability, which is one of the primary objectives in encouraging policy development. But an equally important objective, in making the policy visible, is to subject it to a form of review that will ensure it is supported by a defensible rationale and reflects an appropriate concern with both fairness and effectiveness. The worst possible result would be to have the appearance of rules but the retention of practices that have not been thought through.

It has often been argued that policymaking cannot possibly address the infinite variety of unpredictable situations the police confront.[62] Those most strongly supporting the articulation of policy would probably agree. At best, policymaking closes the gap. Recognizing this, progressive police administrators have invested substantial effort in instilling, through training and supervision, a set of values that, in the absence of specific guidance, will serve as general standards for the discretionary decisions that must be made. If the administrators succeed, they will have taken a major step toward providing the basis for attributing to the police a new form of professionalism such as is commonly attributed to administrators in other areas of government—an attribution that has resulted in a willingness on the part of the courts to recognize the propriety of these administrators setting policy within broad legislative bounds.[63]

The Police Decision Not to Arrest

In sharp contrast with the recognition of various forms of discretion exercised by the police and the significant advances in attempting to deal with this discretion, much less has been accomplished regarding the most troubling form of police discretion—the decision not to arrest, even though there is adequate basis for arrest, and the related decision to enforce a given law selectively. Police have taken the initiative to try to achieve some consistency in the enforcement of specific statutes through training and informal guidelines. Some agencies have set forth their recommended criteria in writing but restricted such documents to internal use. Rarely has a department publicly announced its intention not to enforce a given law or to enforce a law selectively and, if so, the criteria that would be employed in doing so.

Unlike the actions taken by legislatures in acknowledging the discretion exercised, for example, in stopping and questioning, in using force, and in conducting high-speed chases, they have, with one exception, avoided the reality that police engage in less than full enforcement. The exception relates to assaults by a person on another person living in the same household. Anxious to send a strong message that such assaults are as criminal as all other assaults, legislatures in some states have mandated that the police arrest whenever evidence of an assault is present.[64] In a somewhat backward manner, these enactments probably did more to raise the full enforcement issue than was ever intended. The requirement that arrests be made in all cases has stimulated much discussion about the feasibility, fairness, and effectiveness of such a legislative policy. But more broadly, the enactment carries the implication that the police *are not required* to enforce all other statutes fully—an implication with ramifications that have yet to be explored.

Why the enormous reluctance on the part of the police to assert what they are already doing or intend to do? Quite simply, the potential costs are considered too high, in the absence of legislative support, with much uncertainty as to the benefits. The naive assumption that the police enforce all of the laws all of the time is so strong among legislators, elected officials, the courts, and the public generally, the police make themselves vulnerable to the charge that they are acting improperly in exercising discretion. Police administrators have been chastised, even when only alluding to the reality of less than full enforcement, for preempting the legislature, violating the "rule of law," and ignoring the separation of powers that gives legislatures the job of enacting laws and the executive branch the job of enforcing them. Police worry that open acknowledgment of partial or full nonenforcement will encourage conduct that they want to deter. They worry that published criteria will be used to challenge the legality of arrests when they do choose to arrest. And in some jurisdictions that have experienced problems of corruption in the past, they worry that any acknowledgment of less than full enforcement will increase the potential for corruption—the opportunity for officers to solicit bribes in exchange for exercising their newly recognized discretion not to make an arrest.

Each of these concerns has been aired. In rebuttal, it is argued that it is preferable to provide realistic guidance to police officers to achieve adherence to thoughtfully developed standards and to achieve uniformity and fairness; that it is preferable to share honestly with the public the criteria used in deciding whether to enforce the law and the rationale in developing those criteria; and that it is healthy to engage the community in an open discussion of the issues that arise in deciding on enforcement policies.

But whatever support has been expressed for greater openness has been dampened in recent years as the police have increasingly been held liable for their decision making in suits brought as tort actions in state courts and under the federal Civil Rights Act. Although the cases generally involve egregious police actions that a quality police department would not defend under any circumstances,[65] the judgments have carried a broad, overpowering message that failure of the police to arrest if there was a basis for arrest was a major factor in establishing liability. A careful reading of the cases would not lead one to conclude that police ought never to exercise discretion or, if they do, that they ought not acknowledge it. The effect, however, has been to all but stamp out whatever support existed for opening up the complex issues associated with the exercise of discretion in deciding whether an arrest should be made, because it is easier to defend a decision on the basis that the law requires it than to adequately defend even the sensible exercise of administrative discretion. As a result, most police continue to live with the widespread belief that they have a responsibility to enforce all laws fully. This means that, with regard to one of the most important aspects of their operations, they are precluded from taking those steps—through greater openness, honesty, and the development of rational policies—that could substantially improve the quality of their performance.

The Criminal Justice System as a System

"Criminal justice system" was used in the ABF survey to describe the systemic character of the intricate interrelationships and interdependence of the police, the prosecutor, the courts, and the correctional agencies. The survey made visible the important decisions in the criminal process and the way in which these decisions were affected by the actions of the several agencies.

The term—and the concept it conveyed—had enormous appeal. The president's commission made the term an indelible part of the vocabulary in thinking about the response to crime. The very organization of the commission study reflected an awareness of the importance of recognizing the systemic nature of the criminal process. And throughout its reports, the commission and its staff argued that it was imperative that the functions of each of the agencies in the criminal justice system be viewed as interrelated if there were to be progress in improving the apparatus for dealing with crime.

The emphasis on the system had its greatest and most lasting impact in academia.[66] It not only dramatically changed what was being taught about crime and the response to crime but served as the organizing vehicle for texts, programs, and entire schools. The students in these programs would learn that several agencies are involved in the total response to crime. It is less clear how successful the programs have been in conveying and further exploring the complexities of the system—the interrelationships of the various actors in the system and the effect that decision making at one point in the system has on operations at another point. Once brought under a single roof, the natural tendency has been to segregate studies relating to each of the agencies, usually reflecting the specialized interests of faculty members.

Another major consequence of the increased awareness of the systemic character of the response to crime was the creation, through the incentive and financing of the federal government, of coordinating councils on criminal justice in all of the states and in the larger cities. The objective was to require that states and cities, in their planning for improvement in the criminal justice area, coordinate changes so that the implications for each of the agencies would be taken into consideration.[67] When the federal funds used to staff these efforts were eliminated, the majority of states moved to a slimmed-down institutional arrangement to supervise the funneling to localities of whatever remained of federal support—abandoning the emphasis on coordinating developments in the criminal justice agencies.

Though firmly established as part of our vocabulary, the original messages that "criminal justice system" was intended to convey, reflecting the complexity of the system, have been largely ignored in those quarters where an understanding of them is most important—in the development of public policies affecting crime. It was once suggested, for example, that, given what had been learned regarding the operations of the criminal justice system, all legislative proposals should have an "impact statement" attached to them that alerts legislators to the systemic implications of their proposals. What has happened, instead, is that legislators, in their desire to lash out at various forms of behavior, have mandated arrest, restricted plea bargaining, and enacted minimum sentences without any regard for what the likely effect of such actions might be. Likewise, state and municipal governments have increased the number of personnel at one point in the system, as with a greater number of police officers, without recognizing the need for comparable increases to handle the increased workload elsewhere.

Based on what is known about the complexity of the criminal justice system, it is predictable, with a high degree of certainty, that efforts to reduce discretion at one point in the system or to increase sanctions will cause accommodations elsewhere in the system and often produce results quite different from those that are intended. The requirement that the police arrest in all alleged domestic abuse cases in which there is probable cause is bound to overload the rest of the system. It will also eliminate the opportunity for the police to respond to domestic violence cases in ways that give appropriate consideration to some factors, like age, that a commonsense response requires be considered. An increase in sanctions for drinking drivers is destined to reduce the number of arrests police will make. And the most recent tendency of legislators to lash out at truancy, drug possession and sale, and other nondriving offenses through the suspension or revocation of driving licenses will increase the number of drivers without licenses and insurance and load the police, prosecutors, courts, and jails with persons charged with driving after suspension or revocation. Legislation that fails to anticipate such predictable consequences ignores the most elementary insights acquired in the ABF survey. It is especially misleading if proposed as constituting an improvement in the operation of the criminal justice *system*. The use of the term in this loose manner strips it of all its meaning. It disregards the complex, intricate interrelationships that the emphasis on *system* was originally intended to convey. It ignores, for example, tough issues like the need to decide on the appropriate locus for the making of critical decisions or the need to strike a balance between achieving adequate control and achieving flexibility in responding to the infinite variety of situations the system is expected to handle.

CONCLUSION

The ABF survey was a novel undertaking. It experimented with new methods for inquiring into the operations of the police and other agencies in the criminal justice system. It identified critically important issues about the functioning of the police that had not previously received attention. And through subsequent analysis and dissemination, it made available a large amount of data and many new insights regarding these issues. By its accomplishments, the survey marked the beginning of a period in which the issues of importance in policing were redefined.

Some of this redefinition may be attributed directly to the survey. Much is due to the work of others in various forums, often totally independent of the survey. Whatever the source or the influences, the combination of research, debate, and action in the years since the survey has raised to a much higher level efforts to improve police operations. And as a consequence, significant changes have occurred in the definition of the police function, the refinement of police authority, the structuring of discretion, and the establishment of new systems of accountability. These changes have special importance because they are of such a fundamental nature. Unlike many of the more technical and organizational changes that have been associated with police reform in the past, they confront basic problems in striving to create that form of policing that best meets the peculiar needs of policing in a free society. The changes ultimately enable the police to function in a more straightforward, forthright manner, thereby reducing both the need to operate sub rosa and the pressure to act improperly or even illegally. They have contributed to creating a healthier atmosphere within police agencies, in which atmosphere a premium is placed on openness rather than secrecy, on addressing issues rather than ignoring or suppressing them.

Much of the progress that has been realized stems from increased recognition of the complexity of the police task. The ABF survey was the first major research project that surfaced this complexity, due in large measure to the unique, penetrating and nonjudgmental nature of the inquiry. The survey demonstrated that it was essential, in research relating to the police, to observe directly the day-to-day operations of the police in the field. Although there obviously is a need, in any field of endeavor, to examine the lowest level of execution and the end product of one's work, that need had been largely ignored in the modest research efforts relating to the police, in part because of the impediments to doing such research—the strong commitment to secrecy that pervades policing, the sensitivity of the police to potential criticism, and the costly, time-consuming effort that is required. The ABF survey, since reinforced by the experience of other ethnographic studies, established a standard for the depth that is required in research relating to the police if one is to have confidence in one's findings.

If the primary product of the ABF survey, as it related to the police, can be characterized as an increase in understanding of the complexity of policing, it is important to recognize that the product was not presented in the form of a series of policy recommendations or even a set of conclusions. The results of the survey, rather, were a somewhat amorphous collection of observations and insights that took shape only in the analysis of the data and in the developments that have occurred since the survey. Especially prominent among these new insights into the complexity of policing were the points described in this chapter: the multifaceted and often conflicting roles of the police, the endless array of variables present in the incidents police handle, the varied uses made of the authority conveyed to the police through the criminal law, the discretion exercised at the lowest levels in the organization (including the decision whether to arrest), and the manner in which the police affect and are affected by the different elements in the criminal justice system.

As one reflects on developments relating to these new insights since the ABF survey, summarized in this chapter, the picture that emerges is not neat and smooth. If examined closely or at any one point in time, it reflects uneven progress, frequent slippage, and occasionally even some retrenchment. When considered in its entirety and over a larger span of time, however, the cumulative picture reflects major advances—the results of a continuous and rather natural process of refinement. The reasons for the uneven progress are obvious. The new visibility acquired into policing— especially the gradual recognition of the need for discretion—was understandably disconcerting. It identified major vacuums in guidance, authority, and accountability. In a variety of different contexts, the new visibility aroused concern on the part of administrators, judges, legislators, civil rights advocates, and the public. It invited conflict over who should make important policy decisions, over how much discretion ought to be allowed and who should exercise it. It raised new concerns about controlling police conduct, and it led to attempts to control police decision making through new legislation and administrative rules. These reactions have led to the realization that the task of confronting complexity is itself complex and often frustrating to those engaged in it. Despite these difficulties, however, major progress has been realized in the past several decades toward achieving greater effectiveness and fairness—and ultimately in raising the quality of policing.

In examining this progress, one is prompted to ask what distinguishes those responses to complexity that appear to have been most productive from those that have led to dead ends or that have encountered major difficulties. A partial answer, it appears, is in the extent to which the response—whether advanced by an academic, a legislature, or a court—takes note of the full range of complexities (i.e., the six "findings" described in this chapter) or engages with but one of them.

For example, Ronald Allen, in his often-cited dialogue with Kenneth Davis, confronts the complexity inherent in the exercise of discretion by the police.[68] But his attack on proposals that the police use administrative rule making to indicate when they do not intend to enforce a criminal law is weakened because it ignores what has been learned about the complexity of the police function. In support of his arguments, Allen writes: "We do not say to the police: 'Here is a problem. Deal with it.' We say to the police: 'Here is a detailed code. Enforce it.'"[69] Consideration of all of the complexities surfaced by and since the ABF survey make it abundantly clear that we do, indeed, say to the police: "Here is a problem. Deal with it." Likewise, the action of legislatures in mandating arrest in domestic violence situations also engages the issue of discretion, opting to eliminate it, but such legislation creates problems because it fails to deal with the infinite variety of factors that distinguish the cases police are required to handle and because it does not give adequate consideration to the capacity of the criminal justice system to process the greatly increased number of arrests likely to be made.

By contrast, one finds the rewards for more comprehensively confronting complexity in the optimism that pervades the current movement to implement a radically different model of policing that focuses on solving problems and on engaging the community. Problem-oriented policing and the more advanced forms of community policing engage with the full range of complex factors given visibility by the ABF survey and by subsequent research on the police. The movement acknowledges the multifaceted nature of the police function, recognizing that the job of the police is not simply to enforce the law but, more accurately, to respond effectively to a wide variety of community problems. It acknowledges that each such problem differs from every other and that the highly individualized character of the incidents that together constitute a problem require that the police be equipped with a broad range of appropriate responses, including new resources, authority, and skills. It recognizes the need for flexibility in choosing from among these responses, including discretion in the use made of arrest and prosecution. It acknowledges the need to recognize the limited capacity of the criminal justice system and the need to engage problems in accord with public expectations that transcend the obligations for enforcement. Finally, it acknowledges the need to make discrete use of the criminal justice system when it appears to be the most effective means available for dealing with a problem.

Skeptics of change in policing tend to view all new initiatives as fads, not likely to take root and have a lasting impact. They can cite much in the recent history of efforts to improve policing to support their view. The major distinctive quality of problem-oriented policing and the more advanced forms of community policing is that they grow out of a recognition of all the complexities uncovered in policing and that they are designed to connect with these complexities. As a conceptual model for the future, they are in many respects the culmination of efforts to think through the implications of all of the insights that have been acquired into policing since the results of the ABF survey first became available. Resting on so solid a foundation, the enormous potential they hold should be an incentive to maintain their purity, to resist pressures to return to simplistic responses, and to support those efforts that continue to confront the complexity inherent in the policing of a democratic society.

NOTES

1. *Report of Citizen's Committee Appointed by Mayor Peters to Consider the Police Situation, The Boston Police Strike: Two Reports* (1919; reprint, New York: Arno Press, 1971).

2. *The Chicago Memorial Day Incident,* Hearings on S. Res. 266 before a Subcommittee of the Senate Committee on Education and Labor, 74th Cong., lst sess., pt. 14 (1937; reprint, New York: Arno Press, 1971).

3. *Report of National Commission on Law Observance and Enforcement* (Wickersham Commission), vol. 11, *Report on Lawlessness in Law Enforcement*; and vol. 14, *Report on Police* (Washington, D.C.: U.S. Government Printing Office, 1931; Montclair, N.J.: Patterson Smith, 1968).

4. Raymond B. Fosdick, *American Police Systems* (1920; reprint, New York: Century Co., 1968); Bruce Smith, *Police Systems in the United States*, rev. ed. (New York: Harper and Bros., 1960); O. W. Wilson, *Police Administration* (1950). O. W. Wilson's second edition of *Police Administration* appeared in 1963, reflecting the experiences of his first years in administering the Chicago Police Department. Roy C. McLaren joined Wilson in revising the third edition and assumed responsibility for the publication after Wilson's death in 1972. A fourth edition by McLaren was published in 1977. (All four editions published by McGraw-Hill, New York.)

5. Arthur Woods, *Crime Prevention* (New York: Arno Press, 1918).

6. Arthur Woods, *Policeman and Public* (New Haven: Yale University Press, 1919).

7. August Vollmer, *The Police and Modern Society* (1936; reprint, Berkeley and Los Angeles: University of California Press: 1971).

8. Roscoe Pound and Felix Frankfurter, *Criminal Justice in Cleveland: Report of the Cleveland Foundation Survey of the Administration of Criminal Justice in Cleveland, Ohio* (Cleveland: The Cleveland Foundation, 1922); The Missouri Association for Criminal Justice, *Missouri Crime Survey* (New York: Macmillan, 1926); Illinois Association for Criminal Justice, *The Illinois Crime Survey*, ed. John H. Wigmore (Chicago: Illinois Association for Criminal Justice in cooperation with the Chicago Crime Commission, 1929).

9. Raymond Moley, *Politics and Criminal Prosecution* (1929; reprint, *Politics and People*, New York: Arno Press, 1974), 234.

10. Sam B. Warner, "Investigating the Law of Arrest," *American Bar Association Journal* 26 (1940):151–55, reprinted in *Journal of Criminal Law and Criminology* 31, no. 1 (1940):111–21.

11. William A. Westley, *Violence and the Police: A Sociological Study of Law, Custom and Morality* (Cambridge: MIT Press, 1970).

12. Arthur H. Sherry, *The Administration of Criminal Justice in the United States: Plan for a Survey to Be Conducted Under the Auspices of the American Bar Foundation* (Chicago: American Bar Foundation, 1955), 107–27.

13. See "American Bar Foundation Survey of Criminal Justice: Pilot Project Reports," 7 vols. (Dec. 1957, Mimeo., on file with the Criminal Justice Reference and Information Center, University of Wisconsin-Madison, Law School).

The American Bar Foundation published the results of its survey in a five-volume series. See p. 13.

14. For a comprehensive description of these findings, see Wayne R. LaFave, *Arrest: The Decision to Take a Suspect into Custody,* ed. Frank J. Remington (1965), 437–82.

15. See Joseph Goldstein, "Police Discretion Not to Invoke the Criminal Process: Low-Visibility Decisions in the Administration of Justice," *Yale Law Journal* 69, no. 4 (1960):554–62.

16. Frank J. Remington and Victor G. Rosenblum, "The Criminal Law and the Legislative Process," *University of Illinois Law Forum* 1960, no. 4:481–99. J. Goldstein, "Police Discretion Not to Invoke"; Herman Goldstein, "Police Discretion: The Ideal Versus the Real," *Public Administration Review* 23, no. 3 (1963):140; LaFave, *Arrest.*

17. See Frank J. Remington and Herman Goldstein, "Law Enforcement Policy: The Police Role," in President's Commission on Law Enforcement and Administration of Justice, *Task Force Report: The Police* (Washington, D.C.: U.S. Government Printing Office, 1967), 13–41. See also Herman Goldstein, "Police Policy Formulation: A Proposal for Improving Police Performance," *Michigan Law Review* 65, no. 6 (1967):1123–46; Kenneth C. Davis, *Discretionary Justice: A Preliminary Inquiry* (Baton Rouge: Louisiana State University Press, 1969); Carl McGowan, "Rule-Making and the Police," *Michigan Law Review* 70, no. 4 (1972):659–94; Gerald M. Caplan, "The Case for Rulemaking by Law Enforcement Agencies," *Law and Contemporary Problems* 36, no. 4 (1971):500–14.

18. Kenneth C. Davis, "An Approach to Legal Control of the Police," *Texas Law Review* 52, no. 4 (1974):703–25; Ronald Allen, "The Police and Substantive Rulemaking: Reconciling Principle and Expediency," *University of Pennsylvania Law Review* 125, no. 1 (1976):62–118; Kenneth C. Davis, "Police Rulemaking on Selective Enforcement: A Reply," *University of Pennsylvania Law Review* 125, no. 6 (1977):1167–71; Ronald Allen, "The Police and Substantive Rulemaking: A Brief Rejoinder," *University of Pennsylvania Law Review* 125, no. 6 (1977):1172–81.

19. The most valued results of these observations are available in Albert J. Reiss, Jr., *The Police and the Public* (New Haven: Yale University Press, 1971).

20. The connection between the ABF survey and the President's Commission on Law Enforcement and Administration of Justice was, in some respects, a personal one. Lloyd E. Ohlin, who had been consultant on field research for the ABF survey, was associate director for

research for the commission. Frank J. Remington, who had been director of field research for the ABF survey and editor of the summary volumes, was a general consultant for the commission. And Herman Goldstein, who had been a field researcher for the ABF and had responsibility for some of the initial analysis, was a consultant on the police. Ohlin, Remington, and Goldstein met with James Vorenberg, director of the commission, in the planning stages of the commission's work, and several memorandums were exchanged—especially regarding the direction of the commission's inquiries relating to the police. Subsequently Remington and Goldstein wrote chapter 2 of the task force report on the role of the police in developing law enforcement policy.

21. President's Commission on Law Enforcement and Administration of Justice, *The Challenge of Crime in a Free Society* (Washington, D.C.: U.S. Government Printing Office, 1967), 98.

22. Ibid., 108–9.

23. Egon Bittner, "The Police on Skid Row: A Study of Peace Keeping," *American Sociological Review* 32 (1967):699.

24. Egon Bittner, "Police Discretion in Emergency Apprehension of Mentally Ill Persons," *Social Problems* 14 (1967):278.

25. Egon Bittner, *The Functions of the Police in Modern Society: A Review of Background Factors, Current Practices, and Possible Role Models* (Chevy Chase, Md.: National Institute of Mental Health, Center for Studies of Crime and Delinquency, 1970).

26. Elaine Cumming, Ian Cumming, and Laura Edell, "Policeman as Philosopher, Guide and Friend," *Social Problems* 12 (1965):276; Jerome H. Skolnick, *Justice Without Trial: Law Enforcement in Democratic Society* (New York: Wiley, 1966); James Q. Wilson, *Varieties of Police Behavior: The Management of Law and Order in Eight Communities* (Cambridge: Harvard University Press, 1968); Joseph M. Livermore, "Policing," *Minnesota Law Review* 55 (1971):649–729; Jonathan Rubinstein, *City Police* (New York: Farrar, Straus and Giroux, 1973); William K. Muir, Jr., *Police: Streetcorner Politicians* (Chicago: University of Chicago Press, 1977).

27. Maurice Punch, "The Secret Social Service," *British Police*, ed. Simon Holdaway (Beverly Hills: Sage Publications, 1979).

28. American Bar Association, "The Urban Police Function" (Institute of Judicial Administration, New York, 1973, Approved draft), 30.

29. George Kelling, Tony Pate, Duane Dieckman, and Charles E. Brown, *The Kansas City Preventive Patrol Experiment: A Summary Report* (Washington, D.C.: Police Foundation, 1974); Kansas City, Missouri, Police Department, *Response Time Analysis 2* (Washington, D.C.: Department of Justice, Law Enforcement Assistance Administration, National Institute of Law Enforcement and Criminal Justice, 1978); Birmingham Police Department, Police Executive Research Forum, *Differential Police Response Strategies,* ed. Michael T. Farmer (Washington, D.C.: Police Executive Research Forum, 1981); J. Thomas McEwen, Edward F. Connors, and Marcia I. Cohen, *Evaluation of the Differential Police Response Field Test* (Washington, D.C.: Department of Justice, National Institute of Justice, 1986).

30. Kelling et al., *Kansas City Preventative Patrol.*

31. James Q. Wilson and George L. Kelling, "Broken Windows: The Police and Neighborhood Safety," *The Atlantic Monthly,* March 1982, 29.

32. Herman Goldstein, "Improving Policing: A Problem-Oriented Approach," *Crime and Delinquency* 25 (1979):236–58; Herman Goldstein, *Problem-Oriented Policing* (New York: McGraw-Hill, 1990).

33. Remark of President Johnson to members of the President's Commission on Law Enforcement and Administration of Justice (Sept. 8, 1965) quoted in Frank J. Remington, Donald J. Newman, Edward L. Kimball, Marygold Melli, and Herman Goldstein, *Criminal Justice Administration: Materials and Cases* (Indianapolis: Bobbs-Merrill, 1969), 3.

34. President's Commission on Law Enforcement and Administration of Justice, *Challenge of Crime* (see n. 21), 3.

35. Morton Bard, *Training Police as Specialists in Family Crisis Intervention* (Washington, D.C.: U.S. Government Printing Office, 1970).

36. H. Goldstein, *Problem-Oriented Policing,* 38–40.

37. Ibid., 32–34; John E. Eck, William Spelman, Diane Hill, Darrel W. Stephens, John R. Stedman, and Gerard R. Murphy, *Problem Solving: Problem-Oriented Policing in Newport News* (Washington, D.C.: Department of Justice, National Institute of Justice, 1987), 1–32.

38. For a summary of police practices as of 1980, see Nancy Loving, *Responding to Spouse Abuse and Wife Beating: A Guide for Police* (Washington, D.C.: Police Executive Research Forum, 1980).

39. As of 1988, two states had passed laws providing for mandatory

arrest in domestic violence cases. Sarah Mausolff Buel, "Mandatory Arrest for Domestic Violence," *Harvard Women's Law Journal* 11 (Spring 1988):213. By 1990, the number had grown to twelve. See Conn. Gen. Stat. Ann. § 46b–38b (West Supp. 1987); Iowa Code § 236.12 (West 1989); La. Rev. Stat. Ann. § 46:2140 (West 1989); Me. Rev. Stat. Ann. tit. 19, § 770(5) (West 1987); Nev. Rev. Stat. Ann. § 171.137 (Michie 1989); N.H. Rev. Stat. Ann. § 173–B:9 (1989); N.J. Rev. Stat. § 2C:25–5 (1989); Or. Rev. Stat. § 133.055 (1989); R.I. Gen. Laws § 12–29–3 (1988); S.D. Codified Laws Ann. § 23A–3–2.2 (1990); Wash. Rev. Code § 10.31.100 (1990); Wis. Stat. § 968.075 (1987–88). In addition, police departments in a growing number of cities have instituted mandatory arrest policies even where state statutes do not so provide.

40. American Bar Association, "Urban Police Function" (see note 28), 93–95.

41. Raymond T. Nimmer, *Two Million Unnecessary Arrests* (Chicago: American Bar Foundation, 1971).

42. *Powell v. Texas*, 392 U.S. 514 (1968).

43. The movement was spurred by the National Conference of Commissioners on Uniform State Laws, which, in 1971, adopted the Uniform Alcoholism and Intoxication Treatment Act. For a description of the evolution of the act, see Norman R. Kurtz and Marilyn Regier, "The Uniform Alcoholism and Intoxication Treatment Act: The Compromising Process of Social Policy Formulation," *Journal of Studies on Alcohol* 36, no. 11 (1975):1421–41.

44. Am. Jur. 2d Desk Book Item no. 124 (1979 and Supp. 1990).

45. See President's Commission on Law Enforcement and Administration of Justice, *Task Force Report: Drunkenness* (Washington, D.C.: U.S. Government Printing Office, 1967), 1. For an overview of the problem, see Nimmer, *Two Million Unnecessary Arrests*.

46. Federal Bureau of Investigation, *1988 Uniform Crime Reports* (Washington, D.C.: Federal Bureau of Investigation, 1989), 168.

47. See Samuel J. Brakel, John Parry, and Barbara A. Weiner, *The Mentally Disabled and the Law*, 3d ed. (Chicago: American Bar Foundation, 1985). For a description of the way in which this authority has been implemented, see Gerard R. Murphy, *Special Care: Improving the Police Response to the Mentally Ill* (Washington, D.C.: Police Executive Research Forum, 1986).

48. *Nelson v. City of Chicago,* No. 83–C–1168 (N.D. Ill., E. Div., July 7, 1983) (consent decree).

49. Charles Rosenbleet and Barbara J. Pariente, "The Prostitution of the Criminal Law," *American Bar Association American Criminal Law Review* 11, no. 2 (1973):373–427; Ellen F. Murray, "Anti-Prostitution Laws: New Conflicts in the Fight Against the World's Oldest Profession," *Albany Law Review* 43, no. 2 (1979):360–87.

50. Robert Force, "Decriminalization of Breach of the Peace Statutes: A Nonpenal Approach to Order Maintenance," *Tulane Law Review* 46, no. 3 (1972):367–493. See also Robert C. Black, "Police Control of Street Disorder: Legal Bases and Constitutional Constraints" (Report submitted to the Fear Reduction Project of the Police Foundation, Jan. 18, 1983).

51. For example, in responding to gang violence, the Los Angeles Police Department in 1988 used one thousand officers in conducting "sweeps" that resulted in the arrest of as many as one thousand persons in a weekend. At least half the cases were dropped immediately for lack of evidence. *Criminal Justice Newsletter* 19, no. 19 (Oct. 3, 1988):2–3.

52. For a summary of these developments, see Danny Scott Ashby, "Fourth Amendment Pretexts: Are Two Reasons to Stop the Defendant One Too Many?," *Baylor Law Review* 41, no. 3 (1989):495–540.

53. J. Goldstein, "Police Discretion Not to Invoke" (see note 15); Wayne R. LaFave, "The Police and Nonenforcement of the Law—Part I," *Wisconsin Law Review* 1962, no. 1 :104–37; H. Goldstein, *Police Discretion* (see note 16).

54. J. Goldstein, "Police Discretion Not to Invoke" (see note 15); LaFave, "Police" (see note 53); Davis, *Discretionary Justice* (see note 17); Gregory H. Williams, *The Law and the Politics of Police Discretion* (Westport, Conn.: Greenwood Press, 1984).

55. President's Commission on Law Enforcement, *Challenge of Crime* (see note 21), 103–6.

56. President's Commission on Law Enforcement, *Task Force Report: The Police* (see note 17), 13–41.

57. American Bar Association, "Urban Police Function" (see note 28), 121–44.

58. Commission on Accreditation for Law Enforcement Agencies, Inc., *Standards for Law Enforcement Agencies* (Fairfax, Va.: Commission on Accreditation for Law Enforcement, 1989).

59. See chapter by Wayne LaFave in this volume.

60. *Tennessee v. Garner,* 471 U.S. 1 (1985).

61. Strong support exists for the development of policies relating to, for example, the use of informants; conducting a surveillance; stopping and questioning suspects; the use of force in making an arrest; conducting a high-speed chase; deciding whether to issue a citation or make a physical arrest and detain; choosing, if the option exists, between charging a violation of a state statute or a city ordinance; conducting in-custody questioning; providing access to counsel; and conducting lineups.

62. See, e.g., Wilson, *Police Behavior* (see note 26), 293–95; Bittner, *Functions of the Police* (see note 25), 109–12; Michael K. Brown, *Working the Street: Police Discretion and the Dilemmas of Reform* (New York: Russell Sage Foundation, 1988), 292–94 ; H. Richard Uviller, *Tempered Zeal* (Chicago: Contemporary Books, 1988), 158–62.

63. In *Youngberg v. Romeo,* 457 U.S. 307 (1982), for example, the Supreme Court declared that a prime factor in determining whether a state agency adequately protects the constitutional rights of retarded persons in its custody is the extent to which professional judgment has been exercised in treatment and other decisions affecting such persons. See also *Central School District v. Rowley,* 458 U.S. 176 (1982), and *Irving Independent School District v. Tatro,* 468 U.S. 883 (1984). I am indebted to Prof. Victor G. Rosenblum for suggesting the analogy and for directing me to these cases.

64. See note 39, above.

65. Most often cited in this regard is *Thurman v. City of Torrington,* 595 F. Supp. 1521 (D. Conn. 1984), in which damages were awarded for the repeated failure of the police to respond appropriately to the plaintiff's request for help in protecting herself from an abusive spouse.

66. See chapter by Donald J. Newman in this volume.

67. A helpful summary of the rapid movement toward coordinated planning for the criminal justice system is contained in the report of the National Advisory Commission on Criminal Justice Standards and Goals, *Criminal Justice System* (Washington, D.C.: U.S. Government Printing Office, 1973), 5–31.

68. Ronald Allen, "Police and Substantive Rulemaking: Reconciling Principle and Expediency" (see note 18), 62.

69. Ibid., 97.

CHAPTER 3

The Decision to Charge, the Decision to Convict on a Plea of Guilty, and the Impact of Sentence Structure on Prosecution Practices

Frank J. Remington

INTRODUCTION

As a young law school graduate I had an opportunity in 1949 to work with a great scholar, John Dawson of the University of Michigan. His primary interest was in unjust enrichment—the problem in contract law of people attempting to obtain money in inappropriate ways, such as by threatening to accuse a person of a crime unless that person agreed to pay them some money. He suggested that I spend time in the prosecutor's office in Detroit to see if the office used the threat of criminal prosecution to force a person to agree to compensate a victim of fraud, a practice that, in theory at least, resulted in an agreement that was unenforceable and illegal under contract law and that might arguably violate the criminal statute prohibiting extortion by threats to accuse a person of a crime. I found that the practices in the real world of the prosecutor's office differed sharply from what one would expect if formal contract law was applied in practice. Many of the poor of Detroit who felt that they had been defrauded, and who were unable to afford legal assistance,

73

looked for help from the prosecuting attorney, whom they considered to be the public's lawyer. Their expectation was that the prosecutor would assist the poor by attempting to see that a just result was achieved. In many respects, this expectation was fulfilled. Prosecutors used informal, extralegal methods for dealing with minor frauds and other community problems that affected the poor, who were unable to afford legal assistance.

In handling a case involving a poor person who had been defrauded by conduct that may or may not have constituted a violation of the criminal law, the prosecutor commonly notified the suspect that a criminal prosecution was being considered. The hope was that the suspect would respond by returning the money obtained from the poor victim. Ultimately the important objective was to solve the problem. It was thought less important to decide whether the problem was a criminal fraud or a legal problem civil in nature.

Trial judges in Detroit also often used informal methods to assist victims. For example, a victim injured in an accident caused by a motorist from nearby Windsor, Canada, might confront a difficult, multinational civil law suit. The common practice was for the judge to postpone action on the driving violation until the question of compensating the victim had been settled. Under this pressure, cooperation of the defendant's insurance company commonly was forthcoming. The assumption was that a refusal to be concerned about the victim's loss would be reflected in a severe sentence for the traffic violation, perhaps jail.

This was my first in-depth experience with the "law in action" and the extent to which it differed from the "law on the books." It was my first experience in looking at the way government responded, often informally, to community problems that needed attention. It was also my first opportunity to confront the important question of whether primary reliance should be placed on "legality" and "rule" or on "choice" and the exercise of "discretion."

Although my Detroit experience was my first opportunity to look carefully at the "law in action" as reflected in prosecutor offices, it was not my last. In the mid-1950s I served as the director of field research for the American Bar Foundation Survey of Criminal Justice. This afforded me a second opportunity to learn firsthand about the practices of prosecutors and trial judges.

I was again impressed with the wide variety of problems that confronted prosecutors and trial judges, with the incredible complexity of most of those problems, and with the importance of prosecutor and trial judge practices for victims, defendants, and the larger community.

In the ensuing decades, important changes in practice have occurred. Some of these seem to be the result of changes in public attitudes and changes in ideology, particularly of those holding political power. But some changes have resulted, in large part, from empirical research, from understanding more completely what the problems are, how government responds to these problems, and the extent to which the responses contribute effectively to a resolution of these problems.

The purpose of this chapter is to describe some of the major survey research bearing on prosecutor and trial judge practice that has taken place during the past seventy years,[1] to indicate what was learned, and to try to determine whether the results of empirical research had an impact on the changes that have taken place. Primary emphasis is given to the ABF research that took place more than three decades ago because it was the first major effort to employ the survey methodologies of field observations and interviews to explore the practices of first line decision makers.

In the sections that follow, the charging and guilty plea decisions are looked at in three chronological stages: the pre-ABF research period, the ABF research, and the three decades or so since the ABF research. Guilty plea practices are given particular emphasis because these have been most controversial, more numerous than contested trials, and historically less visible to the public than the formal trial. The principal research efforts in these three periods had both strengths and weaknesses. Understanding them should enable us to do more productive research in the future and to be wiser because of the experience of the past.

Briefly stated, the strength of the pre-ABF research and the great crime surveys of the 1920s and 1930s was in making evident, by statistical analysis, where important decisions resulting in case mortality were being made in the criminal justice system. The weakness lay in the naive assumption that case mortality was necessarily undesirable and that it was caused by incompetence and political corruption. Further, the surveys ignored important aspects such as the police's low-visibility decisions that were not reflected in the case mortality statistics.

The great strength of the ABF research was methodological: a concentration on the decision making of frontline actors as a way to determine the important aspects of criminal justice administration.[2] As a consequence, the ABF research made visible previously low-visibility practices, such as the informal practices used by prosecutors and judges. In so doing, the research documented the system's great complexity by describing in detail the problems being confronted. The weakness of the ABF research lay in its overemphasis on the criminal justice system as the appropriate vehicle for responding to a wide variety of social problems, ignoring alternatives such as the mental health system and the ability of prosecutors to solve community problems without resorting to the criminal justice system. Also, observational methodology in the limited time available in each jurisdiction produced little information on the long-term results of the practices observed. Thus the prevalent informal prosecutor responses to cases of domestic violence were reported, but no systematic effort was made to study the impact of these informal practices on the frequency of repetition of the violence.

Research in the post-ABF decades has increased in volume. Numerous efforts have been made to measure the impact of practices, including previously low-visibility practices disclosed by the ABF research, such as the response to domestic violence.[3] The emphasis, however, has tended to be limited to single agency practices, and the results have been overshadowed by a heavy academic emphasis on formal, ideological positions rather than on conclusions adequately supported by factual, empirical information. Too often the major empirical studies have succumbed to the temptation to claim proof of the desirability of ideologically popular programs rather than making more appropriate and modest claims for their findings until the results have been put to the test of replication.[4]

Why thirty years later is it important to again describe and reexamine the ABF research results relating to charging and guilty plea practices?[5] The response is simple. It is because the ABF work was the first major effort to describe the practices of frontline actors in detail. By giving attention to the practices that existed before and after the ABF research, one is able to ask what difference it makes whether we know in detail what problems are faced by prosecutors and trial judges and whether we know in detail how prosecutors and judges respond to those problems in day-to-day practice. Frank Allen has recently reminded us this is particularly important today: "We are passing through a period in our public life characterized by policy initiatives based on ideology and hunch, supported by incorrect factual assumptions, partial knowledge or no knowledge at all."[6]

The basic issues, which will be given greater emphasis in the following material, can be stated briefly:

First, is it desirable or undesirable for a prosecutor to charge less than the formal law allows? If the answer is that it is sometimes desirable and sometimes undesirable, what factors are of significance in deciding which it is and how that decision should be made in an individual case?

Second, is it desirable or undesirable to negotiate the result in a criminal case by means of a guilty plea agreement? And once again, if the answer is that it is sometimes desirable and sometimes undesirable, what factors are of significance in deciding which it is and how that decision should be made in the individual case?

THE CHARGING AND GUILTY PLEA DECISIONS AS SEEN IN THE PRE-ABF RESEARCH

In response to widespread suspicions that criminal justice systems were inefficient, numerous American cities in the 1920s appointed blue-ribbon crime commissions to gather and analyze data on the disposition of criminal cases. Beginning with Cleveland in 1922, successive commissions published their findings. The surveys provided for the first time a comprehensive statistical analysis of how cases were disposed of in the criminal justice system. The data were assembled in "mortality tables," a straightforward model intended to provide a more scientific and less anecdotal image of the justice process than was previously available. The Wickersham Commission, in its 1931 analysis of the surveys, noted that

> The purpose [of the tables] is to set up the statistics in such a way as to give a picture of the number and percentages of cases which fall away or die, so to speak, at the various stages of the prosecution and trials, and thereby throw some light upon the relative responsibility of the various organs of the administration for the dispositions of cases as actually made.[7]

These early surveys are especially noteworthy because they attempted to gather system wide data. For the first time, they called attention to the flow of cases through the system as a whole, rather than focusing on the response of a single agency.

The Charging Decision

Because the mortality tables rendered a stage-by-stage image of the criminal justice process, the researchers were able to determine the point in the system at which a case "died." The picture revealed that a high number of cases "died" at the prosecution or charging stage. In St. Louis the prosecuting attorney rejected 40 percent of felony arrests brought by the police,[8] and in Cleveland 46 percent were not prosecuted.[9] The *Illinois Crime Survey*, commenting on the public concern over the escape of a particular defendant, noted the uninformed nature of the citizenry:

> The public gets excited about the sole individual who...escapes the toil of the law by climbing through a skylight, but fails to note the failure of the 10,658 prosecutions wherein the defendants were solemnly charged with major offenses but returned to the streets unnoticed. Here is a fact which the average citizen should ponder long and earnestly.[10]

The surveys revealed a wide array of means by which cases were terminated. Among these, the prosecutor had the greatest impact by declining to charge a person who had been arrested or by dismissing a case that initially had been charged. The *Missouri Crime Survey* commented on the enormous power of prosecutors in the charging decision:

> Not only in starting prosecutions, but in terminating them after they start, does the enormous importance of the prosecutor appear. The public is accustomed to thinking that arrests are followed by trials and that juries and judges decide the fate of persons accused of crime. The prosecutor is to the public a person who must prosecute all who fall into the toils of the criminal process. This conception is far from correct. In fact, the prosecutor makes most of the decisions; he terminates most of the cases, and upon him falls the responsibility of freeing most of those who are charged with crime.[11]

Most troublesome to the authors of the surveys was the enormous amount of unchecked discretion prosecutors possessed. Rarely, if ever, were prosecutors required to give reasons for case terminations. When cases were "no papered"—refused prosecution after an arrest occurred—frequently no reason was provided.[12] Prosecutors regularly terminated prosecutions without any accompanying explanation, even when explanation was required by the formal law. If there was to be judicial review, it was usually pro forma, with the court invariably accepting the decision of the prosecutor.[13]

The unstructured discretion of prosecutors was highlighted by the Cleveland survey in its description of informal screening conferences in which prosecutors disposed of cases by refusing to charge in those situations not considered major felonies. At such conferences prosecutors tried to "soothe" the anger of complaining witnesses. The survey estimated that more cases were handled by this means than were actually prosecuted, with each conference taking approximately three minutes.[14]

The surveys also revealed that many cases were discontinued by the prosecutor after an initial decision to prosecute had been made. In Cleveland in 1925, more than 11 percent of all cases indicted were nolled. In St. Louis in 1923–24 that figure was 10.2 percent, and in Minneapolis in 1923, 28.61 percent.[15]

The response of the crime survey authors to the significant case attrition rates was decidedly mixed. Most believed the high rates of attrition demonstrated a chronic inefficiency within the system. The members of the Cleveland survey believed that the rates of attrition resulted from an inefficient, politically biased system where decisions were fragmented among too many agencies with too much discretion. In such a system, with so little control over initial charging or dismissal decisions, cases inevitably were lost in the careless tumult of the system.[16] Some remarked that too little communication existed among those involved in the charging decision, especially police and prosecutors, and that cases were prepared poorly, resulting in higher case termination rates than were otherwise necessary.[17] More generally, the screening process was seen as outmoded, an "apparatus disproportionate to the job at hand" in times of markedly increased case volume.[18] Whatever the cause of the attrition rates, said the Wickersham Commission, the conclusion that the system as a whole is not an efficient one is justified.[19] Echoing this view, the Illinois Crime Survey concluded that "society has a curiously ineffective way of protecting itself."[20]

At the same time, however, in reviewing the surveys one gets the distinct feeling that many analysts, although not happy about the situation, nevertheless saw attrition as a necessary and perhaps inevitable phenomenon.[21] From this perspective, "sifting" had to occur if only the guilty were to be prosecuted and ultimately convicted.[22] Refusals to prosecute were often justified: an indictment may be faulty, witnesses may be unreliable, or a suspect may have been convicted of a more serious charge in another jurisdiction.[23] Moreover, according to the Wickersham Commission, frequently the cases prosecutors received were "slipshod" in nature, the products of a "tendency to arrest first, and find a case, if at all, afterwards, which unhappily prevails in too many localities. The sifting which must be done somewhere, and in a proper system should be done at the outset, has had to be done by the prosecuting attorney."[24] Alone among the surveys, the Missouri Crime Survey reinforced such a "systemic" view with its provision of data indicating that the more mechanical the arrest by police, that is, the less discretion exercised in the arrest decision, the greater the proportion of cases eliminated in the preliminary examination.[25] Although never explicitly stated, the assumption was that the desirable norm was charging to the full extent allowed by the formal law.

The Guilty Plea Decision

The crime surveys and related research of the 1920s and 1930s documented for the first time the enormous dependence of the American justice system on plea bargaining. To the astonishment of these early criminal justice researchers, trial by jury largely had been displaced by "justice by compromise."[26] In Chicago 85 percent of all felony convictions were based on guilty pleas; in Detroit that figure was 78 percent; in Minneapolis, 90 percent; in Cleveland, 86 percent; in St. Louis, 84 percent; and in Los Angeles, 81 percent.[27] Moreover, research showed the practice to be widespread in other, less urbanized areas: upstate rural New York registered a 91 percent guilty plea rate, and in twenty-five smaller counties within Minnesota 85 percent of all convictions derived from pleas of guilty.[28] Reflecting on these findings along with those relating to dismissals, Raymond Moley, an active force in a great many of the surveys, commented: "It is not an over-statement to point out that the practical application of criminal law is, in substance if not in form, as truly a process of administration as are such routine governmental functions as the collection of taxes."[29] What Moley meant was that decisions were driven as much by a conception of what would be an appropriate outcome in light of all circumstances that the available evidence could provide as they were by formal legal considerations.

The early researchers' focus on the practice of defendants pleading to lesser offenses than those originally charged was also enlightening. Although the practice is not mentioned in the Cleveland survey in 1922, successive surveys in Missouri, New York, and Illinois dedicated considerable attention to the phenomenon. The New York survey revealed that in 1925 in Kings County 57 percent of all pleas were to a lesser offense, but only 12 percent were to the offense charged.[30] In Chicago in 1926, 78 percent of all guilty pleas in felony cases were to lesser charges. In fact, the majority of guilty pleas were not to felonies at all but rather to misdemeanors.[31] This occurrence, the authors of the Illinois survey concluded, accounted for "the most serious loss of force and energy in the prosecution of felonies in Chicago."[32] The Illinois survey authors continued:

> Thus the meaning of the term "guilty" must be carefully analyzed in order to evaluate the quality of law enforcement in the City of Chicago. When we come to such an analysis we find the most appalling difference between the charges which are originally made against defendants and the crimes of which they are finally found guilty. This is a serious problem involved in the administration of prosecution in Cook County.[33]

As with charging, early researchers disagreed as to what explained the prevalence of plea bargaining. Poor record keeping, incompetent prosecutors and clerical staff, and poor communication among those involved were thought to account for the rampant plea bargaining revealed by the early research.[34] The Wickersham Commission in its review of the early crime survey research commented:

> A high percentage of pleas of guilt would be an indication of efficiency, as it would indicate that a low percentage of unjustified cases are instituted or that cases are so well prepared by the police and prosecution as to reduce the elements of chance on which the accused would rely in demanding a trial. When, however, these pleas are not to the offense as charged but to a

lesser offense, then this satisfaction can not be drawn; for the high percentage of such pleas is not inconsistent with considerable carelessness in the institution of cases and may represent careless or inefficient disposition of cases which would result otherwise if given thorough and efficient work.[35]

By far the most frequently perceived cause of bargaining, however, was widespread political manipulation. To an even greater extent than with charging, the research on plea bargaining disclosed plea decisions based on apparent political considerations. The problem, it was believed, was a lack of control over the discretion of prosecutors—allowing "back-stair wire-pulling and fixing."[36] The period of time after the preliminary hearing was seen as the "weakest spot" in the justice process, a time when pragmatism and politics had the capacity to predominate over justice.[37] "It is not surprising...that prosecutors have indulged to their heart's desire in the politically profitable enterprise of making friends among the friends of accused persons while at the same time and by the same acts they were building an apparent record of vigorous and successful prosecutions."[38]

In Chicago, this suspicion of political machinations implicated the bench when, in the early 1920s, three circuit court judges were temporarily removed pending an inquiry into their having reduced felonies to misdemeanors in exchange for guilty pleas.[39] The three were ultimately vindicated, with the investigators determining that the judges were not acting improperly; they were merely sanctioning the recommendations of the state's attorneys.[40]

The survey authors and commentators of the era condemned the rampant plea bargaining on many grounds. One recurrent concern stemmed from the perceived unseemly character of plea bargaining. Throughout the surveys one finds repeated accounts of the plea bargaining process either in the anarchic tumult of the criminal courtroom or in the unsupervised corridors of the courthouse. Such a process was a far cry from the measured, rational ideal of the justice process; "the spirit of an auction had come to dominate the process of justice."[41] According to Moley, plea bargaining "is not a search for the truth; it is an attempt to get as much from an unwilling giver as is possible."[42]

Related to this concern was a belief that the bargaining process was irrational and in a sense dishonest. Crimes of conviction were not reflecting the original charge. According to the

Illinois Crime Survey, "[i]f the defendant is to be prosecuted at all it should be for the crime of which he is guilty."[43] In this sense, the "appalling difference" between charges and convictions amounted to a corruption of the process.[44] The Illinois survey added: "This tendency to plead guilty is no abject gesture of confession and renunciation; it is a type of defense strategy."[45] The Illinois survey portrayed the process as nothing less than disingenuous behavior on the part of the state:

> [T]he state is not making good on its prosecutions. Either it is "bluffing" in the charges that are originally brought and pressed against criminals, that is, charging persons with more serious crimes than they should be charged with, or it is permitting the strength of the defense and the complementary feebleness of the prosecution to whittle down the force of law administration to a mere fragment of its basic seriousness.[46]

The surveys also expressed concern over the practical effects of such "bluffing." Because the penal sanction of the state so often was mitigated in instances of bargains, many argued that deterrence of criminal behavior was proportionately lessened. The *Illinois Crime Survey* claimed that plea bargaining

> gives notice to the criminal population of Chicago that the criminal law and the instrumentalities for its enforcement do not really mean business. This, it would seem, is a pretty direct encouragement to crime....
>
> [T]hrough this process of legerdemain dangerous criminals are permitted to develop an attitude toward the public which holds in utter contempt all attempts to restrain their pernicious activity.[47]

Finally, even persons partial to the interests of offenders expressed some displeasure over bargaining in the early research. Research indicated that the system potentially most harmed the least sophisticated and novice criminals and perversely most benefited hardened, experienced offenders. Defendants unfamiliar with the system were less likely to strike advantageous deals, but veteran offenders and those savvy enough to retain counsel managed the opposite.[48] Moreover, there was a concern that plea bargaining had the unintended effect of inducing some defendants to plead guilty when otherwise they would not have been convicted at trial.[49]

These negative views notwithstanding, not all research of the time saw plea bargaining as dysfunctional. Rather some believed the practice was desirable. Several reasons were given. Most commonly it was said that accepting pleas was essential given the enormous and increasing volume of cases entering the system[50] and that, because of plea bargaining, the resulting decrease in the number of cases to be tried made it possible to dedicate more attention to the jury trials. It was also said that if the state's case was weak, a plea of guilty ensured that at least some punishment would result ("half a loaf is better than none"). Finally, some pointed out that often original charges were more serious or numerous than justified and the acceptance of a plea to a less serious offense or a lesser number of offenses would more accurately reflect the seriousness of the facts of the case.[51]

Roscoe Pound asserted that plea bargaining was a predictable phenomenon in the faster, modern society that looked more to "results" than to "procedure." Legal proceedings were coming to be "judged by their results in action, not by their conformity to some abstract, ideal scheme."[52] This assertion of Pound gave renewed emphasis to the important distinction between a decision that reflects a careful consideration of a desirable case outcome under all circumstances, on the one hand, and a decision that reflects a relatively mechanical application of the law without concern for the desirability of the result.

Some saw plea bargaining as a way to mitigate the severe penalties prescribed for many criminal acts. In New York, for instance, the so-called Baumes Law required that four-time felony offenders receive automatic life sentences. In effect, discretion to mitigate punishment of offenders was taken from sentencing judges and parole boards. In actual administration, however, this discretion was reinserted in the form of prosecutorial discretion to allow, with court approval, pleas of guilty to misdemeanors in the belief that the strict application of the law would have resulted in unjust punishments.[53]

The Wickersham Commission, in its review of the results of the crime surveys, concluded that the justice system had to be viewed as an "organic whole," an interrelated system of decision points, the nature of which precluded the hope of uprooting discretion.[54] The commission concluded by inquiring to what extent, not whether, plea bargaining is an acceptable mode of criminal justice administration.[55] Moley added: "The remedy...is not a direct attack upon the practice of prosecutors. The range of methods by which criminal charges can be disposed of is so great that merely to shut off one practice will open up others."[56]

Summary

In the final analysis, the crime surveys and related research of the 1920s and 1930s were laudable first attempts to chronicle the pervasive and persistent phenomenon of case attrition at the charging and guilty plea stages. Alarmed at the impact of the practices and concerned with the specter of their justice systems spinning out of control under the weight of increased caseloads, most of the crime survey authors concluded that inefficiency and politics were at fault. Decisions were largely seen by them as being discrete and isolated events, enabling blame to be apportioned readily in accord with the particular juncture at which "mortality" became evident. With the exception of the *Missouri Crime Survey*, which effectively demonstrated the impact of nondiscretionary arrests on charging, none of the surveys critically examined such issues as the relation between the nature of an offense and the charge or the degree of charge and the ultimate plea. In its analysis of the surveys, the Wickersham Commission spoke to this need: "There is a reason for everything; but the whys and wherefores of this development can not be thoroughly explored by the simple process of locating the agency which does most of the disposing of cases and then attributing full and exclusive responsibility to that agency."[57]

The various states sought to remedy their faltering justice systems by suggesting formal means, such as the requirement of judicial approval of a decision to dismiss a prosecution.[58] However, as noted by the Wickersham Commission, "[t]he more one reads and examines the surveys, the more one becomes possessed with a sense of the complexity of the problem and the impossibility of meeting it through easy remedies."[59] Full recognition of this and its programmatic implications would have to await future research efforts.

THE CHARGING AND GUILTY PLEA DECISIONS IN THE ABF RESEARCH

Unlike the early crime surveys, the ABF research did not start with an assumption that prosecutors ought to charge to the full extent of the law or that the compromise of cases by means of a plea agreement was necessarily undesirable. Rather, the ABF research tried to understand in objective terms the decisions made by criminal agencies, including the charging and guilty plea decisions. Judgments about whether what was being done was desirable were left for others to make at another time.

The following descriptions reflect, almost exclusively, the observational research conducted in Milwaukee, Wisconsin, and Detroit, Michigan. These metropolitan areas are concentrated on for two reasons. First, the research data are more detailed than those gathered in smaller communities, where less time was spent in observation. Second, the data obtained in Milwaukee and Detroit were compiled in descriptive form in two "Pilot Project Reports"[60] making these data the easiest to retrieve. Finally, differences in the formal legal requirements in Michigan and Wisconsin make a comparative analysis of the impact of those legal requirements possible. Moreover, the ABF research in smaller communities and in Kansas did not produce data that conflicted to a significant degree with those in Detroit and Milwaukee.

The Charging Decision

The Prosecutor's Decision to Handle the Matter by Methods Other Than Prosecution   Most often a prosecutor first confronts the charging decision after the police have decided to make an arrest and have referred the case to the prosecutor so the prosecutor can decide whether to initiate a prosecution by the issuance of a complaint. In some situations, however, cases come first to the prosecutor's attention, without police involvement, and sometimes police refer victims to the prosecutor, but not on the assumption that a prosecution will be instituted.

Most cases that involve loss of money by the victim as a result of fraud come directly to the prosecutor without police involvement. The victim hopes the prosecutor can persuade the alleged offender to repay the victim the money believed to be deserved. Those cases referred by the police for reasons other than prosecution are cases in which the police have concluded that some use of the criminal justice system is desirable but that an informal method, rather than a formal prosecution, is thought to be most appropriate.

The question of whether a case comes directly to the prosecutor or comes first to the attention of the police is usually determined by whether immediate action or the use of force is needed, as in domestic violence cases to which police commonly respond.[61] In contrast, if these factors are absent, such as in fraud cases, the prosecutor has the resources needed to respond without police assistance.

Borderline Criminal Frauds and Bad Check Cases   Typically, minor fraud cases and bad check cases came directly to the prosecutor's office. At least two groups of people looked to the prosecutor for help in situations in which they believed that they had been defrauded in some way or that their property had been stolen or damaged. One group, consisting of the poor who were unable to afford counsel to bring a civil action, looked to the public prosecutor as their lawyer. A second group, merchants, found that the prosecutor was best able to help in recurring situations such as those involving the receipt of a bad check.

In both situations, the prosecutors in Milwaukee and Detroit saw their job as solving the problem by getting the victim's money returned. Typically this could be accomplished by contacting the person who had committed the offense and at least implying that a prosecution might be brought if restitution were not made. Though this was an almost universal response, prosecutors were somewhat uneasy about the practice because it conflicted with the image that the prosecutor represented the public interest, not the more limited interest of the victim. Such "law" as existed seemed to indicate that "settlement" of money and property disputes by a threat of prosecution was itself illegal, constituting both criminal extortion and an illegal agreement under contract law. The common response of prosecutors was "we say we are not a collection agency but we really are."

Family Matters—Nonsupport and Domestic Violence Cases
·Nonsupport cases were handled through a threat of prosecution if informal methods of arranging for support were unsuccessful. Although the responsibility for working out a support arrangement was left to an appropriate social service agency, clearly the ability of the agency to work out informal methods of arranging for support was dependent on the ability to threaten prosecution if support payments were not made. The prosecutor was a cooperating participant in this method of dealing with this problem.

Domestic violence cases were dealt with differently, although at least in Detroit the major responsibility for the decision as to what to do was shared by police and the prosecutor, with the decision of the prosecutor influenced by factors other than sufficiency of the evidence. The police were reluctant to arrest and commonly would refuse to do so unless the offense was committed in their presence.[62] Most cases were handled by the police at the scene. In some situations an arrest was made, but the defendant was released because the victim declined to sign a complaint. Some cases, usually if the facts were not entirely clear, were referred to a mediation process presided over by a detective, assigned to the prosecutor's office, who was commonly referred to as "judge." The most common result was to place the offender on a "peace bond." Although the so-called peace bond was not formally authorized by law, it was assumed by the combatants to be significant and appeared to satisfy the victim in most situations. That someone listened and made a decision seemed to help. This was another illustration of an informal response that was believed to constitute a practical solution of the problem. Thus, the decision of the prosecutor was influenced more by judgment of how best to deal with the problem, particularly frequently occurring problems, than it was by considerations of whether the available evidence was sufficient to justify charging with the expectation of conviction.

The various problems handled by the prosecutor by informal means had some common characteristics. They were low-visibility practices, hidden almost entirely from public view. Pre-ABF research focused not on the variety of problems confronting communities and criminal justice systems, but rather on crimes, principally felonies, in which an arrest had been made by the police. As to these latter cases it was assumed that they could best be dealt with by arrest, prosecution, conviction, and sentence. In contrast, the ABF research demonstrated that prosecutors were also confronted with a variety of important social and economic problems that were dealt with by means other than the formal processes of the criminal justice system.

The administration of the criminal law can be viewed in two quite different ways. One, that of the pre-ABF surveys, is to assume that the substantive criminal law determined what constitutes a desirable outcome. Thus a person who commits a burglary should be arrested, prosecuted, convicted, and sentenced for burglary. The second way is to look at day-to-day practice and ask the basis for deciding that an outcome is desirable. Often, as in the situations just described, the substantive criminal law is looked to not as a definition of desirable case outcome but rather as authority for the prosecutor to intervene and to "solve the problem" in the way thought best by the prosecutor. Getting a victim's money back in minor fraud cases and resolving conflict in domestic violence cases is thought more desirable than prosecution of the defendant for theft or for battery and sentencing that person after conviction.

The Prosecutor's Decision to Charge the Person with Crime   In cases in which a suspect had been arrested by police and the arrest report stated that a felony was committed, the police usually asked the prosecutor to charge the person with a crime—typically the crime specified in the arrest report.

In these cases the question was not whether there was an alternative to prosecution but rather what offense or offenses should be charged. Again in making this decision one could look to the substantive criminal law for the answers or, instead, ask the more difficult question of what is a fair and just outcome based on the facts of the individual case. In both Detroit and Milwaukee it was clear that the prosecutors were very much concerned about achieving a fair and just outcome in the individual case. But in both cities reliance on the formal, substantive criminal law was feasible because there were later opportunities to consider whether reliance on the formal criminal law would produce a fair and just outcome. In Detroit it was at the guilty plea stage when charges were reduced to make it possible to impose an appropriate sentence. In Milwaukee it was at the sentencing stage, because in Wisconsin's indeterminate system the trial judge had almost unlimited discretion in sentencing.

In Detroit, except in a few situations in which the prosecutor might have doubts about the desirability of prosecuting a clearly guilty person, the usual concern of the prosecutor was limited to whether the available evidence was sufficient to support a reasonable expectation of conviction. If the evidence was sufficient, the person was charged with a criminal offense. Commonly the effort was to charge an offense that conformed most closely with the facts of the individual case. Concern over the outcome that would result from a conviction and sentence seldom played a primary role at this stage. This was deferred to the guilty plea stage.

In Milwaukee the charging decision, as in Detroit, involved concern over whether the evidence was adequate to sustain a charge for the offense or offenses specified in the police report.[63] But in Milwaukee there was also an opportunity to consider, more broadly, whether a criminal prosecution was in fact desirable. This was reflected in the precharge conference which afforded the police, the defendant, defense counsel, and, on occasion, the victim a chance to participate with the assistant district attorney in a discussion about what, if anything, should be charged. As in negligent homicide or obscenity cases, the conference might be adjourned to allow defense counsel to submit views and argument in writing. Usually, however, the decision was made at the time of the initial precharge conference. This procedure enabled the prosecutor to give attention to the facts of the individual case and also afforded defense counsel, if counsel had been retained, an opportunity to participate in the important decision of whether to prosecute and, if so, for what offense or offenses.[64]

Similar to the situation in Detroit, the charging decision in Milwaukee was influenced by concerns about the appropriate offense of conviction but not about the sentence that would be imposed for that offense. This was not because concern about appropriate sentence would be reflected at the guilty plea stage. Rather it was because the trial judge had discretion as to sentence, a discretion that was not usually limited by the charging decision, and counsel had an opportunity to speak to the issue of appropriate sentence at the time of sentencing. With only a few exceptions, Wisconsin statutes provided the sentencing judge with a choice between probation and prison and, if a prison sentence was to be imposed, discretion to impose a sentence as short as a day or as long as the maximum provided by the statute.

It was abundantly clear in practice in both Milwaukee and Detroit that the prosecutor made the charging decision, although in both cities the attitude of the police was important in cases initiated by an arrest. Though the practice was clear, the theory of who had authority to charge was not clear in either Wisconsin or Michigan. If the decision was to charge, a judge was commonly asked to issue a complaint and arrest warrant if an arrest without a warrant had been made. This created the appearance, but not the reality, of judicial responsibility for the decision to prosecute.[65]

The Guilty Plea Decision

The ABF research, especially in Detroit, made clear that the guilty plea process was driven primarily by considerations of what was thought to be a proper outcome in the individual case. This had to be done at this stage because of the existence in Detroit of mandatory sentences. The trial judge, prosecutor, and defense counsel agreed that flexibility was needed to ensure that the outcome of the case reflected the facts of the individual case.[66] In individual cases there was disagreement between the prosecutor and defense counsel as to what an appropriate case outcome would be. However, there was no disagreement over the desirability of adjusting the offense of conviction if to do so was necessary to produce the outcome thought by prosecutor and defense counsel to be appropriate.[67] The trial judge was willing to approve of these pleas to less serious offenses almost routinely, with only occasional concern expressed by the judge if the reduction was to an offense that could not logically be related to the facts of the case. Milwaukee defendants were less likely than Detroit defendants to plead guilty to reduced charges. This was the case because of the prosecutor's unwillingness to reduce the charge because in Milwaukee, unlike Detroit, the trial judge was not bound to give a mandatory sentence based on the offense of conviction.

In Milwaukee, both prosecutor and defense counsel appeared willing to leave the choice of sentence to the trial judge.[68] Although this would seem to create a risk that the judge would impose a sentence thought inappropriate by counsel, this risk was minimized by an informal practice of discussing the sentence with the judge in chambers before the sentence was actually imposed and obtaining an early indication of what sentence the judge was willing to impose. This was done despite the fact that the judge in accepting the guilty plea would routinely state, on the record, that he was not bound by any recommendation or representation as to what sentence he would impose and that he reserved the right, in every case, to impose the maximum sentence required by law.

The Manner in Which a Guilty Plea Was Entered and Accepted by the Judge in Detroit   The guilty plea process in Detroit was brief. The judge typically asked whether the plea was voluntary, without coercion, and whether it was entered because the defendant and defense counsel had consulted before deciding whether to plead guilty. Apparently a great deal of responsibility for ensuring that the guilty plea was in the defendant's interest lay with counsel rather than with the trial judge. And it was clear that defense counsel was expected to understand the system and take appropriate steps to ensure that the mandatory sentence did not result in undue severity, given the facts of the individual case.

The Manner in Which a Guilty Plea Was Entered and Accepted by the Judge in Milwaukee   The guilty plea procedure in Milwaukee placed great emphasis on whether there was a factual basis for the plea.[69] Thus the plea procedure was more lengthy and more formal than in Detroit, with the primary concern of the Milwaukee trial judge being to learn enough about the facts of the case to be able to decide whether the offense to which the defendant was pleading guilty actually was committed by the defendant. This was accomplished by taking testimony from a number of persons—the victim, the police, and others who had knowledge about the case. If the defendant was willing to answer the judge's questions, the defendant was also encouraged to testify with respect to what actually had happened.

*Lessons Learned in the ABF Research
on Charging and Guilty Plea Decisions*

The first lesson in the ABF research was that those administering the system believed that, as to some forms of behavior, an alternative to prosecution and conviction was often the preferable response. In part this was because the societal problems confronting the prosecutor were so numerous that charging to the full extent would not have been possible with the resources available. More important, alternatives to charging and conviction were thought to produce a more appropriate outcome and a more effective response.

Second, whether the decision to charge was an executive or a judicial responsibility was unclear, an ambiguity created in part by the issuance of a postarrest warrant that served no practical purpose and that, probably for that reason, was viewed as a ministerial function of the clerk of court.[70] Though in theory who was responsible for making the charging decision was uncertain, in practice the decision was made by the prosecutor.

Third, in cases in which the decision was to prosecute, there was a willingness at the guilty plea stage to take those steps necessary to prevent what was thought to be an inappropriately severe outcome in the case.[71] This was particularly so if sentences were legislatively mandated.

Fourth, there was no system studied during the ABF research in which judgment as to what an appropriate outcome would be was not exercised at some stage, based on the facts of the individual case. At what stage this judgment was exercised, however, differed from jurisdiction to jurisdiction, depending primarily on whether there was a legislative effort to preclude the trial judge from exercising sentencing discretion.

Fifth, both the charging and guilty plea procedures were relatively informal, although in Milwaukee the precharge conference and the "minitrial," designed to ensure a factual basis for the plea existed, were somewhat more formal.

Sixth, in both Detroit and Milwaukee defense counsel played an important role. This was particularly true in Detroit where assistance was often needed by a defendant faced with a charge thought by the judge and often the prosecutor to be unduly severe. It was the function of counsel to negotiate a more appropriate outcome. In Milwaukee, if counsel was available early in the process, an important role was played in the precharge conference.

Seventh, and perhaps most significant, was the discovery that the charging and guilty plea decisions are as complex and difficult as they are important and that simple solutions, such as requiring judicial approval of the prosecutor's decision to dismiss a case, would be totally ineffective. The charging and guilty plea decisions are complex for at least the following three reasons.

The Charging and Guilty Plea Decisions Are Interrelated and Are Affected by Decisions Elsewhere in the Process   If the decision is made to issue a complaint and to proceed with prosecution, the guilty plea procedure and the charging decision usually become intimately related. For example, one course of action for a prosecutor is to charge the most serious offense possible or the greatest number of offenses possible on the basis of available evidence and then reach what the prosecutor believes to be a proper level of charge or number of offenses by agreeing to accept a plea of guilty to a lesser charge or a fewer number of offenses.[72] For some time, common practice in Wisconsin has been for prosecutors to charge first-degree intentional homicide, even if the facts would more appropriately call for a charge of a less serious degree of homicide.[73] In this situation, the prosecutor typically is willing later to reduce the charge to the appropriate level in return for a plea of guilty to the reduced charge. The result is the same as it would have been if the original charge had been for the less serious offense thought appropriate on the basis of the evidence and the subsequent conviction were for that same offense. Thus one can understand the significance of the guilty plea decision only in relation to how the charge originally brought relates to the facts of the particular case. This is a point almost universally overlooked in the evaluation of guilty plea practice.[74]

Equally true is the fact that one cannot adequately understand either the charging decision or the guilty plea decision without relating them to the sentencing practice.[75] At the time of the ABF research in Milwaukee, the judge had great discretion in sentencing. The outcome of any individual case was in large part under the control of the trial judge, who could decide on an appropriate sentence. The prosecutor had little ability to control the outcome of the case by means of either the charging decision or the decision to accept a guilty plea and thus little incentive to use either the charging decision or the guilty plea decision as a means to influence or control the judge's sentencing decision. In contrast, in a situation like that in Detroit, where mandatory sentences were common, the outcome of the case could be determined almost entirely by the charging and guilty plea decisions of the prosecutor. In a system with legislatively mandated sentences, flexibility and individualization can be introduced only by reflecting desired case outcome in the selection of charge or, when this is not accomplished by the charging decision, by the willingness to accept a plea to an offense that carries a penalty thought appropriate to the facts of the particular case.[76]

The significance of the charging and guilty plea decisions is thus directly related to the presence or absence of choice elsewhere in the system, at an earlier stage by the police or at a later stage by the trial judge in sentencing or by a correctional agency, such as the parole board, with discretion to fix the date of release from prison.

The Charging and Guilty Plea Decisions Are Complex Because of the Wide Variety of Social Problems Dealt with by Prosecutors and Trial Judges   Herbert Packer said: "We use the criminal law for as many ends today as there are ends of social control. It is widely doubted that all of these uses are equally wise."[77]

If there was ever a doubt about this, the ABF research put that doubt to rest. Shortly after the ABF field research was completed, I commented on the wide variety of social and economic problems that confronted prosecutors:

> The prosecutor and court do a lot of things....Nonsupport is given a great deal of attention by the prosecutor solely because it is the community's feeling that husbands ought to support their families and should be threatened with a severe sanction if they do not do so....In the bad check case, reliance on the prosecutor is not a result of a philosophical decision that it is desirable to subject to criminal liability the person who writes a bad check. Rather, it is because the ability of most of us to cash a check with ease is dependent upon a workable system of enforcement against those who write checks and have insufficient funds in their accounts. To date the alternative to the criminal process is a different credit system, a price we have been unwilling to pay.
>
> So when we talk about the limits or the philosophy of the criminal law, it is sort of like talking about the philosophy of a wastebasket. It is the place where all things go that are not wanted. To analyze its content is difficult because it is filled with all kinds of stuff that has been rejected by other less drastic methods of social control whether governmental, family, or religious.[78]

The Charging and Guilty Plea Decisions Are Complex Because of the Tension between the Objective of Applying the Law as Written and the Desire to Achieve a Sensible Outcome on the Facts of the Individual Case   In most situations the task of the prosecutor involved more than deciding whether the evidence was sufficient to charge a particular offense or offenses. The prosecutor commonly tried to determine the most effective response to the particular social or economic problem rather than just enforcing the law in an unthinking manner.[79] This was, for example, usual in minor fraud cases and bad check cases in which restitution for the

victim was usually thought to be better than prosecution, conviction, and sentence. Diversion of a mentally ill person to a treatment program was often preferable to prosecution. Resolving interpersonal conflict, as in the Detroit misdemeanor-complaint practice, was believed to be a better response than prosecution of the offending spouse.

Tension existed between the desire to rely on "the law" to determine a proper charging or conviction decision, on the one hand, and the desire to allow for the exercise of discretion to achieve the best result, on the other hand. Often this was a tension between the desire for severity and the desire to deal with the individual compassionately. Although there was an ideological commitment to enforcing the law by prosecuting and to the formal trial as the preferable method of adjudication, there was also a more practical commitment to use alternatives to prosecution and, if the decision was to prosecute, compromise by means of the guilty plea whenever the formal law would produce an outcome thought inappropriate in the individual case.[80]

POST-ABF DEVELOPMENTS

The Charging Decision

The trend in the decades following the ABF research has been to limit, even eliminate, the exercise of discretion at some stages of the criminal justice system. Illustrative are the increasingly common mandatory sentences for a great many offenses and mandatory arrests in domestic violence and drunken driving cases. The exception to this trend has been the prosecutor's charging decision as to which a great deal of discretion continues to exist. In fact the significance of the prosecutor's discretion has greatly increased because of the elimination of discretion at other stages of the criminal justice system, particularly the sentencing stage.

Ignored has been Raymond Moley's early admonition that if discretion is to exist it should be exercised whenever possible in the open, in court, rather than behind the closed doors of the prosecutor's office. Instead, the trend seems to be the opposite—to eliminate discretion where it is most visible, as in the courtroom, while tolerating its continued existence where it is less visible, as it is at the charging stage.

The importance of the prosecutor's charging discretion has also increased because of the failure of earlier efforts at codification and clarification of the substantive criminal law. Joe Goldstein recently wrote: "full enforcement is a program for the future. That future never arrived. I share with you that today is more like the past than any future we might have contemplated or hoped for when the ABF survey was undertaken."[81]

In his frequently quoted statement, Herbert Wechsler, the reporter for the American Law Institute's Model Penal Code, said, "A society that holds, as we do, to belief in law cannot regard with unconcern the fact that prosecuting agencies can exercise so large an influence on dispositions that involve the penal sanction, without reference to any norms but those that they may create for themselves."[82]

In fact, progress was made in the 1950s and 1960s toward codification and clarification of the traditional crimes that historically made up the substantive criminal law. But the escalating concern about crime in more recent decades has resulted in a proliferation of new criminal statutes that often duplicate, overlap, or conflict with existing statutes. The result is that the prosecutor has an almost unlimited choice of statutes under which to prosecute. Herbert Packer anticipated the problems that would result:

> [T]he character of the processes of criminal justice is formed by the substantive tasks allotted to them. A criminal law that deals centrally with gross injuries to persons and property...requires very different institutional processes for its administration than does a criminal law that plays a role in every sphere of social policy in which government takes a hand, as Anglo-American criminal law has increasingly come to do."[83]

Appellate courts have made the problem worse by holding that charging and convicting a person under two similar, even identical, statutes is appropriate. Any thought that one could look to the substantive criminal law as a basis for rational charging decisions no longer exists.[84]

Judge Charles D. Breitel's defense of prosecutorial discretion is truer today than ever before: "If every...prosecutor...performed his...responsibility in strict accordance with rules of law, precisely and narrowly laid down, the criminal law would be ordered but intolerable."[85]

At the same time that the prosecutor's decision to charge was becoming more and more important, there were also developments that significantly affect the way prosecutors use their charging authority. This is particularly true with respect to the rise of the victims' rights movement.

The growth of the victims' rights movement has resulted in increased pressure on the prosecutor's charging decision. Tension has been created in some cases between the prosecutor's assessment of the public interest and the victim's assessment of his or her own interest. At the time of the ABF survey, ambiguity existed as to whether the decision to prosecute was a judicial responsibility of the trial judge or an executive responsibility of the prosecutor.[86] This seemed to be of only theoretical concern, because reliance was uniformly placed on the prosecutor to make the decision. The victims' movement, particularly the women victims' concern about sexual assault, has made what was of theoretical concern now a problem in day-to-day practice, because victims increasingly request the judge to issue a complaint on less evidence (probable cause) than is commonly required by the prosecutor (reasonable expectation of conviction).[87] Finally, what was, at the time of the ABF research, a largely invisible use of the criminal law to reimburse victims of crime for the financial loss they suffered has been replaced by a more recent formal emphasis on reimbursing the victim, usually in the form of a requirement that restitution be ordered and, more recently, that a civil judgment for the amount of loss caused the victim be entered as part of the criminal proceeding.

These changes have increased pressure to enforce the law as written, particularly with respect to conduct of concern to victims, rather than exercising discretion to reflect the facts of the individual case. But limitations of jail and prison space, high corrections cost, and concern over the high percentage of young black males in prison raise important questions about the trend toward increasing severity. How these conflicting pressures will bear on prosecutors' charging practices is a question of central importance.

With respect to the charging decision today there are some things we know; there is much that we do not know.

We know that the charging decision is, in many situations, the single most important decision made in the individual case.

We know that efforts to limit discretion at other stages, such as sentencing, have greatly increased the power of the prosecutor and the importance of the charging decision. For example, one federal judge, reflecting a view widely held by members of the federal judiciary, recently said: "Congress, through the minimum mandatory sentencing statutes and the sentencing guidelines, has severely curtailed the discretion of the court at sentencing, but no similar limitation has been placed on the exercise of discretion of...prosecutors. This situation results in de facto sentencing by...prosecutors."[88]

We do not know whether shifting discretionary power from judge and correctional agency to the prosecutor is wise. If the objective is an overall reduction in the amount of discretion exercised in criminal justice administration, it obviously follows that greater controls over the charging decision will be needed. If the policy judgment is that power is better lodged in the prosecutor than in the court, then it is necessary to identify more clearly why this is believed to be so[89] and to determine whether the objectives of change are being achieved in day-to-day administration. Certainly it has long been assumed that it is preferable in a democratic society that important governmental decisions be made in the open, visible to public view. The shift of discretion from the trial judge in sentencing to the prosecutor in charging is contrary to this assumption.

We know that the problems confronted by the prosecutor are so wide ranging and so factually diverse that no single approach to charging will sensibly deal with the many problems confronted. Yet pressures continue in the direction of single, simple solutions such as strict mandatory punishment.

Finally, and perhaps most important, we know that proper charging practices cannot realistically be based on the "law." The legislative proliferation of criminal statutes, repeater provisions, and sentencing enhancers has so greatly increased the scope of authority of the prosecutor that charging all the law would support and giving sentences in proportion to the charges would produce sentences so severe that it would be economically impossible to maintain a prison and correctional system large enough to handle the resulting offender caseload. Courts have completely abandoned any effort to insist on a principle-based, systematic criminal code and have held, instead, that it is proper to prosecute, convict, and sentence under two overlapping statutes that prohibit identical conduct. Add to this the reduction or elimination of trial judge discretion, and the result is that the only standards that exist to guide prosecutor charging are those developed by prosecutors themselves.

What we do not know is what, if anything, should be done about the immense amount of discretion possessed by the prosecutor.

Frank Miller believed that "some system which would ensure uniformity of treatment in the charging process should be devised."[90] Kenneth Davis has been a principal proponent of the requirement of administrative rules to control prosecutor discretion.[91] Following suggestions such as that of the National Advisory Commission on Criminal Justice Standards and Goals[92] and the American Bar Association Standards for Criminal Justice,[93] some prosecutors such as Attorney General Edward Levi developed guidelines for the charging decision.[94] Some state prosecutors have adopted guidelines and believe the guidelines to be effective.[95] Yet there is reason to doubt that guidelines will be effective: "[E]xperience suggests that prosecutors' offices today do not necessarily generate the incentives and rewards that would motivate prosecutors either to discover circumstances where formal policy is appropriate, to formulate it wisely, or to abide by it when made."[96] An alternative suggestion is to change the structure of the charging decision by utilizing the precharge conference.[97] This contributes to the information available to the prosecutor, and the opportunity for discussion prior to making the important charging decision may give greater emphasis to "whether the ways prosecutors make decisions encourage substantive rather than formal rationality."[98]

We lack the knowledge necessary to decide whether giving increased power and discretion to the prosecutor is wise and lack also the knowledge necessary to decide how best to structure the charging decision so that it does focus on the substantive concern of how best to achieve the social control objectives of the criminal justice system.

The Guilty Plea Decision

In the decades following the publication of the ABF research, there have been increasing efforts at critical analysis of guilty plea practice and a number of empirical research studies designed to test whether guilty plea practice is an undesirable, if expedient, aspect of criminal justice administration, on the one hand, or a normal and useful way to reach a "just" result on the facts of the individual case, on the other hand. Efforts also have been made to guide and control guilty plea practice by imposing increasingly formal requirements for the taking of the guilty plea, including an obligation on the part of the trial judge to review and to accept or reject a negotiated plea.[99]

Increased Formal Requirements for Taking a Guilty Plea   The lead was taken at the federal level through changes in the Federal Rules of Criminal Procedure. Rule 11 of the federal rules has influenced both court decisions and statutory developments throughout the country. The changes that have occurred have greatly increased the responsibilities of the trial judge in taking a guilty plea and, in the process, may have had the unintended effect of lessening the significance of counsel, particularly of defense counsel. The new, formal requirements have been mainly of four types:

1. A requirement that there be a finding that there is a factual basis for the plea
2. A recognition of the propriety of plea negotiation and a clarification of the relative control of the judge and counsel over the extent to which an agreement can properly affect case outcome, particularly the sentence to be imposed
3. Increased requirements to ensure that a defendant knows what rights are given up by pleading guilty
4. Increased requirements to ensure that a defendant knows the consequences of the plea, particularly the maximum penalty that can be imposed

The change requiring that there be a factual basis for the plea seems clearly a reflection of the ABF research reporting guilty plea practice in Milwaukee.[100] The requirements of openness and judge approval of a negotiated plea reflect increased recognition of the importance of guilty plea practice demonstrated by ABF and pre-ABF research. Notice to the defendant of the consequence of the plea and of the rights being relinquished seems not to have been influenced by ABF or earlier research.

Research on the Costs or Benefits of Current Guilty Plea Practice
Recent research, such as that done in Alaska and in El Paso, Texas, is instructive. Both research projects conclude that an effort to eliminate the negotiated plea of guilty is unlikely to be successful.

Although the results are not conclusive, studies such as the one conducted in El Paso suggest that the reason for the persistence of plea bargaining is the desire in many situations to reach an agreement as to an appropriate case disposition. The advantage, particularly from the point of view of the defendant, is either to avoid an overly severe mandatory sentence or, in a system in which the judge has sentencing discretion, to eliminate the uncertainty as to what the judge will do: "Since in most instances it is not possible to predict either the outcome of trial or the sentence upon conviction, when a defendant receives an offer with a firm sentence commitment he may voluntarily choose the sentence over the added uncertainty of a trial."[101] There is less reason to believe in the alternative explanation that plea bargaining is caused by caseload pressures. For example, the El Paso study concluded that evidence that caseload pressure was the cause was largely lacking and that the evidence was stronger that the real influence was a desire by counsel to cooperate in reaching a mutually satisfactory solution.[102]

Even if successful, abolition of the opportunity to negotiate a plea agreement is unlikely to substantially change case outcome, particularly the sentence, at least in serious cases in jurisdictions in which the trial judge has discretion to impose the sentence thought appropriate on the facts of the individual case. (This is in contrast to mandatory sentence jurisdictions, like Detroit, where charge bargaining has a direct impact on the sentence.) A report on the Alaska experience, at a time when the Alaskan trial judge had sentencing discretion, concludes: "The negotiated arrangements in these kinds of cases were, therefore, more in the nature of insurance against an unexpectedly harsh sentence than true 'concessions' or 'bargains.'"[103] A careful study of an effort to eliminate plea negotiation in El Paso, Texas, "shows that the ban did not affect the duration of prison sentences imposed by judges" in Texas where the judge had sentencing discretion.[104]

The perception that the elimination of plea negotiation would necessarily change sentence outcomes seems clearly to be without empirical support. The evidence strongly suggests that in serious cases, of greatest public concern, the results achieved by negotiation and compromise approximate the sentences in cases that have been tried to the court or jury.

Questions do, however, remain. The El Paso study indicated that overcharging by prosecutors was more common in a system that has plea negotiation than in a system that does not. As used in the El Paso study, the term *overcharging* refers to a lawyer's judgment that the charge was "more than [the case] was worth." This confirms the close relationship between the charging and guilty plea decision and the temptation in a negotiated plea system to charge at a higher level and reduce to an appropriate level in return for a guilty plea.

In contrast, a 1991 study of the Alaska plea bargaining ban concluded that prosecutor screening increased after the ban.[105] In fact, most prosecutors adopted a "beyond a reasonable doubt" standard for charging.

The tendency to charge more than the case is worth when plea bargaining is common gives rise to questions whether negotiated pleas create a risk that an innocent person will plead to an offense not committed to avoid a risk of conviction of the more serious offense. This risk is minimized by the now common requirement that the trial judge accept a guilty plea only if there is a finding of a factual basis for the plea. This was a prominent part of the practice observed in Milwaukee during the ABF research and, in subsequent decades, has become common throughout the country.[106] Questions remain, however, whether the practice puts undesirable pressure on a defendant to plead guilty and whether some defendants who refuse to plead are sentenced to more than the case is worth.

With respect to guilty plea practice there is much that has been learned; much we know too little about. But no one today doubts the central importance of guilty plea practice.

Controversy about the desirability of the negotiated guilty plea continues today. It has become an increasingly common political issue raised by candidates for public office who assert that plea negotiation results in both undue leniency to defendants and a risk that innocent defendants will be tempted to plead guilty to offenses they did not commit. Thus the basic question of whether guilty plea practice is an aberration or a normal and desirable part of the criminal justice system remains an important question.

In situations in which "solving the problem" is the objective of the criminal justice system, compromise, as in civil litigation, is an effective way to accomplish this. Illustrative is a fraud case in which there is a guilty plea, probation, and a requirement of restitution. Satisfaction with compromise in these cases probably reflects the fact that the crimes are not thought to be especially serious and restitution accomplishes the principal objective of the victim. On the other hand, if the objective is dramatizing the wrongfulness of the conduct as a way to educate the public, it is commonly assumed that the trial more effectively accomplishes these objectives.[107]

Although it is true that the formal trial does give the greatest visibility to the societal response to the criminal conduct, opponents of the compromise of criminal cases by means of a guilty plea usually assert also that the practice detracts from the deterrent value of the process because it results in undue leniency. Such research as has been conducted indicates that this is not the case, because the abolition of plea bargaining does not impact on the actual sentence given to the serious offender. Rather the difference between a system that recognizes the propriety of compromising criminal cases and those that do not is much more subtle. The difference is in public perception of leniency and differences in the stage of the process at which discretion is in fact exercised. More specifically:

1. If the trial judge has sentencing discretion, the recognition of the propriety of a plea agreement shifts discretion as to sentence from the judge to counsel. The elimination of plea bargaining shifts discretion back to the trial judge.[108]

2. If plea bargaining has been abolished and sentencing discretion is left to the trial judge, guilty pleas continue to be common if the sentence to be imposed by the judge is predictable and is believed by counsel to be reasonable.[109] Predictability can be achieved either formally through sentence guidelines or informally through a private, in camera conference with the judge. This was the practice in Milwaukee during the ABF survey and was the practice in El Paso after plea bargaining was abolished.[110]

3. If the trial judge is required to impose a legislatively mandated or guideline-mandated sentence that is thought to be overly severe in light of the facts of the individual case, discretion is reintroduced, often through a plea of guilty to a less serious offense. This was reflected in the Detroit practice during the ABF survey,[111] appears to be happening in the federal courts since the mandatory guideline system was adopted,[112] and happened in Alaska after a presumptive sentence system was adopted.[113]

4. In a system that prescribes the sentence the trial judge must impose and that prohibits plea bargaining (in theory, today's federal system), one would anticipate that pressure to compromise will shift to the prosecutor either in the selection of the initial charge[114] or in a stipulation of fact that will affect the application of a mandatory guideline. There is some evidence that this is occurring in the federal system.[115]

5. If plea bargaining is not recognized as proper so that it can be exercised in the open and particularly if the trial judge also lacks sentencing discretion, the risk is that negotiation will continue to take place and compromises will be made in secret. The obvious disadvantage is the resulting lack of visibility and accountability. This is what happened when the effort was made to abolish plea bargaining in El Paso.[116]

6. In a system in which sentences are mandatory, plea bargainings are prohibited, and discretion is not exercised at charging, one would anticipate an increase in the number of trials. This happened in El Paso.[117] The exception might be a system in which the mandated sentences were thought to be moderate.

The Alaska experience is clearly the best illustration of the operation of the factors just identified. *Alaska's Plea Bargaining Ban Re-evaluated,* published in 1991, points out that when the Alaska trial judge had sentencing discretion, the prohibition against plea bargaining was effective because the sentences trial judges imposed were consistent with the sentences previously agreed on through plea negotiations. This was similar, therefore, to the Milwaukee experience during the ABF survey. When judges are given discretion and exercise that discretion in a consistent, predictable, and reasonable fashion, sentencing responsibility can be exercised almost entirely by the trial judge. Subsequently in Alaska, the legislature adopted a system of presumptive sentences that limited the sentencing discretion of the judge. This led to a very significant increase in charge bargaining resembling the situation in Detroit during the ABF survey, when restrictions on trial judge sentencing discretion produced a prevalent practice of charge bargaining to avoid what was perceived to be the overly harsh consequences of mandatory sentences.

The lesson of the Alaska experience seems clear and seems to confirm the conclusion of the ABF research. It is that the effort to eliminate or substantially reduce discretion at one stage, for example, trial judge sentencing, creates apparently irresistible pressure to exercise discretion at another stage, such as charge bargaining. In this contest between the legislative desire for uniformity and often severity and the desire of frontline practitioners to reflect the circumstances of the individual case, the desire for individualization is the stronger force and usually prevails.

The guilty plea procedures have become more lengthy and more formal. Important questions remain whether the increasingly detailed formal procedures are implemented primarily to make a record of judicial concern over whether the defendant has made an informed plea or whether the procedures are implemented in a way that actually does ensure that the plea is both informed and voluntary. Recent research[118] suggests that the formal procedures are not an effective way to either communicate information to defendants or make the defendants feel that they have had an opportunity to be heard—to tell their story.

The Changing Roles of Trial Judge, Prosecutor, Defense Counsel, and Victim in the Charging and Guilty Plea Decisions

In the decades since the ABF research was conducted, significant changes have occurred in the roles of judge, counsel, and victim. To briefly recapitulate, at the time of the ABF research the prosecutor clearly played the dominant role in the charging decision. Although there was ambiguity in legal theory as to whether the decision was an executive decision for the prosecutor to make or a judicial decision for the trial judge to make, in practice the judge did not participate in any significant way in the charging decision.[119] With the exception of the Milwaukee precharge conference utilized when the defendant could afford retained counsel,[120] no significant role was played by defense counsel or the victim in the charging decision.

In guilty plea practice the prosecutor and defense counsel played a very significant role in reaching a negotiated agreement. In the court hearing on the acceptance of the guilty plea, the trial judge, especially the Milwaukee trial judge, played a significant role in ensuring that the defendant was guilty of the offense to which he pleaded guilty. The victim did not play a significant role in guilty plea practice at the time of the ABF survey.

The availability of counsel for indigent defendants has changed. The earlier system in which counsel was appointed at the guilty plea stage has been replaced in many areas by a public defender system with staff available as early as the charging stage. Yet despite the fact that in Wisconsin a major argument in favor of the public defender system was early availability, the new system does not afford representation at the charging stage. This has happened notwithstanding the increased recognition that the charging decision is the single most important decision that will be made affecting the life of the defendant. The reason is said to be a shortage of staff though it seems more likely to be a continuing failure to recognize the important role that can be played by defense counsel at stages other than the guilt phases of the criminal justice process.

The influence of the victim at the charging stage has greatly increased as a result of the efforts of organizations, such as Mothers Against Drunk Driving, that monitor prosecutor charging practices in cases with interest by a group identifying with victims. Individual victims also play an increasingly important role in cases such as sexual assault, and victims have in some situations persuaded judges to issue a complaint charging a person with the commission of a sexual assault after the prosecutor has declined to do so. This has, in turn, given the trial judge an increased role, at least in some charging decisions.[121]

In summary, the prosecutor continues to play the dominant role in the charging decision, though both the victim and the trial judge increasingly are involved. Even when a precharge conference is available, the public defender staff has chosen not to participate in the charging decision.

The post-ABF trend in guilty plea cases is to impose increased responsibility on the trial judge to ensure that the plea is a voluntary, informed, and accurate plea of guilty. The expansion of Federal Rule 11 illustrates this. In the early 1960s, in its initial consideration of guilty plea practice, the Advisory Committee on Criminal Rules, and particularly its reporter Edward Barrett, gave emphasis to the important role played by both the trial judge *and* defense counsel. Indeed, in early drafts, Professor Barrett resisted the placing of additional burdens on the trial judge, preferring to leave the responsibility on defense counsel. For example, in 1963, he opposed requiring the trial judge to find a factual basis for the plea, stating, "I think we need to rely...upon efforts to increase the availability and quality of representation by counsel."[122] Barrett's proposed rule would have prohibited a defendant from pleading guilty if not represented by counsel.

Some also objected to the proposal that the judge address the defendant personally and explain various aspects of the plea. These objections were based in large part on the assertion that it "would be a useless formality where the defendant is well represented and the lawyer can assure the court that the defendant knows what he is doing."[123]

Despite early recognition of the important role that counsel might play, the trend in the development of rule 11 very soon switched to total, at least formal, reliance on the trial judge to ensure fairness and care in the guilty plea process or at least to establish a formal record that the judge had tried to ensure that the plea of guilty was an informed decision by the defendant. Additional requirements were added to rule 11. Each new addition was motivated by a desire to respond to a problem that had arisen in practice and a desire to be more specific about the detailed responsibilities imposed on the trial judge.

Although increased emphasis was given to the duties of the trial judge, certain important objectives could not realistically be achieved by the trial judge. Thus, in a 1974 amendment, the rule was changed to eliminate the requirement that the judge inform the defendant of the "consequences of the plea" and substituted instead that the judge ensure that the defendant understands "the mandatory minimum penalty...and the maximum possible penalty." In explanation it was pointed out that this information is readily available to the trial judge but other important consequences cannot realistically be known at the time of taking the guilty plea if the judge has not seen the presentence report.

Unfortunately, the recognition that the judge lacked the

capacity to do certain things was not followed by a recognition that the defense counsel must do so if the defendant is to be adequately informed. The early assumption of the important role of counsel was not reflected in the development of the more formal guilty plea requirements in rule 11.

Santos v. Kolb illustrates the absence of any formal, required role for defense counsel.[124] In *Santos*, defense counsel forgot to inform the client that the plea of guilty would result in his being sent back to Cuba unless the trial judge issued an order providing that the conviction should not be the basis for expulsion to Cuba. Absent the request, the trial judge did not issue the order within the required period of time. Although the courts that decided the postconviction motion agreed that expulsion was the most important and serious consequence for this defendant (he may be executed if returned to Cuba), they also held that it was a collateral consequence concerning which the court need not inform the defendant. The court need not inform the defendant, knowing the consequence is not essential to a valid plea, and therefore the failure of counsel to inform the defendant does not constitute ineffective assistance of counsel.

The implication of this is significant. It means that if there are to be requirements for taking a valid plea, those requirements have to be imposed on the trial judge; otherwise neither the judge nor defense counsel needs to meet the requirement. The obvious question is why not impose on defense counsel those responsibilities that are better performed by counsel than by the trial judge? The answer seems to be a lingering belief, perhaps held over from an earlier day when counsel often was not available, that counsel cannot be relied on.

Obviously, competent counsel will spend time explaining the alternatives and the consequences of a plea of guilty to the client. But doing so is despite, rather than because of, the requirements of law. Legally a defense counsel has served the client competently, rendered effective assistance, if a defense counsel has done absolutely nothing.

CONCLUSION

Great attention is commonly given to research results that support a current, popular ideology. In contrast, much less attention is given to research, like the ABF research, that stresses the complexity of the problems and, as a consequence, the need for varied, individualized responses. This latter type of research is more difficult to understand and is less widely publicized, probably because it does not give support to simple, easy-to-understand solutions to the complex problems. For example, understanding research results that claim that plea negotiations reduce the charge originally filed and thus are undesirable because they lessen the severity of the punishment[125] is obviously easier than understanding research results that indicate that negotiation and compromise are sometimes appropriate (as when the original charge was overly severe) and sometimes inappropriate and that the task is to decide when the practice is appropriate and when it is inappropriate.

Although this fact limits the impact of research like the ABF research, there are also encouraging signs that careful ethnographic research that makes modest claims of significance does make a contribution over a period of time. Some of the contributions of the ABF research that relate to charging and guilty plea practices are:

First, the ABF research findings contributed to an increased understanding that an effort to eliminate or reduce discretion at one stage in the process where it is visible, such as in trial court sentencing, will create a risk that discretion will merely shift to another stage where its exercise is less visible, such as the charging and guilty plea stages.[126] In the implementation of the federal sentencing guidelines, it has been recognized that the objective of uniform treatment of defendants based on the seriousness of defendant's conduct may be defeated unless prosecutor discretion is controlled. The underlying assumption is that "rule," rather than "judgment" and "discretion," should determine appropriate case outcome. What has not been determined is whether it is possible, even if desirable, to eliminate discretion entirely and, if it is, how to accomplish that objective. The ABF research results suggest, but do not conclusively prove, that the complete elimination of discretion is neither possible nor desirable.

Second, the ABF research, which gave emphasis to the work of the frontline practitioner, demonstrates that the practitioner does not utilize nondiscretionary responses, ideologically popular though they may be. Practitioners who confronted difficult social-behavioral problems firsthand practically always adopted the flexible, discretionary response thought to work best under the individual circumstances. Thus, prosecutors exercised discretion in charging, and both prosecutors and trial judges did so in plea negotiations. In contrast, the attempt to eliminate discretion in the implementation of the federal sentencing guidelines has required an effort to control prosecutor discretion "by those at the pinnacle of the criminal justice pyramid (Congress, the commission, and the Department of Justice) to get those on the diffuse lower ranks, who have potentially conflicting interests and agendas, to comply with centrally determined policies."[127]

Third, at the time of the ABF research, low visibility was a principal characteristic of prosecutor and trial judge discretionary practices such as the precharge conference and plea negotiations.

Fourth, practitioners expressed concern that exposing discretionary practices to public view as a result of the ABF research would lead to criticism and efforts to substitute formal rules and procedures for the informal, discretionary practices. Subsequent experience has demonstrated that this was a realistic fear.[128] As the negotiation and compromise of criminal cases became more visible, efforts increased to eliminate the practice largely because the discretionary practices often do not conform to ideological preferences even though the discretionary practices may serve utilitarian objectives. Pamela Utz makes this point in her perceptive book, *Settling the Facts*: "Substantive justice considerations take hold when prosecution and defense also wear the mantle of judge and learn to collaborate in determining 'really what happened' and what sanction is warranted." But she adds that, despite this fact, "Unfortunately the criticism of negotiated and discretionary justice has remained largely ideological."[129] When emphasis is on utilitarian objectives, flexibility and discretion are commonly exercised; when emphasis is on ideology, rule and formality commonly prevail. An increasing amount of research data indicates that people's response to a general policy question, such as whether the compromise of criminal cases results in undue leniency, differs from the response to the same questions in the context of the detailed facts of an individual case.[130] The public opinion polls measure responses to general questions such as whether plea bargaining is desirable or undesirable; the practitioner faces that issue in the context of an individual case, involving an individual offender and often mitigating circumstances.

Fifth, discretionary practices are likely to survive after they become publicly visible only if the practices achieve objectives that have public support. Thus, the earlier ABF study described informal practices of prosecutors to get money back for victims who were defrauded rather than to prosecute the offender, and these have survived. This is in contrast to many practices designed to rehabilitate offenders, about which there was greater professional and public skepticism. Even when practices serve utilitarian objectives, however, visibility tends to lead to formality. Thus, the very popularity of restitution for victims has led to rules mandating that restitution be ordered without regard for the facts of the individual case.[131] In other words, increased visibility tends to result in the elimination of discretion by mandating the use of practices thought desirable and by prohibiting the use of practices thought undesirable.

Sixth, the difficulty with formal rules is the tendency in practice to see a rule as the objective rather than as a means to achieve a substantive objective. This is illustrated in guilty plea practice. In an effort to prevent the inadequate guilty plea practice of the past, detailed rules have been adopted to ensure that the careless or incompetent trial judge at least complies with the detailed formal procedures. But the good trial judge then has little incentive to modify the guilty plea procedure even when to do so will better achieve the objective of an informed guilty plea.[132] Compliance by the trial judge with formal procedures will be affirmed on appeal, but a departure can conceivably result in a reversal, and even if it does not, there is no reward for trying to improve a standard procedure.[133] The most difficult task in developing rules of procedure—for example, a guilty plea procedure—is to do so in ways that facilitate and reward the work of the excellent trial judge who strives to achieve the substantive objective in the individual case, departing from literal compliance with the rule when it is necessary to do so, while at the same time discouraging the use of clearly inadequate methods by the incompetent trial judge.

In brief, the ABF research suggests, but does not conclusively prove, that it is naive to believe that the criminal justice system can operate sensibly by rules alone without the exercise of discretionary judgment. The problems are too complicated, the factual variations are too numerous, and the experiences of the frontline practitioners are clearly to the contrary. A recent study of prosecutor circumvention of sentencing guidelines indicated that one reason is a "commitment to the prosecutor's own conception of a fair sentence rather than to full enforcement of the law."[134]

This is the clear message of the ABF research. It is also the conclusion reached by those who, in the ensuing three decades, have studied prosecutor day-to-day practices. For example, Carter concludes after studying practices in a California prosecutor's office: "This book argues that, on balance, we should prefer that such control efforts fail, that criminal justice reform should instead seek primarily to develop men and organizations that change, innovate, and learn in a sustained rather than haphazard fashion."[135] A similar conclusion is reached by Weninger in his study of prosecutor practices in El Paso[136] and by Utz, who studied prosecutor offices in San Diego and Alameda County. She recommends "a strategy that informs instead of only limiting the exercise of official discretion and reduces the obstacles that now frustrate sensible and sensitive problem solving."[137] Arthur Rosett and Don Cressey, who spent months in a California prosecutor office, conclude: "As long as decisions are the results of formulas for processing cases rather than of informed human judgments, justice will not be done."[138]

Sensible and sensitive problem solving requires the exercise of judgment in charging and guilty plea practices.[139] The quality of the decision made is dependent not on whether the law is fully enforced, as was the assumption of the early crime surveys, or whether the appearance of equal treatment is achieved by mandating decisions based on statistical analysis of past practices, as is popular today. Rather, the quality decision is the decision that most sensibly responds to the social problem involved, whether it be a case of domestic violence, bad checks, sexual assault, homicide, or the infinite variety of other problems confronting prosecutors and trial judges.[140] Achieving quality in decision making requires an informed, experienced, and sensitive exercise of judgment; decisions made, not at "the pinnacle of the criminal justice system," but rather at the "lower ranks" by those who see the problems firsthand and who are capable of assessing the circumstances of the individual case.

Albert Alschuler, in a recent analysis of the experience with mandatory sentence guidelines, reaches a conclusion very similar to that reached by this analysis of the ABF research; that is, the choice is not between an individualized decision in which the decision makers "are free to indulge their whims and biases," on the one hand, or a full enforcement or mandatory guidelines system "in which cases are grouped on the basis of a few characteristics and in which [as a consequence] unlike cases are treated alike."[141] Alschuler's conclusion is similar to that reached by the Administrative Law Section of the American Bar Association, which concluded that both rules and guidelines ought not preclude "needed individualizing in applying the policy...to the facts and circumstances of each particular case."[142]

Statutes can and should limit discretion, and standards can and should guide its exercise.[143] But the test, whether of effectiveness or of fairness to the individual, is whether all of the circumstances of the individual case are taken into account in making the decision. To date, neither rules nor mandatory guidelines alone can do this. Only the mind of the decision maker has the capability of taking into account all of the significant facts of the individual case and giving them such weight as they deserve.[144] The fact that this is well understood by most prosecutors, defense counsel, and trial judges who remain committed to achieving both effectiveness and fairness explains why legislative efforts to eliminate the exercise of discretion have failed, why they have merely moved the exercise of discretion to a different place in the system.

NOTES

I am indebted to Wayne Logan, who prepared an excellent draft of the material dealing with the great crime surveys of the 1920s and 1930s. Wayne is author of an excellent comment, "A Proposed Check on the Charging Discretion of Wisconsin Prosecutors," *Wisconsin Law Review* 1990, no. 6: 1695, and is coauthor of Frank J. Remington and Wayne A. Logan, "Frank Miller and the Decision to Prosecute," *Washington University Law Quarterly* 69, no. 1 (1991): 159. Steve Bauer provided helpful research assistance. I am obviously indebted to Frank Miller, who wrote the ABF book *Prosecution: The Decision to Charge a Suspect with a Crime* (1969), and to the late Don Newman, who wrote the ABF book *Conviction: The Determination of Guilt or Innocence Without Trial* (1966).

1. Seven decades are picked because the original, major research project, Criminal Justice in Cleveland, started in 1922.

2. See Lief H. Carter, *The Limits of Order* (Lexington, Mass.: Lexington Books, 1974), 6: "When prosecutors frequently asked what I was up to, I usually replied that I was interested in learning about the practical problems they faced and how they tried to solve them." The Carter book is one of the most useful studies of prosecutor practices.

3. See Lawrence W. Sherman and Richard A. Berk, "The Minneapolis Domestic Violence Experiment," in *Police and Law Enforcement,* vol. 4, ed. Robert J. Homant and Daniel B. Kennedy (New York: AMS Press, 1987), 335–47; Lawrence W. Sherman and Ellen G. Cohn, "The Impact of Research on Legal Policy: The Minneapolis Domestic Violence Experiment," *Law and Society Review* 23, no. 1 (1989): 117–44.

4. See, e.g., James W. Meeker and Arnold Binder, "Experiments as Reforms: The Impact of the 'Minneapolis Experiment' on Police Policy," *Journal of Police Science and Administration* 17, no. 2 (1990):147–53; Sherman and Cohn, *Impact of Research*; Richard Lempert, "Humility Is a Virtue: On the Publicization of Policy Relevant Research," *Law and Society Review* 23, no. 1 (1989):145–61.

5. See Frank W. Miller, *Prosecution: The Decision to Charge a Suspect with a Crime,* ed. Frank J. Remington (Boston: Little, Brown, 1969); Donald J. Newman, *Conviction: The Determination of Guilt or Innocence Without Trial,* ed. Frank J. Remington (Boston: Little, Brown, 1966).

6. Frank Allen, "The Dophin and the Peasant: Ill Tempered, But Brief, Comments on Legal Scholarship," *The Northwestern Reporter* 88 (1990):8.

7. *Report of the National Commission on Law Observance and Enforcement* (Wickersham Commission), vol. 4, Report on Prosecution (Washington, D.C.: U.S. Government Printing Office, 1931; Montclair, N.J.: Patterson Smith, 1968), 53 [hereinafter *Wickersham Report*].

8. The Missouri Association for Criminal Justice, *Missouri Crime Survey* (New York: Macmillan, 1926), 290 [hereinafter *Missouri Crime Survey*].

9. Roscoe Pound and Felix Frankfurter, *Criminal Justice in Cleveland, Report of the Cleveland Foundation Survey of the Administration of Criminal Justice in Cleveland, Ohio* (Cleveland: Cleveland Foundation, 1922), 236 [hereinafter *Cleveland Crime Survey*].

10. Illinois Association for Criminal Justice, *The Illinois Crime Survey*, ed. John H. Wigmore (Chicago: Illinois Association for Criminal Justice in cooperation with the Chicago Crime Commission, 1929), 295 [hereinafter *Illlinois Crime Survey*].

11. *Missouri Crime Survey*, 125. This newly discovered power was commented on by the Wickersham Commission at p. 11 of its 1931 report.

> In the States the great majority of those who are apprehended for violations of law never come to trial. Their cases are disposed of by the prosecuting attorney. In every way he has much more power over the administration of criminal justice than the judges, with much less public appreciation of his power. We have been jealous of the powers of the trial judge, but careless of the continual growth of power in the prosecuting attorney. His office is the pivot on which the administration of criminal justice in the States turns. (*Wickersham Report*)

12. *Cleveland Crime Survey*, 143–44.

13. Ibid., 144.

14. Ibid., 136. The *Cleveland Crime Survey* further observed:

> Complainants frequently desire to use the prosecution or threat of prosecution for purposes of collecting a claim or debt and have little interest in criminal proceedings except as it may serve this purpose. A danger arises, therefore, that in this preliminary and unofficial court of conciliation the prosecutor will permit himself to be used to further this purpose, and even a danger that, through inadvertence or favoritism, he will permit himself to use his position to aid in the collection of doubtful or trumped-up claims. (136)

15. Raymond Moley, *Politics and Criminal Prosecution* (1929; reprint, *Politics and People*, New York: Arno Press, 1974), 152.

16. *Cleveland Crime Survey*, 98, 209, 246.

17. *Wickersham Report*, vol. 4, 137.

18. *Cleveland Crime Survey*, 193–94. According to Roscoe Pound, "Transition from rural to urban and thence to metropolitan conditions has not been met by intelligent reconstruction, but simply by addition of more men and expenditure of more money." Ibid., 621.

19. *Wickersham Report*, vol. 4, 56.

20. *Illinois Crime Survey*, 295–96.

21. See Moley, *Politics*, 191:

It is not the exercise of discretion that we should attempt to prevent. The tendency to create out of the law a loose pattern with details to be supplied in individual cases is a wise and happy portent of an age which recognizes that in the criminal law there is need of a wide individualization of application. Discretion, however, should be granted with a nice sense of the fitness of things.

22. In this regard the Wickersham Commission commented:

[T]he theory of the law is that an innocent man should not be convicted, and as arrests may be freely made without any judicial determination of probability of guilt, a large percentage without convictions is as compatible with the conclusion that an excessive number of innocent persons were arrested as with the conclusion that an excessive number of guilty persons escaped punishment. (*Wickersham Report*, vol. 4, 55)

However, the commission hastened to add that the idea that police

should arrest most freely in order to place into the mill all possible cases, the weakest as well as the strong cases...is a fallacious conception. It assumes the necessity for an extremely wasteful system, one requiring a much larger and more complex machinery than could administer those cases in which prosecution is justified. It assumes that police departments cannot be made efficient. It assumes a necessity for doing injustice to those who, though ultimately freed, are required to contest cases through police departments, courts of preliminary examination, and trial courts. An assumption that carelessness and poor work at any stage of a successive process can have a productive value would seem to be fallacious on its face. (56–57)

The Illinois survey commented that it is obvious that there is no standard by which to determine how many cases ought to be eliminated, but the current system clearly manifested an excessive degree.

23. *Illinois Crime Survey*, 301.

24. *Wickersham Report*, vol. 4, 20.

25. *Missouri Crime Survey*, 123. The Wickersham Commission, agreeing, advised that "any attempt to trace the sources and causes and factors [of case attrition] should evidently be carried back to the arrest stage." (*Wickersham Report*, vol. 4, 87).

26. Moley, *Politics,* 150. Moley added: "The very difficulty with which the facts concerning this practice have been unearthed show how

easy it has been for prosecutors to indulge in this sort of compromise without exciting the public interest. It has cost thousands of dollars in Missouri, Cleveland, New York and Illinois to develop the facts here summarized" (189).

27. Ibid., 160.

28. Ibid., 161.

29. Ibid., 149–50.

30. Ibid., 169.

31. *Illinois Crime Survey*, 47.

32. Ibid., 318.

33. Ibid., 311.

34. *Wickersham Report*, vol. 4, 97.

35. Ibid., 70–71.

36. Raymond Moley, *Our Criminal Courts* (New York: Minton, Balch, 1930), 29.

37. Ibid., 30.

38. Moley, *Politics,* 190.

39. Ibid., 181–85.

40. Ibid., 184–85. In response to the investigation's findings, one judge remarked:

[I]t is a dangerous and unfortunate statement when they say a judge is not responsible for his own acts....While the state's attorney must be depended upon for much information, still any judge who depends entirely on the state's attorney for his decisions is mistaking the functions of his office. The waiving of felonies and bargaining with criminals is a crying evil in the administration of justice in this country. (185)

41. Ibid., 172–73.

42. Ibid., 189.

43. *Illinois Crime Survey*, 319.

44. Don Newman, in his ground-breaking research on pleas some thirty years later, observed that plea bargains had an effect on sentence outcome, rather than on the nature of charge "so that the offenses for which [defendants were] convicted did not usually deviate greatly from

the crime actually committed" (Donald J. Newman, "Pleading Guilty for Considerations: A Study of Bargain Justice," *Journal of Criminal Law and Criminology* 46, no. 6 [1956]:786–90).

45. *Illinois Crime Survey*, 310.

46. Ibid. In response to this notion Raymond Moley commented: "There is no justification for such unadulterated bluffing. It means that a false charge is brought against the defendant in order to frighten him into confessing to a lesser offense. A solemn indictment is turned into a false threat. This deserves nothing but condemnation" (Moley, *Politics,* 186).

47. *Illinois Crime Survey*, 318, 319.

48. *Cleveland Crime Survey* observed: "The business of justice is like a complicated game, the odds favoring him who has the intense desire to win plus the skill of an expert on his side. As between defendants, the advantage lies wholly with the habitual defendant, who has played the game and knows the expert to employ" (238). See also Newman, "Pleading Guilty," 790.

49. Hugh N. Fuller, *Criminal Justice in Virginia* (New York: Century Co., 1931), 78.

50. *Wickersham Report*, vol. 4, 97.

51. Moley, *Politics,* 185–86.

52. *Cleveland Crime Survey, 585.*

53. Moley, *Politics,* 172.

54. *Wickersham Report*, vol. 4, 175.

55. Ibid., 183.

56. Moley, *Politics,* 191. To Moley, the solution was to vest wider discretionary powers in judges, who operated more publicly and—arguably—were less prone to political manipulation.

57. *Wickersham Report*, vol. 4, 146.

58. Moley, *Politics,* 153–59.

59. *Wickersham Report*, vol. 4, 174.

60. "American Bar Foundation Survey of Criminal Justice: Pilot Project Reports," 7 vols. (Dec. 1957, Mimeo; on file with the Criminal Justice Reference and Information Center, University of Wisconsin-Madison, Law School).

61. See Egon Bittner, *The Functions of the Police in Modern Soci-*

*ety: A Review of Background Factors, Current Practices, and Possible
Role Models* (Chevy Chase, Md.: National Institute of Mental Health,
Center for Studies of Crime and Delinquency, 1970), 36–47.

62. See chap. 5 by Raymond I. Parnas in this volume.

63. The only exception seems to have been in homicide cases,
where the practice of both the police and the prosecutor was to charge
the higher degree and leave to the defendant the task of producing the
evidence of mitigation that would call for a conviction for a less serious
degree of homicide than that originally charged.

64. In his excellent study of prosecutor practices, Lief H. Carter
urges as desirable the kind of charging decision practice that is involved
in the Milwaukee precharge conference. He says: "If, however, we put
ourselves in the position of the judged, we shall also be concerned that
those who make judgments about us—...[e.g.,] a prosecutor...—learn
enough about us to treat us not as a member of a category but as an
individual" (Carter, *Limits of Order* [see note 2], 9).

65. See Frank J. Remington and Wayne A. Logan, "Frank Miller
and the Decision to Prosecute," *Washington University Law Quarterly*
69, no. 1 (1991):159–74, for a detailed analysis of the use, without reason, of the postarrest warrant.

66. See Lynn M. Mather, "Comments on the History of Plea Bargaining," *Law and Society Review* 13, no. 2 (1979):282: "It was a way
for judges and prosecutors to reach a sentence that, in their view,
would be more appropriate for the needs of the individual offender" at
a time when rehabilitation was an important objective. See also Pamela
J. Utz, *Settling the Facts: Discretion and Negotiation in Criminal Court*
(Lexington, Mass.: Lexington Books, 1978), 138, 139: "Sentencing is
what plea bargaining is all about....Plea bargaining is best understood
as an adaptive process in which prosecutor, defense attorney, and judge
attempt to rationalize the penal code and infuse a sense of realism
in...the penal code...'notorious' for its 'repetitive and overlapping' provisions."

67. See Todd R. Clear, John D. Hewitt, and Robert M. Regoli,
"Discretion and the Determinate Sentence: Its Distribution, Control,
and Effect on Time Served," *Crime and Delinquency* 24, no. 4
(1978):428–45, indicating that in Indiana the determinate sentence
increased the prosecutor's discretion in determining the final sentence,
often in a low-visibility manner. Compare Terance D. Miethem,
"Charging and Plea Bargaining Practices: An Investigation of the
Hydraulic Displacement of Discretion," *Journal of Criminal Law and
Criminology* 78, no. 1 (1987):155–76, suggesting that the shift of dis-

cretion to the prosecutor in a determinate sentencing system is not inevitable. However, it is widely assumed, even by the proponents of eliminating discretion at sentencing, that it will increase discretion at the charging and guilty plea stages. See David F. Greenberg and Drew Humphries, "The Cooptation of Fixed Sentencing Reform," *Crime and Delinquency* 26, no. 2 (1980):218.

68. In general, the sentencing structure has a profound effect on bargaining. The more restraints the penal code places on the prosecutor's and the court's capacity to affect the sentence, the more tortuous and covert is the charging and disposition process. In states with strict legislative determination of sentence, the system exhibits considerable charge manipulation. But in states where judicial sentencing discretion is large, defendants more frequently plead "on the nose" (simply as charged), leaving to accommodating judges the adjustments that must be made to achieve sentencing realism.

69. The emphasis on the factual basis for the plea of guilty was clear in a speech by Judge Steffes of Milwaukee who, at the time of the ABF survey, handled about 50 percent of the felony cases prosecuted in any year in the entire state of Wisconsin. In his 1959 address to the Wisconsin Board of Circuit Judges, Steffes said in part:

> I consider it important that when a defendant thus confesses his guilt through a plea of guilty that the record, at least prima facie, support such plea of guilty, and I have always made it a practice to make sure that enough testimony is adduced so that the validity and trustworthiness of such confession is corroborated. I have had occasional necessity, in cooperation with the prosecutor appearing in court, of suggesting to the defendant during or at the conclusion of the testimony that he withdraw his plea of guilty because the facts did not substantiate his judicial confession—his plea of guilty—both in cases when he was represented by counsel and when he was not.

Herbert J. Steffes, "Admissions and Confessions in Criminal Cases," (January 7, 1959, Mimeo.; on file with the Criminal Justice Reference and Information Center, University of Wisconsin-Madison, Law School), 2–3.

70. See Remington and Logan, "Frank Miller and the Decision to Prosecute."

71. Malcolm M. Feeley, "Perspectives on Plea Bargaining," *Law and Society Review* 13, no. 2 (1979):204. "I do not want to claim that efforts to alter the guilty plea process are foredoomed. I only wish to reiterate what students of mandatory and determinate sentencing sys-

tems have long maintained: eliminating discretion at one stage in the process fosters it in others."

See also Samuel H. Pillsbury, "Understanding Penal Reform: The Dynamic of Change," *Journal of Criminal Law and Criminology* 80, no. 3 (1989):765: "Yet, in some respects, determinate sentencing simply shifted the institutional balance of power. Legislators gained power by eliminating the administrative authority of parole boards and restricting the sentencing powers of judges through either direct enactment or delegation to a sentencing commission. By design or by default, legislators also increased the powers of prosecutors."

72. See Utz's discussion of "tactical charging" in *Settling the Facts* (pp. 20–26). She comments:

> The form of overcharging that is most easily observed and most likely to aid plea bargaining does not depend on fabrication. Rather it involves filing charges at the highest level the evidence will permit, with the expectation that an appropriate plea for the behavior in question would be to a somewhat lesser charge. Negotiations will follow, with a reduction of charges in return for the guilty plea. A closely related form is "horizontal overcharging," or "multiplying 'unreasonably' the number of accusations against a single defendant."

Ibid., 23. See also Fred Kray and John Berman, "Plea Bargaining in Nebraska: The Prosecutor's Perspective," *Creighton Law Review* 11, no. 1 (1977):94–149.

73. See James A. Dillon, "Wisconsin Homicide Conviction Disparities" (LL.M. thesis, 1989) (available in University of Wisconsin-Madison, Law School Library).

74. There are exceptions. See William F. McDonald, *Plea Bargaining: Critical Issues and Common Practices* (Washington, D.C.: Department of Justice, National Institute of Justice, July 1985), 14: "Much of the difficulty with defining 'overcharging' arises from the fact that there is no clear consensus of what constitutes proper charging." McDonald explains the difficulty is that the nature and significance of charging have changed with developments like mandatory sentences that make the charging decision also the sentencing decision. See, e.g., Feeley, "Perspectives on Plea Bargaining," 201: "Although critics often charge that the rise of plea bargaining represents the triumph of administrative and organizational interests over justice, they overlook the fact that many charge reductions are made 'in the interests of justice.'" See also Mather, "Comments on Plea Bargaining," 282: "An important question, of course, is the extent to which plea compromises actually did reflect a concern for substantive justice in the individual case rather

than the pressures of administrative expediency or simply political influence."

75. See Utz, *Settling the Facts,* 10: "In most criminal cases the issue of guilt has been effectively resolved by police and prosecutor screening practices that tend to eliminate the doubtful cases early....Rather the issue is: Of what is he guilty, and what should be done with him? In this context, the defendant's primary concern is his eventual sentence, and plea bargaining enables him to affect that interest."

76. See Pillsbury, "Understanding Penal Reform," 773: "A second institutional concern with determinate sentencing...is the failure to control prosecutorial discretion. While schemes have restricted or eliminated discretion by parole authorities, and many have restricted discretion by judges, prosecutorial discretion has been largely ignored. As a result, prosecutors have the power to change the nature of determinate sentencing."

See also Milton Heumann and Colin Loftin, "Mandatory Sentencing and the Abolition of Plea Bargaining: The Michigan Felony Firearm Statute," *Law and Society Review* 13, no. 2 (1979):395: "In short, mandatory sentences reduce judicial discretion but are handled by an increase in prosecutorial discretion; plea bargaining proscriptions reduce prosecutorial discretion but are handled by an increase in judicial discretion. Plug up the system at one point and analogous processes seem to emerge at another."

See also Utz, *Settling the Facts,* 11: "In states where there is strict legislative determination of sentence, the system exhibits considerable charge manipulation. But in states where judicial sentencing discretion is large, defendants more frequently plead 'on the nose' (simply as charged) leaving to accommodating judges the adjustments that must be made to achieve sentencing realism."

77. Herbert L. Packer, "The Model Penal Code and Beyond," *Columbia Law Review* 63, no. 4 (1963):605.

78. Frank J. Remington, "The Limits and Possibilities of the Criminal Law," *Notre Dame Lawyer* 43, no. 6 (1968):865–66. See also Wayne R. LaFave and Jerold H. Israel, *Criminal Procedures,* vol. 2, sec. 13.2 (St. Paul: West Publishing Co., 1984), 162, for a brief discussion of "overcriminalization."

79. Malcolm Feeley suggests the problem-oriented approach as the most realistic way to reform court processes. Malcolm Feeley, in *Court Reform on Trial: Why Simple Solutions Fail* (New York: Basic Books, 1983), 209, suggests "[T]his policy of flexibility breeds a suspicion all its own, and it is not surprising that, periodically, efforts to restrict it gain

prominence. But this in turn brings forth a new set of concerns, and the cycle begins anew" (150).

80. See Utz, *Settling the Facts,* 137, in which the author points to the tension between the desire for the formal procedure of the trial and the desire for a fair case outcome. Speaking of formal rules she says: "Because they speak to the manner not the outcome of decisions, standards of fairness are inherently weak supports for justice." She concludes later: "These problems require a strategy that informs instead of only limiting the exercise of official discretion and reduces the obstacles that now frustrate sensible and sensitive problem solving" (139).

81. Letter from Joseph Goldstein to Frank J. Remington (copy on file with the Criminal Justice Reference and Information Center, University of Wisconsin-Madison, Law School). Goldstein wrote the influential early article "Police Discretion Not to Invoke the Criminal Process: Low-Visibility Decisions in the Administration of Justice," *Yale Law Journal* 69, no. 4 (1960):543–94. In his article he urged legislative revision of the substantive criminal law to make full enforcement a more realistic objective.

82. Herbert Wechsler, "The Challenge of a Model Penal Code," *Harvard Law Review* 65, no. 7 (1952):1102.

83. Packer, "Model Penal Code," 604.

84. See *State v. Wolske,* 143 Wis. 2d 175, 420 N.W.2d 60 (1988) (two homicide prosecutions proper although only one death occurred); *Mack v. State,* 93 Wis. 2d 287, 286 N.W.2d 563 (1980) (prosecution proper for both forgery and credit card fraud based on the same conduct).

85. Charles D. Breitel, "Controls in Criminal Law Enforcement," *University of Chicago Law Review* 27, no. 3 (1960):427. See also "United States Department of Justice Materials Relating to Prosecutorial Discretion," *Criminal Law Reporter* (BNA) 24, no. 8 (1978):3001; and United States Department of Justice, Prosecutors Handbook on Sentencing Guidelines and Other Provisions of the Sentencing Reform Act of 1984 (Nov. 1, 1987), discussed in Stephen J. Schulhofer and Ilene H. Nagel, "Negotiated Pleas under the Federal Sentencing Guidelines: The First Fifteen Months," *American Criminal Law Review* 27, no. 2 (1989):231–88.

86. The situation is described in detail in Samuel Becker, "Judicial Scrutiny of Prosecutorial Discretion in the Decision Not to File a Complaint," *Marquette Law Review* 71, no. 4 (1988):749–68.

87. See *State v. Unnamed Defendants,* 150 Wis. 2d 352 (1989),

upholding the authority of a judge to issue a complaint on probable cause after the prosecutor had refused to charge. The case is discussed in Wayne A. Logan, "A Proposed Check on the Charging Discretion of Wisconsin Prosecutors," *Wisconsin Law Review* 1990, no. 6:1695–1743. For a description of the Cook County, Illinois, system in which the judge controls the charging decision, see Donald M. McIntyre, "A Study of Judicial Dominance of the Charging Process," *Journal of Criminal Law, Criminology and Police Science 59*, no. 4 (1968):463–90.

88. *United States v. Williams*, 746 F. Supp. 1076, 1082 (D. Utah 1990).

89. At a recent conference, a federal prosecutor offered this explanation:

> If in fact power has been shifted from the judicial branch to the prosecutor's office, there's a reason for that....That's because in the '60s and '70s, something happened to this country. There was an explosion of crime. People weren't very happy with it....[T]hey thought the judicial branch wasn't doing a whole heck of a lot about it. So it's natural, in that climate, to expect a shift of power away from a branch of government that has proven inadequate to the problem toward a branch of government that is there to enforce the law. (4 *BNA Criminal Practice Manual* No. 24 at 568 [1990])

90. Miller, *Prosecution* (see note 5), 350. See also a helpful discussion in Wayne R. LaFave, "The Prosecutor's Discretion in the United States," *American Journal of Comparative Law* 18 (1970):532–48.

91. Kenneth C. Davis, *Discretionary Justice: A Preliminary Inquiry* (Baton Rouge: Louisiana State University Press, 1969).

92. National Advisory Commission on Criminal Justice Standards and Goals, *Courts,* standard 1.2, "Procedure for Screening" (Washington, D.C.: U.S. Government Printing Office, 1973), 24–26.

93. American Bar Association, *Standards Relating to the Prosecution Function*, vol. 1 of *ABA Standards for Criminal Justice*, 2d ed. (Boston: Little, Brown, 1980), standard 3–2.5.

94. "United States Department of Justice Materials Relating to Prosecutorial Discretion," *Criminal Law Reporter* (BNA) 24 (1978): 3001.

95. See Norm Maleng, "Charging and Sentencing: Where Prosecutors' Guidelines Help Both Sides," *Criminal Justice* 1, no. 4 (1987):6.

96. Carter, *Limits of Order* (see note 2), 161. See Gregory H. Williams, "Good Government by Prosecutorial Decree: The Use and

Abuse of Mail Fraud," *Arizona Law Review* 32, no. 1 (1990):146: "Thus U.S. Attorneys...decide largely on their own what improper practices warrant federal prosecution."

97. The precharge conference is recommended in the President's Commission on Law Enforcement and Administration of Justice, *Task Force Report: The Courts* (Washington, D.C.: U.S. Government Printing Office, 1967), 7–8.

98. Carter, *Limits of Order,* 14.

99. A helpful discussion of plea negotiations and the various issues involved is found in LaFave and Israel, *Criminal Procedure*, vol. 2, chap. 20.

100. I was a member of the Advisory Committee on the Criminal Rules in 1963 when the rule was amended to require the judge to find a factual basis for the plea. The committee was concerned that the requirement would be difficult to implement in practice. That it is used in Milwaukee and has not caused difficulty in practice is obviously helpful at least to the proponents of the change.

101. Carter, *Limits of Order*, 154.

102. Robert A. Weninger, "The Abolition of Plea Bargaining: A Case Study of El Paso County, Texas," *UCLA Law Review* 35, no. 2 (1987):311–13. See also Francis W. Laurent, *The Business of a Trial Court* (Madison: University of Wisconsin Press, 1959), which is a study of the work of a rural Wisconsin court during the 1800s. Pleas of guilty were more numerous than trials even though caseload pressures were not a significant factor.

103. Michael L. Rubinstein, Stevens H. Clarke, and Teresa J. White, *Alaska Bans Plea Bargaining* (Washington, D.C.: Department of Justice, National Institute of Justice, 1980), 227.

104. Weninger, "Abolition of Plea Bargaining," 303.

105. Alaska Judicial Council, *Alaska's Plea Bargaining Ban Reevaluated (Executive summary)* (Anchorage: Alaska Judicial Council, 1991), 12.

106. The extent to which a factual basis is required in the various states and how effective the requirement is in safeguarding the innocent is helpfully discussed in McDonald, *Plea Bargaining* (see note 74).

107. Arguing in favor of the contested trial, Stephen J. Schulhofer says that the lack of a "day in court" is demeaning to the American concept of the individual. See, e.g., Stephen J. Schulhofer, "Criminal

Justice Discretion as a Regulatory System," *Journal of Legal Studies* 17, no. 1 (1988):43–82; Stephen J. Schulhofer, "Is Plea Bargaining Inevitable?" *Harvard Law Review* 97, no. 5 (1984):1037–1107; Stephen J. Schulhofer, "No Job Too Small: Justice Without Bargaining in the Lower Criminal Courts," *American Bar Foundation Research Journal* 1985, no. 3:519–98.

108. Weninger, "Abolition of Plea Bargaining," 292; Alaska Judicial Council, *Alaska's Plea Bargaining Ban*, 4.

109. Ibid., 293, 301, 304–5.

110. Ibid., 307. The abolition of plea bargaining in Tyler, Texas, was accompanied by a judicial practice of allowing withdrawal of an unconditional plea of guilty if the defendant is dissatisfied with the sentence imposed. Mark Curriden, "Banning Bargaining," *American Bar Association Journal* 78 (March 1992):18.

111. See note 66 and accompanying text.

112. This is the conclusion of the Federal Court Study Committee. See July 1, 1990, the memorandum from associate reporter Sara Sun Beale to the committee regarding sentencing guidelines: "The net effect of the guidelines has been to increase at least some forms of prosecutorial discretion while circumscribing the court's discretion. This is most apparent in the covert bargaining that is going on outside of the guidelines, which is subject to little or no judicial control" (Federal Court Study Committee, *Working papers and Subcommittee Reports,* vol. 1), 16.

Albert W. Alschuler has written very ably and extensively on the disadvantages of plea bargaining, on prosecutorial discretion as it relates to plea bargaining, and on the effects of federal sentencing guidelines on plea agreements. Alschuler has argued that a formal trial is far superior to a plea agreement in emphasizing society's serious attitude toward crime and in stressing the significance of society's decision to deprive an individual of liberty. He also points out potential systemic flaws in the plea bargaining procedure that lead to ineffective representation of defendants. Alschuler also believes that the cost and efficiency of the judicial system should not be given great weight in the design of an effective criminal system because these procedural policies pervert other substantive criminal policies. The abolishment of plea bargaining, he argues, would force prosecutors to charge only with regard to substantive criminal policies, which may result in fewer charges backed by stronger evidence. Finally, Alschuler fears that without tight control on plea bargaining, the federal sentencing guidelines will decrease the discretion of judges and shift much of this discretion to the prosecutor. He argues that this shifting of discretion is undesirable because prosecutors value procedural policies more than judges, again leading to sentences that are substantively incorrect. See, e.g., Albert W. Alschuler, "Departures and Plea Agreements Under the Sentencing Guidelines," *F.R.D.* 117 (1987):459–76; Albert W. Alschuler, "The Changing Plea Bargaining Debate," *California Law Review 69*, no. 3 (1981):652–730; Albert W. Alschuler, "Personal Failure, Institutional Failure, and the Sixth Amendment," *New York University Review of Law and Social Change* 14, no. 1 (1986):149–56; Albert W. Alschuler, "Plea Bargaining and Its History," *Law and Society Review* 13, no. 2 (1979):211–45; Albert W. Alschuler, "Implementing the Criminal Defendant's Right to Trial: Alternatives to the Plea Bargaining System," *University of Chicago Law Review 50*, no. 3 (1983):931–1050.

Michael H. Tonry concludes that, although Minnesota's presumptive sentencing system initially did equalize sentencing patterns, prosecutors and defense counsel later started to plea bargain, resulting in a return to inequitable sentences. The plea bargaining, in the form of offense class bargaining, he believes, will still exist with presumptive sentencing because of prosecutors' continued need for incentives to entice a guilty plea and the participants' personal and institutional need for cooperation and therefore that prosecutorial guidelines are needed. See, e.g., Michael H. Tonry, *Sentencing Reform Impacts* (Washington, D.C.: Department of Justice, National Institute of Justice, Office of Communication and Research Utilization, 1987); Michael Tonry and John C. Coffee, Jr., "Enforcing Sentencing Guidelines: Plea Bargaining and Review Mechanisms," in *The Sentencing Commission and Its Guidelines,* ed. Andrew Von Hirsch, Kay A. Knapp, and Michael Tonry (Boston: Northeastern University Press, 1987), 142; Michael H. Tonry, "Real Offense Sentencing," *Journal of Criminal Law and Criminology* 72, no. 4 (1981):1550–96; Michael Tonry, "More Sentencing Reform in America," *Criminal Law Review* 1982:157–67; Michael Tonry, "Criminal Law: The Missing Element in Sentencing Reform," *Vanderbilt Law Review* 35, no. 3 (1982):607–41.

See also Schulhofer and Nagel, "Negotiated Pleas" (see note 85).

113. Alaska Judicial Council, *Alaska's Plea Bargaining Ban* 27.

114. See note 107. An interesting illustration arose during oral argument in the U.S. Supreme Court over the constitutionality of Michigan's life sentence without parole for drug possession:

JUSTICE O'CONNOR. What if...the grandson said, "Grandma, there's cocaine in this suitcase. I'm going to keep it in your closet for a few days."

THOMPSON [ASS'T ATTY. GENERAL FOR THE STATE OF MICHIGAN]. In that case, the prosecutor would have discretion whether or not to charge.

JUSTICE KENNEDY. So the statute permits an exercise of discretion by the prosecutor but not by the judge? (*Criminal Law Reporter* [BNA] 48, no. 7 [1990]:3065)

115. See, e.g., *BNA Criminal Practice Manual*, Current Reports, 3, no. 26 (Dec. 27, 1989):631: "In the real world, despite the probation officer's kicking and screaming, the district court accepts what the defense and prosecution agree to." Thus the application of the guidelines can be substantially affected by agreements as to what the facts are.

116. See Weninger, "Abolition of Plea Bargaining," 313. This is also occurring in the federal system. See *Report of the Federal Courts Study Committee*, April 2, 1990, 138, where the report discusses "promotion of hidden bargaining."

117. Ibid., 303.

118. Under a grant from the State Justice Institute, staff of the University of Wisconsin Law School made an effort to determine the effectiveness of guilty plea procedure by interviewing one hundred prison inmates who had pleaded guilty and had been sentenced recently. The interviews disclosed that the principal complaint was not that the inmates did not understand the rights that were given up by pleading guilty, but rather it was that the inmates felt that the process did not allow them adequate opportunity to tell their story. See Dan Schneider, "Inmate Interviews: What Really Is and Is Not Important" (1990 manuscript; on file with University of Wisconsin Law School, Continuing Education and Outreach, 905 University Avenue, Madison, Wisconsin 53705).

119. Frank J. Remington and Wayne A. Logan, "Frank Miller and the Decision to Prosecute," *Washington University Law Quarterly* 69, no. 1 (1991):159–74.

120. Volker Knoppke-Wetzel, *Defense of Criminal Cases in Wisconsin* (Madison: University of Wisconsin Extension Department of Law, 1974):2-6–2-8.

121. Logan, "Proposed Check" (see note 87), 1695.

122. Memorandum from reporter Edward L. Barrett to the Advisory Committee on Criminal Rules, Sept. 3, 1963 (on file with the Administrative Office of United States Courts, Washington, D.C.).

123. Ibid.

124. 880 F.2d 941 (7th Cir. 1989), *cert. denied*, 493 U.S. 1059 (1990).

125. See Ralph A. Fine, *Escape of the Guilty* (New York: Dodd, Mead, 1986), reviewed in David E. Schultz, "Escape of the Guilty, What a Wisconsin Trial Judge Thinks of the Criminal Justice System," *Marquette Law Review* 70, no. 4 (1987):633–45.

126. See Arthur Rosett and Donald R. Cressey, *Justice by Consent: Plea Bargains in the American Courthouse* (Philadelphia: J. B. Lippincott, 1976), 170: "The exercise of discretion is a response to a fundamental need for flexibility....Like a closed tube of toothpaste, if squeezed in one spot it merely pops out in another."

There is ample evidence that limiting the trial judge's sentencing discretion adds to the power of the prosecutor. See, e.g., Judge Henry H. Greene in *United States v. Adonis*, DDC No. 88–0358–01 (HHG) 8/2/90: "[T]he events of this case support what this Court has been noting...that to vest the bulk of sentencing authority in partisan prosecutors rather than dispassionate judges is bound to do harm to the maintenance of due process" (*BNA Criminal Practice Manual* 4, no. 18 [1990]:427).

See Albert W. Alschuler, "The Failure of Sentencing Guidelines: A Plea for Less Aggregation," *University of Chicago Law Review* 58, no. 3 (1991):925–28.

127. Schulhofer and Nagel, "Negotiated Pleas" (see note 85), 253.

128. The relationship of visibility and decision making is effectively pointed out in Franklin E. Zimring and Gordon Hawkins, *The Scale of Imprisonment* (Chicago: University of Chicago Press, 1991), 173–74:

> We believe, for example, that the information revolution in criminal case processing has increased accountability throughout the system and that this may lead to greater use of imprisonment. If prosecutors, judges, and sentencing commissions *feel more visible* in making decisions and are more conscious of the capacity of others in the system to tie them to their decisions and the results of those decisions, this is bound to affect their performance. Thus, the fact that information is cheaper, of better quality, and easier to retrieve will engender a feeling of accountability and will tend to produce a large number of "safe" decisions.
>
> In many systems, the safe decision is likely to involve the continuation of prosecution rather than its abandonment; a sentence of imprisonment rather than probation; a decision to hold in prison rather than to release. (Emphasis added.)

For an analysis of the "problem" of discretion and the argument in favor of eliminating at least unnecessary discretion, see LaFave and Israel, *Criminal Procedure*, vol. 2, sec. 13.2, 167–69.

129. Utz, *Settling the Facts* (see note 66), xi, x.

130. See Loretta J. Stalans and Shari S. Diamond, "Formation and Change in Lay Evaluation of Criminal Sentencing," *Law and Human Behavior* 14, no. 3 (1990):199–214. See also Robin West, "The Supreme Court 1989 Term, Foreword: Taking Freedom Seriously," *Harvard Law Review* 104, no. 1 (1990):87: to have "morally responsible decisions" it is necessary to have individualized decisions that give consideration to all mitigating circumstances.

131. For a very useful discussion of the growing popularity of restitution, see Stephen A. Saltzburg, *American Criminal Procedure,* 3d ed. (St. Paul: West Publishing Co., 1988), 1090–92. For example, Saltzburg points out that Colorado requires that restitution be ordered, and the trend nationally appears to be in that direction, even in cases in which the offender is sentenced to a long prison term. See Wis. Stat. § 973.20 (1991–92) for a statute that both mandates that restitution be ordered and provides a detailed method of computing the amount of restitution.

132. Wayne LaFave, with whom I shared a copy of my draft, asked if there is proof that the existence of a formal rule discourages rather than encourages the good trial judge to achieve the substantive objectives of the rule. In fact, no conclusive evidence exists, but that this is true is adequately indicated. In monthly meetings with Wisconsin trial judges for more than twenty-five years, I have heard frequently the statement that the formal procedures are followed to satisfy the appellate court more than to inform the defendant.

In interviews with more than one hundred prison inmates, the universal answer was that the formal procedures had little meaning for them, and the prevalent view was that the procedure hindered rather than advanced communication of information thought by the inmate to be important. See Daniel J. Melzer, "State Court Forfeitures of Federal Rights," *Harvard Law Review* 99, no. 6 (1986):1235, in which he points out that the effort to have the trial judge ensure fairness in guilty plea practice is not very effective.

Even so, Wayne LaFave is right in suggesting that things would not be better if there were no guilty plea procedures. What appears clearly to be needed is a way to ensure that procedures are viewed as a means, not an end, and that any generalized procedure has to be adapted to the circumstances of the individual case if the substantive objectives are to be achieved.

133. See Mark Tushnet and Jennifer Jaff, "Critical Legal Studies and Criminal Procedure," *Catholic University Law Review* 35, no. 2 (1986):382–84, in which the effort of a trial judge to really communi-

cate with a guilty plea defendant is explained by the fact that the judge "is a sincere warm-hearted human being." Ibid., 384. This article suggests that the effort to achieve substantive objectives will probably require more than the existence of a formal rule.

134. Schulhofer and Nagel, "Negotiated Pleas" (see note 85), 285. In James Garofalo, "Police, Prosecutors, and Felony Case Attrition," *Journal of Criminal Justice* 19, no. 5 (Sept.–Oct. 1991):448, the author concludes "the present research suggests that most case attrition derives…from efforts by prosecutors to reach just outcomes when applying the broad mandate of the law to the specific features of individual cases."

135. Carter, *Limits of Order* (see note 2), 3.

136. Weninger, "Abolition of Plea Bargaining" (see note 102), 313.

137. Utz, *Settling the Facts* (see note 66), 139. The same point is effectively made in Nick Schweitzer, "Plea Bargaining," *Wisconsin Bar Bulletin* 61 (June 1988):22: "The reason, I believe, lies in the differing expectations held by experienced criminal attorneys and the general public.…[A]n essential aspect of plea bargaining is the need to be fair. Plea negotiations…reflect the need to individualize justice."

138. See Rosett and Cressey, *Justice by Consent* (see note 126), 172.

139. A New York Times editorial recently concluded: "Problem-oriented prosecution puts…discretion to creative, positive use" *New York Times*, Feb. 15, 1989).

140. Martha A. Fineman reaches a similar conclusion in her book *The Illusion of Equality: The Rhetoric and Reality of Divorce Reform* (Chicago: University of Chicago Press, 1991), where she is critical of liberal feminists who advocate equality of treatment rather than equality of outcome.

For a discussion of the difficulty in determining the effectiveness of prosecution practices, see Richard S. Frase, "The Decision to File Federal Criminal Charges: A Quantitative Study of Prosecutorial Discretion," *University of Chicago Law Review* 47, no. 2 (1980):246–330.

141. Alschuler, "Failure of Sentencing Guidelines" (see note 126), 949.

142. Frank J. Remington and Victor G. Rosenblum, "The Criminal Law and the Legislative Process," *University of Illinois Law Forum* 1960, no. 4:487.

143. The resolution of the Administrative Law Section of the American Bar Association was adopted in 1977.

144. Support for individualized decision making is found in Robin West's thoughtful article, in which she recommends that liberals give less emphasis to abstract civil rights and more emphasis to the responsibility of the individual (citing Havelian liberalism as a model). To accomplish this, West urged that "individualized verdicts are a central aspect of morally responsible decisions" and that one has a "right to be dealt with in one's particularity rather than a right to generality" (West, "Supreme Court 1989 Term" [see note 130], 43).

A thoughtful analysis of experience under the federal sentencing guidelines reaches a similar conclusion. "Sentencing reform...must begin by aiming to optimize the ability of discretion to account for individual differences among offenders" (Steve Y. Koh, "Reestablishing the Federal Judge's Role in Sentencing," *Yale Law Journal* 101, no. 5 [1992]:1134).

An interesting example of trial court dissatisfaction with the restriction on sentencing discretion is found in David Margolick, "Chorus of Judicial Critics Assail Sentencing Guides: 5-Year Effort Is Called Hobgoblin of U.S. Courts," *New York Times*, Apr. 12, 1992. Federal trial judge dissatisfaction with the guidelines can be explained either by a natural inclination of public officials to oppose restraints on their authority or, more charitably, as a recognition by trial judges that guidelines do not adequately take account of all the relevant facts of the individual case. The ABF research suggests that the latter is the accurate explanation.

CHAPTER 4

Sentencing, Parole, and Community Supervision

Walter J. Dickey

INTRODUCTION

In 1987, when I resigned as director of the Wisconsin correctional system and returned to the University of Wisconsin Law School, I struggled with the question of how I could best contribute to this perplexing field. Developments in sentencing and corrections have always involved a complex interplay of ideology, politics, and public attitudes. However, it seemed to me that the direction of change could be influenced by more detailed knowledge and understanding of how the system functions in reality at the level of the frontline actors who make daily decisions about offenders. Such knowledge, for example, might help me evaluate the current tendency of policymakers who, by imposing guidelines embodied in grids and matrices, remove responsibility for decision making from those most involved with offenders. Confronted with such proposals in Wisconsin, I was worried that offenders were becoming score values without a human face. But I know offenders do not neatly fit into distinct categories. Their lives are turbulent, with more variation than matrices of variables can capture adequately. I worried that these developments would ignore complexity and sacrifice justice and effectiveness for a superficial consistency.

I decided to spend months in the streets of Wisconsin communities with probation and parole agents to observe and record

what they actually do day-to-day in making decisions. I wanted
to learn from them how they respond to the complexities in the
circumstances and behavior of offenders, what works, and why.
It later came as a surprise to read the "Field Reports" of the
"American Bar Foundation Survey of Criminal Justice" that
describe the practices of probation and parole agents in rural
Wisconsin and to find them to be almost identical to notes of my
own observations.

I thought it would be especially instructive to accept the invi-
tation to compare sentencing and correctional practices prior to
the ABF study, during the study, and in the post-ABF period, as
authors of this volume do the police, prosecution, and guilty plea
stages of the criminal justice system.

In the following sections of this chapter, I shall review the state
of practice in sentencing and corrections along with its ideological
and factual justification. The presentation is divided into four
main sections: the state of affairs prior to the ABF survey, the findings of the ABF research, the post-ABF period, and a final review
of the major findings in light of the situation today. The first three
sections will review sentencing and parole release, probation and
parole supervision, and probation and parole revocation.

PRE-ABF RESEARCH AND DEVELOPMENTS

Classical and Positivist Theories

Pre-ABF research into sentencing, probation, and parole practices can be understood only in the context of the ideological
shifts in penal theory that took place in the early part of this century. Prior to about 1900, sentencing in America was based on
the "classical" or "justice" model. In the classical model, articulated most prominently by the eighteenth-century Italian theorist
Cesare Beccaria, punishment of an offender should be proportional to the seriousness of the offense, not the character of the
offender. Classical theory posited three purposes of sentencing:
punishment of the wrongdoer, retribution by society for the
offender's breach of the social contract, and deterrence of others
from committing the same offense. This theory envisioned the
offender as a free, rational individual who balanced the likelihood and severity of punishment against the potential benefits of

the criminal act and who should be held personally responsible if he or she chose to commit a crime.

Around the turn of the century, classical penal theory was challenged in fundamental ways by the "positivists." They argued that crimes were not always committed voluntarily, since many people committed offenses because of inherited or environmental deficiencies.[1] The offender's individual deficiencies, they argued, could be cured, just as physical ailments could be cured. Thus, positivist theory asserted, offenders could be classified according to type—inebriates, the mentally disturbed, psychopaths, and so forth—and a plan of scientific treatment devised for each individual to cure him or her of criminal tendencies. As Sanford Bates stated in 1926, the extent of punishment was based not on the crime but on the criminal: "[P]unishment depends not upon [the offender's] crime but upon his particular type of personality; the length of punishment depends on his reaction to treatment; and the place and character of such punishment likewise depend upon his needs and his reaction to correctional treatment."[2]

For positivist theorists, three crucial elements of a proper rehabilitative penal system were probation, parole, and the indeterminate (i.e., open-ended) sentence. Probation (as a substitute for custodial punishment) and parole (following custodial punishment) allowed a trained expert to assess the offenders' needs; provide the education, training, and mental health assistance necessary to treat their particular problems; and monitor how well they adjusted to the demands of "straight" society. An indeterminate judicial sentence was deemed necessary for the success of probation and parole, since it provided the state with a legal basis for surveillance and control of offenders until such time as they were properly adjusted. The probation or parole authorities, rather than the court, would determine how much time the offender would actually spend in prison and under supervision upon release.

In the United States throughout the nineteenth century and into the twentieth, classical theory provided the ideological basis for statutes by which legislatures would fix penalties for specific crimes. Such statutes allowed trial judges little or no discretion in sentencing. As the twentieth century progressed, however, trial courts increasingly attempted to adapt fixed sentences to the mitigating circumstances of individual offenders, by creating judicial versions of probation and parole through such devices as sus-

pended sentences, conditional suspended sentences, or continua-
tions.[3] These adaptations portended more fundamental changes
later in the century, particularly in the years after World War II.

Implementation of Rehabilitative Theory in American Practices

As penal theory began to shift toward rehabilitation, states
began to adopt indeterminate sentencing, probation, and parole.
However, these three practices, theoretically all part of a single
package, developed along separate lines and at different rates
throughout the country.

In 1904 the report of the national correctional census noted
that the most significant change in sentencing patterns since 1880
was the introduction of the indeterminate sentence, which took several forms, none "purely" indeterminate.[4] However, most indeterminate sentencing laws delegated authority over the amount of time
the offender actually spent in prison not to the courts but to administrative tribunals. California's system, considered the most extreme
indeterminate system in the country, was an example. In 1917, the
California legislature conferred broad discretion over sentencing to
administrative bodies such as the Adult Authority. The court had
the power to state that the offender must go to prison, but the sentence of imprisonment was stated within a range of six months to
life. The administrative authority would actually determine how
long a sentence the offender served within this range.[5]

Adult probation was also an element in the rehabilitative
package. Massachusetts passed the first adult probation statute in
1878. By 1917, only Wyoming lacked a juvenile probation law,
but adult probation spread more slowly. Nonetheless, by 1937
only twelve of the forty-eight states had no adult probation laws,
and these twelve states used suspended sentences to achieve the
same ends. A 1935 survey of thirty states found that about 30
percent of adults convicted were placed on probation, although
the use of probation ranged from 62 percent in Rhode Island to
14.9 percent in Utah.[6]

Parole originated with the indeterminate sentence and reformatory system. However, parole soon became separated from
these two concepts and spread more rapidly than either, because
it could be combined with preexisting definite sentencing and
prison systems. By 1922, forty-four states had parole laws.[7]

Parole, eventually widespread, was often poorly implemented.

By 1931, only 64 percent of parolees were under the supervision of a full-time, salaried parole officer. In the same year, the most common length of parole was twelve to fourteen months.[8] In the 1930s, the short length of the parole period and the inadequate supervision of parolees led critics such as J. Edgar Hoover to label parole as "soft," and one concern of the crime surveys of the period was the adequacy of parole as it was being practiced.

Ideological Framework of the Pre-ABF Research

The state, local, and national crime surveys of the 1920s and 1930s examined sentencing, probation, and parole in some detail.[9] In addition, several studies of the effects of probation and parole were published during the same period, most notably Sheldon and Eleanor Glueck's *500 Criminal Careers* and *Later Criminal Careers*.[10] What is most notable about all of these studies is their rejection of the classical model of retributive, proportional punishment and their wholesale acceptance of the "scientific" treatment model. Even when their own research demonstrated that scientific rehabilitation was not working as it should, the authors of the pre-ABF studies attributed problems to holdovers from the older, punitive system and to inadequate numbers of trained probation or parole officers; and they forecast a sunny future if the scientific model could only be fully implemented.

The survey authors showed nearly complete disillusionment with the efficacy of classical, proportional punishment to control crime. Writing in the *Cleveland Crime Survey* of 1922, for example, Roscoe Pound attacked the older model as composed of "abstractly just, formal, rigid rules, mechanically administered."[11] Pound argued that fear of fixed punishment could never completely deter offenders who believed they would not be caught and that harsh fixed penalties were counterproductive, since juries would refuse to convict defendants.[12]

By contrast, the crime survey authors enthusiastically embraced the rehabilitative model of the positivists. They frequently couched their discussions in terms of an analogy between penal and medical treatment. Thus Bates stated that the function of the sentencer was to "look into the individual's case as that of a human being, study it, diagnose it, prescribe for it, and administer the cure."[13]

The crime survey writers showed a touching, if naive, faith in the efficacy of "science"—that is, psychology, psychiatry, and the social sciences—to solve the crime problem. In the Oregon Crime Survey, Wayne Morse and Ronald Beattie described the new ideological climate: "It is becoming more and more recognized that many of the major concepts of criminal law theory...are untenable when checked against the findings of modern criminologists, psychologists, psychiatrists, and other social sciences."[14] Specifically, Morse and Beattie pointed out that the "psychology of equality" underlying classical penal theory had been replaced by the "psychology of individual differences" posited by the human and social sciences. Thus, as the Wickersham Commission asserted in 1931, "[i]ndividualization is the root of adequate punishment and the proper basis for parole."[15]

Pre-ABF Research Findings

The focus of the research conducted by the crime surveys of the 1920s and 1930s indicates the writers' concerns and assumptions. One concern was whether the criminal justice system was adequately processing the cases before it or offenders were wrongly "getting off." The crime surveys extended their "mortality tables" to indicate the percentage of cases that lasted from arrest warrant through sentencing and at which points in the process other cases were eliminated.

The assumptions behind the mortality tables are interesting. The *Illinois Crime Survey*, for example, treated pleas to lesser offenses than charged, as well as convictions of lesser offenses, as "mortality."[16] In terms of sentencing, the imposition of probation (as opposed to a custodial sentence) was lumped along with vacated or modified sentences as "mortality."[17] Similarly, the *Missouri Crime Survey* presented numerous mortality tables that tracked cases from arrest warrant through sentencing to "punishment." Judicial parole was not considered punishment. Rather it was viewed as mortality, reducing the percentage of cases that resulted in punishment.[18]

The crime surveys viewed probation, parole, and plea bargaining as "mortality," despite commentators' ideological commitment to rehabilitative penal practices, in part because of their findings on the actual nature of conditional release and sentencing practices during the period. The writers found that conditional release was often poorly implemented. Parole, in particular, was used as a means to empty overcrowded prisons through automatic conditional release, which, due to inadequate parole supervision, constituted de facto absolute discharge.[19]

The Missouri survey documented the extent to which the parole board's decision on whether to release an offender was influenced by such factors as political pressure and the views of the sentencing judge, the prosecutor, and the victims. The *Illinois Crime Survey*, while presenting less statistical evidence than the Missouri survey, provided numerous examples of the parole board's decisions in individual cases. In both surveys, the purpose of the research was to evaluate how well the parole board operated— whether it appeared to be reasonably competent and free from political pressures—a repeated concern in all the crime surveys.

The crime surveys did not call for the abolition of individualized sentencing, probation, or parole, however. Rather, they noted that probation and parole staffs were inadequate in number, underfunded, and often made up of incompetent political appointees rather than trained experts. The inadequacy of staff levels at the time was notorious: the Wickersham Commission recorded an instance in which a state parole board handled ninety-five cases in four hours.[20] The researchers called for larger numbers of professional, well-paid, well-trained probation and parole officers, free from political pressure, who could provide proper assistance and supervision to offenders.

The crime surveys also attempted to document, through tables that linked individual traits with rates of violation, the factors that led to success or failure on probation or parole. These traits included the offender's age, race, offense, prior record, family background, and urban or rural environment. The purpose of the research was to come up with a set of criteria—a "prognostic table"—that the judge or parole board could use to predict the likelihood of success on conditional release. Many of these criteria are the very ones relied on in parole and sentencing guidelines today to "fix" the time an offender is to serve. They are precursors of the matrices currently used by such authorities as the federal parole commission and the federal sentencing commission.

In their writings, the pre-ABF researchers emphasized the inadequate staff and resources devoted to the supervision of offenders in communities. However, aside from their examination of successes and failure rates in probation and parole supervision, the researchers spent little time studying the actual processes of probation and parole supervision or revocation.

The crime survey writers also noted the correlation between original guilty pleas and imposition of probation or suspended sentences in jurisdictions where judges had some discretion to individualize sentencing. The Missouri survey, for example, found that in the city courts defendants who originally pleaded guilty received custodial sentences only 41.9 percent of the time, whereas defendants who originally pleaded not guilty received custodial sentences 80.28 percent of the time.[21]

The major problem with which the pre-ABF researchers had to contend was that their own data rarely provided conclusive support for their argument that scientific rehabilitation worked better than the old fixed penalty system. To be sure, a number of writers asserted confidently that at least 70 percent of probationers and parolees finished their supervision periods successfully.[22] However, as the Gluecks pointed out, the data on which such assertions were based were highly suspect, since an offender could change his or her name, move to another state, or otherwise drop out of sight before reoffending. In an era before fingerprinting, it was almost impossible to trace an offender's criminal career.[23]

The most comprehensive research into the subsequent careers of "rehabilitated" offenders was that of the Gluecks. In *500 Criminal Careers*, they traced the activities of 510 men who left the Massachusetts reformatory between 1917 and 1922, examining what each individual did for five years after the expiration of his sentence. Their findings were not encouraging: 61 percent of the men failed to succeed on parole, and nearly 80 percent had reoffended within five years of the end of their sentences.[24] However, neither the Gluecks nor other crime survey writers viewed such statistics as evidence of the failure of the rehabilitative model.[25] Rather, they argued that the model had never been given "a fair chance"[26] due to inadequate funding and "the residue of an archaic system of penal justice"[27]—that is, fixed, retributive sentences—which undermined the individualizing efforts of probation and parole authorities.

The survey writers made remarkably uniform recommendations for the future of individualized sentencing: (1) indeterminate sentences; (2) clearinghouses that would classify convicted offenders according to their rehabilitative potential; (3) separate prisons for different types of offenders; (4) educational, vocational, and recreational programs in prisons; (5) full-time, well-paid, centralized parole boards free from political interference; (6) "scientific" probation and parole and the use of prognostic tables; (7) properly trained probation and parole officers; (8) sufficient numbers of such officers to allow adequate supervision of released offenders; (9) preparation of communities for acceptance of released offenders; and (10) no automatic conclusion to conditional release—the sentence would end when, and only when, the offender was rehabilitated.[28]

Sentencing Discretion in Pre-ABF Research

The pre-ABF writers recognized that in an individualized sentencing system, the court or tribunal that decided on the extent and severity of an offender's sentence was in a very powerful position. As Louis N. Robinson stated in 1921:

> It is clear that it has not yet been settled where this power to fix the length of a man's stay in prison is to reside. Taken out of the hands of the judiciary through the efforts of the Classicists and given to the hands of the legislative branch of the government; then handed back in part to the judiciary through the minimum and maximum sentence laws; taken from them again and turned over to the prison authorities, and, later, in some instances, put into the hands of an independent board or commission of parole; grasped at by the chief executive, this power to determine the length of sentence, a power that ought clearly to be exercised under all due legal restraint, safeguarded in every way that the liberty of no individual may be unduly infringed, is still a prize fought for by all branches of the government.[29]

In general, the writers of the period believed that classical theory was wrong to leave the decision on punishment to the legislature. They agreed with the Gluecks that sentences should not be determined by "the inexpert views of legislators as to the relative seriousness of various crimes."[30] However, the writers disagreed over whether sentencing discretion was best left to judges or to administrative tribunals such as parole boards.

Bates, for example, argued that the courts should have the power to individualize dispositions: society must "free the hands of the authority which prescribes the treatment."[31] The advocates of judicial discretion opposed transferring sentencing authority to an administrative board because they feared abuse of low-visibility administrative discretion.

On the other hand, many writers argued that sentencing authority should be vested completely in an administrative tribunal. As Pound stated, "administrative discretion...is the chief agent of individualization."[32] Some writers pointed to evidence of bias, corruption, and abuse of discretion by the courts in sentencing decisions.[33]

However, there was a more fundamental argument for administrative, as opposed to judicial, discretion over sentencing. This argument was an extension of the medical analogy to rehabilitation. A court ordering a specific sentence was seen as acting like a doctor ordering that a patient be released from the hospital long before it would be possible to determine whether the patient was cured. As Tom Clark stated in 1945, "men who administer correction, like doctors, must be permitted to decide when the cure has been effected."[34] Similarly, the Wickersham Commission asserted that "no court could determine in advance" when the offender would be reformed.[35] Such a decision, these writers asserted, should be left to the penal authorities who provided the treatment and assessed its effectiveness.[36]

The writers of the early crime surveys were sensitive to criticism that they were "soft" on criminals. Yet they seem to have been curiously insensitive to the possible unfairness of incarcerating individuals on the basis of what they might do in the future rather than on the basis of what they have done in the past. This insensitivity is a logical outcome of the medical model: if the state is providing "treatment" to a "sick individual" rather than imposing punishment on a criminal, then that individual is hardly in a position to complain about unfairness. This is the utilitarian purpose taken to the extreme.

Conclusions on Pre-ABF Research

Several important points emerge from the pre-ABF research. First, although their language emphasized empiricism and the scientific method, the writers' arguments for rehabilitation appear to have been based more on ideology than on facts. If the facts did not fit their positivist argument, the writers asserted that rehabilitation had not yet had a fair chance.

The facts available were usually bare statistics, often gathered into mortality tables and without helpful explanation about their significance. The actual operation of the sentencing and correctional systems was not carefully observed. This may have been, in part, simply because researchers had little access to the workings of the system. The writers of the time, therefore, relied on reformers and casual observers for information. This lack of information explains, at least in part, why ideology dominated the early writing on sentencing and corrections and why suggestions for reform were speculative.

Second, there was no "pure" implementation of either classical theory or positivist rehabilitative theory. For one thing, history shows that sentencing authority has always been shared among the courts, administrative agencies, and legislature. Both "pure" theories would have removed sentencing authority from the courts: in the classical model it would have been given to the legislature and in the rehabilitative model it is given to an expert administrative tribunal. Because American criminal justice has never implemented either theory in its pure form, courts have retained some authority over sentence authority, usually shared with the legislature and a parole authority.

Third, the writers of the crime surveys demonstrated a fundamentally different theory of what constituted fairness and uniformity in sentencing than did the classical theorists. In classical theory, every individual was equal in the eyes of the law. Sentencing variations came about because of the various social harms caused by different criminal acts. For the positivists, this formal equality of individuals was a "dangerous fiction."[37] Because people differ in their social and economic background, intelligence, and general aptitudes, the positivists considered it unfair to give the same sentence to two very different individuals simply because they happened to have been convicted of violating the same statute.

These underlying theories explain how each system would allocate sentencing authority. For the classical theorists, like those who advocate fair and certain punishment today, the judge played a limited role in sentencing because the individual characteristics of the offender were of no importance and, without parole, there was no need to set parole eligibility. A sentence based on the offense could be set by the legislature or, in more sophisticated systems, by guidelines. For those favoring rehabilitation, the parole authority played the critical role because it was expert at the assessment of treatment progress. Both the legislature, so distant from the individual, and the court had only a limited role in such decision making.

THE AMERICAN BAR FOUNDATION RESEARCH

The research took place during the 1950s, a period of continued commitment to the objective of rehabilitation. As in earlier periods, there were significant differences in the way responsibility was allocated for making sentencing and correctional decisions. In Michigan, the legislature reserved power to itself by means of mandatory prison sentences and by limiting the ability of the trial judge to determine the length of a prison sentence. As Frank J. Remington pointed out in chapter 3 of this volume, flexibility denied the sentencing judge was reintroduced into the Michigan system through the process of plea negotiation condoned, often encouraged, by the trial judge.[38]

In Wisconsin, the trial judge had broad sentencing discretion limited only by the legislatively set maximum sentence, and much less emphasis was placed on plea negotiation as a way of affecting sentence.

At the time of the ABF research, the Wisconsin correctional system was widely recognized as one of the most capable of this country's correctional systems. It was a system committed to professional standards with a heavy emphasis on social work education and on casework as an approach to the supervision of offenders in the community.

Prior to the ABF survey, the Division of Corrections, which included the parole board, a unified state system of probation and parole, and the prison and reformatory system, had undergone a major change in its organization and operational objectives. The previously independent division was incorporated in 1948 under the control of the Department of Health and Social Services. This change coincided with a shift of ideology and objectives toward a social work orientation stressing the primacy of rehabilitation over purely punitive or custodial goals. New administrators with social work training and commitments were appointed to head the Division of Corrections and the parole and field services. Friction developed in the early years between the newly recruited social workers and older employees less committed to rehabilitation objectives or not trained in treatment procedures. However, by the time the survey field staff began its work in Wisconsin in 1956, the parole and probation services and the parole board were widely regarded as one of the most progressive systems in the nation.

The ABF research in Wisconsin is instructive, particularly the descriptions of the work of the judge at sentencing, the actions of the parole board, and the supervising actions of the state probation and parole agents outside Milwaukee County. During this research, the Milwaukee Probation Department was a county-run department in contrast to the rest of the Wisconsin that was run by the Wisconsin Division of Corrections. Emphasis in this description of the ABF research is given to the Wisconsin data because doing so enables one to view a state system with an indeterminate sentence structure and a state correctional system highly regarded for its professionalism. Doing so enables one to look particularly at trial judge sentencing practices in a system that gave broad discretion to the sentencing judge in contrast to the system in Michigan in which the legislatively mandated sentences shifted discretion to the prosecutor and the guilty plea stage. It also affords an opportunity to look at parole board practices in a system committed to rehabilitation and broad discretion by the parole board and at probation and parole supervision practices in a system oriented toward social work training and casework methods.

Trial Judge Sentencing in Wisconsin as Described by the ABF Research

In Wisconsin at the time of the ABF research, the trial judge had complete discretion either to place an offender on probation or to impose a prison sentence. If the decision was to impose a prison sentence, the judge had complete discretion to set a term within the maximum fixed by the legislature and specified in the statute defining the crime. For example, a sentence for armed robbery could be anywhere between one day and twenty years, the prescribed maximum.

This broad discretion obviously meant that the trial judge could impose a sentence thought by the trial judge to be appropriate under all of the circumstances of the case. The disadvantage, apparent during the ABF research, is that judges differ in their assessment of the seriousness of the offense and what is needed to deter or change the offender for the better. The result is disparity among sentences imposed by different judges, a problem, however, that was at least moderated by the authority of the parole board to take account of disparity when deciding on the proper time for release of offenders into the community on parole. Although disparity in sentencing became a major issue in some jurisdictions, including the federal system, during the ABF research there appeared not to be a great deal of concern with this problem on the part of anyone in the Wisconsin system.

In a system in which the trial judge is expected to individualize the sentence and to take account of the possibility of rehabilitation, detailed information about the offender is needed. The practice in Wisconsin was to request from the probation service a presentence report that contained detailed information about the offender from birth to the date the offense was committed. Although some trial judges still gave primary emphasis in sentencing to information concerning the current offense and the offender's prior record, it was assumed that more detailed information would be significant, if not in sentencing, then later during correctional treatment and consideration for parole.

In general, Wisconsin trial judges took sentencing seriously. They would read the presentence report carefully and, in guilty plea cases, often conduct a postplea hearing to obtain further information about the circumstances of the current offense and other matters relevant to the sentencing decision.

Parole Release in Wisconsin

The Wisconsin Parole Board was made up of career correctional officers who had extensive prior experience as probation and parole agents or in various prison assignments. The board believed strongly in its ability to time release on parole in a way that would reflect the seriousness of the offense, moderate disparity if the sentence was unusually severe, and maximize the chances of success under supervision in the community. A preparole report, indicating where the offender would live, what kind of employment he would have, what conditions of supervision should be imposed, and the like, was usually available. The primary concern, of course, was the board's estimate of the risk that another offense would be committed after release, although this was less a factor if the current offense was a nonviolent property offense.

The members of the parole board were firmly committed to the value of parole. It was common for the board to hold mock hearings for community groups, and the board took pride in the fact that the community was supportive of current parole practices. Usually the board members in addressing community groups noted that law enforcement officers in the mock hearings frequently voted to release offenders earlier than would the board members. It was a way to demonstrate that parole practices and law enforcement objectives were not inconsistent, despite the prevalent assumption by parole boards generally that the prisoner given parole could best succeed if notice of release was not shared widely, for example, with police.

Probation and Parole Supervision in Wisconsin

My recent examination of the ABF "Field Reports" about probation and parole agents outside Milwaukee County shows that their orientation and practices are virtually identical to those I observed recently in the rural community of Lancaster, Wisconsin, and of a specialized unit in Milwaukee, which is staffed by persons thought to be among the most able in the city at the supervision of offenders in the community. My summary of the characteristics of probation and parole supervision in rural Wisconsin written in 1988 reflects the practices of social work trained agents described in the "Field Reports" of the ABF research.[39] Following is a brief description of these practices.[40]

The practices involved the resolution of family and community problems of offenders, the provision of assistance to offenders under economic and social stress so that they were better able to cope with life, and the building of stronger community support. The agents manifested a strong commitment to people and made sustained efforts to individualize treatment and supervision. Adjustments in objectives and supervision practices were made as circumstances, people, and opportunities changed. Contacts with clients were frequent. The most important ones occurred outside the office; from them the agents gained a better perspective on the client and his life circumstances. Emphasis was placed on encouraging the client to genuinely embrace the goals of supervision, which were individualized to take into account the significant differences among offenders and their circumstances. Thus, the nature of supervision was defined less by the offense than by the needs of the offender and the community.

The agents communicated to the clients that they cared about them, and they sought to create a bond that allowed each agent to assist the individual client's reintegration into the community. The clients appeared to understand what was expected of them. This meant that they knew the specific limits on what they were permitted to do as well as the goals to be achieved. The agents extensively involved the families of clients in the programs of supervision. Because the problems of clients were sometimes related to the problems of the family, the family frequently became a focal point of assistance. In addition, individual community members, particularly potential employers, were enlisted as a source of help for clients. The agent's knowledge of the community, developed through extensive contacts, was critical to tapping such assistance. An important reason corrections functioned as well as it did in Wisconsin at the time of the ABF research was because of the accessibility of community resources.

Although planning played an important role in successful supervision, many decisions had an "opportunistic" quality. This meant that the agent waited for the right time to intervene, using every violation, every source of stress, every apparent problem as an opportunity to induce proper behavior and provide a catalyst for significant change in their lives.

The probation and parole system in rural Wisconsin that is described in the "Field Reports" had a strong casework–social work orientation at a time when the rehabilitative ideal was at its zenith. The methods described above were driven by the need to deal in a sensitive and responsive way with offenders in the community. Offender behavior and agent efforts to control and modify it shaped the system. The methods used were complex and individualized. The parole and probation agents' apparent rapport with the community suggests that there was strong community support for what was going on. The agents had enormous discretion and their decisions were of low visibility. They attempted to "render justice" individually, and they required and used great flexibility in so doing.

Significance of the ABF Research

The main contributions of the ABF research include the following:

1. The research captured processes and decisions that had never been described so fully before in sufficient detail to

understand their significance. The work gave visibility to factors in decisions, to the decisions themselves, and to practices reflecting those decisions that were seldom visible or were only emerging in the mid-1950s. This is particularly true of parole and probation supervision and revocation.

2. The research detailed the prevalence of discretionary decisions in the correctional process. In so doing, it highlighted the apparent uncontrolled nature of this discretion—uncontrolled in practice by statutory criteria, formal guidelines, administrative review, or judicial review. The research also revealed the informal guidelines and controls that did exist.

3. The research painted a picture of a very complex world in which multiple objectives and factors, often individualized to the particular case, substantially influenced the decisions made. Actors in the system were encouraged to *improvise* in order to fit sanctions and treatment to the needs of individual offenders.

4. The research also revealed the interplay of actors in the correctional system. For example, the parole agent is under pressure from the police to revoke an offender's probation and acts as a buffer to keep the offender in the community. The judge relies on the recommendation of the probation agent in determining whether to imprison or place an offender on probation. The judge agrees to a charge reduction by the prosecutor to avoid a mandatory sentence. Not only is this interplay revealed, but at times the actors are partners in the development of improvisational solutions to problems. (The prosecutor agrees to drop charges, probation is not revoked, or the offender agrees to enlist in the army.)

5. In general, the research described a system in which decisions affecting offenders are decentralized and dispersed, with frontline actors allotted large areas of discretion to adjust their actions in a highly individualized fashion.

POST-ABF RESEARCH AND DEVELOPMENTS

Although rehabilitation was an important factor in most sentencing and correctional decisions during the decades of the 1950s and 1960s, a major change occurred thereafter. Persons who identified themselves politically as from either the right or the left expressed increasing concern about disparity in the treatment of persons convicted of crime.[41] In part this was the legacy of leaders like James Bennett, director of the United States Bureau of Prisons, who devoted a great deal of effort to pointing out the problems created by disparity in the sentencing practices of federal judges. Bennett's solution was to make sentences more indeterminate, thus allowing the United States Parole Commission to reduce disparity by granting an early parole for those offenders given an unduly severe sentence. He also advocated sentencing institutes in which federal judges could come together to discuss types of cases in the expectation that adequate discussion would produce a consensus among federal judges, thus making their sentences less disparate.

Other pressures were brought to bear on sentencing practices in the federal courts and in most states. Many people argued that an effective response to crime was compromised by the existence of parole, which was perceived as a form of leniency. Others, less concerned about leniency, feared that the broad discretion afforded judges and parole boards would be used arbitrarily or, worse, to the disadvantage of those expressing unpopular political views such as opposition to the Vietnam war. Many believed that current sentence practice was dishonest because a ten-year sentence did not mean ten years in prison due to the possibility of earlier parole. Perhaps most significantly, faith in rehabilitation declined as faith in government and faith in behavioral sciences, psychiatry in particular, also declined.[42]

In 1974, Martinson, in a much cited study, had asked "what works?" as he examined research on the question of the effectiveness of rehabilitative programs.[43] His answer—"nothing"—received far more attention than his qualifying note of caution published five years later.[44]

An earlier and very influential report of the Working Party of the American Friends Services Committee[45] severely criticized the indeterminate sentence and its underlying assumptions about discretion and rehabilitation. One commentator summarized these criticisms as follows:

> The final report of the group specifically criticized the indeterminate sentencing structure for its assumption that: 1) crime is the product of individual pathology; 2) penology has the

knowledge to affect treatment of criminals; 3) experts have established a significant body of knowledge to diagnose the particular factors resulting in a criminal activity; 4) knowledge for practice in criminology is free from biases of race, class, or status; 5) useful and accurate means of measuring the success of treatment exists; and finally that 6) discretionary power is a necessary attribute of a fair and efficient criminal justice system (American Friends Committee, 1971). The critique provided by *Struggle for Justice* was both technical and political. At the technical level, the group emphasized that the present status of knowledge available to criminologists, prison staffs, and others was insufficient to support claims for indeterminacy, discretionary power, and rehabilitation. At the political level, *Struggle for Justice* argued that the discretionary exercise of power by the criminal justice system had contributed to the development and continuation of a dual system of justice which was unfair to the poor, the non-white, and the politically weak.[46]

Two other influential works, Alan Dershowitz's *Fair and Certain Punishment* and Andrew Von Hirsch's *Doing Justice: The Choice of Punishments*,[47] also argued for determinate sentencing systems. They emphasized that sentencing and parole discretion should be greatly limited; that punishment ought to be the purpose of the system; that fairness could best be achieved through uniformity in sentencing; and that honesty in sentencing should require the abolition of "invisible" decisions, such as parole and good time, which are inconsistent with "open" decisions. These works were the theoretical spawning ground for the grids and matrices used in many jurisdictions to set sentences, to determine parole release dates, and for other sentencing reforms. In these systems, both uniformity and individualization (it is claimed) are achieved through the assignment of numerical weights to individual characteristics of the crime and the offender.

The form the systems take varies from state to state. In Maine, the judge sets the maximum term, within legislatively prescribed limits, from which there is no parole.[48] In California, the judge selects one of three legislatively prescribed sentences and presumptively sets the middle sentence, unless mitigating or aggravating factors permit selection of the alternative lower or higher sentence.[49] Again, parole release is abolished.

In the federal system from 1977 until 1987, judges set parole eligibility and the maximum term within legislated limits.[50] The parole release date was set by the parole commission according to the salient factor score. This score was obtained by assigning points to the offender's characteristics at the time of the offense. The characteristics were identified by actuarial studies of factors predicting future behavior and weighing them accordingly. All these characteristics existed at the time of sentencing, so the offender could do relatively little while in prison to affect release. (The score resulted in the assignment of a narrow range of months to be served by the offender, and prison behavior could affect movement or placement of the offender within the range or out of it.)

In 1987, the federal system abolished parole and adopted a sentencing guidelines system.[51] These "guidelines" are in fact numerical ranges within which the judge must sentence, with limited exceptions. The ranges were established by assigning weights to offense and offender characteristics.

The critical reaction to the federal sentencing guidelines has been increasingly severe because of a variety of undesirable effects. One observer, Michael Tonry, formerly a proponent of guidelines, describes this reaction as follows:

> The guidelines developed by the U.S. Sentencing Commission, which took effect on November 1, 1987, are the most controversial and reviled sentencing reform initiative in United States history. They are commonly criticized on policy grounds (that they unduly narrowly limit judicial discretion and unduly shift discretion to prosecutors), on process grounds (that they foreseeably cause judges and prosecutors to circumvent them), on technocratic grounds (that they are too complex and hard to apply accurately), on fairness grounds (that by taking only offense elements and prior convictions into account, they require that very different defendants receive the same sentence), and on normative grounds (that they greatly increased the proportion of offenders receiving prison sentences and are generally too harsh).[52]

The criticisms of the federal system of sentencing guidelines echoes objections to the imposition of mandatory sentences encountered in the ABF research. Mandatory sentences enacted by the legislature provide for a fixed term of years, whereas the sentencing guidelines provide a presumptive sentence with a range of years, depending on mitigating or aggravating circumstances. Since the guidelines require judicial conformity to specified terms, they are generally regarded as mandatory, in a sense similar in effect to the fixed mandatory sentence. However, the United States Sentencing Commission makes much of this difference. In a detailed study mandated by Congress on the work of the federal courts, the commission reached conclusions about the undesirability of legislatively fixed mandatory sentences. Michael Tonry commented:

> The Commission concluded that mandatory penalties are unwise and unsound policy because they remove incentives to plead guilty and thereby increase trial rates, case processing times, and workloads; they foster prosecutorial manipulation in charging and plea bargaining both to induce guilty pleas and to avoid imposition of sentences prosecutors believe to be unduly harsh; they often result in imposition of sentences that are unduly harsh; they do not permit judges to take into account special circumstances concerning the defendant that might suggest some other sentence. These are, of course, precisely the same charges that critics lay against the Commission's guidelines. Capturing this point precisely, in what may be a Freudian slip, the Commission, on the first page of its mandatory sentencing report refers to its own "mandatory guidelines."[53]

The lessons of the ABF research were ignored in these developments. The experience in Michigan at the time of the ABF research, when legislatively mandated sentences were common, was that strong pressure was exerted on the prosecutor to make concessions necessary to achieve a sentence believed by the prosecutor and the judge to be appropriate under all of the circumstances. Although the same shift of power from sentencing judge to prosecutor was predicted by some commentators, the response of the later proponents of mandatory sentences or guidelines was that this is a problem that can be dealt with later. Some also were in favor of giving authority to the prosecutor, who was believed likely to be tougher on crime than judges had been.

Today, after almost two decades of experience with mandatory sentences, there is adequate corroboration of the ABF conclusion that the mandatory system does result in a shift of sentencing discretion from the judge, who formally exercised discretion in open court, to the prosecutor, who exercises discretion in the confines of the prosecutor's office. One explanation of support for this system is that public concern is greater when discretion is exercised openly and visibly by the judge than when there is the appearance of cer-

tainty because the exercise of discretion is in the office of the prosecutor, not visible to the public.

Less anticipated was the great increase in prison populations
that has resulted, at least to some degree, from high, mandatory
sentences. Because the Michigan mandatory sentences were routinely evaded by plea bargaining, the ABF research did not offer
any experience with respect to the likely impact of mandatory sentences on prison populations. Although it was predicted by some
that mandatory sentences would be severe, some proponents of
mandatory sentences seemed convinced that such sentences could
be both honest (not subject to reduction by parole) and moderate.
This has not been the experience in most jurisdictions.

It would be an oversimplification to attribute the unprece-
dented growth in prison populations in this county between
1975 and 1990 solely to the changes in sentencing systems.
Indeed the jurisdictions that did not change systems also experienced significant increases in the number of prisoners, while one
state (Minnesota) that adopted a definite sentencing system did
not experienced such explosive growth.[54] Crime rates, public fear
of crime, the political exploitation of this fear, media reporting
about crime and the criminal justice system (often stressing dramatic cases of the system misfiring, such as the Willie Horton
case),[55] and the shift of public values away from individualization
and toward certainty, consistency, and punishment are among
the factors that explain the increase.

The experience with mandatory sentences has given rise to at
least three significant issues, as to which attitudes seem to be in
the process of change. These are:

1. Does the mandatory sentence shift sentencing discretion
   from the judge to the prosecutor? Most observers conclude
   that it does.

2. Does the mandatory sentence, including mandatory guidelines, adequately take into account the circumstances of
   the individual case? Is there less disparity under mandatory sentences than existed when the judge had sentencing
   discretion? Increasingly observers are concluding that
   mandatory guidelines do not take adequate account of the
   important factual variations that exist between cases and
   that disparity may in fact be increased.

3. Do mandatory sentences and mandatory guidelines contribute to prison overcrowding and the immense cost of
   prison construction and operation that most states are
   finding they cannot afford? Increasingly, the answer seems
   to be yes, and there is rapidly increasing support for the
   creation of alternatives to prison, alternatives more significant than ordinary probation but less costly than prison.

The signs of change are increasing as criticism of mandatory
sentences and mandatory guidelines increases among both practitioners and academics. Some indication of this is reflected in a
Sunday front page article in the *New York Times* titled, "Chorus
of Judicial Critics Assail Sentencing Guides: 5-Year Effort Is
Called Hobgoblin of U.S. Courts."[56] The article detailed what
has been known for some time: that is, that federal trial judges,
facing individual defendants, feel that the sentence mandated by
the guidelines is not appropriate when one takes into account all
of the circumstances in the individual case.

Nor do the federal guidelines serve to eliminate disparity.
Gerald W. Heaney, a senior judge of the Eighth Circuit Court of
Appeals, in a study of the operation of guidelines in four district
courts, concluded:

> The roles of the prosecutor and the probation officer in the
> sentencing process have been enhanced and that of the district
> judge diminished. While district judges are required to devote
> more time to sentencing, their discretion has been severely lim-
> ited....There is little evidence to suggest that the Congressional
> objective of reducing unwarranted sentencing disparity has
> been achieved....Voluminous anecdotal evidence and case law
> show the unfairness of the guidelines and the disparities cre-
> ated through their application.[57]

One of the most perceptive of the current academic
researchers in the field of criminal justice administration, Albert
W. Alschuler, concludes:

> "But weren't sentencing commissions always supposed to focus
> on the specific, to consider paradigmatic cases, to listen to
> experienced sentencing judges, to become experts on particular
> offenses, and to try to understand the world of criminal con-
> duct that they punished?" I once thought that the answer to
> this question was yes. The aggregative style seems so ingrained,

however, that sentencing commissioners have apparently assumed that their task was to consider categories, not cases, and to allocate punishment wholesale.[58]

A recent *Yale Law Journal* "Note" sounds remarkably similar to a conclusion reached by Frank J. Remington in the decade following the ABF research, when the trend toward mandatory sentences first became apparent. He concluded:

> The danger, as I see it, is that disenchantment with rehabilitation will lead us back to punishment, where we have been before. After a period of time, disenchantment with punishment will cause us once again to try to individualize sentences. The reason for the vacillation probably will be that neither rehabilitation nor punishment is a panacea. Rather, what is needed are carefully worked-out governmental responses to significantly different kinds of socially deviant behavior, responses that are calculated to deal both fairly and effectively with the conduct involved.[59]

Twenty years later, Steve Y. Koh, writing in the *Yale Law Journal,* concludes:

> Those who concluded that the pre-Guidelines system was a failure traced the fault to judges exercising discretion inconsistently and unfairly. This Note argues that restraining judicial discretion with a Guidelines matrix was both an ineffective and ill-advised response. Not only did the sentencing process lose the potential benefits of discretion, but the process became skewed in a way that promoted new, and arguably more troubling, forms of disparity. Sentencing reform that aspires to eradicate unwarranted disparity must begin by aiming to optimize the ability of discretion to account for individual differences among offenders. It should tap the abilities and experiences that judges bring to the sentencing process in a manner that elicits dialogue yet checks abuse. Only in this way can sentencing theory evolve.[60]

The historical pre-ABF data, discussed earlier, noted a shift from a heavy emphasis on punishment fixed by legislation in proportion to the harm caused to an equally heavy emphasis on the indeterminate sentence enabling the judge to fix the sentence to meet the needs of the offender, a change endorsed by the early crime surveys. We appear to be witnessing the early stages of a similar shift today from heavy reliance on mandatory sentences and mandatory guidelines to the reintroduction of greater discretion in sentencing. The question is whether we have learned enough, through criminal justice research like that of the ABF, to avoid another complete swing of the pendulum.

The state of Wisconsin, carefully studied during the ABF research, did not change to a system of mandatory penalties, nor did it abolish parole in the past decades, during which most states and the federal government did. Looking carefully at post-ABF developments in Wisconsin affords us an opportunity to perhaps learn how to avoid swings between reliance on mandatory sentences at one extreme and total, unguided, and uncontrolled discretion at the other extreme. Albert Alschuler said recently,

> Discussions of sentencing procedures sometimes have posed a false dilemma—the choice between an individualized sentencing system in which judges are free to indulge their whims and biases and an aggregated system in which cases are grouped on the basis of a few characteristics and in which unlike cases are treated alike.[61]

Whether Wisconsin has steered an appropriate middle course between uncontrolled discretion and undue rigidity is a question to which I now turn my attention. In doing so I rely on the experience I had as head of the Wisconsin Division of Corrections and on the opportunity I have had more recently to study first-hand the practices in Wisconsin of both rural and urban probation and parole agents.

The Experience in Wisconsin After the ABF Survey— *Sentencing and Parole Release*

It is a simple matter to describe the structure of the Wisconsin criminal justice system and a much more complex one to describe and analyze its performance. In sentencing, parole release decision making, and probation and parole supervision, Wisconsin remains indeterminate and flexible. Few crimes carry mandatory sentences of any kind and, except for intentional murder, all of them are misdemeanors.[62] A person sentenced to prison is eligible for parole release after serving one-fourth of the sentence, more than was the case at the time of the ABF, but not a substantial limit on parole release.[63] The parole board is able to release a prisoner at any time after one-fourth of the sentence is served and must release when two-thirds of the sentence has been served.[64] Probation and parole agents prepare presentence reports that are usually influential at sentencing, and they retain substantial discretion with regard to the circumstances of community supervision and the decision whether to seek its revocation.

Guidelines now exist for sentencing, parole release, and probation and parole supervision and revocation.[65] These guidelines are not mandatory and take two forms. Sentencing judges and the parole board have numerical information about the treatment of offenders said to be similarly situated. Probation and parole agents have rules that require them to take a variety of factors into account in their decision making regarding both supervision and revocation.

In a nutshell, Wisconsin has retained the basic sentencing and correctional structure that existed at the time of the ABF survey. Although mandatory sentencing and the abolition of parole were proposed, these were not adopted, largely because the legislature took the advice of criminal justice leaders that such change would inappropriately shift power to prosecutors, inordinately limit or shift discretion, and make the system less flexible and less fair. Implicit and sometimes explicit in the decisions Wisconsin has made in the past two decades is a continuing commitment to the rehabilitative ideal.

What have changed in Wisconsin, as in the rest of the nation, are political attitudes toward crime and corrections. No laws required change, but from 1975 on, judges have sentenced people to prison who, in an earlier time, might not have been imprisoned; sentences have been longer; until recently, parole release has been less frequent and has come later in the sentence; and parole and probation of offenders in the community have been revoked more often. Difficult as it is to say with certainty, it appears that these shifts have been less extreme in Wisconsin than in most states. For example, although Wisconsin has experienced prison growth, it has not been the explosive growth of California, Illinois, or many other states.[66]

Whether this is attributable to the retention of the indeterminate system is impossible to say. That was certainly a factor, as were the culture and tradition of the state, the high degree of professionalism in corrections, the rural character of the state, the leadership of legislators and criminal justice officials, and the cost of more extreme prison growth.

At the risk of oversimplifying, let me share my impressions of how judges, the parole board, and probation and parole agents have functioned in the past two decades with respect to sentencing, parole release, and the revocation of community supervision.

Judges have continued to individualize sentences, taking as many circumstances into account as they can. Utilitarian objectives continue to dominate sentencing, especially individual deterrence and rehabilitation, though increased emphasis is generally given to punishment. Sentencing guidelines are used in various ways throughout the state. Many judges use them as a benchmark in imposing the appropriate sentence but still emphasize their own assessment of the individual in the imposition of sentence. A minority, but apparently growing number, rely more directly on guidelines as a starting point for sentencing. These judges, in effect, ask whether individual characteristics argue for deviation from the guidelines, which are themselves stated as broad ranges.

The parole board's performance has not been consistent throughout the past two decades. Until about 1980, discretionary parole was granted with great frequency as well over half the releases from prison per year were discretionary parole releases. These decisions reflected individualized evaluation of the offender, giving greatest emphasis to the prospects for successful completion of parole, but also considering the amount of time served, the seriousness of the crime, and other factors. In the 1980s, the number of releases on parole (as opposed to release at the mandatory release date) declined. During this period, the parole board gave greater emphasis to punishment. Although individual circumstances were considered, the weight they received declined substantially in board decisions. This was also a period in which guidelines were used, both numerical categories that indicated when similar offenders had been released and policy statements such as whether the time served for punishment was sufficient. During the ABF survey, the parole board worked closely with field agents assigned to offenders in prison to ensure continuity and a commitment to successful reintegration. This practice was stopped during the 1980s, but it was started again, consistent with the other changes I will now briefly describe.

In the 1990s, there has been a decided shift in parole board practices. Individualized decisions are again the rule. Greatest emphasis is given to successful reassimilation of the offender into the community. The board now accepts the service of the sentence to parole eligibility (i.e., 25 percent of the sentence fixed by the judge) as sufficient time for punishment. The board has abandoned the use of numerical ranges and continues to use policy statements as standards.

Three factors appear to explain this latest change in parole practices. The prisons in Wisconsin are crowded, and parole offers a way to alleviate this. A new board chair was appointed who had extensive experience with offenders in the community, and he brought a different outlook to parole than that which had been prevalent in the 1980s. Finally, reflecting a legislative and executive mandate to rely less on prison, an intensive sanctions program was created to give judges, the parole board, and agents greater options in dealing with offenders.[67] The board uses these options extensively to implement its policies, emphasizing reintegration of offenders. The enthusiasm among judges for alternative sentences also reflects their desire to individualize sentences.

The experience in revocation is also a mixed one. There were more revocations of probation and parole in the past two decades than in the previous period. This does not signal any less emphasis on individualized decision making, which continues to dominate revocation decision making. Rather, two factors explain the increase. The first is the increase in serious crime by people under supervision. Revocation is virtually automatic in such situations, particularly if the offender is sentenced to prison for the new crime. The absence of alternatives to revocation—the diminution of resources—also explains the increase in revocations. Again, the increased alternatives available through the intensive sanctions program both address this problem and signal a strong commitment to individualized decision making for sentencing judges, the parole board, and probation agents considering the revocation of community supervision.[68]

The intensive sanctions program emphasizes successful reintegration of offenders and short periods of confinement for punishment.[69] Substantial state funds have been allocated to this alternatives program. The commitment to the intensive sanctions program signals a renewed commitment in Wisconsin to individualized decisions. This program creates resources that give meaning to a system that, in structure and theory, is an open-ended, indeterminate one. That it has been well received among criminal justice professionals is an indication that there continues to be a deep-seated commitment at the line level to such a system and to the rehabilitative ideal.

As I noted earlier, the probation and parole system of supervision described in the ABF "Field Reports" is virtually identical to the one existing today, especially in rural areas. A strong commitment to the rehabilitative ideal remains. The methods are consumer and community driven, responsive to the needs of client and society. These methods are complex and highly individualized to the client and situation and are strengthened by the agent's rapport with the community. The agents treat offenders individually and flexibly, exercising low-visibility discretion.

The setting in which these qualities flourish deserves emphasis. Rural Wisconsin of the 1950s and of today remains relatively free of crime, compared to large cities. The caseloads of probation agents are, if not low, manageable. The agents are professional—most have a master's degree in social work—and are experienced and committed to remaining in the communities in which they live and work. The criminal justice system entrusts them with extensive authority over the clients they supervise and similar discretion as to its exercise. Their day-to-day decisions are not highly visible or regulated by numerical formulas, but they are accountable because they are "checked" by guidelines, supervisors, the people in the community with whom they work, and the culture of the correctional system of which they are a part, a culture that retains a strong social work orientation.

However, I would by no means solely limit these observations to supervision in rural areas. Although cities do present some unique problems, the quality of supervision is similar to rural areas, when the resources are available, caseloads are reasonable, and the agents are experienced. My experience gained in creating a special supervision unit in Milwaukee has convinced me that we can transfer the successful model of supervision used in rural areas to urban areas.[70]

What comes of probation supervision in such settings? Perhaps most important is the intensive and extended contact among probation agent, client, and community. Whatever the initial orientation of the probation agents, the nature of the situation forces them to be consumer oriented, the consumer being the community and client. The extensive contact permits the agents to see the offenders more clearly for what they are and results in a highly individualized plan to assist them. Coping with life is usually the offenders' greatest need and is a means toward the avoidance of crime. Individualizing this needs compels the agent to devise various strategies for supervision that invoke the community's assistance. Ultimately, the agent does care about the client and guides the client toward a better-adjusted life in the way a skillful parent guides an adolescent toward adulthood and independence. Doing so requires close contact, flexibility, authority, and good judgment. With these conditions, the supervision or guidance afforded offenders on probation can become responsive to individualized differences and caring (a desperate need for many offenders). This kind of supervision is opportunistic and geared toward strengthening the communities' capacity to cope with crime through improving the quality of life of offenders who have extensive interactions with their communities each day. Done well, probation supervision is responsive to and enriches both the lives of offenders and the communities in which they live.

Conclusion: Discretion in Sentencing and Corrections on the National Scene

The activities and decisions of the sentencing courts, parole boards, and correctional agencies described in the ABF survey are highly complex. They deal with a wide range of behavior and people, and a variety of factors and values are reflected in the decisions that are made. These decisions tend to be highly individualized attempts to "render justice," usually defined as properly responding to the behavior to hold the offender accountable while seeking to avoid future crime. The system, as described in the ABF survey, is a loosely integrated, loosely interdependent one, in which the actors work, if not together, at least with reference to one another and sometimes serve as checks on one another.

Today, the range of behavior with which the sentencing and correctional systems deal remains complex. However, in dealing with the behavior, the factors and values taken into account are fewer, since individualization and effectiveness have given way to other objectives, such as uniformity, certainty, predictability, and punishment. The actors in the system are now more isolated from one another, and the term *system* seems even more inaccurate. Because of the nature of the values sought to be achieved, decision making has become more rigid and less capable of responding in a flexible way in confronting problems.

Sentencing, parole decisions, probation and parole revocation, and supervision strategies were highly discretionary decisions in the system described by the ABF survey. The amount of discretion was not well publicized at the time and was not regulated by rule, though it was checked by custom. Certainly, it was not "legalized" in the sense that the written rule of law was applied to it to any substantial degree. In part, this was due to the low visibility of the decisions. Many of the practices of parole boards and parole agents were not widely known prior to the ABF survey or were visible mainly to those close to the system.

By contrast, today sentencing, parole release, and revocation are very rule bound. Even when the rule is called a "guideline," it is hardly this, since today's guidelines are matrices that dictate a result. Not only is the system far more regulated by rules, but the rules are rigid. They assign point scores or dictate responses, such as a parole date or sentencing term. These results (it is hard to call them "decisions") are more visible, both to the public and to other actors in the system. They are subject to judicial review, if only of a limited kind, as are the parole release and revocation decisions. And the public tends to be more aware of the decisions, if only when the system misfires.

If by control is meant influence over decision at the line level, the situation today is markedly different than at the time of the ABF survey. Then the sentencing and correctional decisions were for the most part made at the operational level. Parole boards, parole and probation agents, and judges actually made judgments and decisions while directly confronting the person who was the subject of the decision.

Today, decisions are more likely to be made at higher levels, in the legislature, in the sentencing commission, or at the top of the administrative agency. The decision makers, then, are distant from those affected by the decisions. They do not "know" offenders and are not forced to put a human face on them. The principal device for this change, this exercise of control, this removal of decisions from the front line, is the rule or matrix that dictates the result, once certain events have been factored into the process. The claims for such a system's achievements (whether in fairness or in effectiveness) remain essentially untested.

History has changed little in our reliance on the criminal justice system for solutions to problems that typically emerge at sentencing and corrections. The trouble is that decisions to deal with problems that may become very apparent in the correctional process (like the lack of employment, vocational training, and housing in the urban community for offenders and many other poor people) are largely viewed as the responsibility of others. The failure of corrections to become partners in any meaningful way with other community agencies or of others in the community to deal with such problems that directly affect correctional clients is puzzling. By and large, the correctional system focuses on correctional issues within the limits of the criminal justice system. Widespread reliance on and involvement with other systems of social justice are not apparent, even in community corrections.

Although the above describes the situation today, signs indicate that change may be in the winds. The rigidity of the present system and the limit it places on individualized decision making are generating a need for reevaluation. What have we learned to suggest that a greater degree of discretion should be introduced into the sentencing and correctional process? Certainly, unchecked discretion, like unchecked power, is undesirable and is an extreme to which the system is likely to return, since unacknowledged discretion will be exercised invisibly and will not be subject to systematic control. Only if we admit the desirability and need for various forms of accountable discretion can we avoid such a result in the effort to avoid a mandatory system of decisions.

Between the extremes of no discretion and unchecked discretion lies a good deal of territory for experimentation. The experience with probation supervision in rural Wisconsin suggests that the best decisions in the criminal justice system are made by the person closest to the problems. Not only are good decisions made about the individual case, but the compelling nature of the problems leads to a vitality and ingenuity in the resolution of problems that the system desperately needs. The nature of the problems leads officials to think more broadly about the criminal justice system and relations with the community. It involves the agents and corrections in community problems as partners and breaks down the deadly isolation that has stifled corrections where practiced in more traditional ways. The challenge is to devise ways to ensure accountability in such situations without sacrificing the creativity that broad discretion encourages.

In reality, we already have experience with combinations of accountability and flexibility. Whether it is rural Wisconsin or elsewhere, no correctional system has escaped developments to make it more accountable. In some, creativity has been smothered, along with flexibility. Others have adjusted and avoided extremes and function quite well. The situations I observed in rural Wisconsin and Milwaukee are examples of good programs that combine discretion with accountability. We need to find more of them, learn from them, and build on the principles that help them flourish. We need to apply these principles in sentencing, parole decisions, and probation supervision. This will make a better system.

NOTES

I am indebted to Merideth Ross, who prepared an excellent draft of the material on pre-ABF research. Ross is a clinical instructor in the University of Wisconsin Law School's Legal Assistance to Institutionalized Persons Program.

1. The most important of the early positivists was Cesare Lombroso, whose 1876 work *Criminal Man* was enormously influential both in Europe and in America. See C. Lombroso, *L'Uomo delinquente: In rapporto all anthropologogia, alla quirisprudenza, ed alle discipline carcerarie* (1876; reprint, Rome: Napoleone Editore, 1971); see also C. Lombroso, *Crime, Its Causes and Remedies* (1911).

2. Sanford Bates, "What May Be Done to Forward the Judicious Application of the Principle of Individualization of Punishment by the Judge Who Assigns the Penalty to Be Inflicted on the Offender?," *Journal of Criminal Law and Criminology* 16, no. 4 (1926):485.

3. Charles H. Z. Meyer, "A Half Century of Federal Probation and Parole," *Journal of Criminal Law, Criminology and Police Science* 42, no. 6 (1952):707–28.

4. Margaret W. Calahan, *Historical Corrections Statistics in the United States* (Washington, D.C.: Department of Justice, Bureau of Justice Statistics, 1986).

5. Sandra Shane-DuBow, Alice P. Brown, and Erik Olsen, *Sentencing Reform in the United States: History, Content, and Effect*

(Washington, D.C.: Department of Justice, Office of Development, Testing, and Dissemination, 1985) [hereinafter *Sentencing Reform*]. The first indeterminate sentencing law in the country was passed by the Michigan legislature in 1869. By 1922, thirty-seven states had some form of indeterminate sentence. In 1904, 15 percent of those convicted in state and federal courts received indeterminate sentences. By 1923, that figure had increased to 55 percent. Calahan, *Historical Corrections Statistics*, 40.

6. Calahan, *Historical Corrections Statistics*, 172.

7. Ibid., 169.

8. Ibid., 177.

9. See, e.g., Hugh N. Fuller, *Criminal Justice in Virginia* (New York: Century Co., 1931); Illinois Association for Criminal Justice, *The Illinois Crime Survey*, ed. John H. Wigmore (Chicago: Illinois Association for Criminal Justice in cooperation with the Chicago Crime Commission, 1929) [hereinafter *Illinois Crime Survey*]; Leon C. Marshall, *Comparative Criminal Statistics: Ohio and Maryland* (Baltimore: Johns Hopkins Press, 1932); The Missouri Association for Criminal Justice, *Missouri Crime Survey* (New York: Macmillan, 1926) [hereinafter *Missouri Crime Survey*]; Wayne Morse and Ronald Beattie, *Survey of the Administration of Criminal Justice in Oregon* (Eugene, Ore.: University Press, 1932); *Report of the National Commission on Law Observance and Enforcement* (Wickersham Commission), vol. 3, *Report on Criminal Statistics*; vol. 8, *Report on Criminal Procedure*; vol. 9, *Report on Penal Institutions, Probation and Parole* (Washington, D.C.: U. S. Government Printing Office, 1931; Montclair, N.J.: Patterson Smith, 1968) [hereinafter *Wickersham Report*]; eds. Roscoe Pound and Felix Frankfurter, *Criminal Justice in Cleveland: Report of the Cleveland Foundation Survey of the Administration of Criminal Justice in Cleveland, Ohio* (Cleveland: Cleveland Foundation, 1922) [hereinafter *Cleveland Crime Survey*]; United States Department of Justice, *Attorney General's Survey of Release Procedures* (Washington, D.C.: U.S. Government Printing Office, 1939) [hereinafter *Attorney General's Survey*].

10. Sheldon Glueck and Eleanor Glueck, *500 Criminal Careers* (New York: Knopf, 1930) and *Later Criminal Careers* (New York: Commonwealth Fund, 1937).

11. *Cleveland Crime Survey*, 585.

12. *Cleveland Crime Survey*, 582. Not all writers were as restrained as Pound in their condemnation of the classical model. Writing in 1927, Charles Chute, a probation officer, attacked the "undis-

criminating, childish penology of the past" (Charles L. Chute, "The Development and Needs of Probation Service," *Journal of Criminal Law and Criminology* 18, no. 4 [1927–28]:514–21). In the *Cleveland Crime Survey,* Pound emphasized that times had changed: "[W]e can no more return to the old methods than we can return to horse-carts or ox-teams or flails or sickles. We must go forward scientifically" (*Cleveland Crime Survey,* 588). In the same vein, the Virginia crime survey quoted Proskauer's statement that "society does not adequately protect itself against the criminal by ignoring the facts of modern science and continuing blindly along the paths which were marked out in ignorance of what we [now] know" (quoted in Fuller, *Criminal Justice,* 162).

13. Bates, "What May Be Done," 480.

14. Morse and Beattie, *Criminal Justice in Oregon,* 165.

15. *Wickersham Report,* vol. 9, 172.

16. *Illinois Crime Survey,* 43.

17. Ibid., 53.

18. *Missouri Crime Survey,* 286, 290.

19. The *Missouri Crime Survey,* for example, found that in 1923 only 4.73 percent of the prisoners in Missouri served their full sentences. Virtually all inmates were released after serving one-fifth of their time (*Missouri Crime Survey,* 438). Moreover, there was no relation between the length of sentence and time served. The Missouri survey noted that such automatic release of inmates, without regard to their conduct, violated the principle of individualized sentencing and treatment that was the basis of parole. The Missouri writers argued that most prisoners were released before they had been adequately punished and attributed the rise in crime in that state to the failure of deterrence caused by this policy. The writers concluded that "[o]ur study of parole shows an astonishing breakdown of the whole system of punishment for crime in this state" (ibid., 5).

20. Cited in Thomas E. Murphy, "The New Penology," *Journal of Criminal Law and Criminology* 27, no. 6 (1936–37):795.

21. *Missouri Crime Survey,* 314. Similarly, the *Illinois Crime Survey* found that probation was $2^{1}/_{2}$ times more likely if a defendant originally pleaded guilty (*Illinois Crime Survey,* 101). The Oregon crime survey found a high correlation between original guilty pleas and suspended sentences (Morse and Beattie, *Criminal Justice in Oregon,* 141. At a time when most writers viewed the plea bargain with suspicion (see chap. 3 of this volume), it is not surprising that the survey writers

were disturbed by the possibility that sentencing authority was being used to pressure defendants to plead guilty.

22. See, e.g., Chute, "Development and Needs" (see note 12); Meyer, *Half Century* (see note 3); *Wickersham Report*, vol. 9. Sheldon Glueck and Eleanor Glueck set out to demolish earlier claims of the efficacy of parole in *500 Criminal Careers*, 5.

23. Glueck and Glueck, *500 Criminal Careers*, 5–6.

24. The results of the Gluecks's research in *500 Criminal Careers* were summarized in their work *Later Criminal Careers*, 6–7.

25. One notable exception to the general rule of optimism was Richard C. Cabot, who stated in his foreword to the Gluecks's *500 Criminal Careers*: "I doubted whether any improvements which could now be suggested would result in reforming the type of habitual offender who is now sent there [to the Massachusetts reformatory] from the courts of Massachusetts. Either he must be prevented (if anyone can do it), or he must be kept indefinitely in confinement or he must be turned loose—as he is now—to continue his life of crime until he gets tired of it" (xii–xiii).

26. Chute, "Development and Needs," 515.

27. Murphy, "The New Penology," 794.

28. See, e.g., *Cleveland Crime Survey*; Fuller, *Criminal Justice* (see note 9); and *Wickersham Report*, vol. 9.

29. Louis N. Robinson, quoted in Helen Leland Witmer, "The History, Theory, and Results of Parole," *Journal of Criminal Law and Criminology* 18, no. 1 (1927–28):52.

30. Glueck and Glueck, *Later Criminal Careers*, 206.

31. Bates, "What May Be Done," 484.

32. *Cleveland Crime Survey*, 585.

33. See, e.g., Bates, "What May Be Done," 488, citing a 1914 survey of New York state courts; Morse and Beattie, *Criminal Justice in Oregon*, 164.

34. Tom C. Clark, "Foreword to Symposium on Fitting the Punishment to the Criminal," *Iowa Law Review* 31, no. 2 (1945–46):194.

35. *Wickersham Report*, vol. 9, 142.

36. Even Bates agreed with this argument to the extent that he believed the court should sentence the offender to a particular institu-

tion, but "should not attempt to determine in advance what kind of treatment the offender should receive there" (Bates, "What May Be Done," 486).

Many of the pre-ABF writers questioned whether the courts, trained in the law, were competent to determine rehabilitative sentences. The Virginia crime survey quoted Proskauer: "We must question whether we do not throw upon the courts, judge and jury, the burden of making determinations which can fairly be made only by the psychiatrist, the social workers and the specialist" (quoted in Fuller, *Criminal Justice* [see note 9], 163).

This argument over which body should have sentencing discretion was especially significant because of the enormous power over individual lives inherent in the rehabilitative model. In a purely rehabilitative system, the Gluecks pointed out, "the length of incarceration would not be determinable in advance and might in some cases endure throughout life" (*Later Criminal Careers,* 210–11). The determining factor would be whether, in the opinion of the experts, the offender was sufficiently cured of his or her criminal tendencies to be released. The Gluecks themselves had little doubt that the experts, with their scientific knowledge, could predict how the offender would behave on release: "[I]t is possible to forecast, with sufficient accuracy for practical purposes, the probable behavior of an offender or ex-prisoner over a long span of time" (ibid., 210).

37. Raymond Saleilles, quoted in Bates, "What May Be Done," 489.

38. This section on the ABF research relies heavily on Robert O. Dawson, *Sentencing: The Decision as to Type, Length, and Conditions of Sentence,* ed. Frank J. Remington (Boston: Little, Brown, 1969) and the "American Bar Foundation Survey of Criminal Justice: Field Reports" (1956; on file with the Criminal Justice Reference and Information Center, University of Wisconsin-Madison, Law School) [hereinafter "Field Reports"]. The Michigan experience is also the basis of an article by Lloyd E. Ohlin and Frank J. Remington, "Sentencing Structure: Its Effect Upon Systems for the Administration of Criminal Justice," *Law and Contemporary Problems* 23, no. 3 (1958):495–507.

39. See, e.g., "Field Reports," nos. 40062, 40064, 40066, 40068, 40085, 40093, 40114, 40115; Walter Dickey, "From the Bottom Up: Probation Supervision in a Small Wisconsin Community" (on file with the Criminal Justice Reference and Information Center, University of Wisconsin-Madison, Law School, 1988).

40. Cf. "Field Reports," nos. 40062, 40066, 40068, 40085, 40093, 40114, 40115; and Dickey, "From the Bottom Up."

41. Shane-DuBow, Brown, and Olsen, *Sentencing Reform* (see note 5), 7–8. To do justice to the influential work of the past fifteen years that urges change in sentencing would require an extensive bibliography. Only a representative sample can be provided here. See Norval Morris and Michael Tonry, *Between Prison and Probation* (New York: Oxford University Press, 1990); Albert W. Alschuler, "Sentencing Reform and Prosecutorial Power," *University of Pennsylvania Law Review* 126, no. 3 (1978):550–77; Pete Du Pont, "A Governor's Perspective on Sentencing," in *Crime and Punishment in Modern America,* ed. Patrick B. McGuigan and Jon S. Pascale (Washington, D.C.: Free Congress and Research Foundation, 1986); Marvin E. Frankel, *Criminal Sentences: Law Without Order* (New York: Hill and Wang, 1972); Don M. Gottfredson, Leslie T. Wilkins, and Peter B. Hoffman, *Guidelines for Parole and Sentencing* (Lexington, Mass.: Lexington Books, 1978); Peter W. Greenwood, *Selective Incapacitation* (Santa Monica: Rand, 1982); Joan Petersilia, *Expanding Options for Criminal Sentencing* (Santa Monica: Rand, 1987); Michael Tonry, "Structuring Sentencing," in *Crime and Justice: A Review of Research,* vol. 10, ed. Michael Tonry and Norval Morris (Chicago: University of Chicago Press, 1988), 267–337; Franklin E. Zimring, "Making the Punishment Fit the Crime: A Consumer's Guide to Sentencing Reform," *Hastings Center Report* 6, no. 6 (1977):13–17; Paul H. Robinson, "Hybrid Principles for the Distribution of Criminal Sanctions," *Northwestern University Law Review* 82, no. 1 (1987):19–42.

42. Andrew Von Hirsch, *Doing Justice: The Choice of Punishments* (New York: Hill and Wang, 1976); Alan M. Dershowitz, *Fair and Certain Punishment* (Twentieth Century Fund Task Force on Criminal Sentencing; New York: McGraw-Hill, 1976); American Friends Services Committee, *Struggle for Justice* (New York: Hill and Wang, 1971).

43. Robert Martinson, "'What Works?'—Questions and Answers About Prison Reform," *Public Interest* 35 (Spring 1974):22–54.

44. Robert Martinson, "New Findings, New Views: A Note of Caution Regarding Sentencing Reform," *Hofstra Law Review* 7, no. 2 (1979):243.

45. American Friends Services Committee, *Struggle For Justice.*

46. Shane-DuBow, Brown, and Olsen, *Sentencing Reform* (see note 5).

47. See note 42.

48. Me. Rev. Stat. tit. 17–A, ch. 51, § 1253 (1983).

49. Cal. Penal Code § 1170(a), (b) (1985).

50. See, e.g., 18 U.S.C. §§ 4201–4218 (1984).

51. The Sentencing Reform Act of 1984, Pub. L. 98–473, tit. II, ch. II § 218(a)(5), 98 Stat. 2027 (1984), which went into effect November 1, 1987, repealed the parole provisions of 18 U.S.C. § 4202 and established a determinate sentencing system in the federal courts. See United States Sentencing Commission, *Federal Sentencing Guidelines Manual,* rev. ed. (Washington, D.C.: U.S. Sentencing Commission, 1991).

52. Michael Tonry, "Judges and Sentencing Policy—The American Experience," in *Sentencing, Judicial Training, and Discretion,* ed. Martin Wasik and Colin Munro (London: Butterworths, 1992).

53. Ibid.

54. The yearly average population of the Minnesota adult correctional institutions was 1,945 in 1976, 1,509 in 1978, 1,994 in 1980, 2,440 in 1985, and 3,180 in 1990. "Adult Correctional Institutions— Average Population" (Minnesota Department of Corrections, 1990). See Alfred Blumstein, "Prison Populations: A System Out of Control?" in *Crime and Justice: A Review of Research,* vol. 10, ed. Michael Tonry and Norval Morris (Chicago: University of Chicago Press, 1988), 231.

55. Willie Horton was an offender who committed a serious crime while furloughed in Massachusetts. He became a symbol of what George Bush called Michael Dukakis's "softness on crime" in the 1988 presidential campaign and was a major issue.

56. David Margolick, "Chorus of Judicial Critics Assail Sentencing Guidelines: 5-Year Effort Is Called Hobgoblin of U.S. Courts," *New York Times,* Apr. 12, 1992.

57. Gerald W. Heaney, "The Reality of Guidelines Sentencing: No End to Disparity," *American Criminal Law Review* 29, no. 2 (1991):163–64, 167.

58. Albert W. Alschuler, "The Failure of Sentencing Guidelines: A Plea for Less Aggregation," *University of Chicago Law Review* 58, no. 3 (1991):950–51.

59. Frank J. Remington, "Fair and Certain Punishment," review of *Punishing Criminals,* by Ernest van den Haag (New York: Basic Books, Inc., 1975), and *Thinking About Crime,* by James Q. Wilson (New York: Basic Books, Inc., 1975), *Vanderbilt Law Review* 29, no. 5 (1976): 1320.

60. Steve Y. Koh, "Reestablishing the Federal Judge's Role in Sentencing," *Yale Law Journal* 101, no. 5 (1992):1134.

61. Alschuler, "Failure of Sentencing Guidelines," 949.

62. Cf. Wis. Stat. §§ 940.01 and 343.43(2) (1991–92).

63. Wis. Stat. § 304.06 (1991–92).

64. Wis. Stat. § 302.11 (1991–92).

65. Wis. Stat. § 973.01 (1991–92).

66. See Wisconsin Correctional System Review Panel, "Final Report" (Submitted to Walter Kunicki, speaker, Wisconsin Assembly, June 4, 1991).

67. Ibid.; 1991 Wis. Act 39; Wis. Stat § 301.048 (1991–92).

68. Wisconsin Correctional System Review Panel, "Final Report."

69. 1991 Wis. Act 39; Wis. Stat. § 301.048 (1991–92).

70. Dickey, "From the Bottom Up" (see note 39); Walter Dickey, "From the Bottom Up: Probation and Parole Supervision in Milwaukee" (on file with the Criminal Justice Reference and Information Center, University of Wisconsin-Madison, Law School, 1990).

CHAPTER 5

Criminal Justice Responses to Domestic Violence

Raymond I. Parnas

Almost everyone today is aware that acts of physical violence in the home between spouses and other adult intimates are common occurrences. The cycle of repetition, injury escalation, and ultimate homicide occurs worldwide. Books on the subject abound.[1] Newspapers and magazines periodically run features on the subject. Documentaries and movies, such as the highly publicized prime-time movies "The Burning Bed" and "Cry for Help," are shown on television.

National, state, and local organizations, both private and public, have been created to focus attention on the issue. In 1984 Congress passed the Family Violence Prevention and Services Act.[2] Every state now has some kind of legislation—civil, criminal, or both—directed at coping with this problem. These statutes establish, among other things, crisis shelters, protective orders, specialized police training, altered arrest requirements, charging guidelines, and treatment programs. Litigation to mandate remedial action is abundant, and research is ongoing. Police, prosecutors, judges, and others hold meetings and promulgate policy statements on the issue.

It was not always so. Until 1967 not a single book or journal article focused on the law's response to intrafamily violence.[3] There was practically no legislation on the subject, nor were there focused organizations, reported litigation, or published research. Immediately prior to 1967, knowledge of the extent and complexity of the problem was almost totally within the confines of the families affected, the responsible agencies, commonly the police officer called to the scene, and, of special significance here, those familiar with the empirical data derived from the ABF survey of criminal justice conducted in Michigan, Wisconsin, and Kansas in 1956 and 1957.[4] In this chapter, I will revisit the findings and insights about domestic assaults revealed by the ABF survey and explore subsequent developments and policy issues up to the present time. Unquestionably the use of the survey data by subsequent analysts of domestic violence, including my own work, served to make highly visible the problem of spousal assaults. This visibility, made possible by the ABF research, in turn led to a reevaluation of whether the response to an incident of spousal abuse should be left to the unguided discretion of the individual police officer responding to the scene, on the one hand, or ought to be resolved for all cases by a legislatively mandated arrest, on the other hand. There are obviously alternatives in between, such as requiring the police to develop administrative standards.

It is this story and its significance for our present and future policies of coping with this social and criminal problem that I wish to present, in addition to the dilemmas and difficulties I have encountered in confronting the complexities of domestic violence and the adequacy of our responses to it. In doing so the reader will note my early conversion to a strong belief in the value of arrest and my conclusion sometime later that even though an arrest can constitute an effective response, mandating an arrest in every case is undesirable and, therefore, the police must be allowed to exercise some discretion in responding to the incredible variety of situations involved in domestic violence cases.

THE ABF SURVEY'S CONTRIBUTION TO DOMESTIC VIOLENCE ISSUES

ABF survey researchers, committed to recording all that they observed, repeatedly chronicled domestic disputes as they described the daily activities of the criminal justice agencies. Accordingly, several writers having early access to the ABF data published works implicitly or expressly including the issue of domestic violence within their focus. For example, Joseph Goldstein, in his classic article "Police Discretion Not to Invoke the

Criminal Process: Low-Visibility Decisions in the Administration of Justice," stated: "Confidential reports detailing the day-to-day decisions and activities of a large municipal police force have been made available to the author by the American Bar Foundation. These reports give limited visibility to a wide variety of police decisions not to invoke the criminal process."[5] Drawing on those reports, Goldstein devoted several pages to a description of routine nonenforcement practices in admittedly very common felonious assault cases. The major reason cited for nonarrest was the victim's refusal to prosecute. Other reasons mentioned included the extensive paperwork required by so many arrests, limited resources to investigate other crimes, cross-cultural bias by white police regarding intra-Black assaults, and the prediction of dismissal by the court or prosecutor due to an uncooperative victim.

Goldstein's work was clearly very important in illuminating the common occurrence of assaults, describing the police response, discussing the reasons for this practice, and questioning its appropriateness. However, he never mentioned or dealt in any way with the context of these assaults. In other words, the intimate, spousal, family, or domestic nature of many of the assaults he reviewed was never mentioned. Is that complicating factor irrelevant to the victim's lack of cooperation in prosecution? Is it irrelevant to the routine response of nonarrest, prosecution, or conviction? Is it irrelevant to fashioning an appropriate governmental response to a clear violation of the penal code? Despite these possible analytical omissions, Goldstein urged arrest in that seminal article as a more appropriate response to felonious assault long before arrest became fashionable in domestic violence cases (as it is today). But is that because he, like today's domestic violence-arrest advocates, failed to adequately comprehend the complexity and implications of the "family" context of so many of these assaults? Although I concentrate on the complexity of domestic violence because of the family or other close relationship, I recognize that important differences also exist between families and that other close relationships are not, by any means, all of one kind. When reference is made to domestic violence, it must be kept in mind that the phrase includes a wide variety of conduct, and, as a consequence, any single response, such as arrest, is unlikely to be effective in all situations. These differences need to be taken into account in evaluating the adequacy of the response to a specific instance of domestic violence. But I am getting ahead of myself. For now let us see what followed Goldstein's very influential 1960 piece.

In 1965 the ABF published the first volume analyzing its field data. In *Arrest*,[6] Wayne LaFave used a variety of domestic violence incidents from the field studies as illustrations for many of the factors he thought played a role in police decision making. Thus not only did he increase the visibility level of common assaults, a task begun by Goldstein, but now, for the first time, the domestic nature of much of the violence was publicized. Additionally, the use of specific illustrations drawn directly from the field studies highlighted the complexity of a variety of family violence situations. For example, LaFave dramatically illustrated Goldstein's cross-cultural bias nonarrest factor by using a spousal stabbing incident in a section entitled "Conduct Thought to Reflect the Standards of a Community Subgroup."

Taking Goldstein's work still further, LaFave established three categories of cases in which "victim does not or will not request prosecution." Two of these involved close contact between the participants as a discrete discriminating factor: (1) victim in continuing relationship with offender and (2) victim a member of offender's family. He acknowledged that "[t]he reluctance of the victim to prosecute makes conviction difficult or impossible and is at least some indication that the offense is not serious enough to justify the expenditure of time and effort of the police and prosecutor."[7]

But LaFave also found exceptions to the nonarrest rule. For example, arrests would occur when police had knowledge of repeated offenses, when a brief lecture did not close the incident, or when the offender threatened subsequent harm (even though the victim did not wish to prosecute).

Like Goldstein before him, LaFave in 1965 considered full arrest, but explicitly referred to the domestic dispute using ABF examples. One Michigan police chief, disturbed by the number of domestic complaint calls received, issued a directive requiring an arrest in all domestic disputes, believing presumably that this would end the calls for service. However, no evaluation of this policy change was possible, because the city attorney reversed it after only one week. LaFave's comment about that policy is interesting in light of the current full-enforcement craze. It contrasts with Goldstein's earlier more positive view of a full-arrest policy, perhaps due to LaFave's better appreciation of the complexity of these incidents. He said:

> More likely the effect would be to reduce the number of complaints when it became known that the spouse would be put in jail as a consequence of any complaint made. Such a consequence would not necessarily be desirable, particularly if no other agency were ready to assume the task of mediating family disputes which had been handled by the police.[8]

The Misdemeanor Complaint Bureau, a very imaginative quasi-judicial response to domestic violence, fashioned by the Detroit police and prosecutor, was also discovered in the ABF data and reported for the first time by LaFave.[9] Frank Miller's later ABF survey book, *Prosecution*,[10] gave it greater prominence in the chapter, "The Decision Not to Charge Because Informal Administrative Procedures More Satisfactorily Achieve Objectives Underlying Criminal Statutes." Miller reported that, despite the vast number of family assault complaints and victims' initial insistence on prosecution, few prosecutions occurred. Resource and priority considerations were only partly the cause of this practice. Prosecutors generally discouraged victims from pressing charges against their attackers because they found that most victims changed their minds before trial, making successful prosecution impossible or difficult. Another complicating factor in prosecutions was said to be the frequent shared "guilt" of the parties. Additionally, it was felt that charging would "place an additional strain on an inevitably continuing relationship."[11] Prosecutors therefore preferred amicable solutions to these problems, an alternative to prosecution.

It was apparently in this contextual understanding of domestic violence that the Misdemeanor Complaint Bureau was born. An assistant prosecutor screened complaints for dismissal, charge, or referral to the complaint bureau. Most domestic assaults were referred. A hearing date was set about one week after the complaint, and notices were delivered. If no one appeared, reconciliation was assumed and the case was dropped. Second notices were sent if the victim appeared without the defendant and wanted to proceed. A subsequent failure by the defendant to appear resulted in a charge and a warrant. The hearing, held in a room in the prosecuting attorney's office, was conducted by a detective, often referred to as "judge." Mediation or referral was the goal, and four general dispositions were available to promote this goal: (1) dismissal because of minor or equal guilt or due to victim's decision to cease further prosecution efforts, (2) recommendation of formal judicial process by warrant (in cases of severe physical injury), (3) adjournment without date, and (4) "peace bond."

Adjournment without date implied official action if further difficulties arose, but in fact a new offense was necessary. The "peace bond" was the most frequent disposition, though it had no foundation in Michigan law and indeed no bond was actually posted. Nonetheless an informal record was kept, and imposition of the bond was sometimes taken into account (if known) in subsequent charging or complaint bureau decisions. What can be said of a creative, arguably successful, but legally unfounded, sham perpetrated on the public by our legal system? Miller, discussing similar use of a "peace bond" by Chicago courts, concluded:

> When the active endorsement of the system by police, prosecutors, and private defense attorneys is combined with the complainant's and defendant's unawareness of the lack of any official standing of the peace bond, it is not surprising that the procedure is effective both to satisfy the complainant that there has been "official" action taken with respect to the complaints, and to deter the defendant from future infractions.[12]

RELATED DEVELOPMENTS
ON DOMESTIC VIOLENCE ISSUES

In between the publication of the two aforementioned ABF books, the President's Commission on Law Enforcement and Administration of Justice issued its report, *The Challenge of Crime in a Free Society*, and supporting task force reports. Many of those who had worked on the ABF survey and books were on the commission staff, and the ABF data were used in the commission reports.[13] *The Challenge of Crime* focused greater attention than ever before on many of LaFave's earlier observations about domestic violence. But it went further by specifying issues in need of further research and recommending policy guidelines for the exercise of police discretion. For example:

The police should seek to accumulate information about families that cause repeated disturbances, to discover whether certain kinds of disturbances are more likely than others to lead to serious assaults or to homicides, to compile statistics on the typical effects of having one of the parties swear out a complaint against the other, to become familiar with the social-service agencies, if any, to which troubled families can be referred. For the police to mediate, arbitrate or suppress each dispute that they encounter as if it were unique—or as if all disputes were alike—contributes little, in the long run, either to law enforcement or to community service.[14]

One year later the *Report of the National Advisory Commission on Civil Disorders* also seemed to emphasize nonarrest by focusing on the service, nonadversary functions of the police in a domestic violence context:

The Commission believes that police cannot, and should not, resist becoming involved in community service matters. There will be benefits for law enforcement no less than for public order.

First, police, because of their "frontline position" in dealing with ghetto problems, will be better able to identify problems in the community that may lead to disorder. Second, they will be better able to handle incidents requiring police intervention, particularly marital disputes that have a potential for violence.[15]

All of the cited publications written in the 1960s drew upon the ABF data and asked questions about the adequacy of societal responses to domestic violence. But these early public references, as important as they were, treated the topic only briefly and then in the context of other primary concerns—police discretion, arrest, crime, charging, and civil disorders.

Toward the end of the 1960s two researchers focused their energies on domestic violence alone. Two psychologists, Morton Bard, then of the Psychological Center of the City University of New York, and Sydney Berkowitz, began training police in family crisis intervention. Their program subsequently influenced police training programs throughout the United States.

Just as the National Advisory Commission on Civil Disorders later emphasized the police "service" function respecting marital disputes, Bard's and Berkowitz's Family Crisis Intervention Unit project emphasized crime prevention by training police to intervene not only as law enforcers but as subprofessional mental health specialists using mediation and referral techniques primarily. The Bard-Berkowitz approach included family crisis specialist selection, intensive mental health pretraining, and in-service training, which resulted in special patrol units responding to all family crises.[16] Indeed the *Kerner Report* expressly cited the project as a program of special interest to improve police performance of the "service" function. Whether due to political reasons, resource limitations, or uncertain evaluative data, however, the Bard-Berkowitz comprehensive approach was not fully implemented in New York or elsewhere beyond the early 1970s. But cities like Oakland, California, and Louisville, Kentucky, attempted to replicate many aspects of the approach; and departments everywhere, learning from the publicity it received, added or increased training in family crisis intervention techniques for all police officers and especially new recruits. Thus the Bard-Berkowitz work, at a minimum, increased awareness of the problem, documented its complexity, and greatly stimulated police training.

According to Bard, the experiment did not have its origin in the ABF data. Rather, it was born of Bard's and Berkowitz's prior personal job experience as police officers.[17] However, about the same time, in 1967, I began to publish a series of law journal articles describing the problem of intrafamily violence and the variety of existing public and private responses to that phenomenon.[18] The catalyst for my work on this subject was Frank Remington, director of the ABF survey project staff and editor of the ABF survey books. My initial data were drawn directly from ABF data printouts, the ABF survey books, and the few other ABF-influenced works discussed above. Like Bard, I focused solely on domestic violence, but my scope was much broader, encompassing all of the available intrafamily dispute information. Thus in five law journal articles published from 1967 to 1973, I described intrafamily violence in the context of police, prosecutor, judicial, and other community responses to it. In addition to using the ABF material gathered in 1956 and 1957, I made personal observations of the Chicago response network in 1966, analyzed those data, and also had access to empirical data acquired in other key areas around the country in the late 1960s and early 1970s. The resulting articles were the first to focus in detail on the phenomenon of domestic violence, explore it in depth, and describe the various societal responses to it. Equally important, the articles illustrated incidents, categorized practices, and offered explanations for the various responses. In addition, they attempted to quantify the extent of the problem whenever data were available and suggested recommendations for future action.

Based on my work, I reiterated *The Challenge of Crime*'s important call to the police for a clearly stated departmental policy on field practices and for changes in the recruitment and training of officers.[19] I also raised related practical issues concerning the use of specialized units, beat assignments, dispatcher guidelines, repeat offender information in the field, referral mechanisms, follow-up, record keeping, and the relevance of subcultural criteria. I further recommended that charging decisions be made only by lawyers, that social service adjuncts be used if mediation and referral were needed, and that the use of prosecutors be completely replaced in most domestic assaults by civil family court jurisdiction.[20] Commenting on the criminal judicial response, I recommended the elimination of sham procedures like the Misdemeanor Complaint Bureau's detective "judges" and fictional "peace bonds."[21] "The traditional [criminal] judicial process is neither an effective solution nor a deterrent, and in fact can aggravate an inflamed situation by imposition of a fine against already depleted finances or a jail sentence which removes whatever earning capacity or family stability exists."[22] Once again I called for increased resources for mental health and social service court adjuncts. A myriad of innovative responses needed to be explored including: arbitration, mediation, and conciliation through peer, neighborhood, or ecclesiastical entities, school classes on family living, and better community services outreach programs.[23]

As many of these recommendations suggest, underlying all of these early articles were two overriding themes: (1) prevention of the initial incident or of repetition and escalation of prior incidents and (2) service and support to the disputants and adjustment of the problem rather than arrest, prosecution, and conviction in those cases involving nonserious injury.[24] These articles sought to remove any remaining semblance of low visibility from the problem of domestic violence as well as to highlight the complexity of this phenomenon and the difficulties in fashioning adequate and appropriate responses to it.

The first journal article dealing solely with family violence, and written by someone other than myself, was not published until 1971.[25] At least seven more specifically focused law journal articles were written by others and published in the 1970s.[26] Beginning in 1974 books on the subject began to appear. More than ten books on the subject were published in the 1970s. By 1980 public attention intensified. In 1980 alone, seven law journal articles and at least five books on the issue of battered women were published. And by the end of 1988 more than 120 law journal articles and 50 books focusing on domestic violence had been published in that partial decade. My ABF-generated seminal articles were repeatedly cited by the next early writers on the subject and continue to be referred to despite the subsequent glut of literature on the subject. A comprehensive English language bibliography, which includes government publications, conference papers, master's theses, doctoral dissertations, directives, handbooks, pamphlets, and popular periodicals, had 1,783 entries through 1983.[27]

Focused research, specialized lobbying organizations, voluminous legislation, and litigation demanding appropriate governmental action followed closely upon this inverse publication pyramid. The ABF survey data, publicized and expanded upon by Goldstein, LaFave, Miller, myself, and the President's Crime Commission in the 1960s, contributed to the dramatic change in public and institutional recognition of the domestic violence problem. But undoubtedly much more important focusing influences were the women's and victims' rights movements, which were well underway by the early 1970s. Individual adherents, popularized writing, burgeoning quasi-political organizations' rapid growth and actions, and the consequent coverage of a "new" hot topic by the mass media all greatly contributed to pushing domestic violence to the front of public consciousness much faster than scholarly articles and books could.[28] The possible negative implications of this all too common public policy scenario will be discussed later. Virgie Lemond Mouton is probably correct in writing that, "With the advent of Women's Liberation,...women began speaking out against wife abuse and demanding solutions from the police, the legislatures, other women, churches and other social help organizations."[29]

Erin Pizzey is credited, by those unfamiliar with the earlier writings, with first bringing the problem of wife abuse to public attention. In 1971 she organized a center where women could discuss mutual problems. Pizzey published the first book about abused women in England in 1974.[30] By 1975 the National Organization for Women established the National Task Force on Battered Women and Household Violence. In 1976 the International Tribunal on Crimes Against Women met in Brussels to hear testimony about the victimization of women. Del Martin's *Battered Wives* (San Francisco: Glide Publications, 1976) was also quite influential as was Faith McNulty's *The Burning Bed* (1980), particularly in its graphic television movie adaptation starring Farrah Fawcett. After these efforts, the news media and city and state government officials recognized wife abuse as a serious social problem.

Organizations on a national, state, and local level proliferated and began to gather and distribute information, lobby for legislation and policy changes, institute litigation, form new organizations, and provide direct victim assistance. At the national level are the National Coalition Against Domestic Violence, the National Woman Abuse Prevention Project, the Family Violence Project of the Center for Women's Policy Studies, and the National Clearing House on Domestic Violence. Most states, if not all, have similar organizations such as Minnesota's Coalition for Battered Women. There are also relevant state attorney general's task forces. At the local level, direct services to victims exist in many places (for example, Sacramento's WEAVE—Women Escaping a Violent Environment). Now available are domestic violence hot lines, crisis shelters, handbooks, victims' guides, and pamphlets that try to lead uneducated victims step-by-step through the filing of a protective order.

INFLUENCES ON THE DEVELOPMENT OF FULL-ENFORCEMENT POLICIES

The current fuller enforcement trend originated in some of the early ABF scholarly writing, a Police Executive Research Forum report, litigation, and Minnesota research.

As noted above, Joseph Goldstein raised the general issue of fuller enforcement in 1960. He favorably described a late 1950s program in full enforcement by the Oakland Police Department. Before the program, between 1952 and 1956, the number of unspecified felonious and misdemeanor assaults reported had increased from 93 to 161 and from 618 to 2,630, respectively. According to the Oakland Police Academy Instructor's Manual cited by Goldstein, these figures were seen as reflecting

> an increasing lack of respect for the laws of society by a measurable segment of our population, and a corresponding threat to the rest of the citizens of our city. The police have a clear responsibility to develop respect for the law among those who disregard it in order to insure the physical safety and well-being of those who do.[31]

As a result, a full-enforcement policy was implemented in Oakland and coordinated with prosecutors and judges. The district attorney was to deny a complainant's request to drop charges and suggest it be directed to the court. Then the judge was to advise that the case would not be dismissed and that perjury, contempt, or false-report charges would be brought against the victim if she failed to follow through. Goldstein acknowledged that the subsequent drop in reported assaults and batteries needed follow-up evaluation to determine whether the actual number of such incidents had been reduced or only the reporting of them. Nonetheless his conclusion in the overall theoretical context of generalized police discretion was:

> The ultimate answer is that the police should not be delegated discretion not to invoke the criminal law. It is recognized, of course, that the exercise of discretion cannot be completely eliminated where human beings are involved. The frailties of human language and human perception will always admit of borderline cases....But nonetheless, outside this margin of ambiguity, the police should operate in an atmosphere which exhorts and commands them to invoke impartially all criminal laws within the bounds of *full enforcement*. If a criminal law is ill-advised, poorly defined, or too costly to enforce, efforts by the police to achieve *full enforcement* should generate pressures for legislative action. Responsibility for the enactment, amendment, and repeal of the criminal laws will not, then, be abandoned to the whim of each police officer or department, but retained where it belongs in a democracy—with elected representatives.[32]

LaFave's view was more pessimistic than Goldstein's: "The precise outcome of a continued policy of full enforcement in such cases is difficult to predict....More likely the effect would be to reduce the number of complaints when it became known that the spouse would be put in jail as a consequence of any complaint made."[33] In my first article in 1967 I also briefly discussed the two extremes of full enforcement and no response and concluded: "Neither of the two extremes in the spectrum of police alternatives in handling the domestic disturbance is practical."[34]

Ten years later, however, I switched my emphasis from adjustment to invocation of the criminal law by arrest. I summed up the reasons for this switch as follows:

> The compassion and humanity of the social services has been increasingly interjected to effect more organized and "knowledgeable" efforts at diversion, counseling, referral, mediation and treatment....The trouble with such a trend for inter-spousal violence *now* is that the juvenile and adult processes, in the United States at least, confronted with intolerable rates of delinquency and criminality, have recently been discarding and rethinking the commendable, but still unproven, facets of models based on sickness, treatment and rehabilitation, and have been returning to the known entities of personal public accountability for bad acts, with appropriate and acknowledged punishment, enlightened and softened somewhat by prior experience with the social services.[35]

Using Frank Allen's classic 1964 analysis[36] of the "problems of socializing criminal justice" with regard to other incidents on "the borderland of the criminal law" to answer the central question regarding an appropriate process response for intrafamily violence, I concluded:

> Efforts at therapy can, and I suppose should, be included in the process but should not be given undue emphasis, for there is simply no evidence that we know how to diagnose, much less treat, disputants' problems in a manner that will prevent repetition. Simply put, we must go with what we know. And we know that we cannot ignore or condone acts or threats of imminent violence. We know that the police are best equipped to protect others and themselves. We know how to punish, whether by fine, incapacitation, other denials of full liberty, embarrassment, inconvenience, *etc.* And we know punishment is a clear statement of the personal responsibility of the offender and the condemnation and retribution of society. We also know that where punishment is to be imposed, the crimi-

nal process provides the best safeguards that such punishment is imposed on the appropriate person under the most adequate circumstances. We know that incapacitation prevents repetition during the period of incarceration. Finally I submit that we are increasingly coming to believe that punishment, quickly, fairly, proportionately and appropriately imposed, may deter or reduce the quality and quantity of some kinds of bad conduct at least as well, if not better, than attempts at speculative therapy, and thus may serve the rehabilitation function even better from the perspective of non-repetition....Thus the criminal law, the police, the prosecutor and the courts should not only continue to respond to incidents of inter-spousal violence, but should emphasize the importance of the traditional response of arrest, prosecution and sanction as a sign of public disapprobation and protection, not only at the upper levels of violence, but also at the first minimal signs of trouble.[37]

At the prosecution level, many in 1978 at the Center for Women's Policy Studies and the National District Attorneys Association Family Violence Conference in Memphis urged fuller enforcement.[38] "No-drop" policies, however, are considerably more controversial among domestic violence reformers than is mandatory arrest, probably because its onus falls more on the alleged victim. For example, in a few instances subsequently uncooperative complainants have arguably been victimized a second time by being held in contempt and jailed for refusing to testify. The arguments against "no-drop" policies by many proponents of mandatory arrest illustrate both the complexity and variety of domestic violence incidents and the gender politics surrounding the ongoing reforms in this area over much of the last two decades. For example:

> In family violence cases, the pressure not to prosecute can be overwhelming. Many battered women face verbal harassment and intimidation not to press and pursue charges, and the threat of further physical violence, even murder, if they do. Given the alarmingly high rates of spousal homicide, these fears are legitimate. Sometimes a battered woman drops charges against her husband because he pleads with her not to carry through with prosecution, promising not to hurt her again. Hoping that he will keep that promise, she may decide to give him another chance. Many battered women fear that their husbands will be jailed if they proceed with prosecution. Concern about loss of financial support if their husbands are

incarcerated, fear of family reprisal, and a wish to save face in the community by settling the dispute as quietly as possible, all act as deterrents to pursuing criminal prosecution....Some argue that any policy that denies victim discretion is patently offensive. Others oppose no-drop policies on the grounds that they are not effective.[39]

If charges are brought and not dismissed, what is the effect of judicial intervention? A National Institute of Justice study reported that only one-half of such cases resulted in conviction, and one-third of these victims suffered renewed abuse within two to three months. Nevertheless, because the rearrest rate was only 10 percent and more than half of the victims were satisfied with the arrest outcome, researchers concluded that judges play a critical role in deterring future violence: "The study postulates that the judges' conduct is especially critical to those individuals, both victims and defendants, who appear in court for the first time, and suggest that the effects of a judge's conduct on the cessation or resumption of violence is a topic worthy of further study."[40]

One of the two most important causes of the full enforcement trend of the 1980s, other than the effect of social movements, is the growth of litigation about the issue, much of which has been fostered by battered wives' advocates.[41] (The other important cause is the Minnesota research discussed at the end of this section.)

Research Findings on Full Enforcement

On the research side, a report and an experiment conclude this description of developments leading to the current emphasis on fuller enforcement of the criminal law regarding domestic violence. In 1979 the Police Executive Research Forum [PERF] visited seventeen police departments, interviewed fifty police officials, administered 130 patrol officers' questionnaires, and solicited written police procedures and training materials concerning policing of incidents of adult intrafamily abuse. A report by Nancy Loving was published in 1980 as the result.[42] The text of the report itself recommends upgrading written policies, procedural guidelines, and training, without any clear explicit emphasis on mandatory or even fuller arrest. However, a brief executive summary and a preface by the PERF president, Bruce Baker, chief of police, Portland, Oregon, both give greater emphasis to arrest as a response more effective than conflict resolution. The executive summary concludes: "The traditional police response to these calls, emphasizing crisis intervention skills and reconciliation of the parties, is inappropriate and unhelpful." To his credit, Chief Baker points out that "Further research is needed to test the...impact of police actions in a variety of spousal conflicts."[43]

The research that most influenced the fuller enforcement trend of the 1980s was the Minneapolis Domestic Violence Experiment.[44] Three types of responses to misdemeanor-assaults were tested: arrest, advising and counseling the parties (or negotiating the dispute), and separating the parties by ordering the assailant to leave.[45] Police patrol officers participating in the experiment used one of the three responses, determined by a random selection process, for each domestic disturbance case they handled. A research staff worker made a follow-up visit to the victim, followed by telephone interviews every two weeks for twenty-four weeks, to see if violence had recurred.

Any research project is subject to design and methodological and evaluative criticism, as well as the problems of monitoring and human error. This project was certainly no exception.[46] However, most commentators seemed to accept the results, based on both department records and a victimization survey, that arrest resulted in about half the repeat violence rate of the other responses (table 5.1). Those arrested typically were held overnight in jail and then released. Only 3 of the 136 arrestees received a formal judicial sanction.[47]

TABLE 5.1
Repeats within Six Months

	Arrest	Advise	Send Defendant Away
Official Records	10%	19%	24%
Victimization Survey	19%	37%	33%

Homant and Kennedy acknowledged that "the [Minnesota] experiment is not totally immune to criticism" (citing, for example, that 28 percent of the cases derived from just three of forty-one officers involved), but like most they nonetheless generally accepted the results. However, they offered a well-balanced analysis when, in their book *Police and Law Enforcement*, they introduced a chapter on the subject by the researchers Sherman and Berk:

We are reasonably convinced that in this particular case arrest did produce a significant deterrent effect. This, we feel, places a strong burden of proof on any who would support the crisis intervention model to the exclusion of a law enforcement model for dealing with spouse abuse.

The better approach, however, may be to try to find common ground for the two models. Sherman and Berk found that arrest plus "listening" was more effective than simple arrest. They also concede their "advise" condition did not make use of any special training programs or referral resources....

While some increase in the typical level of arrest is certainly called for, research is needed to try to determine the optimum balance between an arrest and a crisis intervention response.[48]

Interest in and criticism of the Minnesota experiment has led to research, funded by the National Institute of Justice, in Omaha, Miami, Atlanta, Charlotte, Milwaukee, and Colorado Springs. Not only do these research programs replicate the Minnesota experiment but they expand the kind of police alternatives used and the length of the follow-up period. Although the results for all are not available, the final report of the Omaha Domestic Violence Police Experiment casts substantial doubt on the generalizations to be derived from the Minnesota project:

First, arrest in Omaha, *by itself*, did not appear to deter subsequent domestic conflict any more than separating or mediating those in conflict, i.e., arrest and the immediate period of custody associated with arrest, was not the deterrent to continued domestic conflict that was expected....Second, while arrest, by itself, did not act as a deterrent to continued domestic conflict for the misdemeanor domestic assault cases coming to the attention of the Omaha police, neither did it increase continued domestic conflict between parties to an arrest for assault....Arrest, therefore, did not appear to place victims in greater danger of increased conflict than did separation or mediation....

Since arresting suspects is expensive and conflicts/assaults do not appear to increase when arrests are *not* made, one response to these data might be a recommendation to effect informal dispositions (separate or mediate) in cases of misdemeanor domestic assaults in Omaha. A significant problem with this approach, however, is that it seems ethically inappropriate, it violates the recommendations of the Attorney General's Task Force on Family Violence...and it may be illegal...to patently ignore the rights of victims....

A policy that encourages, but does not mandate arrest may be useful from several points of view. First, it would allow officers in Omaha to respond to the wishes of victims who do not want, for a variety of reasons, suspects arrested....Second, when an arrest is seen as an entry point into a coordinated criminal justice system rather than an end point, it may shift the burden of deterrence from a single official police intervention (arrest) to a sequence of other interventions, each of which may have some salutary effect. This view recognizes that suspects chronically involved in domestic violence most frequently do not admit to having a problem in this regard...are not easily treated...and do not seek help voluntarily...to deal with such problems and thus might require sustained long-term interventions to change their ways. It supports arrest in domestic assault instances in which probable cause for an arrest is present and when victims support the arrest of suspects, not because arrest is a panacea for deterring domestic violence, but because of penalties and the *leverage* that an arrest implicitly facilitates.[49]

Similar results from the Milwaukee replication have Lawrence Sherman, the principal researcher in the Minnesota experiment, now also seriously reconsidering the benefits of arrest for domestic violence misdemeanors.[50] The experiment included twelve hundred misdemeanor domestic violence nighttime calls from specific high-poverty districts of Milwaukee over a period of sixteen months from April 1987 to August 1988. The calls were responded to by members of a special thirty-five-officer team using three randomized responses: no arrest with a warning, short-term arrest averaging 2.8 hours, and long-term arrest averaging 11.1 hours. As in the Minneapolis study, virtually none of the cases were ultimately prosecuted. Outcome measures included initial and six-month follow-up victim interviews as well as a variety of official records entered up to thirty-three months after the incident.

In Milwaukee, short-term arrest did have an *initial* deterrent effect. For example, whereas there were 7 percent immediate repeat attacks after the police left with only a warning, there were only about 2 percent immediate repeats upon return from a short- or long-term arrest. However, the initial deterrent effect decayed by six months after to no difference in deterrent effect between the three responses. More important, the study concludes that after one year the short-term arrest cases had a significantly higher recidivism frequency than the other cases in the experiment. In trying to understand the relationship between the initial deterrence and the apparent long-term criminogenic effect of short-term arrest, Sherman and his colleagues may have stumbled across what to my mind is the most significant finding of their many years of research into domestic violence, namely: "There is no law of social science that says humans have to be consistent, and no reason why the same stimulus cannot have contradictory effects as time elapses."[51]

Interestingly, the long-term criminogenic effect of short-term arrest did not develop in the eleven- to twelve-hour arrests. Surprisingly, however, Sherman et al. seem to reject this longer period of custody as the appropriate policy response by acknowledging the old arguments that question the use of arrest because of its disruptive effect on employment and on the domestic relationship of the parties "in situations of mutual conflict more properly labeled disputes."[52]

Sherman et al. make the following findings from the Milwaukee study. The premise that mandatory arrest results in long-term specific deterrence is "clearly refuted." Indeed, "arrest can actually increase domestic violence."[53] The relatively low level of awareness of the mandatory arrest policy suggests a lack of general deterrence. And mandatory arrest is also hard to justify on the grounds of a high probability of serious violence in the near future because of the very rare occurrence of any subsequent serious injury.

Thus in 1991, Sherman and his present colleagues find "good reason to challenge."[54] Sherman and Berk's 1984 "recommendation of presumptive arrest policies regardless of time in custody." Reverting once again to ideas discovered in the ABF survey thirty-five years ago, and elaborated on by the early writers on this subject, they now conclude: "Other kinds of legal innovation may be far more useful, such as nonarrest strategies to forestall violence immediately after police leave. The initial deterrence period may also offer a window of opportunity for new approaches to intervention, either by police or others."[55]

THE FUTURE: FROM LOW VISIBILITY TO HIGH VISIBILITY; FROM ADJUSTMENT TO ARREST; SO WHAT?

All of the foregoing clearly shows that for some time now the problem of domestic violence has been highly visible. Recent studies and arguments suggest the possible intergenerational transmission of domestic violence to children who witness assaultive behavior in their homes. This possibility has further heightened concern for the problem.[56]

The impact on the criminal justice process has been immense.[57] Domestic violence training of police is now commonplace. Arrest is now mandated in some places and preferred most everywhere else.[58] In San Francisco, arrests increased by 46 percent in the early 1980s, and written reports of domestic violence increased 100 percent.[59] The Los Angeles police arrested five thousand alleged spouse batterers in both 1986 and 1987 (as compared with six hundred in 1985).[60]

One of the new Sacramento district attorney's first administrative actions was to increase staffing of its vertical prosecution program, thereby placing a greater emphasis on the crackdown on domestic violence. In San Francisco, filed charges increased 136 percent, and the conviction rate in felony cases increased 44 percent, in the early 1980s.[61] On the beautiful island of Maui the prosecutor employs a "no-drop" policy. Victims are subpoenaed. The use of voice video cameras by responding officers as a subsequent aid in charging, convicting, and sentencing is being considered.[62] Diversion programs are under attack for having "only" a 50 percent success rate; critics claim that they allow defendants to escape the wrath of the criminal justice process and merely function as valves to relieve the pressure resulting from the increase in the number of court cases.[63] New domestic violence courts in Chicago and Los Angeles are being established and highly touted as a way to reduce case and participant confusion and to increase efficiency, sensitivity, and expertise.[64]

Judicial training programs and lengthy bench books for dealing with domestic violence cases are being provided. Batterer's treatment programs have proliferated from Connecticut to Hawaii and in between. Mandated by legislation or practice, some programs attempt to explain domestic violence as a product of cultural sex-role expectations and attempt reeducation; most employ support group therapy techniques; and all in various ways place responsibility on the offender and offer alternatives to violence through stress- or anger-control management methods. Meanwhile, protective orders and other civil remedies proliferate, and crisis shelters continue to be available.[65]

The emphasis of all of these changes is on publicizing that

domestic violence is a very serious crime and that the batterer will be held accountable for his acts by arrest, prosecution, and incarceration if necessary. The victim's realization of empowerment through access to a justice process that is sensitive and responsive to her need for protection has the highest priority. There are no signs of battered women's advocates letting up the pressure to continue in the direction of maximum use of the criminal justice process.[66] Nor are there many signs that legislators, police officials, prosecutors, judges, and even academics are any less influenced by that pressure. That is the direction we seem to be going in the 1990s. But is this a reasonable, sensible, realistic approach?

The 1981 Minnesota experiment seemed to show that arrest, if used instead of the two nonarrest response alternatives, reduced repeat offenses by about 50 percent for a period of six months. And a subsequent Bureau of Justice Statistics analysis of 1978–82 National Crime Survey victimization data concluded that just calling the police reduced repetition by as much as 62 percent over the subsequent six months.[67] But here the ultimate conclusion of the more recently reported study from Omaha (subsequently reaffirmed in Milwaukee) bears repeating and may return us to square one: "It is clear, however, that arrest, by itself, was not effective in reducing or preventing continuing domestic conflict in Omaha, and that a dependence upon arrest to reduce such conflict is unwarranted, perhaps erroneous and even counterproductive."[68]

Annette Jolin, comparing pre-1977 Oregon homicides with post-1977 homicides in an effort to gauge the impact of Oregon's mandatory-arrest law, found a 10 percent decrease in domestic homicides, although nondomestic homicides increased by 10 percent.[69] But again, the implications of these data are unclear and further confused by another more recent research report on domestic violence, which concluded "that there is no way police can predict that a particular situation is likely to lead to murder."[70]

Despite all of the chronicled changes, there is really no sign that domestic violence is diminishing! Statistics used by full-enforcement advocates in their continual lobbying efforts to show the extent of the problem may just as well be used to show a lack of overall success in stemming the tide of domestic violence after a decade of mass publicity and legal changes. Of course, a decade is perhaps not long enough for any significant reduction to have occurred or any definitive evaluation to be published. It is also possible, however, that nothing the legal system does will alter the rate of domestic violence.[71] Indeed, some battered spouse advocates acknowledge, at least in private, that what is required is a nationwide reversal of a whole generation of children's sex-role understanding. This may be true; it may also be unrealistic. Whether this could happen soon, if at all, is uncertain.

In fact, the criminal justice process in a free society probably has little to do with the rates of most crimes. Fluctuations have long seemed to have more to do with unpredictable, indirect, external societal influences than any criminal process responses. As difficult as apprehension and conviction often are, once accomplished, recidivism continues to skyrocket, with the period of incapacitation as the only really effective deterrent. But with our jails and prisons bulging, should incarceration be a priority for domestic offenders, even though we believe repetition and escalation may occur? We continue to hope that one day rehabilitation programs will work. Yet their lack of significant success has in part led to the incarceration explosion.

Also in 1988, fifteen battered women were murdered in Minnesota, the model state for the arrest experiment and a state with a comprehensive protective order statute. Julie Tilley, lobbyist for the Minnesota Coalition for Battered Women, referring to one of these victims, said: "She did everything right, the system did everything right. The police had arrested him several times. She had an order for protection several times, and she had one when she died."[72] In Brentwood, New York, a protective order, augmented by a burglar alarm and a hand emergency beeper, failed to protect a homicide victim from her former husband three days after he was arrested for attempting to murder her and was released on bail.

The Bureau of Justice Statistics *National Crime Survey Report of Criminal Victimization in the United States for 1987* (published in June 1989) shows 53 percent of simple assaults and 39 percent of aggravated assaults are by nonstrangers. F.B.I., *Crime in the United States—1986*, reported 30 percent of female homicide victims were killed by husbands or boyfriends, with 6 percent of male homicides similarly attributed. Other statistics vary, depending on the source, but the extent of the problem is rarely minimized. For example, women's rights advocates variously report that from 1.8 to 4 million American women are subject to domestic violence each year; that violence will occur at some time in one-fourth to two-thirds of all marriages; and that 20 percent of women seeking emergency surgical procedures are victims of domestic violence.[73] Closer to home than all these statistics are the incidents of domestic violence reported daily in our own academic communities—highly educated, upper-middle-class individuals, supposedly the most sensitive to the goals of sexual equality, knowledgeable of the problem of domestic violence, and aware of the availability of enlightened law enforcement agencies.[74]

While paying lip service to the complexity of incidents of domestic violence, single-issue advocates for reform continue to look for a solution. Many more years of searching for solutions to much less complex crimes than these have taught that no solutions may exist. Eliminating judicial discretion in sentencing by mandatory prison legislation[75] and preventive detention[76] has contributed to the prison and jail overcrowding problem and undoubtedly caused the release or nonincarceration of others who should be locked up. Similarly, mandatory arrest and prosecution or fuller enforcement in domestic violence cases not only will exacerbate the overcrowding problem but will reduce or eliminate law enforcement efforts directed at other crimes. Perhaps domestic violence is that important, but crime prioritizing, resource allocation, and sentencing judgments have traditionally been made by police, prosecutors, and courts with public input, not by the difficult-to-change mandates of legislatures subject to the pressures of the moment.

Should domestic violence be taken seriously? Of course. Should arrest be a serious alternative, exercised more often than in the past? Definitely. Should prosecutors charge and go to trial frequently even when confronted with an uncooperative victim? Yes. Should judges dismiss less and incarcerate more even though the family may require public funds for its sustenance? Surely. Accordingly, I continue to stand by what I wrote in 1978:

> Incidents of inter-spousal violence, no matter how minimal, must remain subject to police intervention. For years a disproportionate number of disturbances, assaults, batteries, uses of deadly weapons, mayhem, and homicides have involved family

members. Despite the resources necessary and the danger inherent in responding to such calls, no entity other than a police agency has the authority and ability to cope with such volatile situations. Central to the function of the police and the criminal law is the protection of life and limb.

The basic question is: what response, if any, should the legal system make after the dispute has been halted by police intervention? This is a crucial stage for another reason. It is at this point that an offender and a victim in a continuing volatile situation have been identified. All of the data showing the extent of inter-spousal violence and the experience of escalation from minimal to aggravated injury indicate that it would be irresponsible governmental action to drop the matter at this point. In fact, however, what we have been doing is to ignore the extremely important preventative, corrective, retributive, incapacitative, and deterrent implications of this early official knowledge of subsequent potential violence. At the very least, an adequate record keeping procedure must be implemented so that all those responding to subsequent incidents will know of the disputants' prior history so that an appropriate relevant additional response can be made. But even more important than our criminal law's traditional escalation of meaningless slaps on the wrist until too late, is recognition of the need for a breakthrough at the outset to the consciousness of the disputants as to the seriousness of their behavior and not later than the second time around at most.

In my judgment, only the coercive, authoritative harshness of the criminal process can do this.[77]

But fuller use of the criminal process need not be followed by a loss of administrative discretion. Rather a change in emphasis and a restructuring of the exercise of that discretion may be necessary. Indeed, anything else would diminish our knowledge of the incredible complexity inherent in incidents of domestic violence and the need for appropriate societal responses thereto first discovered in the ABF data. The police may not have always dealt with this problem in the most appropriate ways. But the early research clearly shows that they, *better than anyone*, recognized its complexity and frequently tried novel approaches to deal with it.

Pressures from the women's movement largely brought about the high visibility of domestic violence. They took up where the ABF data began and rightly forced the law enforcement and legal processes to better acknowledge the problem and to be more responsive to the needs of all victims of violence. Lerman correctly stated that "the premise of the Model Act is that violence is caused by and is the responsibility of the perpetrator."[78] But to go on and state, as she does, that "violence is not the product of a relationship or the result of the interaction of the individuals" totally overlooks the complexity of domestic violence and thus the necessity of allowing discretion, albeit better trained and guided, to be exercised by those responding to individual cases.

The constant possibility of domestic strife is inherent in all adult living situations. The opportunity and motive for violence are always present because of the intimate, continuing, and largely private contact between the parties that necessarily gives rise to the frustrations and friction of daily living. When intoxication is thrown into this setting, as it frequently is, the risk of lashing out increases dramatically.[79] In this milieu, police, prosecutors, judges, and other outsiders must make decisions. The parties themselves are frequently uncertain what they want the intervention to be. Indeed they may not know what future relation they want with each other. The interveners know that whatever they do, or do not do, will affect the relationship between the parties, their economic status, and any children involved. But they cannot really be sure how. Is it always better for the disputants and society that sometimes-violent couples be apart rather than together? Is it always better for children and society to be in single-parent homes rather than with a quarreling, sometimes violent couple? Each incident is different in hundreds of ways. I submit we simply do not know, and may never know with any certainty, the answer to these basic questions, much less how best to respond to the myriad types of incidents arising each day.

For example, in a recent Sacramento case, a thirty-four-year-old woman, after being in a coma for two and one-half months and undergoing eight operations, helped convict her boyfriend who had punched and kicked her, puncturing her kidney. Though she was glad she testified, she did not want him to go to prison. "'You spend nine years of your life with this one person,' she said. 'That person was there when you went into the hospital to have your kids. That person was there when nobody else was. You cannot hate this person. It's just like cutting off part of your arm.'"[80] The boyfriend was subsequently sentenced to six years in prison (three with maximum good time). His attorney said that the sentence was too long for a man with no criminal history, who worked steadily and had been a good father to all four of the children (two of them his own). The defense attorney said, "I understand the reasons for the sentence, given the hue and cry about this kind of offense. But I think the law as it presently stands and is implemented by the judges because of the public pressure is too rigid."[81]

Decision making, of course, should be absolute in rejecting the consideration of some facts. For example, one's race certainly should not be considered as a reason for not enforcing the law, as the ABF data found it to have been in the past.[82] It is ironic, however, that race may again become an indirect factor, but this time under a mandatory-arrest policy, because impoverished victims tend to call the police for assistance more often than those better able to afford other alternatives. Frank Allen's essay "The Borderland of the Criminal Law: Problems of 'Socializing' Criminal Justice" is again pertinent. Allen asserts that, "When penal treatment is employed to perform the functions of social services, selection of those eligible for penal treatment proceeds on inadmissible criteria...by reference to their poverty or their helplessness." In such instances, he says, neither effective social services nor equity prevail.

Many other factors, however, appear to be worthy of consideration for appropriate decision making in these cases. Thus, was the draft set of guidelines for a proposed settlement of a class action suit against the Los Angeles police well founded in telling police that they must make decisions "according to the same standards which govern the decision to report to, remain at, or leave the scene of similar or identical crimes that do not involve an incident of domestic violence"? The guidelines may not even consider such factors as (1) whether the victim and suspect are living together, (2) whether society would prefer keeping family units intact, and (3) speculation about reconciliation.[83]

Certainly violence, whatever the cause, must be taken seriously and the offender held accountable in some way unless the act was legally justifiable. Victim precipitation is a crucial part of the battered woman syndrome defense to conviction and in amelioration of sentence, yet its mere use as a factor in decision making if the victim is a woman is deemed objectionable sexism. Is this reasonable? In other words, are not all of the facts surrounding the incident under question, particularly those going to motive, at least relevant to appropriate arrest, charging, diversion, and sentencing decisions? For most other less complicated offenses they are. Why not in complex domestic violence cases?

Frank Allen and Anthony Platt shed some light on this question. Allen said:

> We should not overlook the fact that, in many areas, our basic difficulties still lie in our ignorance of human behavior in its infinite complexities....
>
> Ignorance, of itself, is disgraceful only so far as it is avoidable. But when, in our eagerness to find "better ways" of handling old problems, we rush to measures affecting human liberty and human personality on the assumption that we have the knowledge which, in fact, we do not possess, then the problem of ignorance takes on a more sinister hue.[84]

The parallel to where we are in dealing with domestic violence and how we got there is apparent in the theme of Platt's book *The Child Savers: The Invention of Delinquency*. He argued that the juvenile court had its origin in largely middle-class women reformers who

> viewed themselves as altruists and humanitarians [who nonetheless] brought attention to—and, in doing so, invented—new categories of...misbehavior which had been hitherto unappreciated....Granted the benign motives of the savers, the progress they enthusiastically supported diminished...civil liberties and privacy....Although the savers were rhetorically concerned with protecting..., their remedies seemed to aggravate the problem.[85]

My point is a simple one. We have come about as far as we can or should go toward the full enforcement of laws against domestic violence. Indeed, we have gone too far with mandatory provisions. Victim advocates have had a tremendous impact by heightening visibility and pushing largely positive reforms. But it is time now for them to stop their narrow gender-focused arguments for further changes. More important, it is time for policymakers to resist pressures from them. It is time for everyone to regroup and evaluate what more can or should be done. And it is time to recognize the tremendous complexity of dealing with crime in general, accentuated in cases of domestic violence. This was true at the time of the ABF research and remains true today.

The result is that there is probably no solution in a free society, but the wisest course is to allow decision makers adequate leeway to utilize scarce resources within the bounds of structured exercises of discretion, considering all relevant factors.[86]

NOTES

With invaluable assistance by Scott Taryle, Melissa Hill, and Allison Hughes, University of California at Davis School of Law.

A somewhat longer article with a similar emphasis is found in Raymond I. Parnas, "The American Bar Foundation Survey of the Administration of Criminal Justice and Past, Present, and Future Responses to Domestic Violence," *Washington University Law Quarterly* 69 (1991): 107. This article includes a description of the experience in California and an analysis of the litigation dealing with domestic violence.

1. For a recent and excellent summary of many issues, see Lloyd Ohlin and Michael Tonry, eds., *Family Violence* (Chicago: University of Chicago Press, 1989).

2. 42 U.S.C. §§ 10401–10413 (1988).

3. But see Robert Adams, *Wife Beating as a Crime and Its Relation to Taxation* (1886), cited in Elizabeth Pleck, "Criminal Approaches to Family Violence, 1640–1980,' in Ohlin and Tonry, *Family Violence,* 19.

4. The American Bar Foundation published the results of its survey in a five-volume series. See chap. 1, p. 13.

5. Joseph Goldstein, "Police Discretion Not to Invoke the Criminal Process: Low-Visibility Decisions in the Administration of Justice," *Yale Law Journal* 69, no. 4 (1960):554.

6. Wayne R. LaFave, *Arrest: The Decision to Take a Suspect into Custody,* ed. Frank J. Remington (Boston: Little, Brown, 1965).

7. Ibid., 114.

8. Ibid., 145–46.

9. Ibid., 123, 144–46.

10. Frank W. Miller, *Prosecution: The Decision to Charge a Suspect with a Crime,* ed. Frank J. Remington (Boston: Little, Brown, 1969).

11. Ibid., 267.

12. Ibid., 270–71.

13. President's Commission on Law Enforcement and Administration of Justice, *Task Force Report: The Police* (Washington, D.C.: U.S. Government Printing Office, 1967), 50–51.

14. President's Commission on Law Enforcement and Administration of Justice, *The Challenge of Crime in a Free Society* (Washington, D.C.: U.S. Government Printing Office, 1967) [hereinafter *Challenge of Crime*].

15. *Report of the National Advisory Commission on Civil Disorders,* also known as the *Kerner Report* (New York: Bantam Books, 1968), 167.

16. See, e.g., Morton Bard and Bernard Berkowitz, "Training Police as Specialists in Family Crisis Intervention: A Community Psychology Action Program," *Community Mental Health Journal* 3, no. 4 (1967):317.

17. Conversation with Bard, summer 1989.

18. My works include: "The Police Response to the Domestic Disturbance," *Wisconsin Law Review* 1967, no. 4:914–60; "The Response of Some Relevant Community Resources to Intra-Family Violence," *Indiana Law Journal* 44, no. 2 (1969):159–81; "Police Discretion and Diversion of Incidents of Intra-Family Violence," *Law and Contemporary Problems* 36, no. 4 (1971):539–65; "Prosecutorial and Judicial Handling of Family Violence Matters," *Criminal Law Bulletin* 9, no. 9 (1973):733–69; "Judicial Response to Intra-Family Violence," *Minnesota Law Review* 54 (1970):585–644; "The Relevance of Criminal Law to Interspousal Violence," in *Family Violence: An International Interdisciplinary Study,* ed. John M. Eekelaar and Sanford N. Katz (Toronto: Butterworths, 1978).

19. Parnas, "Police Response," 957; Parnas, "Police Discretion," 560–65.

20. Parnas, "Judicial Response," 641–44.

21. Parnas, "Police Discretion," 562; Parnas, "Judicial Response," 600–605, 642–43.

22. Parnas, "Judicial Response," 642.

23. Parnas, "Response of Some Resources."

24. However, compare this second goal with a revised position taken in 1977 in Parnas, "Relevance of Criminal Law."

25. Elizabeth Truninger, "Marital Violence: The Legal Solutions," *Hastings Law Journal* 23, no. 1 (1971):259–76.

26. Jeffrey W. Allister and Sue Schleifer Levy, "Impact of the New Family Offense Legislation," *New York State Bar Journal* 50, no. 8 (1978):648–52; Eva S. Buzawa and Carl G. Buzawa, "Legislative Responses to the Problem of Domestic Violence in Michigan," *Wayne Law Review* 25, no. 3 (1979):859–81; Alan D. Eisenberg and Earl J. Seymour, "The Self-Defense Plea and Battered Women," *Trial* 14, no. 7 (1978):34–42; Noel H. Thompson, "Representing the Accused Charged with an Intra-Family Violence Offense," *Practical Lawyer* 18, no. 8 (1972):41; Deborah Flynn, "Domestic Relations: The Protection From Abuse Act," *Temple Law Quarterly* 51, no. 1 (1978):116–26; Barbara H. Schickling, "Relief for Victims of Intra-Family Assaults: The Pennsylvania Protection from Abuse Act," *Dickinson Law Review* 81, no. 4 (1977):815–22; "Panel Workshop: Violence, Crime, Sexual Abuse, and Addiction," *Contemporary Drug Problems* 5, no. 3 (1976):385.

27. Eugene A. Engeldinger, *Spousal Abuse: An Annotated Bibliography of Violence Between Mates* (Metuchen, N.J.: Scarecrow Press, 1986).

28. The intentional use of the mass media to publicize the Minneapolis Domestic Violence Experiment, which led to subsequent emphasis on the arrest response, is acknowledged by one of the primary researchers, Lawrence Sherman. Lawrence W. Sherman and Ellen G. Cohn, "The Impact of Research on Legal Policy: The Minneapolis Domestic Violence Experiment," *Law and Society Review* 23, no. 1 (1989):117–44. For criticism of that intentional publicity, see Richard Lempert, "Humility Is a Virtue: On the Publicization of Policy-Relevant Research," *Law and Society Review* 23, no. 1 (1989):145–61.

29. Virgie Lemond Mouton, "Wife Abuse Legislation in California, Pennsylvania and Texas," *Thurgood Marshall Law Review* 7, no. 2 (1982):282–89.

30. This work was later published in the United States: Erin Pizzey, *Scream Quietly or the Neighbors Will Hear* (Baltimore: Penguin, 1977).

31. J. Goldstein, "Police Discretion Not to Invoke" (see note 5), 577, n. 71, citing Police Academy, Oakland, Calif., *Police Department Instructor's Material,* vol. 6, bull. no. 35 (Aug. 26, 1957), 2.

32. J. Goldstein, "Police Discretion Not to Invoke," 587.

33. LaFave, *Arrest* (see note 6), 145–46.

34. Parnas, "Police Response," 948.

35. Parnas, "Relevance of Criminal Law." This paper was first presented at the Second World Conference of the International Society of Family Law in Montreal.

36. Francis A. Allen, "The Borderland of the Criminal Law: Problems of 'Socializing' Criminal Justice," in *The Borderland of Criminal Justice* (Chicago: University of Chicago Press, 1964).

37. Parnas, "Relevance of Criminal Law," 190–91.

38. For an article on prosecutorial discretion in spouse abuse cases, see Janell Schmidt and Ellen H. Steury, "Prosecutorial Discretion in Filing Charges in Domestic Violence Cases," *Criminology* 27, no. 3 (1989):487–510.

39. Center for Women Policy Studies, "'No-Drop' Prosecution Policies Sometimes Backfire Against Victims," *Response* 7, no. 3 (1984):5–6.

40. Center for Women Policy Studies, "Courts' Response to Battered Women Evaluated," *Response* 5, no. 2 (1982):4, discussing and quoting from Barbara E. Smith, *Non-Stranger Violence: The Criminal Courts' Response* (Washington, D.C.: Department of Justice, National Institute of Justice, 1981).

41. The litigation experience is discussed in detail in Raymond I. Parnas, "The American Bar Foundation Survey of the Administration of Criminal Justice and Past, Present, and Future Responses to Domestic Violence," *Washington University Law Quarterly* 69 (1991):107.

42. Nancy Loving, *Responding to Spouse Abuse and Wife Beating: A Guide for Police* (Washington, D.C.: Police Executive Research Forum, 1980).

43. Ibid., xvi.

44. First reported in Lawrence W. Sherman and Richard A. Berk, "The Specific Deterrent Effects of Arrest for Domestic Assault," *American Sociological Review* 49, no. 2 (1984):261.

45. Lawrence W. Sherman and Richard A. Berk, "The Minneapolis Domestic Violence Experiment," in *Police and Law Enforcement,* vol. 4, ed. Robert J. Homant and Daniel B. Kennedy (New York: AMS Press, 1987), 331, 335.

46. See, e.g., Delbert S. Elliott, "Criminal Justice Procedures in Family Violence Crimes," in *Family Violence* (see note 1), 453–58. However, to his credit, at least one of the primary researchers acknowledges a wide range of possible "limitations" of his research including

internal validity concerns of (1) randomization, (2) differential victim reporting by treatment, (3) sample size, (4) analysis, (5) follow-up period, and (6) displacement, as well as external validity issues of (1) jail time, (2) mediation quality, (3) interaction of interview and arrest, (4) absence of theory, (5) victim perception of officer, (6) city context, and (7) alternative procedures. He admits that this "list of possible threats to the internal and external validity of the 'arrest-works-best' finding is clearly quite extensive." However, he concludes that "the Minneapolis experiment actually suffered quite minor threats to validity" in comparison with most other policy studies and randomized experiments.

In support of his research and the publicity he actively sought for it, he states that "the appropriate test is a comparison of the evidentiary strength of the recommendations derived from the Minneapolis experiment with the strength of the evidence in support of the pre-experiment status quo" (Sherman and Cohn, "Impact of Research on Legal Policy" [see note 28], 134).

47.   Sherman and Berk, "Specific Deterrent Effects," 342–44.

48.   Robert J. Homant and Daniel B. Kennedy, eds., *Police and Law Enforcement*, 5 vols. (New York: AMS Press, 1987), 332.

49.   Franklin W. Dunford, David Huizinga, and Delbert S. Elliott, "Final Report: The Omaha Domestic Violence Police Experiment" (Submitted to the National Institute of Justice and the City of Omaha, June 1989), 61–67. See also their published account, "The Role of Arrest in Domestic Assault: The Omaha Police Experiment," *Criminology* 28, no. 2 (1990):183–206. The Milwaukee replication is expected to show the same results as the Omaha report. Milwaukee, like "about 20% of the nation's medium to large cities, has mandatory arrest laws or policies" as a "direct result" of the Minnesota experiment ("Mandatory Arrest Doesn't Deter Domestic Abuse, Study Concludes," *Milwaukee Journal*, Sept. 13, 1989).

50.   This study and the observations of Sherman and his colleagues are reported in Lawrence W. Sherman, Janell D. Schmidt, Dennis P. Rogan, Patrick R. Gartin, Ellen G. Cohn, Dean J. Collins, and Anthony R. Bacich, "From Initial Deterrence to Long-Term Escalation: Short-Custody Arrest for Poverty Ghetto Domestic Violence," *Criminology* 29, no. 4 (1991):821.

51.   Ibid., 844.

52.   Ibid., 845.

53.   Ibid.

54. Ibid.

55. Ibid., 846.

56. See, e.g., Debra Kalmuss, "The Intergenerational Transmission of Marital Aggression," *Journal of Marriage and the Family* 46, no. 1 (Feb. 1984):11.

57. See generally Elliott, "Criminal Justice Procedures."

58. See "Mandatory Arrest Doesn't Deter." For example, according to Commissioner Anthony Salina, not only is arrest preferred in Connecticut but assaulters are arrested despite the victim's wishes to the contrary (Comments made at Mediation and Domestic Violence Conference, Chicago, Illinois, May 24–25, 1989, sponsored by Association of Family and Conciliation Courts).

59. E. Soler, *The San Francisco Family Violence Project: An Overview* (San Francisco: San Francisco Family Violence Project), available from the project at Building One, Suite 200, 1001 Portrero Avenue, San Francisco, Calif. 94110) M–3.

60. Associated Press, "Domestic Violence Program Comes Under Criticism," *Sacramento Daily Recorder*, July 20, 1988.

61. Soler, *San Francisco Project*, M–5.

62. Remarks by Judge Douglas McNish at conference (see note 58).

63. See, e.g., "Wife Beaters Use Law to Avoid Jail, Critics Say," *Sacramento Bee*, July 18, 1988; "Domestic Violence Program Comes under Criticism," *Sacramento Daily Recorder*, July 20, 1988;

64. See, e.g., "New Protections Help Domestic Violence Victims," *Sacramento Daily Recorder*, Nov. 3, 1987.

65. See generally Daniel G. Saunders and Sandra T. Azar, "Treatment Programs for Family Violence," in *Family Violence*, ed. Lloyd Ohlin and Michael Tonry (Chicago: University of Chicago Press, 1989), 481.

66. In May 1989, in fact, they picketed the National Forum on Mediation and Domestic Violence in Chicago, fearing any turning away from full enforcement of the criminal law, although the focus of the Association of Family and Conciliation Courts' Forum was on how to deal with domestic violence in the process of custody mediation. (My personal observations at Mediation and Domestic Violence Conference, Chicago, Illinois, May 24–25, 1989, sponsored by Association of Family and Conciliation Courts.)

67. Patrick A. Langan and Christopher A. Innes, *Special Report: Preventing Domestic Violence Against Women* (Washington, D.C.: Department of Justice, Bureau of Justice Statistics, August 1986).

68. Dunford, Huizinga, and Elliott, "Final Report," 67.

69. Annette Jolin, "Domestic Violence Legislation: An Impact Assessment," *Journal of Police Science and Administration* 11, no. 4 (1983):454.

70. "Study Finds No Way For Police to Predict Domestic Homicides," *Criminal Justice Newsletter* 21, no. 4 (Feb. 15, 1990):3–4, summarizing and quoting from Crime Control Institute, *Predicting Domestic Homicide: Prior Police Contact and Gun Threats*. The summary continued:

> Researchers at the Washington, D.C.-based Crime Control Institute had hoped to find patterns that could help police intervene and prevent domestic homicides. But after studying more than 15,000 incidents in Milwaukee over a 22-month period, including 33 domestic homicides, they were unable to identify any such indicator.
>
> The institute specifically rejected the "escalating violence" theory (that a domestic homicide often is the culmination of increasingly frequent and severe attacks upon the victim). Contrary to what one might expect, in 32 of the 33 domestic homicides in Milwaukee, there was no police record of previous domestic violence by the suspect against the victim.
>
> Furthermore, in more than 1,000 cases where police were called to protect a particular victim from a particular offender, often repeatedly, no homicide occurred in the period studied. "Even prior pointing of guns with death threats fails to predict domestic homicide," the researchers concluded.

71. Or as Frank Zimring says, in arguing for comparative law research: "Yet the pervasiveness of intimate violence in Western culture suggests that there is a parochial limit to current discussion of the control of such violence in the United States....Family violence, like the poor, may be always with us, but in different proportions and with different outcomes" (Franklin E. Zimring, "Toward a Jurisprudence of Family Violence," in *Family Violence* [see note 1], 567–68).

72. Elizabeth Wiener, "Inadequate Enforcement Seen on Courts' Protection Orders," *Criminal Justice Newsletter* 20, no. 8 (Apr. 17, 1989):4–5.

73. See, e.g., *Domestic Violence Fact Sheets* (Washington, D.C.:

National Woman Abuse Prevention Project, 1988, available from the project at 2000 P Street, N.W., Suite 508, Washington, D.C. 20036).

74. "Why Domestic Violence Exists," *Cal. Aggie* (U.C. Davis campus newspaper) April 13, 1989.

75. See, e.g., Cal. Penal Code §§ 1203.06–.07 (West Supp. 1991).

76. See, e.g., *United States v. Salerno*, 481 U.S. 739 (1987); The Bail Reform Act of 1984, 18 U.S.C. § 3142 (1988); and Cal. Const. art. I, § 12.

77. Parnas, "Relevance of Criminal Law" (see note 18), 190.

78. Lisa G. Lerman, "Statute: A Model State Act: Remedies For Domestic Abuse," *Harvard Journal on Legislation* 21, no. 1 (1984):67.

79. See Irene H. Frieze and Angela Browne, "Violence in Marriage," in *Family Violence* (see note 1), 192–96.

80. *Sacramento Bee*, June 19, 1989, A1, col. 10.

81. *Sacramento Bee*, July 26, 1989.

82. See, e.g., J. Goldstein, "Police Discretion Not to Invoke" (see note 5).

83. *Los Angeles Daily Journal,* Aug. 28, 1985.

84. Allen, "Borderland of the Criminal Law" (see note 36), 12–13.

85. Anthony Platt, *The Child Savers: The Invention of Delinquency* (Chicago: University of Chicago Press, 1969), 3–4.

86. University of Wisconsin Law Professor Herman Goldstein, long a leading researcher and scholar on policing, succinctly summed up much of the problem in his September 4, 1989, memorandum to me as follows:

> In Madison, [Wisconsin,] for example, the police, the prosecutor, and the courts were, on their own initiative, moving toward a rather sophisticated response to spousal abuse cases, with a commitment to arrest and prosecution, but with some room for discretion and the use of alternatives. I felt it led to much progress in both effectiveness and fairness. But the legislative mandate to arrest has swamped the system, eliminating much of the discretion that was being exercised, with results that, in my personal opinion, threaten the progress that was made. I understand that the legislature is being asked to amend the statute to return some discretion to both the police and the prosecutor, and that the amendments are being endorsed by

those who have been most adamant for a blanket form of mandated arrest. Thus, those concerned about the problem are gradually learning what I believe we learned in the ABF study: that responding intelligently to a behavioral problem requires, most importantly, that we recognize its complexity.

CHAPTER 6

Police Rule Making and the Fourth Amendment: The Role of the Courts

Wayne R. LaFave

Over the course of what does not *seem* like three decades, I have spent a good deal of time thinking and writing about the fourth amendment. Despite the single-mindedness of this assiduous endeavor, the work has not been all of the same character. During the earlier years, due to my participation in the analysis phase of the American Bar Foundation survey of criminal justice, the focus was on the actual search and seizure practices of the police as revealed in the empirical data collected during the survey's research phase. In more recent times, my study of search and seizure has been in the form of traditional doctrinal research: the emphasis has been on critical analysis of what the courts (especially the Supreme Court) have had to say about the fourth amendment.

Certainly the latter work has been heavily influenced by the former. In evaluating judicial pronouncements about the fourth amendment, I have rather consistently found that my own views were shaped to a significant degree by my earlier edification concerning how police officers and agencies actually perform. This tie-in between the American Bar Foundation survey of criminal justice and my subsequent forays into fourth amendment law has heretofore been implicit at best. In this chapter, however, it is explicit. I intend to assay the *present* state of fourth amendment jurisprudence from the perspective of some of the key insights of the ABF survey. To begin this undertaking, it may be useful to mention specifically a few of those insights as they bear on the presurvey and postsurvey state of fourth amendment law.

Clearly "the most important single finding of the survey" was "how hard it is to make accurate straightforward statements about criminal law administration" because of the previously unperceived "complexity" of that process.[1] That complexity, the survey established, attends activities of the police that implicate the fourth amendment. In deciding whether to make an arrest or other seizure of a person and whether to search for or seize property, the police are actually called on to make decisions that are quite varied in character and impact and that are influenced by a vast range of factors and considerations.

Because this complexity was not perceived by courts in the presurvey days, the fourth amendment jurisprudence of that era was decidedly one-dimensional. Illustrative is *Henry v. United States*,[2] where FBI agents investigating a theft from an interstate shipment saw two men under surveillance loading cartons into a vehicle from a private residence. The agents' subsequent brief stopping of the vehicle, the Supreme Court concluded, constituted nothing other than an "arrest" necessitating full probable cause (which was lacking). *Henry* stands in sharp contrast to the postsurvey decision in *Terry v. Ohio*,[3] which significantly drew on the findings of the ABF survey regarding the complexity of the stop-and-frisk activities of the police. *Terry* wisely rejected the contention seemingly embraced in *Henry* "that there is not—and cannot be—a variety of [lawful] police activity which does not depend solely upon the voluntary cooperation of the citizen and yet which stops short of an arrest based upon probable cause to make such an arrest." Though not *all* of the Supreme Court's postsurvey fourth amendment decisions manifest a comparable understanding of the complexity of the search and seizure activities of the police, it is nonetheless a fair generalization that the Court now has a much greater appreciation of this complexity than it had at the time of *Henry*. As a result, the Supreme Court is now much more willing to judge discrete search and seizure activity on its own terms.

Yet another recurring theme in the ABF survey concerns "the relatively wide discretion that officials have in enforcing the criminal law."[4] Of particular interest here is that discretion in the criminal process that prior to the survey had been least visible:

that exercised by police in determining when and how to enforce the law. Much of that discretion has to do with determining how to invoke the criminal process and when to utilize a variety of investigative techniques and thus falls within the realm of fourth amendment activity. Included here are such decisions as whether to undertake a custodial arrest, whether to persist in that attempt by using force, whether to stop a suspect for investigation, and whether to conduct a search.

In the presurvey search-and-seizure decisions of the Supreme Court, the Court was largely oblivious to the discretionary practices of the police and the risks they posed to fourth amendment interests. Illustrative is *Harris v. United States*,[5] holding that FBI agents lawfully searched defendant's entire apartment "incident to" his arrest there. The *Harris* majority reassured that this was not "a case in which law-enforcement officers have entered premises ostensibly for the purpose of making an arrest but in reality for the purpose of conducting a general exploratory search."[6] That comment, of course, overlooks the fact that police routinely exercise discretion whether to arrest perpetrators at their home or elsewhere and that the choice in a particular case to arrest at home, because readily explainable in terms of the arrest purpose, could easily be legitimated even if primarily motivated by the opportunity to "piggyback" onto the arrest another, far greater fourth amendment intrusion—a full but warrantless search of the dwelling. The postsurvey decisions of the Supreme Court are not consistently of a better sort. But at least the term *police discretion* has now entered the Supreme Court's lexicon,[7] and in recent years (as I discuss later herein) the Court sometimes has expressly recognized that limits on that discretion are essential to the protection of fourth amendment values.

Given the complex and discretionary character of police search-and-seizure decisions, some limitations on this power are essential. "Half the problem is to cut back *unnecessary* discretionary power. The other half is to find effective ways to control *necessary* discretionary power."[8] One important conclusion of the ABF survey is that this bipartite challenge cannot be completely and successfully met by the legislative and judicial branches alone. The police themselves are perceived to have an important role to play. As the ABF survey concludes, "police ought to acknowledge their exercise of discretion and reduce their enforcement policies to writing and subject them to a continuing process of critical re-evaluation."[9] Over the twenty-five intervening years, this has occurred to an immeasurable but noticeable degree, which accounts for yet another distinction between presurvey and postsurvey fourth amendment jurisprudence: only in the more recent era have courts sometimes taken police regulations into account in ruling on search-and-seizure issues.

As elaborated in the next section, there are ample reasons to conclude that police rule making regarding their fourth amendment activities is a highly desirable undertaking. This being so, it is appropriate to consider whether the judicial branch has a part to play in that enterprise. The answer, quite obviously, is yes: courts "have a role in stimulating this administrative process and reviewing its products."[10] It is the performance to date of this role by the courts (especially the Supreme Court) that constitutes the focus of this chapter. To what extent have the courts performed the "stimulating" function by formulating their decisions in such a way as to mandate or encourage police policymaking? To what extent have the courts performed the "reviewing" function to ensure that law enforcement regulations accomplish the hoped-for benefits of rule making? And, more generally, precisely how has the existence or nonexistence of police rules influenced the quality and character of fourth amendment jurisprudence and, in turn, the quality, consistency, and visibility of search-and-seizure decision making?

POLICE RULE MAKING AND THE FOURTH AMENDMENT

"The police," Kenneth Davis once commented, "are among the most important policy-makers of our entire society. And they make far more discretionary determinations in individual cases than any other class of administrators; I know of no close second."[11] As the pervasiveness of this police discretion became more widely known, there arose in many quarters the understandable concern that this vast discretion must be limited and controlled. To accomplish this, many have concluded, a system of rule making by law enforcement agencies themselves—as proposed in the ABF survey—is imperative. The case for rule making has been made by many thoughtful commentators, including Judge Carl McGowan[12] and Anthony Amsterdam,[13] Herman Goldstein,[14] and

Kenneth Davis.[15] Rule making has been advocated in such law reform efforts as the ALI's prearraignment code[16] and the ABA's criminal justice standards[17] and in such influential studies as those by the President's Commission on Law Enforcement and Administration of Justice[18] and the National Advisory Commission on Criminal Justice Standards and Goals.[19] Consequently, this chapter need not establish the need for development of guidelines by police agencies; it will suffice to summarize the case already made.

In some of this writing (especially that of Davis), the emphasis is on the police discretion related to the substantive criminal law— that is, law enforcement decisions *not* to invoke the criminal process against certain individuals who have apparently violated some provision in the penal code. This is police discretion of the lowest possible visibility. This form of police discretion traditionally has not been a subject of judicial oversight and, by its nature, does not readily lend itself to such supervision. Given these circumstances, it is difficult to quarrel with the proposition that meaningful reform necessitates resort to a regime of police rule making. It may be less apparent that the development of guidelines by the police themselves is essential with respect to their fourth amendment activities. After all, at least since *Mapp v. Ohio*[20] the courts, through the mechanism of the exclusionary rule, have had the responsibility to define the fourth amendment limits of police power and to impose the suppression sanction when those limits have been exceeded. The exclusionary rule ensures a great deal of judicial attention to such police practices and thus has resulted in considerable judicial elaboration of fourth amendment requirements, culminating in an enormous increase in police training and education about constitutional rights. All this being so, police rule making might appear superfluous at best.

That is not the case, however. To appreciate this, it is well to begin with an understanding that this traditional, virtually exclusive reliance on the judiciary for the formulation of fourth amendment standards cannot be taken as an apodictic manifestation that courts possess singular omniscience on these matters. To the contrary, as Amsterdam has pointed out, this judicial activism

> has been the almost inevitable consequence of the failure of other agencies of law to assume responsibility for regulating police practices. In most areas of constitutional law the Supreme Court of the United States plays a back-stopping role,

reviewing the ultimate permissibility of dispositions and policies guided in the first instance by legislative enactments,
administrative rules or local common-law traditions. In the
area of controls upon the police, a vast abnegation of responsibility at the level of each of these ordinary sources of legal rule-
making has forced the Court to construct *all* the law regulating
the everyday functioning of the police.[21]

In the face of this phenomenon, there is no reason to doubt the
contention that a "new allocation of responsibilities is required"
and that the role of the Supreme Court (and courts generally) "is
better adapted to review than to initiation."[22] Indeed, that contention—which presumes a process of administrative regulation at
the police level—makes good sense in the fourth amendment area.

The fourth amendment, whether viewed in terms of its pre-
constitutional history or its current interpretation by the Supreme
Court, is concerned with indiscriminate searches and seizures of
two types: (1) *"unjustified* searches and seizures," that is, those
where "an adequate justification" for such intrusion has not been
shown and (2) *"arbitrary* searches and seizures," that is, those
"conducted at the discretion of executive officials, who may act
despotically and capriciously in the exercise of the power to
search and seize."[23] The first of these concerns is reflected in the
explicit and familiar fourth amendment requirement of "probable
cause," and the second is manifested by the amendment's interpretation "as another harbinger of the Equal Protection Clause,
concerned with avoiding indefensible inequities in treatment."[24]
Protection against arbitrary searches and seizures lies in controlling police discretion, which necessitates a determination that the
police action taken against a particular individual corresponds to
that which occurs with respect to other persons similarly situated.
Judicial assessment of just what the category is (that is, who else
really is "similarly situated") and whether like cases in fact
receive the same disposition will be more meaningful and reliable
if the record in the case reveals a preexisting police regulation on
the subject.

A second characteristic of the fourth amendment is that the
experience and expertise of the police, if properly established in
court, are properly taken into account in determining the legality
of the challenged police conduct. A process of police rule making
makes it possible for the experience and expertise of the entire
department to be focused on the matter at issue and to be more

effectively communicated to the reviewing court. As Goldstein has noted, if police policy has been made through a process of administrative rule making, then

> in the review of police practices initiated by a motion to suppress evidence, a judge could promote a dialogue with the police by affording the law-enforcement agency an opportunity to justify and explain the practice at issue, thereby focusing judicial review upon the legality and propriety of department policies rather than the actions of an individual officer. This would give the police an opportunity to articulate the experience and expertise influential in formulating their policies—factors to be considered in weighing the propriety of their actions. A judge fully informed on all of the circumstances related to a given police practice is obviously in a better position to pass judgment upon its legality and propriety than one whose knowledge of the procedure is limited to what is revealed in the typical hearing on a motion to suppress evidence.[25]

Yet another characteristic of the fourth amendment (or, more precisely, of its exclusionary rule) is that only certain types of police search-and-seizure activity regularly come to the attention of the courts. Because the exclusionary rule ordinarily may be invoked only by a defendant in a criminal case, those police searches and seizures that are undertaken for purposes other than prosecution or that do not result in the discovery of evidence do not receive judicial scrutiny. As acknowledged in *Terry v. Ohio*, the exclusionary rule "is powerless to deter invasions of constitutionally guaranteed rights where the police either have no interest in prosecuting or are willing to forgo successful prosecution in the interest of serving some other goal," a not uncommon occurrence.[26] With respect to these practices, police rule making is needed not so much as an aid to judicial oversight but rather (as with police nonenforcement decisions) because no other meaningful restraint on the activity of individual officers exists. The mere absence of routine judicial review of such activities does not mean that any police regulations adopted would merely approve the established practice. As Amsterdam warns, it is

> a grave mistake...to assume that all of the things that policemen do in a state of rulelessness would continue to be done under a regime of rules. Many practices now tolerated in indi-

vidual cases...would not be approved or authorized by the police command structure itself if it were required to assume responsibility for determining the propriety of those practices as a general mode of departmental operation.[27]

Departmental policymaking regarding the fourth amendment activities of police is desirable because it "improves police performance" in four major ways:

1. *Rule making enhances the quality of police decisions* because it focuses attention on the fact that policy is being made, promotes the placing of decision-making authority in responsible and capable hands, increases the seriousness with which police face up to the implications of their practices for the efficiency of law enforcement and the liberty of citizens, promotes decision-making efficiency, and enhances police prestige and morale.

2. *Rule making tends to ensure the fair and equal treatment of citizens* because rules reduce the influence of bias, provide uniform standards for use in the training of personnel, and serve both to guide and to control police behavior.

3. *Rule making increases the visibility of police policy decisions* because the rule-making process requires the departmental command structure to learn what officers in the field are doing and informs other governmental agencies and the public about what the police are doing.

4. *Rule making offers the best hope we have for getting policemen consistently to obey and enforce constitutional norms that guarantee the liberty of the citizen* because rules made by the police are most likely to be obeyed by the police and, when not obeyed, are most likely to be effectively enforced by the department.[28]

IMPOUNDMENTS AND INVENTORIES: THE *BERTINE* "STANDARDIZED PROCEDURE" REQUIREMENT

In a series of cases culminating in *Colorado v. Bertine*,[29] the Supreme Court has evaluated the reasonableness under the fourth amendment of various police activities related to the impoundment or inventory of effects (usually automobiles). In

South Dakota v. Opperman,[30] the defendant's car was towed to a city impound lot after it received two overtime parking tickets while parked at the same location for more than seven hours. An officer then inventoried the contents of the car and discovered marijuana in the unlocked glove compartment. The Court found the police conduct constitutional, but intimated that the existence of appropriate police regulations on the subject might be a sine qua non. The *Opperman* plurality opinion put forward the proposition "that inventories pursuant to standard police procedures are reasonable," and Justice Powell, concurring separately, stressed that the inventory "was conducted strictly in accord with the regulations of the Vermillion Police Department." *Opperman* was relied on in *Illinois v. Lafayette,*[31] where the Court upheld a station house inventory of the defendant's effects following his arrest for disorderly conduct. Emphasizing an officer had testified "it was standard procedure to inventory 'everything' in the possession of an arrested person," the Court held that "it is not 'unreasonable' for police, as part of the routine procedure incident to incarcerating an arrested person, to search any container or article in his possession, in accordance with established inventory procedures."[32]

Then came *Bertine* where, after the defendant's arrest for driving under the influence, his van was inventoried prior to being towed to an impoundment lot, resulting in the discovery of drugs in a backpack found lying behind the back seat. The Court emphasized that in the present case, "as in *Opperman* and *Lafayette,*... the police...were following standardized procedures," and then proceeded to declare, much more clearly than had the Court's earlier decisions, the central place of police rule making in the constitutional scheme: "We conclude that...reasonable police regulations relating to inventory procedures administered in good faith satisfy the Fourth Amendment, even though courts might as a matter of hindsight be able to devise equally reasonable rules requiring a different procedure."[33] In rejecting the state court's conclusion that Bertine's fourth amendment rights had been violated, the Court took note that both the impoundment of Bertine's car and the opening of containers therein during the inventory were in conformance with Boulder Police Department regulations.

To the extent that *Bertine* either encourages or compels police departments to engage in the promulgation of guidelines on the subjects of impoundment and inventory of vehicles and other effects, it is to be applauded. Especially because (as *Bertine* notes) "an inventory search may be 'reasonable' under the Fourth Amendment even though it is not conducted pursuant to a warrant based upon probable cause," some significant protection in lieu of the two traditional fourth amendment safeguards of probable cause and warrant is essential. As Justice Powell emphasized in his *Opperman* concurrence, to protect against "arbitrary invasions by government officials," it is essential that "no significant discretion is placed in the hands of the individual officer" concerning "the subject of the search or its scope." Thus, it is not sufficient that the challenged impoundment or inventory is of the kind undertaken by police departments generally, nor is it sufficient that it conform to the particular officer's standard practice. What is necessary, says *Bertine*, is that this officer was "following standardized procedures," which certainly can be most convincingly proved by showing that the officer's actions square with the established policy or procedures of his department.

Police rule making on this subject is also desirable because it permits more meaningful input of police expertise. What is at issue here is a routine practice that, as *Bertine* says, serves "to protect an owner's property while it is in the custody of the police, to insure against claims of lost, stolen, or vandalized property, and to guard the police from danger," and thus it is appropriate to expect the police agency in the first instance to make a judgment as to exactly what kind of routine is needed to serve those governmental interests in that particular locality. The result is not statewide uniformity (as likely would be the case if the matter were left entirely to the courts), but this is all to the good; "different procedures might be appropriate for various circumstances in different communities throughout the state."[34] Also, by requiring a relevant police regulation and testing individual instances of impoundment and inventory against such a regulation, the practice is given greater visibility, which in turn serves as an added restraint upon the police and thus ensures greater consistency in future actions of that genre.

In *United States v. Frank*,[35] the Third Circuit upheld an inventory that conformed to "unwritten standard procedures" testified to by a police lieutenant, though the department in question "had no written procedures governing inventory searches."

The court declared: "No Supreme Court case has ever held an inventory search invalid because of the absence of formalized pre-existing standards."[36] This latter statement is unquestionably true, and in defense of *Frank* it might be asserted that *Bertine* does not even contain specific dictum suggesting that if the procedures there had not been in writing the result might be different. But, although *Frank* may in that sense be "correct," it is doubtful that the conclusion reached there is a desirable one. In support of *Frank*, it might be argued that surely an inventory should be upheld when, as in *Madison v. United States*, although the police department did "not have written guidelines for such searches, the officer testified that he had been trained by his supervisors to perform inventory searches in this manner and he did so in accordance with standard operating procedures."[37] But once it is accepted that the *Bertine* "standardized procedures" can be established by police testimony about current practices rather than by proof of preexisting written policies, there are dangers aplenty. As *United States v. Lyons* said of such a situation: "It is far from clear that this sort of vague, customary departmental 'policy' would satisfy the concerns expressed by the Court in *Opperman*."[38] A primary concern, of course, is the possibility of undetected arbitrariness, a risk that takes on much greater proportions if the supposed "standardized procedures" are established only by the self-serving and perhaps inaccurate oral statements of a police officer and are not memorialized in the department's previous written instructions to its officers. Another concern, as reflected by the *Lyons* use of the word *customary,* is that what is represented as department policy may constitute nothing more than a custom, hardly deserving the deference that an actual policy receives pursuant to *Bertine*. One might hope, therefore, that other courts will come to emulate the Massachusetts Supreme Judicial Court, which held that the state constitution "requires the exclusion of evidence seized during an inventory search not conducted pursuant to standard police procedures, which procedures, from now on, must be in writing."[39]

Although *Bertine* itself does not explicitly go this far, the Supreme Court's decision strongly encourages departments to adopt written policies. Given that *Bertine* does require "standardized procedures," a matter on which the prosecution bears the burden of proof, it benefits the police to have these procedures actually set out in a manual or similar directive. This seems particularly apparent when one considers another aspect of *Bertine* not yet mentioned: a majority of the Supreme Court deems it "permissible for police officers to open closed containers in an inventory search only if they are following standard police procedures that mandate the opening of such containers in every impounded vehicle."[40] Establishing this kind of absolute, nondiscretionary policy is likely to be especially difficult absent evidence in the form of written policies.

The positive side of *Bertine*, then, is this encouragement of police rule making with respect to what the Court has sometimes called the "community caretaking functions" of the police,[41] an area in which both the availability of law enforcement expertise and the need to restrict discretion make such administrative action especially appropriate. But *Bertine* has a negative side as well, and it concerns judicial evaluation of relevant police regulations. Although these regulations are entitled to some deference from the courts, there are limits. "Obviously, a policy of deferring to administrative regulations could have undesirable consequences, if the deference were carried too far: constitutional protections would be at the mercy of the most intrusively imaginative police chief or jail administrator."[42] And that is why the Court cautiously stated in *Bertine* that only "reasonable" police regulations satisfied the fourth amendment.

In *Bertine*, the defendant "argued that the inventory search of his van was unconstitutional because departmental regulations gave the police officers discretion to choose between impounding his van and parking and locking it in a public parking place." In response to that contention, the opinion of the Court states:

> Nothing in *Opperman* or *Lafayette* prohibits the exercise of police discretion so long as that discretion is exercised according to standard criteria and on the basis of something other than suspicion of evidence of criminal activity. Here, the discretion afforded the Boulder police was exercised in light of standardized criteria, related to the feasibility and appropriateness of parking and locking a vehicle rather than impounding it. There was no showing that the police chose to impound Bertine's van in order to investigate suspected criminal activity.[43]

This is a most inadequate response, which, unfortunately, fails to recognize the precise function reviewing courts must perform in a system that relies on police rule making to contribute meaningfully to the protection of fourth amendment rights.

For one thing, the passage quoted above fails even to recognize why police regulations providing "standardized procedures" are important in such areas of fourth amendment activity as impoundment and inventory. Their purpose in the fourth amendment scheme of things, as Justice Powell succinctly put it in his *Opperman* concurrence, is "to safeguard the privacy and security of individuals against arbitrary invasions by government officials." "Arbitrary" action is that "depending on choice or discretion" and "arising from unrestrained exercise of the will, caprice, or personal preference,"[44] and thus is hardly limited to those situations where (in the language of *Bertine*) the police acted on "suspicion of evidence of criminal activity." That is simply a matter of motivation, but it is this deviation from established practice or the erratic action attributable to the nonexistence of an established practice that is an appropriate object of fourth amendment concern. If my car is impounded when others are merely parked, if my car is inventoried when others are merely secured, or if the containers in my car are opened in inventorying when others are not, then—absent good reason for singling me out—my privacy and security have been improperly intruded upon, whether it is suspicion of criminal activity or any other reason that accounts for my different treatment.

Moreover, the *Bertine* palliative that there "was no showing that the police chose to impound Bertine's van in order to investigate suspected criminal activity" likewise misrepresents the function of police rule making. It makes *Bertine* appear as a case in which the issue was simply whether the defendant had proved he had been the victim of a pretext or subterfuge search—one purported to be for one reason but in fact motivated by another. But, as noted herein,[45] proving police motivation is a most difficult and seldom successful undertaking, and consequently it is a rather precarious device on which to hang fourth amendment rights. Although arbitrariness can occur for a variety of reasons, the nature of police responsibilities makes especially acute both the risk that supposedly routine noninvestigative activities will be commenced only because of an investigative purpose and the risk that this motivation will never be exposed to the light of day. That is *precisely* why discretion-limiting police regulations are needed regarding impoundment and inventory: to severely restrict the opportunities for undetected (and perhaps undetectable) subterfuge to influence search-and-seizure decisions. Thus the Court in *Bertine* should not have said, in effect, that the defendant's failure to prove an investigative purpose made unnecessary any assessment of the breadth and precision of the applicable police regulations. Rather, the Court should have asked whether those regulations sufficiently confined police discretion so as to provide reasonable assurance against seizures and searches undertaken for reasons unknown to the victims of these intrusions and unknowable to the courts. Only the dissenters in *Bertine* appreciated this point.

Given the Court's erroneous frame of reference in *Bertine*, it is not surprising that the challenged Boulder police regulation, which passed muster in that case, falls significantly short of performing its fourth amendment function of limiting police discretion. As the two dissenters point out, this police directive (never quoted by the majority) states that police may turn the car over to a third party, park it in a nearby public parking lot and merely lock it, or impound and inventory. And, as the dissenters further emphasized, the officer in this case testified that decisions regarding these alternatives "were left to the discretion of the officer on the scene."[46] To this, the *Bertine* majority lamely responds that the regulations establish "several conditions that must be met before an officer may pursue the park and lock alternative," thus ignoring that limitations so stated confine *not at all* the individual officer's power to opt for the impoundment-inventory alternative.

It is possible, and certainly most desirable, to give deference to police regulations—as in *Bertine*, to acknowledge that such a regulation is not unreasonable merely because "courts might as a matter of hindsight be able to devise equally reasonable rules requiring a different procedure"—and at the same time to require that those regulations impose realistic limits on police discretion. The point is not that the regulations must totally eliminate discretion, for that is an impossibility. "[A]s a practical matter, the exercise of some discretion by agents, even if only interpretive, is inevitable since no manual can reasonably be expected to spell out in detail the correct action in light of the almost infinite array of objects an agent may encounter."[47] Thus, even under the *Bertine* concurrence's rule that "it is permissible for police officers to open closed containers in an inventory search only if they are following standard police procedures that mandate the opening of such containers in every impounded vehicle," a carefully drawn police regulation will inevitably require officers sometimes to decide, for example, "whether an object constitutes a 'container.'"

Rather, the question is whether or not the challenged police regulations impose realistic limits on discretion. As the *Bertine* Court highlighted by reaffirming *Lafayette*'s refusal to adopt an "alternative 'less intrusive' means" test, one way to limit discretion is by not even trying to draw lines that, in practice, might be misinterpreted; instead, discretion could be limited by requiring the same police response to a broad category of cases. This is exactly the focus of the *Bertine* concurrence: it might be possible to draft and defend a more selective rule than that of requiring police to open all closed containers in all impounded vehicles,[48] but the virtue of the broader policy is that it "promotes a certain equality of treatment. With a standardized, mandatory procedure, the minister's picnic basket and grandma's knitting bag are opened and inventoried right along with the biker's tool box and the gypsy's satchel."[49] Also, a rule of this broader type may often by its very nature provide us with some assurance that the policy-making police officials carefully balanced the competing interests. As "the cost of law enforcement is more widely distributed,...there is less reason to fear that the governmental decisions to trade off privacy for law enforcement are being made without considering everyone's interests equally."[50] And thus we are more likely to accept the police conclusion that the various objectives of the inventory process can be achieved only by looking inside closed containers when we find that they even intend to look in "the minister's picnic basket and grandma's knitting bag."

It thus appears that an impoundment rule of the broader type, ignoring the turn-over-to-friend and park-at-scene alternatives, is a permissible police regulation. This is not to suggest, however, that a police rule cannot be unreasonable because of excessive breadth. Certainly "a general policy that at any time when there is a felony arrest the vehicle was to be seized," even when the arrestee was not in or by the vehicle and even when "the vehicle was parked at the defendant's residence, at a motel or restaurant parking lot, or at some other place indicating little need for impoundment for safekeeping purposes,"[51] is vulnerable. Nor does this suggest that responsible policymaking at the police level will not sometimes result in the drafting of narrower rules or those requiring decision making by officers on the scene. An impoundment rule might well deal with the turn-over-to-friend and park-at-scene alternatives in a manner so that—unlike the Boulder regulation in *Bertine*—police are advised of those circumstances in which they must forgo resort to the impoundment alternative.[52]

INSPECTIONS: THE *CAMARA* "REASONABLE... ADMINISTRATIVE STANDARDS" REQUIREMENT

Camara v. Municipal Court,[53] holding that a search warrant is ordinarily required to conduct an unconsented housing inspection, marks the origin of a most important fourth amendment doctrine: the so-called balancing test, under which certain discrete investigative and enforcement practices constituting "searches" or "seizures" are permitted on less than the traditional quantum of probable cause. By "balancing the need to search against the invasion which the search entails," the Court in *Camara* held housing inspection warrants did not require probable cause in the sense in which that phrase previously had been used. Rejecting the appellant's claim that an inspection is constitutionally permissible only "when the inspector possesses probable cause to believe that a particular dwelling contains violations of the minimum standards prescribed by the code being enforced,"[54] the Court held that reasonable standards based on such factors as the passage of time, the nature of the building, and the condition of the entire area would suffice. Thus, concluded the Court, probable cause for a warrant exists in this special context "if reasonable legislative or administrative standards for conducting an area inspection are satisfied with respect to a particular dwelling."[55]

The business inspection counterpart of *Camara* is *Marshall v. Barlow's, Inc.*,[56] which involved the constitutionality of a broad warrantless inspection provision of the Occupational Safety and Health Act. Because the Court was "unconvinced...that requiring warrants to inspect will impose serious burdens on the inspection system or the courts,"[57] it held the warrantless inspection provision violated the fourth amendment. As for the grounds to obtain the requisite business inspection warrant, the majority in *Barlow's* followed the *Camara* approach:

> A warrant showing that a specific business has been chosen for an OSHA search on the basis of a general administrative plan for the enforcement of the Act derived from neutral sources such as, for example, dispersion of employees in various types of industries across a given area, and the desired frequency of searches in any of the lesser divisions of the area, would protect an employer's Fourth Amendment rights.[58]

Camara and *Barlow's* are striking examples of the Supreme Court's recognition of how a regime of administrative plus judicial decision making, drawing on the special advantages of each, can contribute to both the protection of fourth amendment rights and the advancement of legitimate government interests. As is evident from a closer look at the *Camara-Barlow's* warrant scheme, the Court's system of promulgation of "administrative standards" and judicial review of contemplated application of those standards permits the full use of expertise at the enforcement level and at the same time ensures against abuse of discretion by those planning and conducting inspections.

Housing inspection programs have traditionally involved administrative decision making. Administrators have selected properties for inspection where there are insufficient personnel to conduct a periodic inspection of all designated buildings and have adjusted the period between inspections according to different rates of neighborhood deterioration. *Camara* obviously recognizes the need for such discretion in the first instance in a sensibly administered inspection system. But are these decisions now to be reviewed by magistrates? Are they to determine the wisdom of once-a-year inspections throughout the community? Are they to pass on the soundness of a particular neighborhood inspection plan? The responsibilities of the magistrate in this regard are not made absolutely clear in *Camara*. In the branch of the opinion dealing with the grounds for an inspection warrant, the Court says that the special type of probable cause needed for inspections exists "if reasonable legislative or administrative standards for conducting an area inspection are satisfied with respect to a particular dwelling."[59] This strongly suggests that the judicial officer has two responsibilities: (1) generally, to determine the reasonableness of the inspection program and (2) specifically, to determine whether the particular inspection requested fits within that program. Yet, in the part of *Camara* imposing the search warrant requirement, the Court seems to assume that judicial review of the grounds for inspection will occur "without any reassessment of the basic agency decision to canvass an area." Post-*Camara* appellate litigation about housing inspections is sufficiently rare that no statement can be made about how courts generally believe this ambiguity in *Camara* should be resolved.

The *Camara* requirement that the warrant-issuing judicial officer must determine that the requested inspection falls within existing legislative or administrative standards is intended as a check on arbitrary searches. It responds to the *Camara* majority's stated concern that a warrantless inspection system would "leave the occupant subject to the discretion of the official in the field"—that, as some of the justices earlier put it, inspections may otherwise be "based on caprice or on personal or political spite"[60] or be conducted "only [as] a front for the police."[61] Once again the scarcity of post-*Camara* appellate litigation does not permit a general statement as to precisely how or how effectively this has worked out. It does seem clear, however, as at least one court has insisted, that for this function of the warrant process to be performed the magistrate must be given details about the nature of the inspection program under which the warrant is being sought, for only then can the magistrate determine whether "the desired inspection fits within that program."[62] Had the *Camara* majority made that point more clearly, they would have blunted the dissenters' objection that the majority's scheme contemplated nothing more than "warrants issued by the rubber stamp of a willing magistrate."[63]

Barlow's, the business inspection case, clarifies that the warrant-issuing magistrate is to perform the two functions mentioned above. The required warrant, the Court emphasized, "would provide assurances from a neutral officer that the inspection...is pursuant to an administrative plan containing specific neutral criteria."[64] The determination of "neutral criteria" requires some review of the plan itself, while the "pursuant to" limitation necessitates a judicial determination that the contemplated inspection falls within that plan. This means that a fairly specific legislative or administrative plan against which to judge the individual inspection contemplated must exist, though unfortunately some appellate courts are not that demanding.

Even more unfortunate is that, in practice, the potential for protecting the fourth amendment rights of businesses through a process of judicially reviewed administrative regulation has been largely unrealized because of another development and its curious ramifications. The development concerns the question of when a business inspection is constitutional absent a warrant. In this area, as in other branches of fourth amendment law, truly exigent circumstances arise in which it would make no sense to insist that a warrant be obtained prior to the search. But in the business inspection field the tendency has been to overstate what circumstances are in fact "exigent." *Donovan v. Dewey*[65] is illustrative. Starting with the congressional finding that safety hazards in mines can be easily concealed, the Court took this to mean that "unannounced, even frequent, inspections" were necessary, which in turn led the Court to the conclusion that, therefore, a warrant requirement would "frustrate inspection." But if, as the Court earlier noted in *Barlow's*, a need for frequent inspections does not mean frequent search warrant applications because most businessmen will cooperate and permit the inspection when the inspector first appears sans warrant, then it is still not apparent that a warrant requirement, limited to the few cases in which the inspector is turned away, would "frustrate" the program. And as for those few, the asserted need for "unannounced" inspections cannot be taken seriously, given the other characteristics of the legislative scheme.[66] Cases such as *Dewey* are troublesome, because it appears that the actual feasibility of obtaining a warrant has little or nothing to do with whether a fourth amendment warrant requirement is recognized.

The absence of a business inspection warrant requirement does not diminish the need for a grounds-for-search standard, as it is still important that inspectors have a basis for assessing what they may do and that a magistrate in a suppression hearing have a basis on which to judge the lawfulness of the inspection. But this logical proposition finds little support in the Supreme Court's warrantless inspection cases. Although the Court in

Dewey does not expressly state that the fact "unannounced, even frequent, inspections are essential" also forecloses inquiry into why the inspector chose this business on this occasion, the implication is that it does, for the Court insists it is not dealing with an inspection scheme that (as in *Barlow's*) confers "almost unbridled discretion" on the inspectors. But in fact, the statutory scheme upheld in *Dewey* does not impose any limits on mine inspectors concerning when or how often any particular mine will be inspected, and thus an administrative plan is still needed. This is equally true of *New York v. Burger*, holding warrantless inspections conducted by police lawful because the "statute informs the operator of a vehicle dismantling business that inspections will be made on a regular basis."[67] The truth, however, as the three dissenters pointed out, is this:

> Neither the statute, nor any regulations, nor any regulatory body, provides limits or guidance on the selection of vehicle dismantlers for inspection. In fact the State could not explain why Burger's operation was selected for inspection....This is precisely what was objectionable about the inspection scheme [in *Barlow's*]: It failed to "provide any standards to guide inspectors either in their selection of establishments to be searched or in the exercise of their authority to search."[68]

Because the no-warrant holding has typically been grounded in the need for "unannounced, even frequent, inspections," perhaps the majority in cases like *Dewey* and *Burger* assume that in such circumstances the *Barlow's* neutral plan approach simply does not apply. So the argument might go, if the inspection scheme requires "frequent" inspections at the businesses covered, then there is already such a pervasive degree of scrutiny and control that it is unnecessary to impose a limitation intended merely as a check against arbitrary selection or concentration. But surely this is not so. For example, even accepting the correctness of the holding in *Dewey* that no warrant is ever required for a mine safety inspection, it hardly follows from this that a particular mine operator may be subjected to, say, ten times as many inspections as the operator's competitors without the government at any point being required to justify this degree of attention. The Supreme Court needs to say so and, in the process, to restore law enforcement policymaking to its rightful place in federal, state, and local inspection activities. Only in that way will reasonable assurances exist (1) that there actually is an inspection program and that expertise has been brought to bear on its formulation; (2) that this program is sufficiently visible to give householders and businesspersons an awareness of what intrusions they may fairly be subjected to, a factor emphasized in the Supreme Court's inspection decisions; and (3) that householders and businesspersons are effectively protected against arbitrary inspection practices.

STOPS: BY "PLAN" OR BY "PROFILE"

Prior to *Terry v. Ohio,* courts were inclined to treat all seizures of the person in exactly the same way. They were "arrests" and consequently could be made only on the traditional quantum of probable cause. But in *Terry* the Court utilized the *Camara* balancing test to support the conclusion that a brief detention on the street for investigation is much less intrusive than a full-fledged station house arrest and consequently is sometimes permissible even absent grounds to make an arrest. From *Terry* emerged the new issue of what facts and circumstances would justify a brief detention on the street. *Terry* also recognized that what it called "street encounters" constituted a low-visibility activity utilized for a variety of purposes and was readily subject to abuse, including "wholesale harassment [of minorities] by certain elements of the police community." The case thus gave rise to special "concern over the need to structure the officer's exercise of discretion,"[69] which quite naturally leads to the question whether courts have perceived police guidelines as being essential or useful for determining when a *Terry* stop is permissible.

Terry itself contains no hints about the apposition of police rules and policies to the just-emerging doctrine. Indeed, the Court said very little about the standard governing brief street detentions other than that their "limitations will have to be developed in the concrete factual circumstances of individual cases." But in its later cases the Court recognized that such a stop might be found lawful on either of two different bases: (1) an individualized suspicion basis, as reflected in the Court's declaration in *United States v. Cortez*[70] that an "assessment...based upon all the circumstances,...seen and weighed...as understood by those versed in the field of law enforcement..., must raise a suspicion that the particular individual being stopped is engaged in wrongdoing";[71] or (2) a standardized procedures basis, as reflected in the assertion of a unanimous Court in *Brown v. Texas* that a brief detention for investigation could "be carried out pursuant to a plan embodying explicit, neutral limitations on the conduct of individual officers."[72] This "plan" alternative is reminiscent of the "standard procedures" and "administrative standards" approaches discussed previously, and consequently it will be examined first.

Although the Court in *Brown* did not elaborate on its dictum, an insight into what the Court apparently was alluding to is revealed by the earlier decision in *Delaware v. Prouse*.[73] The Court there was concerned with a so-called routine stopping of a vehicle to check its registration and the operator's driver's license, done without a reasonable suspicion the car was being operated in violation of law and not "pursuant to any standards, guidelines, or procedures pertaining to document spot checks." The Court held that individual stops were permissible only upon individualized reasonable suspicion, but then added: "This holding does not preclude the State of Delaware or other States from developing methods for spot checks that involve less intrusion or that do not involve the unconstrained exercise of discretion. Questioning of all oncoming traffic at roadblock-type stops is one possible alternative."[74]

Justice Rehnquist, the lone dissenter, objected that the Court, in finding that "motorists, apparently like sheep, are much less likely to be 'frightened' or 'annoyed' when stopped en masse," had "elevate[d] the adage 'misery loves company' to a novel role in Fourth Amendment jurisprudence."[75] But the majority in *Prouse* is correct. For one thing, under the *Camara* balancing-of-interests formula, there *is* a genuine difference in degree-of-intrusion terms between an individual stop and a roadblock stop. As the Court correctly stated in another case upholding checkpoint operations conducted to discover illegal aliens: "At traffic checkpoints the motorist can see that other vehicles are being stopped, he can see visible signs of the officers' authority, and he is much less likely to be frightened or annoyed by the intrusion."[76] For another, random stops without reasonable suspicion are different as a constitutional matter precisely because they do not safeguard citizens against "indiscriminate official interference."[77]

Finally, the distinction drawn by the *Prouse* majority makes sense in terms of representative reinforcement, which "[i]n the context of the fourth amendment [means] that the tradeoff between privacy and law enforcement produced by our political institutions should stand, provided that everyone's interests are equally represented in the making of these political decisions."[78] If it is thus true that the police can be afforded greater leeway "when the privacy costs of law enforcement are spread more widely, and there is a reduced risk that the politically less powerful are being forced to bear disproportionate privacy losses," then we have

> a plausible rationale for the Court's decision [in *Prouse*]. We should be worried that the police on patrol will disproportionately stop the young, the black, and the poor for suspicionless license checks. Those with more political clout will be spared the indignity and inconvenience of these checks. By requiring that the police use full roadblocks, the cost of law enforcement is more widely distributed, and there is less reason to fear that the governmental decisions to trade off privacy for law enforcement are being made without considering everyone's interests equally.[79]

These reasons supporting the *Prouse* roadblock thesis also lend support to the notion that police regulations concerning roadblocks should be encouraged—perhaps even mandated—by the courts. Law enforcement guidelines regarding when, where, and how roadblocks are to be conducted can serve to ensure that the practice has greater visibility and thus is as unthreatening as possible, that unnecessary discretion has not been left to officers on the scene, and that a considered judgment was made by departmental policymakers about exactly how much of an intrusion on the public at large is feasible—including in a political sense—in the interest of law enforcement. In its truncated discussion of roadblocks in *Prouse*, the Court unfortunately said nothing about whether law enforcement guidelines were necessary or desirable in the conducting of roadblocks. But the Court significantly distinguished the random stop in *Prouse* from the alien-check roadblock earlier approved by the Court in *United States v. Martinez-Fuerte*,[80] a case that stresses the significance of law enforcement policies regarding roadblock operations. Moreover, lower courts increasingly are taking positions that make it necessary or advantageous for the police to engage in careful rule making concerning driver's license and automobile registration checkpoints.

The Supreme Court addressed the roadblock issue more directly in *Michigan Dept. of State Police v. Sitz*, upholding the department's sobriety checkpoint program under which "checkpoints are selected pursuant to...guidelines, and uniformed police officers stop every approaching vehicle."[81] In rejecting the state court's conclusion that the checkpoint program was unconstitutional under the *Brown v. Texas* balancing test because it failed the "effectiveness" part of that test, the Court stated:

> The actual language from *Brown v. Texas*, upon which the Michigan courts based their evaluation of "effectiveness," describes the balancing factor as "the degree to which the seizure advances the public interest." This passage from *Brown* was not meant to transfer from politically accountable officials to the courts the decision as to which among reasonable alternative law enforcement techniques should be employed to deal with a serious public danger. Experts in police science might disagree over which of several methods of apprehending drunken drivers is preferable as an ideal. But for purposes of Fourth Amendment analysis, the choice among such reasonable alternatives remains with the governmental officials who have a unique understanding of, and a responsibility for, limited public resources, including a finite number of police officers. [82]

This passage from *Sitz* may be read as encouraging policy-making at the police level, for it reflects a disinclination by the Court to second-guess certain kinds of law enforcement decisions. It also explains or at least intimates the kinds of law enforcement policies that are most likely to receive such deference. For one thing, the Court indicates that the challenged practice arose out of a decision concerning how best to utilize "limited public resources," a kind of police decision that presumably ought to receive considerable respect. For another, the Court emphasizes the propriety of leaving the decision to employ sobriety checkpoints with "politically accountable officials." That squares with the previously discussed concept of representative reinforcement: the decision was, in effect, a decision to enforce the DWI laws by placing a burden on the motoring public at large, and consequently it is the kind of law enforcement decision for which the political process presumably affords an effective check.

Viewed more broadly, however, *Sitz* is rather disappointing. It does *not* reflect a commitment by the Court either to take full account of relevant police guidelines or to submit those guidelines to meaningful judicial review. The necessity for doing either is virtually assumed out of existence by the slight of hand manifested in the *Sitz* excerpt set forth above. By asserting that the case involves nothing more than a decision belonging *entirely* to the police to choose from among what are conclusively characterized as "reasonable alternative law enforcement techniques," the Court finds it unnecessary to assay or even articulate all of the considerations that entered into the law enforcement judgment that checkpoints constitute a "reasonable alternative." That judgment, if made within the framework of *Brown v. Texas*, would be that the benefits of the contemplated practice outweigh its intrusiveness.

But just how intrusive a roadblock is depends, as noted earlier, on the safeguards attending its operation—those that minimize the impact of the seizures on motorists and those that eliminate the risk of arbitrary action by those operating the checkpoint, as reflected in applicable police guidelines. Were there guidelines in *Sitz*? Yes; as the Court noted, an advisory committee "comprising representatives of the State Police force, local police forces, state prosecutors, and the University of Michigan Transportation Research Institute...created guidelines setting forth procedures governing checkpoint operations, site selection, and publicity."[83] However, the *Sitz* majority deemed it unnecessary to reveal in what manner those guidelines minimized the intrusiveness of the checkpoint operation, except to note the extremely important requirement that "[a]ll vehicles passing through a checkpoint would be stopped." This disinterest in the existing guidelines in *Sitz* sharply contrasts to many of the earlier lower court decisions regarding sobriety checkpoints. In those decisions, courts generally accepted that these roadblocks must be established by a plan, formulated or approved by executive-level officers of the law enforcement agency involved, that contains standards with regard to time, place, and similar matters.

As for the perceived benefits underlying the decision by Michigan law enforcement authorities to utilize sobriety checkpoints, the opinion of the *Sitz* majority is again wanting. True, the Court says "empirical data" support the checkpoint's efficiency and then points to trial testimony "that experience in other States demonstrated that, on the whole, sobriety check-points resulted in drunken driving arrests of around 1 percent of all motorists stopped."[84] To this, the three dissenters cogently respond (1) that "there is absolutely no evidence that this figure represents an increase over the number of arrests that would have been made by using the same law enforcement resources in conventional patrols"[85] and (2) that in any event the benefit artic-ulated by law enforcement witnesses at trial was instead deter-rence, about which no evidence was offered. Obviously, mean-ingful judicial review of law enforcement policies cannot occur in such circumstances.

Whether *Terry* stops pursuant to a "plan" rather than on individualized suspicion are permissible in somewhat different situations is unclear. In *Brown v. Texas*, where the Supreme Court asserted that either individualized suspicion or a plan embodying explicit, neutral limitations on the conduct of indi-vidual officers was required by the fourth amendment, the invali-dated stop was of a pedestrian whom two policemen on midday patrol saw walking away from another man in an alley in an area with a high incidence of drug traffic. Because the Court's "plan" thesis was set out in this context, it raises the question of whether stops without individualized reasonable suspicion but pursuant to a neutral plan would be lawful if undertaken for more generalized or more traditional enforcement purposes, where the usual practice has been to focus on particular suspects; that is, if in *Brown* it had been established that the officers stopped the defendant pursuant to a police department "plan" to question all pedestrians found in the "high drug problem area," would the outcome have been different? Most likely not. For one thing, the "high drug problem area" in most municipalities would be an area populated by minorities, and thus this police policy could not be supported by the previously discussed repre-sentation-reinforcement theory. Put differently, this would not be an instance in which a uniform policy had substantially reduced the "risk that the politically less powerful are being forced to bear disproportionate privacy losses."[86] Moreover, this does not seem to be the kind of policy that would in fact substantially eliminate discretion by officers in the field, for the simple reason that stopping *all* pedestrians probably would be well beyond police capabilities. However, if in other circumstances a "plan" could somehow be more carefully and tightly formulated, reflecting application of police expertise in a more particular fashion, then there would be good reason to look with favor on this kind of law enforcement planning by police agencies.[87]

Turning now to the other variety of *Terry* stop, that made on individualized reasonable suspicion, one must ask once again about the actual and potential contribution of police guidelines in articulating clear and proper standards of police conduct. At least as an abstract matter, it seems that administrative regulations on this subject would be helpful. If, as the Supreme Court has emphasized, the requisite degree of suspicion depends upon the evidence "as understood by those versed in the field of law enforcement,"[88] then surely this expertise can be brought to bear not only through the experiences of individual officers in the field but also by the collective learning of the agency as revealed in announced policies. In addition, law enforcement regulations on what amounts to reasonable suspicion might give appellate courts "full appreciation" of the "overall impact and implications" of specific investigative activities and might "govern the exercise of discretion" by police, or so argued one judge with respect to the common practice of DEA agents stopping suspected drug couriers at airports.[89] But the experience of courts with the law enforcement guidelines that emerged in that precise area, the so-called drug courier profile, raises profound questions about what can be accomplished by rules governing this sort of police activity. Profiles are

> an increasingly popular law enforcement tool. Most prominent among the profiles in use today are those used to identify hijackers and those used to identify persons who smuggle illegal aliens into the country. Less prominent are the drug smuggling vessel profile, the stolen car profile, the stolen truck profile, the alimentary-canal smuggler profile, the battering parent profile, and the poacher profile.[90]

But in terms of frequency of use by law enforcement officers and frequency of confrontation by appellate courts, none matches the drug courier profile. "Between 1976 and 1986 over 140 reported cases involved airport stops by DEA agents based on the 'drug courier profile.'"[91] The content of the profile seems not to have always remained constant (which is one of the criticisms of it), but as most commonly confronted in the cases the profile consists of seven primary and four secondary characteristics:

The seven primary characteristics are: (1) arrival from or departure to an identified source city; (2) carrying little or no luggage, or large quantities of empty suitcases; (3) unusual itinerary, such as rapid turn-around time for a very lengthy airplane trip; (4) use of an alias; (5) carrying unusually large amounts of currency in the many thousands of dollars, usually on their person, in briefcases or bags; (6) purchasing airline tickets with a large amount of small denomination currency; and (7) unusual nervousness beyond that ordinarily exhibited by passengers.

The secondary characteristics are: (1) the almost exclusive use of public transportation, particularly taxicabs, in departing from the airport; (2) immediately making a telephone call after deplaning; (3) leaving a false or fictitious call-back telephone number with the airline being utilized; and (4) excessively frequent travel to source or distribution cities.[92]

The Supreme Court's most recent lucubration regarding this profile is *United States v. Sokolow*,[93] holding the police had grounds to stop the defendant as a suspected drug courier on the particular cluster of characteristics present in that case. In marked contrast to some of the Supreme Court cases previously discussed, *Sokolow* does not express any deference toward the law enforcement guidelines—that is, the drug courier profile—relied on by the DEA agents. Indeed, the Court framed the issue not as being whether the profile somehow counted in the government's favor, but rather as whether the profile counted *against* the government. No, the majority responded: "A court sitting to determine the existence of reasonable suspicion must require the agent to articulate the factors leading to that conclusion, but the fact that these factors may be set forth in a 'profile' does not somehow detract from their evidentiary significance as seen by a trained agent."[94] But this was not good enough for the two dissenters, Marshall and Brennan. Though on other occasions (for example, in *Bertine)* these two Justices had decried the failure of administrative regulations to confine police discretion sufficiently, this time their concern was that the profile tended to discourage individual exercise of discretion! They objected:

> It is highly significant that the DEA agents stopped Sokolow because he matched one of the DEA's "profiles" of a paradigmatic drug courier....[A] law enforcement officer's mechanistic application of a formula of personal and behavioral traits in

deciding whom to detain can only dull the officer's ability and determination to make sensitive and fact-specific inferences "in light of his experience," particularly in ambiguous or border-line cases. Reflexive reliance on a profile of drug courier characteristics runs a far greater risk than does ordinary, case-by-case police work of subjecting innocent individuals to unwarranted police harassment and detention.[95]

Though at first such a judicial assessment of law enforcement policy might strike one as curious at best, on reflection the seeming incongruity vanishes. For one thing, the profile differs substantially from the law enforcement guidelines discussed earlier. The others occasionally involve factual determinations of a general nature (for example: Is this a sensible location to place an immigration checkpoint? Is this a sensible place to put a sobriety checkpoint?), but in the main they call for essentially policy judgments (for example: Is there a need to impounded all arrestees' cars, or should some simply be left at the scene? With available resources how often should we inspect auto dismantling shops?). The profile, on the other hand, is intended to establish which air travelers are probably drug couriers, and this is a specific factual determination, that is, one concerning the sufficiency of suspicion regarding particular individuals. Before courts readily accept that kind of law enforcement guideline, they are certainly obliged "to require that the government provide satisfactory empirical evidence that the profile is 'valid' and actually 'works.'"[96] No such showing has been made.

A second reason the drug courier profile deservedly has not received deference from the appellate courts is that it fails to limit meaningfully the discretion of agents in the field (or, more precisely, in the airport). For one thing, as the lower court noted in *Sokolow*, the profile has a "chameleon-like way of adapting to any particular set of observations."[97] As another court put it, "there is no such thing as a single drug courier profile; there are infinite drug courier profiles. The very notion is protean, not monolithic."[98] This is why the profiles tell us that it is suspicious to get off an airplane first *or* last *or* in between, and this is also why they are an object of ridicule. For another thing, the profile does not predetermine just what combination of suspicious factors must exist for a lawful stop, an especially critical matter as some of those factors (for example, traveling from a source city) "describe a very large category of presumably innocent travelers."[99] Given this latter problem, it appears that the lower court's efforts in *Sokolow* to distinguish "ongoing criminal activity factors" (at least one of which would be required in every case) from "personal characteristics" were a meaningful response to such amphibolic law enforcement guidelines.[100]

ARRESTS: POLICE LIMITS ON FORCE AND CUSTODY

Of the important decisions a police officer must make, none carries potential consequences more serious than the determination whether to employ force against a suspect to make an arrest. A mistaken failure to utilize force may result in escape of the offender and, in some instances, subsequent serious harm to others. A mistaken use of force, especially a firearm, may result in serious injury to or even the death of the suspect or bystanders. Moreover, police use of firearms to apprehend suspects often strains community relations or even results in serious disturbances. No wonder, then, that this subject is a matter of special concern to responsible police administrators and that, contrary to the situation at the time of the ABF survey, police guidelines on the use of force are now very common.

When the Supreme Court decided under what circumstances police may constitutionally resort to deadly force in attempting to make an arrest, the Court made use of law enforcement policies in an unusual way. The case was *Tennessee v. Garner*,[101] a wrongful death action brought under the federal civil rights statute. A Memphis police officer had shot and killed an unarmed youth fleeing from the burglary of an unoccupied house. The officer's actions conformed to a state law following the common-law rule, which (as the Court noted) "allowed the use of whatever force was necessary to effect the arrest of a fleeing felon." The action also conformed to police department policy, which was slightly more restrictive but still allowed use of deadly force in cases of burglary. It was not this particular police regulation that grabbed the attention of the Court, however, but rather the pattern revealed in the regulations of other departments across the country:

> Overwhelmingly, these are more restrictive than the common-law rule....A 1974 study reported that the police department regulations in a majority of the large cities of the United States allowed the firing of a weapon only when a felon presented a

threat of death or serious bodily harm....Overall, only 7.5% of departmental and municipal policies explicitly permit the use of deadly force against any felon; 86.8% explicitly do not.[102]

The Court concluded that this narrower position rather than the common-law rule squared with the fourth amendment.

In reaching this result, which was urged on the Supreme Court by many police groups, the Justices found the police guidelines highly relevant in several respects. First, said the Court, "[i]n light of the rules adopted by those who must administer them, the older and fading common law view is a dubious indicium of the constitutionality of the Tennessee statute now before us." This reliance on the police regulations and, in addition, modern statutes on the subject, apparently constituted "an open effort to divine a national trend or consensus concerning the common law rule."[103] This is not to suggest that "the Court was doing nothing more than acting prudently to cover its political flank."[104] Rather, as one perceptive commentator has noted,

> the Court's concern with current practice is both defensible and suggestive of a process that is quite sophisticated. For if the Court is engaged in the explication of values, it makes very good sense to refer to and be guided by the value judgments of other societal decision makers....Thus,...interpretation need not flow from the top down, but may come from the bottom up as well. Indeed, this vertical dialogue is especially appropriate to a process of constitutional interpretation that implicates society's values.[105]

Second, the Court utilized the array of police regulations to rebut arguments by Tennessee that the Court's restrictive standard was impracticable. Asserting that "[w]e would hesitate to declare a police practice of long standing 'unreasonable' if doing so would severely hamper effective law enforcement,"[106] the *Garner* Court concluded, in effect, that widespread existence of the narrower rule in police guidelines demonstrated the absence of such adverse effects. Specifically, the Court noted there had been "no suggestion that crime has worsened in any way in jurisdictions that have adopted, by legislation or departmental policy, rules similar to that announced today."[107] As for the contention that the Court's rule "requires the police to make impossible, split-second evaluations of unknowable facts," the Court responded that "this claim must be viewed with suspicion in light of the similar self-imposed limitations of so many police departments."[108]

Whether the unique use of police regulations found in *Garner* is likely to be repeated in future cases is unclear, though I doubt it will become a common occurrence. There are probably not that many other policy areas in which a consensus will emerge from the police regulations as clearly as in *Garner*. Further, this collective judgment about what the police should or should not do is likely to carry the weight it did in *Garner* only when, as there, it tends to demonstrate that the police are operating more narrowly than existing law would permit. The police establishment was vitally interested in making such a showing in *Garner*, as events had made it politically necessary for law enforcement authorities to circumscribe their deadly force authority more narrowly than the law already demanded. But no comparable pressures exist as to most other search and seizure practices, especially those that lack the inherent visibility of the use of firearms against fleeing felons. But *Garner* does demonstrate that police regulations can strongly influence how the Court comes out on an important issue of constitutional policy when those regulations are adequately presented to the Court, which is an important lesson for *both* prosecutors and defense attorneys to learn.

Although the existence and content of police regulations were very much in the forefront in the *Garner* Court's analysis, quite the opposite was true in two of the Court's other arrest cases: *United States v. Robinson*[109] and its companion, *Gustafson v. Florida*.[110] In *Robinson*, a District of Columbia police officer arrested the defendant for operating a motor vehicle after revocation of his operator's permit, searched the defendant incident to that arrest, and discovered heroin inside a cigarette package in the left breast pocket of the defendant's coat. In a footnote, the Court observed that a general order of the D.C. Metropolitan Police Department mandated custodial arrest for this type of traffic violation and that established procedures in the department required a search of those arrested, but then the Court admonished that "[s]uch operating procedures are not, of course, determinative of the constitutional issues presented by this case."[111] The defendant contended that the bases for search incident to arrest—to find evidence of the crime for which the arrest was made and to find any weapons the arrestee might use to escape—did not exist in this case. The Court responded that it disagreed with the "suggestion that there must be litigated in each case the issue of whether or not there was present one of the reasons supporting the authority for a search of the person incident to a lawful arrest." Thus, concluded the *Robinson* Court, in every "case of a lawful custodial arrest a full search of the person is not only an exception to the warrant requirement of the Fourth Amendment, but is also a 'reasonable' search under that Amendment."[112]

In *Gustafson*, where marijuana cigarettes were found on the defendant's person following his arrest for not having his operator's license with him while driving, the defendant claimed his case was different from *Robinson* in several respects, including that there were no applicable police regulations requiring the officer to take the defendant into custody or to make a full-scale body search incident to arrest. The Court summarily dismissed that argument with the observation that these differences were not "determinative of the constitutional issue."

There is good reason to be concerned about the *Robinson-Gustafson* holding that every custodial arrest, even for a minor traffic violation, permits a full search of the arrestee's person. There is good reason to be even more concerned with the Court's later holding in *New York v. Belton* that in every instance in which "a policeman has made a lawful custodial arrest of the occupant of an automobile, he may, as a contemporaneous incident of that arrest, search the passenger compartment of that automobile."[113] In all such instances, as the *Robinson* dissenters emphasized, "there is always the possibility that a police officer, lacking probable cause to obtain a search warrant, will use a traffic arrest as a pretext to conduct a search."[114] Given that very few drivers can traverse any appreciable distance without violating some traffic regulation, this is indeed a frightening possibility. It is apparent that virtually anyone who ventures out onto the public streets and highways may then, with little effort by the police, be placed in a position where his or her person and vehicle are subject to search.

While the *Robinson-Gustafson* tandem is thus objectionable because it leaves unchecked broad police discretion in determining when to make a custodial arrest for a minor traffic violation, consequently subjecting citizens to a substantial risk of an arbitrary arrest and search, that is not the full extent of the harm fairly attributable to those decisions. If, as in *Gustafson*, a custodial arrest is inherently lawful, notwithstanding the existence of a police regulation conferring unbridled discretion either to ticket or to arrest, then it will remain unnecessary for the actual reason for election of the arrest alternative to be articulated in the particular case. The resulting lack of visibility, a rather pervasive characteristic of police conduct in pre-ABF survey days, is itself highly detrimental. This is because visibility, by which the general public and police administrators become cognizant of the basis underlying critical on-the-street decisions by police, is itself a beneficial restraining influence on the law enforcement enterprise. Finally, and most seriously from the perspective of professionalism in law enforcement, *Robinson* and *Gustafson* are objectionable because they discourage, rather than encourage, the application of police expertise to some of the most difficult problems in policing. For example, if the stopping and searching of a person the police suspect of carrying drugs can so readily be papered over with the explanation that the stopped vehicle had a burned-out tail light or had crossed the highway center line, then there is little incentive for police administrators to confront more directly and explicitly issues deserving their careful attention— not only the narrower question of what congeries of facts ought to suffice for a stop of a suspected drug courier, but also the broader question of how and to what extent law enforcement can be expected to respond to the drug problem.

For all these reasons, the proposition that the fourth amendment should be construed to bar custodial arrests for minor violations is an appealing one. Although as yet "the Court has not directly considered the question,"[115] certainly a persuasive claim can be made that custodial arrest for lesser offenses is unconstitutional. The argument is grounded in two important fourth amendment principles discussed earlier—those having to do with preventing arbitrary exercise of government power and those that require balancing the individual privacy interests and governmental interests regarding custodial arrest. This suggests that if the Court ever does reach this question, a *Garner*-style assessment would be in order, in which case the extent to which police regulations across the country do require use of the citation alternative would be most relevant.

Although the Court in *Robinson* and *Gustafson* had no occasion to consider that broader question, it is unfortunate that the Court did not resolve the narrower issue so dramatically posed by the respective state of applicable police regulations in those two cases: whether the control of police discretion in *Robinson* and the absence of control in *Gustafson* was the dominant characteristic in the cases—one that should have produced different rather than identical results in the two decisions. Had the Court reflected more carefully on the proper relevance of law enforcement guidelines in such cases, it might have realized the ineluctable rationality of this syllogism: "Arbitrary searches and seizures are 'unreasonable' searches and seizures; ruleless searches and seizures practiced at the varying and unguided discretion of thousands of individual peace officers are arbitrary searches and seizures; therefore, ruleless searches and seizures are 'unreasonable' searches and seizures."[116] As Professor Amsterdam has so eloquently put it, if "the Court had distinguished the two cases on this ground, it would...have made by far the greatest contribution to the jurisprudence of the fourth amendment since James Otis argued against the writs of assistance in 1761 and 'the child Independence was born.'"[117] Moreover, it is fair to add, the Court would thereby have ensured that police expertise would be brought to bear on the oft-neglected issue of when the criminal process must be invoked by custodial arrest, and that the custody-versus-citation practice would be given the visibility it needs and deserves.

Perhaps the Court's failure to take this step was grounded in the assumption that the risk of arbitrariness in law enforcement may be sufficiently overcome by allowing a defendant to prove that the officer acted from an ulterior motive. But tangible evidence of subjective motivation is difficult for defendants to produce and difficult for courts to assess, which perhaps explains why Justice White was once moved to observe that "sending state and federal courts on an expedition into the minds of police officers would produce a grave and fruitless misallocation of judicial resources."[118] And this may explain why the Supreme Court ultimately held in *Scott v. United States*[119] that fourth amendment issues should be resolved judicially by use of an objective standard.

The application of *Scott* by lower courts to the issue of pretextual fourth amendment activity has produced these results:

1. If the police arrest X for crime A, as they would have in any event, in the anticipation or hope of thereby finding evidence of crime B on X's person, the latter underlying intent or motivation does not make their action illegal.

2. If the police stop X's car for minor offense A, and they subjectively hope to discover contraband during the stop so as to establish serious offense B, the stop is nonetheless lawful if a reasonable officer would have made the stop in the absence of the invalid purpose.

3. If police obtain a search warrant to search X's premises for evidence of crime A, which again they would have done in any event, the search is not illegal merely because the police suspect they might find evidence of crime B.

4. If X's car is searched in the hope or expectation of finding therein evidence of crime B, but that search is an inventory that would have been made in any event or a search for evidence of crime A that would have been made in any event, again the evidence is admissible.

These decisions are sound, for if the action would have occurred in any event, then there is no *conduct* that ought to have been deterred and thus no reason to bring the fourth amendment exclusionary rule into play for purposes of deterrence.

But some of the allegedly pretextual search and seizure cases are of another kind. The driver of an automobile suspected of unlawful drug activity is placed under custodial arrest for a traffic violation and then searched, though the arrest is not "one which would have been made by a traffic officer on routine patrol against any citizen driving in the same manner."[120] A person suspected of drug activity is arrested late at night inside the premises of another by state police holding city arrest warrants for two minor traffic violations, hardly the usual practice in dealing with outstanding traffic warrants.[121] An arrestee's car is impounded and then inventoried "contrary to the usual procedure followed in traffic cases."[122] Situations such as these involve what the Supreme Court has properly characterized as "serious misconduct by law-enforcing officers,"[123] but this does not mean that the *Scott* rule is inapplicable. These and similar fact situations involve "serious misconduct" *in spite of* rather than *because of* the "underlying intent or motivation" of the police; that is, the proper basis of concern is not *why* the officer deviated from the usual practice but simply that he *did* deviate. It is the *fact* of the departure from the accepted way of handling such cases that makes the officer's conduct arbitrary, and it is the arbitrariness that in this context constitutes the fourth amendment violation.

As a result, the question of what police ordinarily do in a particular set of circumstances becomes critical in these so-called pretext cases. Illustrative are the facts in *United States v. Guzman*,[124] where a New Mexico state patrolman stopped a car because the driver did not have his seat belt fastened. The stop led to other events that uncovered cocaine in the car. The court explained that under the rule stated above:

> If police officers in New Mexico are required to and/or do routinely stop most cars they see in which the driver is not wearing his seat belt, then this stop was not unconstitutionally pretextual at its inception, even if Officer Keene subjectively hoped to discover contraband during the stop. Conversely, if officers rarely stop seat belt law violators absent some other reason to stop the car, the objective facts involved in this stop suggest that the stop would not have been made but for a suspicion that could not constitutionally justify the stop.[125]

In *Guzman* no evidence in the record pointed one way or another, as the district judge had erroneously decided in defendant's favor on a subjective state-of-mind theory. This did not require remand, because the appellate court found another basis on which to rule in defendant's favor. But if remand *had* been necessary, then the district court would have had to make a factual determination of whether drivers violating the seat belt law are, on the one hand, "rarely" stopped or, on the other, "routinely" stopped. In such circumstances, as the reference in *Guzman* to when police are "required" to stop such offenders suggests, it is exceedingly important that the litigants and the court focus on the question of whether a police rule on the subject exists. Admittedly a court might find a practice "routine" even absent such a regulation, but when no applicable law enforcement policy exists there is reason to be uneasy about applying the *Scott* approach. Lacking such documentation, testimony by individual officers as to what they perceive as the "routine" in their department carries at least some of the risk that made the intent-of-the-officer approach unpalatable to courts: a significant chance that the truth of the matter will not be accurately established by the self-serving declarations of the officer whose conduct has been challenged. This suggests that this is an area of fourth amendment litigation within which the existence of and reliance on law enforcement regulations take on special importance.

Some courts have given *Scott* a quite different interpretation, with the unfortunate result that pretext contentions are being dismissed even when it is shown (perhaps by evidence of non-compliance with an existing police regulation) that the established "routine" was not followed. These decisions interpret the *Scott* "objective assessment" test as, in effect, eliminating any meaningful way to mount a pretext claim, for they treat as irrelevant *both* the evidence that may exist as to the actual intentions of the police and the evidence that may exist that the officers in this case did not act as they ordinarily do. These courts thus treat police regulations as having no fourth amendment significance. But noncompliance with a police regulation is powerful evidence that the fourth amendment has been violated, for when a defendant has raised a pretext claim the proper question is not whether the officer *could* have acted as he did but rather whether the officer *would* have so acted absent an invalid purpose. Only by putting the proposition this way is it possible to uncover and respond to arbitrary police conduct that, as we have already seen, is one central concern of the fourth amendment.

THE ROLE OF THE COURTS TO DATE

The foregoing critique of some of the Supreme Court's landmark fourth amendment decisions has both an empirical and a theoretical basis. The empirical basis is to be found in the "American Bar Foundation Survey of Criminal Justice," which (as noted at the outset) revealed that two of the most significant characteristics of policing in our society are (1) complexity and (2) discretion. Because of the complexity of the police task, the ABF survey rightly concluded that "the development of police expertness should be encouraged, and its existence should be recognized when appropriate" by "the development of an 'administrative law' in the enforcement field."[126] And because of the broad range of discretion exercised, the survey rightly emphasized the necessity "of recognizing police discretion and of controlling its exercise,"[127] for in a democratic society the discretion allowed public officials cannot be "unconfined and vagrant."[128] Those two concerns collectively prompted one of the most significant recommendations in the ABF survey (often echoed since by commentators and in law reform proposals): that police agencies draft written policies for the guidance of their officers.

Fourth amendment theory points in precisely the same direction. As detailed earlier, two fourth amendment doctrines that are highly relevant to the present topic are (1) that police experience and expertise is properly taken into account in determining which search and seizure practices are not unconstitutional because "unreasonable" and (2) that the discretion of police to conduct searches and seizures must be sufficiently confined and controlled to ensure that those practices are not unconstitutional because "arbitrary." Once again the two considerations support a regime of police rule making. And thus it may be said as both an empirical and a theoretical matter that such rule making is essential *and* that consequently courts should not only encourage (or sometimes mandate) it but also subject the rules that are made to critical review. Only in this way, it seems fair to conclude, are the benefits of police rule making likely to be fully realized. These benefits, as elaborated earlier, are: (1) enhancing the quality of police decisions, (2) ensuring the fair and equal treatment of citizens, (3) increasing the visibility of police decisions, and (4) raising the level of police compliance with and enforcement of constitutional norms.

It is fair to ask at this point whether, in the new regime of police rule making, the courts (especially the Supreme Court) have substantially contributed to a realization of those benefits. The answer quite clearly is no. With respect to the fourth amendment activities of the police, there has been (presumably) a fair amount of police rule making and (unquestionably) a substantial amount of court review of police searches and seizures. Yet the necessary synergism is lacking. Law enforcement guidelines ordinarily do not constitute the centerpiece of this judicial analysis, and therefore it presently cannot be said that rule making has contributed favorably to our fourth amendment jurisprudence, improving in the process the quality, consistency, and visibility of police search and seizure practices. This is so for three significant reasons.

The first reason is *insufficient judicial encouragement of rule making*. "To the extent that the judiciary seeks out police policy as an aid in its own decisionmaking, instead of focusing only on the conduct of the officers involved in a particular case, it can inspire more rulemaking by the police."[129] Such judicial stimulation of rule making is present to a degree in the Supreme Court's opinions, as several fourth amendment doctrines by their nature encourage the adoption of police policies and regulations. Illustrative are the *Bertine* "standardized procedures" rule; the *Camara* "reasonable...administrative standards" requirement; the *Brown* "plan embodying explicit, neutral limitations" concept; and even the *Scott* "objective assessment" test, which lower courts have often interpreted as necessitating inquiry, on a pretext challenge, into whether the police deviated from their usual practice. Special mention must also be made of *Garner*, because it shows that when the law enforcement community takes pains to educate the Court about what is mandated by police regulations across the country, the Court will take notice.

Closer inspection of some of these and other developments, however, supports the conclusion that the Supreme Court has fallen short of doing all that it might have done. The inventory cases, for example, are sufficiently imprecise to lend themselves to the interpretation that departmental rules on impoundment and inventory are not really necessary. Thus in *Opperman* the Court asserts a "standard police procedures" requirement but never refers to or quotes any regulations of the Vermillion Police Department. Indeed, the Court finally refers to the quoted term as if it simply means what police departments generally often do, leaving it to concurring Justice Powell to invoke the protection-against-arbitrariness concern and to note that this concern was met by the Vermillion department's requirement of complete inventory of all impounded vehicles. (Had the Supreme Court instead stated unequivocally that police regulations were a sine qua non of a constitutional inventory practice, most likely the Court would not have been confronted fifteen years later, as it was, with a case in which a major law enforcement agency had "no policy whatever" on inventory of containers.)[130]

As for the inspection cases, the sad fact is that the Court has created a hypertrophic exception to the warrant requirement and then made the worst of a bad situation by assuming that if no warrant is needed administrative regulations are likewise unnecessary. Perhaps even more noteworthy is the Court's improvident failure on other occasions to make police rule making the focal point of a decision. This has occurred both within the context of the exclusionary rule, as with the *Robinson-Gustafson* tandem, and without, as with *Sitz*. The predictable but unfortunate consequence is that meaningful law enforcement policies are often lacking even today with respect to the practices challenged in those cases, meaning that such searches and seizures lack the quality, consistency, and visibility the ABF survey demonstrated was needed.

The second reason that rule making cannot be said to have contributed favorably to fourth amendment jurisprudence is *nonexistent or inadequate judicial evaluation of rules.* A second important function of courts with respect to police regulations is to pass judgment on their reasonableness; even under a rule-making regime, courts "continue to be, as before, the ultimate shield of the citizen from the improper actions of his government."[131] Here as well, the actions of the Supreme Court are less than encouraging, for the Court has kept as much distance from existing police rules as possible. In such cases as *Opperman, Robinson,* and *Gustafson,* extant rules are discussed only within footnotes and then typically only to disclaim their relevance. Similarly, in *Sitz* the Court largely ignored the guidelines that had been promulgated regarding sobriety checkpoints. *Bertine* is unique in that it is the only case in which the defendant specifically challenged a particular departmental regulation, but the Court summarily dismissed the contention by misreading the regulation as containing "standardized criteria guiding an officer's decision to impound a vehicle." In all of these cases, then, there is lacking an evaluation of the applicable regulation sufficient to give it the necessary visibility and to determine its adequacy in both discretion-limiting and expertise-manifesting terms.

The *Sitz* case is especially disappointing, for the majority seems not to have grasped the fact that the existence of police guidelines does not call for total abdication by the Supreme Court of its fourth amendment responsibilities. The police guidelines in *Sitz*, which authorized resort to DWI checkpoints pursuant to procedures mostly unspecified by the Court, were upheld pursuant to the startling proposition that "the choice among such reasonable alternatives" was entirely for "politically accountable officials" to make. In one stroke, the Court thereby managed to avoid any meaningful review of whether the Michigan guidelines (1) sufficiently minimized the intrusion on those stopped at checkpoints or (2) were sufficiently grounded in a showing of the relative predicted effectiveness of checkpoints. If, as the Court earlier stated in *Robinson*, "such operating procedures are not...determinative of the constitutional issues," then *Sitz* falls well short of even the more limited judicial review appropriate within a regime of police rule making.

Exactly what posture *should* a reviewing court take with respect to a police regulation? Surely there is some middle ground between the *Sitz* approach and that of an earlier era when applicable law enforcement guidelines were treated as if they were totally irrelevant. Without suggesting that the analogy is apt in all respects, it would seem that established administrative law doctrine respecting judicial review of administrative action is useful in this setting as well. Under this doctrine, courts give some deference to professional judgment. As the Supreme Court put it in *Youngberg v. Romeo*,[132] "courts must show deference to the judgment exercised by a qualified professional," that is, "a person competent whether by education, training or experience to make a particular decision at issue." If, as in *Romeo*, the professional judgment of administrators in a state hospital regarding appropriate treatment programs is entitled to deference, then surely deference to professional judgment is likewise appropriate as to police officials who (as put in an unobjectionable part of *Sitz*) "have a unique understanding of, and a responsibility for, limited public resources, including a finite number of police officers."

This is not to suggest, however, that invocation of "professional judgment" commands automatic judicial approval of and deference to any and all administrative decisions. Especially if constitutional limitations are at issue (as they most certainly are when police regulations govern fourth amendment activities), the review function of the courts must be performed with sufficient intensity to ensure accountability and fairness in the rule-making process. The rule-making agency must be required to satisfy the court that the decision making leading to the rule at issue was both informed and rational.

Such was the conclusion in the leading administrative law

case of *Motor Vehicle Manufacturers Association v. State Farm Mutual Automobile Insurance Co.*,[133] where insurance companies petitioned for review of an order of the National Highway Traffic Safety Administration (NHTSA) that rescinded a preexisting safety rule requiring that newly manufactured automobiles be equipped with air bags or seat belts. The Supreme Court, agreeing with the court of appeals that NHTSA had failed to show sufficient justification for this action, first decided that a rule modification or rescission was subject to the same intensity of review as standards initially promulgated via informal rule making. The Court then proceeded to elaborate what such review entailed: the burden is on the agency to "cogently explain why it has exercised its discretion in a given manner," and this explanation must be sufficient to enable the court to conclude that the rule "was the product of reasoned decisionmaking." A greater showing is needed "than the minimum rationality a statute must bear in order to withstand analysis under the Due Process Clause," and consequently "the agency must examine the relevant data and articulate a satisfactory explanation for its action, including a 'rational connection between the facts found and the choice made.'"[134] What this means, the Court in *State Farm* added, is that an agency rule cannot survive judicial review "if the agency relied on factors which [it is not allowed] to consider, entirely failed to consider an important aspect of the problem, offered an explanation for its decision that runs counter to the evidence before the agency, or is so implausible that it could not be ascribed to a difference in view or the product of agency expertise." If such "hard look"[135] review is appropriate for the NHTSA decision on passive restraints in vehicles, then surely no lesser judicial scrutiny should suffice regarding the decision of the Michigan Department of State Police to utilize DWI checkpoints to combat drunken driving (or, for that matter, the decisions of other law enforcement agencies as to precisely when inventories, inspections, stops, and custodial arrests are properly undertaken).

The third reason is *failure of litigants to focus on rules and their rationale.* Although clearly the Supreme Court has on several occasions failed to take advantage of existing opportunities either to stimulate police rule making or to subject such rule making to meaningful review, that is not the entire story. Yet another reason why the perceived benefits of police rule making regarding their fourth amendment activities have not yet been fully realized is that very often the appellate courts (including the Supreme Court) are not provided with the information needed to put the specific conduct at issue into the appropriate context. "The fact material which the appellate judicial tribunal has official liberty to consider in making its decision is largely walled in."[136] It consists of the record made below and such data as may be incorporated in a brief, which in most search and seizure cases collectively includes neither the relevant police regulations nor supporting information that would permit a *State Farm*-style hard-look review of the applicable law enforcement policy.

This lack of information may have a profound effect on the way in which the fourth amendment issue before the court is perceived and resolved, as can be illustrated by comparing one of the decisions from my earlier exegesis with a more typical limited-record case. The former is the *Garner* decision, which is an especially attractive example of reliance on rule making to enhance fourth amendment jurisprudence. In that case, because of the information provided in the record and briefs, it was possible for the Supreme Court to place an important decision of an individual officer (to use deadly force) into the context of his department's official policy regarding such conduct and then to place the rule of that department into the context of law enforcement expertise more generally, as reflected in the relevant rules of a great many other police departments. Because so many departments had authorized the use of deadly force in circumstances significantly narrower than allowed at common law, the Court was able to conclude that there was no police necessity supporting continued adherence to the common-law position.

In stark contrast to *Garner* is *New York v. Belton*, where a New York trooper stopped a vehicle for a traffic violation and then, because he believed the occupants were in possession of marijuana, arrested the four occupants and subsequently searched the passenger compartment of that vehicle. At issue was the lawfulness of the vehicle search, which the Supreme Court resolved by announcing the broad rule that in *any* case in which "a policeman has made a lawful custodial arrest of the occupant of an automobile, he may, as a contemporaneous incident of that arrest, search the passenger compartment of that automobile." Why such a broad rule? Because, the Court explained, the police were entitled to a "straightforward rule," which, by implication, the Court indicated was unachievable by any narrower direction to the police expressed in terms of the arrestee's actual access to the vehicle, notwithstanding his arrest.

At precisely this point, the issue in *Belton* seems remarkably similar to that in *Garner*, for an oft-stated justification for the common-law any-felony rule regarding deadly force is that the police are entitled to a clearly stated and easy-to-apply rule—an argument before the Court in *Garner* and urged by the dissenters in that case. That purported justification failed in *Garner* because the Court learned the police had concluded as a rule-making matter that narrower limits on use of deadly force were feasible and could be expressed in departmental regulations. This strongly suggests that before the "straightforward rule" argument should carry the day in *Belton*, it would again be instructive to know what extant police regulations had to say on this matter. Did the trooper's conduct in *Belton* conform to the New York State Police guidelines on when a vehicle may be searched incident to arrest? If not (or even if so), does that rule identify and articulate in reasonably clear fashion specific circumstances short of the all-cases holding in *Belton,* in which an incident-to-arrest vehicle search is permitted? If so (or, even more important, if not), do the rules of *other* law enforcement agencies on this same subject indicate that police have been able to articulate and live with a less expansive vehicle search rule? Despite the relevance of these *Garner*-style queries, the Supreme Court was in no position to pursue them in *Belton*, as the record and briefs did not include the information essential to their resolution.

Belton, of course, was unlike *Garner* in that it did not appear particularly advantageous to the law enforcement community to have those regulations considered *Garner*-fashion by the Supreme Court. But this only highlights the fact that very often it is defense counsel who must take the necessary steps to ensure that these police rules find their way into the record. Of course, to the extent that fourth amendment doctrine makes certain search and seizure activity unconstitutional *unless* it conforms to an adequate regulation (a possibility discussed later herein), the police and prosecution would not benefit by keeping silent on what the applicable rules are and whether they were complied with in the instant case.

The other point here is that, even if a police regulation is put squarely before the Supreme Court (for example, because the defendant is specifically challenging it, as in *Bertine*), chances are the record will lack the supporting information that would facilitate a *State Farm* kind of judicial review. In *Bertine*, the defendant contended "that the inventory search of his van was unconstitutional because departmental regulations gave the police officers discretion to choose between impounding his van and parking and locking it in a public parking place." At that juncture, it would have helped to know precisely why the Boulder Police Department had formulated the impoundment regulations as they had and, specifically, why the department had concluded that the regulations need not provide any guidance on when the impoundment alternative was permissible. Only in this way could the Court determine whether the regulation was sufficiently grounded in police expertise and whether it narrowed police discretion to the extent reasonably practicable. But nothing on these points is in the record, which merely contains some comments by the inventorying officer on his understanding of the purposes underlying the department's inventory procedures.

REMAINING PROBLEM AREAS

Though these three shortcomings make difficult a more particularized critique of rule making in fourth amendment adjudication, a few additional observations are in order. Six problem areas deserve attention.

First is *the significance of compliance with police rules*. The Supreme Court's general disinclination to mandate or assess police rules raises anew the fundamental question of precisely what significance a pertinent law enforcement regulation should have when a court sets out to determine fourth amendment issues in an exclusionary rule context. In part this concerns how compliance with the regulation bears on the issue of suppression. One possible position is that exclusion is unnecessary if the police officer reasonably relied on a rule of the agency. From the standpoint of deterring the officer who made the search or seizure, one can argue that suppression where the officer relied on a police regulation makes no more sense than one where the officer relied on a statute or a warrant covered by the Supreme Court's "good-faith" exceptions to the exclusionary rule in *Illi-*

nois v. Krull[137] and *United States v. Leon.*[138] Moreover, it can be contended that such an extension of the good-faith exception would have the added advantage, even more so than the possible judicial uses of police regulations discussed earlier, of providing police departments with strong encouragement to engage in careful self-study to produce clear and comprehensive rules governing day-to-day police practices. This would actually *advance* the cause of deterrence: "Police will be most effectively deterred from unconstitutional conduct if police departments respond institutionally to search and seizure decisions by continually promulgating field regulations reflective of developing fourth amendment law, and by training officers to follow such regulations."[139] In addition, so the argument proceeds, this would have the added benefit of focusing the exclusionary rule on instances in which there were institutional failures to protect fourth amendment rights, for (assuming the individual officer complied with the existing policy) the costs of evidence suppression would quite properly not be imposed if "the police department in question has taken seriously its responsibility to adhere to the fourth amendment."[140] So focused, the exclusionary rule would have a much more solid grounding, for it would "be based upon an institutional, or systemic, view of deterrence."[141]

Although these are rather compelling arguments, it is nonetheless doubtful whether such use of police regulations in fourth amendment adjudication is desirable. The Supreme Court in *Leon* and *Krull* asserted that the fourth amendment exclusionary rule has no application to judges and legislators, as it does to police. These distinctions were of central importance in the Court's analysis and in the result reached in these two cases. But it cannot as plausibly be asserted that the exclusionary rule is not directed to those upper-level police officials who are responsible for formulating law enforcement policies touching on fourth amendment rights. It may be true that police administrators, as compared to officers on the beat, are not directly "engaged in the often competitive enterprise of ferreting out crime"[142] and thus are less tempted to cut corners. Yet there is no apparent empirical basis for concluding that law enforcement personnel at the policymaking level are so intensely committed to fourth amendment values that they can always be trusted to draft regulations that sufficiently respect those values. As a result, one can hardly be sanguine about the prospects of such draftsmanship if those officials know—which would be the message of a good-faith exception operating in this area—that even if a regulation does not satisfy the requirements of the amendment, it will nonetheless provide "a grace period during which police may freely perform unreasonable searches."[143]

The suggestion here is *not* that some judgment must be made about the malevolence level of police administrators as compared to, on the one hand, judges and legislators and, on the other, beat patrolmen. The fourth amendment is not concerned merely with calculated and deliberate noncompliance with the amendment's proscriptions, and thus the exclusionary rule is also applicable to the more common fourth amendment violations resulting from carelessness. As the Supreme Court recognized in *Stone v. Powell*, what the exclusionary rule demonstrates is "that our society attaches serious consequences to violation of constitutional rights," which encourages those making critical search-and-seizure decisions "to incorporate Fourth Amendment ideals into their value system."[144] In other words, the exclusionary rule serves not only to deter the occasional ill-spirited officer but, more importantly, to influence police behavior generally by—as the Court put it in *United States v. Johnson*—creating an "incentive to err on the side of constitutional behavior."[145]

As discussed earlier, there are many other ways, without such an extension of the good-faith exception, in which police regulations in fact are and potentially might be brought to bear in a meaningful way on the adjudication of fourth amendment issues. Thus it is especially important that those officers responsible for preparing and promulgating these regulations do "incorporate Fourth Amendment ideals into their value system" and, when in doubt, "err on the side of constitutional behavior." The importance of such a frame of reference is further highlighted by the much greater potential an ill-drafted regulation carries for harm than the single mistake by an officer in the field, which ordinarily affects but one person. In this and other ways, "Fourth Amendment violations become more, not less, reprehensible when they are the product of Government policy rather than an individual policeman's errors of judgment."[146] That is why "any rule intended to prevent Fourth Amendment violations must operate not only upon individual law enforcement officers but also upon those who set policy for them."[147] On balance, grounding a good-faith exception to the exclusionary rule in reliance on police regulations is undesirable.

The second problem area is *the significance of noncompliance with police rules.* What then should be the result in an exclusionary rule context if it is shown that the search or seizure at issue did not comply with some extant and applicable police regulation? Certainly relevant to this issue is *United States v. Caceres,*[148] holding that the failure of an IRS agent to follow IRS electronic surveillance regulations did not require suppression. The Court reasoned that it could not "ignore the possibility that a rigid application of an exclusionary rule to every regulatory violation could have a serious deterrent impact on the formulation of additional standards to govern prosecutorial and police procedures," and it concluded that, "[i]n the long run, it is far better to have rules like those contained in the IRS Manual, and to tolerate occasional erroneous administration of the kind displayed by this record, than either to have no rules except those mandated by statute, or to have them framed in a mere precatory form."[149] This reasoning is rather compelling and seems particularly applicable in the present context, where the police, via rule making, have imposed limits on their own authority beyond those the courts could be expected to inflict as a matter of fourth amendment doctrine.

Clearly, however, this laissez faire approach is not appropriate for all forms of fourth amendment activity, because sometimes the existence of and compliance with administrative regulations is (or ought to be) the very warp and woof of the controlling doctrine. If, as seems to be the case, the *Bertine* "standardized procedures" doctrine is intended both to ensure against arbitrary searches and seizures and to permit departments the opportunity to determine in the first instance how the legitimate objectives of the inventory process can best be served, then surely both the existence of reasonable regulations and compliance with those regulations are prerequisites to a finding of constitutional conduct. Similarly, if the inspection cases mean that when the authorities want to be able to conduct inspections absent individualized suspicion they must act pursuant to "reasonable standards" adopted by legislation or administrative regulation, once again the existence of and conformance to those limits are essential to a finding of "reasonableness" under the fourth amendment. The same may be said of the stop-and-frisk power, where police lacking individualized reasonable suspicion must act pursuant to "a plan embodying explicit, neutral limitations."

In a sense, even the *Scott* doctrine is of this character, for it will not do for the police to contend that on a pretext challenge the courts may inquire into neither their subjective intentions nor whether the conduct deviated from usual practice, as reliably reflected in extant police regulations. Indeed, even absent a pretext challenge, it would seem that the *Robinson-Gustafson* type of situation is one in which conformance with an adequate police regulation should be viewed as essential to a finding of constitutionality. Given the fact that not *all* minor traffic offenses result in arrest, it is appropriate to require that police agencies (1) bring their expertise to bear on the important issue of when custodial arrest is the necessary means of invoking the criminal process for such violations and then (2) delimit the arrest authority of their patrol officers accordingly.

A harder question is whether noncompliance with regulations should be determinative in other fourth amendment circumstances. Consider, for example, execution of a search warrant at premises known to be unoccupied, an action the courts have quite consistently upheld. A police department might for good reason adopt a regulation limiting the circumstances in which warrant execution in the absence of an occupant is permissible. If such a regulation is violated in a particular case, should this require suppression of the evidence obtained in execution of the warrant? The logic of *Caceres* would suggest the answer is no. This would ensure that rule making is not discouraged and yet would not require that courts maintain a disinterest in *compliance* with existing police regulations; that is, even if the failure to comply with a police regulation governing when unoccupied premises may be entered does not per se mandate suppression, compliance with the regulation on another occasion certainly deserves consideration in deciding that the warrant execution process was carried out in a reasonable fashion.

Though all this suggests that the *Caceres* approach is best, there is another possible alternative, which, however, lies somewhat beyond current fourth amendment law. "There remains," as Judge McGowan wrote, "the interesting, albeit presently unresolvable, question of whether the judicial power could be exerted to compel the police to proceed by rule-making."[150] Under this approach, as its principal advocate Amsterdam explains,

> (1) Unless a search or seizure is conducted pursuant to and in conformity with either legislation or police departmental rules and regulations, it is an unreasonable search and seizure prohibited by the fourth amendment. (2) The legislation or police-made rules must be reasonably particular in setting forth the nature of the searches and seizures and the circumstances under which they should be made.[151]

Certainly this alternative deserves further consideration. It would extend the advantages of police rule making across the entire breadth of fourth amendment activity and, of course, would nullify the rationale of *Caceres*, as suppression for nonconformance with rules would not deter rule making if the rule making itself was constitutionally compelled.

The third problem area is *the context of judicial evaluation*. In an exclusionary rule context, as illustrated by *Opperman*, *Bertine*, *Robinson*, and *Gustafson*, the Supreme Court has failed to focus on the applicable police regulations as intensely as it might have. As previously noted, the fault may not be entirely that of the Court, for there is no tradition in such cases for the litigants to put the issues in a manner that would naturally direct attention to the entire range of activity covered by a specific police regulation. "Lawyers striving for victory in adversary litigation cannot be expected invariably to put 'the individual case in the context of the overall enforcement policy involved.'"[152]

Although one would hope that this will change over time as police rule making becomes more commonplace, it may be that the judicial review function would be better performed in another context. Because "judicial review is most effective if it relates to carefully developed administrative policies rather than to the sporadic actions of individual police officers,"[153] perhaps a more direct judicial review prompted by an injunction or declaratory judgment action is preferable. *Sitz*, however, illustrates that meaningful review is not a certainty even in this context. Although the Court there emphasized that it was the sobriety checkpoint program on its face, rather than some particular seizure under the program, that was at issue, the Court nonetheless failed to scrutinize all the program's relevant guidelines.

Another possibility would be some form of judicial review after promulgation but before implementation of the rules, a course that "has increasingly become a characteristic of general administrative law" and that, it has been suggested, "would appear to have significant advantages in respect of police rule-making."[154]

Even if procedural barriers stand in the way of other interested parties obtaining such review, in many instances the police themselves could (and might be well advised to) obtain preimplementation review. The vehicle for doing so, of course, is application for a search warrant. Precisely this kind of review has been mandated in some circumstances (for example, under *Camara*) but not others. Although the courts have not required that warrants be obtained in advance for such activities as establishing a roadblock at a certain place and time, police administrators would be well advised to obtain a warrant. Because these operations can be planned well in advance, there is no reason for not obtaining the prior approval of a magistrate. Such approval would minimize the chance of after-the-fact challenge of the decisions regarding when, where, and how the roadblock should be operated.

Less apparent is the utility of a police-initiated judicial review of some broader policy that does not fit comfortably within the traditional warrant process. For example, if a law enforcement agency were to develop some sort of "profile" for deciding when to stop persons suspected of a particular type of criminal activity, should the agency have available a mechanism to obtain an advance judicial "stamp of approval" on the profile? Especially if the procedure were to be ex parte, as with a warrant application, it is at least debatable whether the review would be sufficiently intense or comprehensive to reveal the full range of fourth amendment concerns threatened by implementation of the policy.

The fourth problem area is *the distinction between custom and policy.* Another troubling characteristic of some of the Supreme Court's cases discussed earlier is that they suggest a willingness to accept a vague and undocumented representation of the established practices of a particular police agency. In *Opperman* and *Lafayette,* for example, the only mention of the practices in Vermillion and Kankakee regarding vehicle inventories and effects inventories, respectively, is that the inventorying officer testified he acted pursuant to "standard procedure" in his department. In neither case is any police regulation ever quoted or even cited, and thus (as we have seen) there is lower court authority that the *Bertine*-mandated "standardized procedure" need not be memorialized in a written departmental communication. This is unsettling for two reasons: (1) there is always the risk that such testimony will be self-serving and thus fail to represent accurately what the usual practice is and (2) even if it is the usual practice, it does not follow that it is the considered policy of the department.

Reviewing courts must be more particular about separating mere custom from policy. As the president's commission cautioned, the trouble with so-called standard procedures or policies that do not appear in a police manual or written set of standard operating procedures is that they "have normally developed through customary practices that rarely are the product of careful analysis and are usually not well understood by patrolmen."[155] Existing custom may on occasion turn out to provide a basis for official policy, but it is not the business of a court to transmogrify the former into the latter. A "re-examination of established methods" must occur at the police level, a "conscious decision as to whether familiar ways of doing things" are actually best.[156] Only if that process has occurred is there really *policy* entitled to deference from reviewing courts under the previously discussed *Romeo* principle, for only then can the courts see clearly

> what it was that the police were doing in a particular case, and why they thought it necessary to do whatever they were doing, and what are the limitations and extensions in police logic of the claim of necessity that is advanced, and whether the claim of necessity advanced by the state's lawyers before the court is in fact the claim of necessity upon which the police acted or will ever act again, and whether the police believe in that claim seriously enough to express it in a general operating procedure.[157]

The fifth problem area is *the distinction between hunch and expertise.* A central feature of our legal system, in the elegant words of Karl Llewellyn, is that it

> entrusts its case-law-making to a body who are specialists only in being unspecialized, in being the official depositaries of as much general and balanced but rather uninformed horse sense as can be mustered. Such a body has as its function to be instructed, case by case, by the experts in any specialty, and

then, by combination of its very nonexpertness in the particular
with its general and widely buttressed expert roundedness in
many smatterings, to reach a judgment which adds balance not
only, as has been argued so often and so hard, against the passing flurries of public passion, but no less against the often deep
but too often jug-handled contributions of any technicians.[158]

With respect to the actions of police agencies and their officers,
then, courts are not the experts but rather the intended recipients
of expertise from the police. One supposed benefit of a rule-making regime is that it necessitates the ordering and communication
of this knowledge and permits "the application of *expertise on a
continuous and systematic basis.*"[159]

But just as distinguishing custom from policy is imperative,
equally compelling is the need to distinguish mere hunch from
expertise, for it is the law enforcement policy grounded in the
latter rather than the former that, under hard-look judicial
review, is entitled to judicial deference. (As suggested earlier, the
unwillingness of courts to embrace the so-called drug courier
profile seems largely attributable to the fact that courts were not
provided solid data supporting its predictive validity.) One difficulty in this area is the long-standing uncertainty about which
police attitudes and practices truly reflect expertise. There "has
been little effort made to capitalize upon police experience or to
attempt to assess its reliability: to distinguish accurate inferences
from inaccurate ones; or to systematize experience so that it can
be effectively communicated...to others, like judges, when the
propriety of police action is challenged."[160] Police agencies need
"to undertake in-depth inquiries in support of policies and rules
they decide to promulgate. It will not suffice, in establishing a
policy, simply to assert an often-repeated but untested claim as to
its value."[161] Moreover, because an unadorned policy statement is
unlikely to be an adequate conduit of its underlying rationale or
empirical basis, police and prosecutors must work together more
effectively to ensure that the supporting data also reach the
reviewing courts. When this occurs, the challenged police action
is much more likely to receive a favorable judicial reaction.

The final problem area is best viewed as a question: *how much
rule and how much discretion?* "There is good discretion and bad
discretion."[162] To this apothegm might be added Llewellyn's pre-
cept that "to be *right* discretion,...the action so far as it affects any

man or group adversely must be undertaken with a feeling, explicit or implicit, of willingness, or readiness, to do the like again, if, as, and when a like case may arise."[163] If a major purpose of police rule making is to place realistic limits on police discretion, then it might be said that one mark of a reasonable regulation is that it serves to eliminate bad discretion by requiring that like cases actually be treated alike. But for the police administrator drafting the rule and the court reviewing it, there is the nagging question of precisely how broadly or narrowly this category of "like cases" ought to be defined. To take an issue considered earlier regarding *Bertine*, which is better: a rule that *all* arrestees' cars should be impounded (with perhaps one limited exception for a vehicle parked at an arrestee's premises) or a rule that an arrestee's car should be impounded only if neither parking it at the scene nor turning the car over to another is feasible (then listing the myriad of factors that bear on the feasibility of each of those alternatives)? What is lurking here, of course, is the old "bright lines" issue, which heretofore has been debated mainly with respect to the rules of police conduct promulgated by appellate courts. Is it better that the police have the easily understood command, or is it better that they make fewer intrusions under a regulation that, by virtue of its complexity, will sometimes be misapplied and may sometimes serve to shield deliberate arbitrariness?

Commentators on both sides of the rule-making fence have warned that decision making in law enforcement is often complex and thus ought not be compassed by overly simple rules. Professor Uviller, apparently swimming against the rule-making tide, has expressed his concern this way:

> The solace of standardized rules and procedures is largely illusory. Rigid rules tend to ossify individual responsibility and discourage individualistic thinking. Those who would shrink discretion obey the precept: "Treat likes alike." However, the overriding lesson of experience in our criminal justice operation is that every case is different. The major worry is that the people out there dealing with the problems will lose their appreciation of the differences between the cases and will begin reacting to them as repetitive.[164]

Similarly, Goldstein, though an advocate of police rule making, cautions that "it is impossible to prescribe with any precision what should be done, since an infinite number of possible circumstances could occur," and thus for him intelligent rule making consists of alerting "officers to the alternatives available for dealing with a given situation, to the factors that should be considered in choosing from among available alternatives, and to the relative weight that should attach to each factor."[165] Doubtless both Uviller and Goldstein would take a dim view of an impound-all-cars rule.

We need to understand, however, that at the police level the pressures will quite naturally push in the direction of the simplest possible rule, thus favoring, for example, the impound-all-cars alternative. This is best illustrated by a rule-making development outside the fourth amendment area. In *Stovall v. Denno* the Court held that the defendant's one-on-one identification in lieu of a lineup was, under the circumstances, "so unnecessarily suggestive and conducive to irreparable mistaken identification that he was denied due process of law."[166] Lower courts, stressing the Court's use in *Stovall* of the "unnecessarily" qualifier and its reference in another case to a police need "swiftly to determine whether they were on the right track,"[167] have held that a one-on-one identification soon after the crime is permissible if a prompt lineup is not feasible. The rule-making response of the District of Columbia police department was not a regulation spelling out the factors bearing on that unfeasibility; rather, what emerged was the so-called sixty minute rule,[168] the operation of which was described by top department officials: "If a suspect were arrested within one hour of the time of the commission of the offense, in an area reasonably proximate to the scene of the offense, he had to be returned to the scene for purposes of identification; if arrested after one hour, he could not be so returned."[169] One leading advocate of police rule making asserted that this was precisely the kind of rule the police needed. In "a large metropolitan police department of 5100 men that investigates 800–1000 robberies a month," the officers must have "a simple, easily-applied rule."[170] This is also the justification offered for the rule by the department. "The result," the department spokesmen asserted, "is a rule more readily understood by those who must use it and therefore more vigorously enforced by those who must enforce it."[171] Perhaps even more compelling proof of the strong police preference for the keep-it-simple approach is the fact that in another large urban department lacking such a straightforward guideline, the officers in the field nonetheless managed to convince themselves that a rule of this kind existed![172]

Much can be said for the Goldstein-Uviller thesis and also for the contrary approach deliberately adopted in the D.C. department. What this manifests is that the art-science of police rule making is bedeviled by a collision of those antithetical dynamics that pervade our entire legal system. Here again, we are confronted with the "conflict between the simplicity of rules and the complexity of human experience."[173] So it is that the "major challenge, in each area of police operations, is in deciding on the appropriate level of specificity for a given set of guidelines."[174]

Although this means there is no ready solution to the previously stated query of how much rule and how much discretion is called for, a few observations are in order regarding the bright lines phenomenon in this setting. First, if there are to be some bright lines in police rules, they should not inevitably be drawn as the Supreme Court has been inclined to draw them—by opting for that form of "brightness" most intrusive on the interests of privacy and liberty.[175] There is some hope here, as experience has shown that a police regulation might well "not seek to use the full authority granted by the case law," as when it "surrenders certain powers that are not seen as needed or helpful, even though granted by the courts."[176] Second, with respect to certain forms of police activity, a bright line may be the only constitutional choice. For example, *Bertine* makes that so with respect to the inventory of containers within vehicles, as the Court left police departments with only two choices: a rule mandating inventory of the contents of virtually *all* such containers[177] or a rule barring inventory of any of them. Doubtless this reflects a judgment that any less precise (even if more logical) intermediate rule provides too great an opportunity for "slippage"—inconsistent action prompted either by misunderstanding or ulterior motives. The Court's holding may also manifest another instance of the previously discussed notion of representative reinforcement at work: the Court may have concluded that the challenged police position, that inventory objectives cannot be realized by merely sealing and storing containers, is entitled to credence only if the department is prepared to bear the political costs of total adherence to such a view by henceforth so intruding upon the privacy of *all* persons whose vehicles happen to be impounded and inventoried.

DENOUEMENT

Twenty-five years ago, the ABF survey declared that police should "reduce their enforcement policies to writing and subject them to a continuing process of critical re-evaluation."[178] With respect to law enforcement guidelines governing the search and seizure activities of police, the further assumption was that judicial review of these regulations would occur and would ultimately result in a fourth amendment jurisprudence that more delicately balanced competing interests. Specifically, such a process of police rule making and judicial review would best serve the interests of law enforcement and of the public at large by enhancing the quality, consistency, and visibility of search-and-seizure decisions.

The point of my assessment is *not* that such a system of rule making and review with such results is beyond accomplishment. Rather it is that the processes of formulating police rules and subjecting them to meaningful review are not without difficulties, at least some of which may have either resulted from or accounted for the Supreme Court's own hesitancy either to *stimulate* rule making or to *review* challenged rules. Clearly much remains to be done.

NOTES

I have benefited greatly from the comments of Herman Goldstein, Lloyd Ohlin, Frank Remington, and Victor Rosenblum.

This chapter is an abridged and revised version of Wayne R. LaFave, "Controlling Discretion by Administrative Regulations: The Use, Misuse, and Nonuse of Police Rules and Policies in Fourth Amendment Adjudication," *Michigan Law Review* 89 (1990):442ff. Because this chapter has been prepared for a general audience, it does not contain the more extensive citations to lower court cases and to the relevant legal literature contained in the aforementioned article.

1. Epilogue to the survey, appearing in Frank W. Miller, *Prosecution: The Decision to Charge a Suspect with a Crime,* ed. Frank J. Remington (Boston: Little, Brown, 1969), 351–52.

2. 361 U.S. 98 (1959).

3. 392 U.S. 1 (1968).

4. Epilogue (see note 1), 352.

5. 331 U.S. 145 (1947).

6. 331 U.S. at 153.

7. See, e.g., *Colorado v. Bertine,* 479 U.S. 367, 375 (1987).

8. Kenneth C. Davis, *Discretionary Justice: A Preliminary Inquiry* (Baton Rouge: Louisiana State University Press, 1969), 51.

9. Wayne R. LaFave, *Arrest: The Decision to Take a Suspect into Custody,* ed. Frank J. Remington (Boston: Little, Brown, 1965), 513.

10. Anthony G. Amsterdam, "The Supreme Court and the Rights of Suspects in Criminal Cases," *New York University Law Review* 45, no. 4 (1970):813.

11. Davis, *Discretionary Justice,* 222.

12. Carl McGowan, "Rule-Making and the Police," *Michigan Law Review* 70, no. 4 (1972):659.

13. Anthony G. Amsterdam, "Perspectives on the Fourth Amendment," *Minnesota Law Review* 58 (1974):409–39; Amsterdam, "Supreme Court," 810–15.

14. Herman Goldstein, *Policing a Free Society*, chap. 5 (Cambridge, Mass.: Ballinger, 1977); Herman Goldstein, "Police Policy Formulation: A Proposal for Improving Police Performance," *Michigan Law Review* 65, no. 6 (1967):1123; Herman Goldstein, "Trial Judges and the Police," *Crime and Delinquency* 14, no. 1 (1968):14.

15. Davis, *Discretionary Justice*, 52–161; Kenneth C. Davis, *Police Discretion* (Baton Rouge: Louisiana State University Press, 1975), 98–138.

16. American Law Institute, *A Model Code of Pre-Arraignment Procedure* (Philadelphia: American Law Institute, 1975), § 10.3.

17. American Bar Association *Standards for Criminal Justice*, vol. 1 of *ABA Standards for Criminal Justice,* 2d ed. supp. (Boston: Little, Brown, 1980), standard 1–4.3.

18. President's Commission on Law Enforcement and Administration of Justice, *Task Force Report: The Police* (Washington, D.C.: U.S. Government Printing Office, 1967), 18–21.

19. National Advisory Commission on Criminal Justice Standards and Goals, *Police* (Washington, D.C.: U.S. Government Printing Office, 1973), § 1.3.

20. 367 U.S. 643 (1961).

21. Amsterdam, "Supreme Court," 790.

22. Francis A. Allen, "The Judicial Quest for Penal Justice: The Warren Court and the Criminal Cases," *University of Illinois Law Forum* 1975, no. 4:542.

23. Amsterdam, "Perspectives on the Fourth Amendment," 411.

24. John Hart Ely, *Democracy and Distrust: A Theory of Judicial Review* (Cambridge: Harvard University Press, 1980), 97.

25. H. Goldstein, "Trial Judges," 24.

26. 392 U.S. at 14.

27. Amsterdam, "Perspectives on the Fourth Amendment," 421.

28. Ibid., 423–28.

29. 479 U.S. 367 (1987).

30. 428 U.S. 364 (1976).

31. 462 U.S. 640 (1983).

32. 462 U.S. at 648.

33. 479 U.S. at 374.

34. *State v. Atkinson*, 688 P.2d 832, 835 (Or. 1984).

35. 864 F.2d 992 (3d Cir. 1989).

36. 864 F.2d at 1003.

37. 512 A.2d 279, 281 (D.C. 1986).

38. 706 F.2d 321, 334 n.22 (D.C. Cir. 1983).

39. *Commonwealth v. Bishop*, 523 N.E.2d 779, 780 (Mass. 1988).

40. *Colorado v. Bertine*, 479 U.S. at 376–77. This language is from the three-Justice concurrence. The two dissenters surely would settle for nothing less. The position of the remaining four members of the Court is unclear, although they joined the opinion of the Court in which some emphasis was placed on the fact that "the Police Department's procedures mandated the opening of closed containers and the listing of their contents." 479 U.S. at 374 n.6.

In the post-*Bertine* case of *Florida v. Wells*, 495 U.S. 1 (1990), this contrary statement appears: "A police officer may be allowed sufficient latitude to determine whether a particular container should or should not be opened in light of the nature of the search and characteristics of the container itself" (ibid., 4). But this language is only dictum and was strongly objected to by four members of the Court.

41. *Cady v. Dombrowksi,* 413 U.S. 433, 441 (1973).

42. *State v. Ridderbush,* 692 P.2d 667, 672 (Or. App. 1984).

43. 479 U.S. at 375–76.

44. *Webster's Third New International Dictionary* (1981), 110.

45. See text at p. 247.

46. 479 U.S. at 381 (Marshall and Brennan, JJ., dissenting).

47. *United States v. Judge,* 864 F.2d 1144, 1145 (5th Cir. 1989).

48. Especially if the somewhat narrower rule did not confer unnecessary discretion. In the *Wells* case, discussed in note 35 above, Justice Blackmun opined that under *Bertine* a state could, for example, "adopt a policy which requires the opening of all containers that are not locked," but yet strongly criticized the majority's "language, unnecessary on the facts of this case, concerning the extent to which a policeman, under the Fourth Amendment, *may* be given discretion in conducting an inventory search" (*Florida v. Wells,* 495 U.S. 1, 11, 10 [1990]).

49. *State v. Shamblin,* 763 P.2d 425, 428 (Utah Ct. App. 1988).

50. Silas J. Wasserstrom and Louis Michael Seidman, "The Fourth Amendment as Constitutional Theory," *Georgetown Law Journal* 77, no. 1 (1988):95.

51. *State v. Kuster,* 353 N.W.2d 428, 432 (Iowa 1984).

52. Of course, even if the regulation sufficiently reduces the need for discretion in the field, the rule must draw sensible distinctions. See *State v. Crosby,* 403 So.2d 1217 (La. 1981), invalidating a university community's regulation permitting only family members to take possession of arrestees' vehicles because it unjustly "imposes a burden on out of town students who have no family members available" (ibid., 1220).

53. 387 U.S. 523 (1967).

54. 387 U.S. at 534.

55. 387 U.S. at 538.

56. 436 U.S. 307 (1978).

57. 436 U.S. at 316.

58. 436 U.S. at 321.

59. 387 U.S. at 538.

60. *Ohio ex rel. Eaton v. Price,* 364 U.S. 263, 271 (1960).

61. *Abel v. United States,* 362 U.S. 217, 242 (1960) (Douglas, J., dissenting).

62. *City of Seattle v. Leach,* 627 P.2d 159, 162 (Wash. App. 1981) (quoting *In re Northwest Airlines, Inc.,* 587 F.2d 12, 14–15 [7th Cir. 1978]).

63. *See v. City of Seattle,* 387 U.S. 541, 548 (1967) (Clark, J., dissenting).

64. 436 U.S. at 323.

65. 452 U.S. 594 (1981).

66. The act forbids use of force when entry is refused and instead requires that the secretary of labor in such instance go to court and seek an injunction against future refusal.

67. 482 U.S. 691, 711 (1987).

68. Ibid., 723 (Brennan, J., dissenting) (quoting *Donovan v. Dewey,* 452 U.S. 594, 601 [1981]).

69. William J. Mertens, "The Fourth Amendment and the Control of Police Discretion," *University of Michigan Journal of Law Reform* 17, no. 3 (1984):594.

70. 449 U.S. 411 (1981).

71. 499 U.S. at 418.

72. 443 U.S. 47, 51 (1979).

73. 440 U.S. 648 (1979).

74. Ibid., 663. Two concurring justices "assume[d] that the Court's reservation also includes other not purely random stops (such as every tenth car to pass a given point) that equate with, but are less intrusive than, a 100% roadblock stop" (ibid., 664 [Blackmun and Powell, JJ., concurring]).

75. 440 U.S. at 664.

76. *United States v. Martinez-Fuerte,* 428 U.S. 543, 558 (1976) (quoting *United States v. Ortiz,* 422 U.S. 891, 894–95 (1975)).

77. *United States v. Brignoni-Ponce,* 422 U.S. 873, 883 (1975).

78. Wasserstrom and Seidman, "Fourth Amendment" (see note 50), 93.

79. Ibid., 95.

80. 428 U.S. 543 (1976).

81. 110 S. Ct. 2481, 2487 (1990).

82. 110 S. Ct. at 2487.

83. 110 S. Ct. at 2484.

84. 110 S. Ct. at 2488.

85. Ibid., 2495 (Stevens, Brennan, and Marshall, JJ., dissenting).

86. Wasserstrom and Seidman, "Fourth Amendment," 95.

87. The chances of drawing up a suitable plan appear greater if the plan addresses a somewhat special problem existing at a certain time and place. See *State v. Hilleshiem*, 291 N.W.2d 314 (Iowa 1980), suggesting that when police administrators have been able to identify a rather unique law enforcement problem in a discrete location such as a park, a carefully drafted "plan" responding to that problem might well authorize stops for questioning at that location without individualized suspicion.

88. *United States v. Cortez*, 449 U.S. 411 (1981).

89. *United States v. Vasquez*, 612 F.2d 1338, 1350, 1352 (2d Cir. 1979) (Oakes, J., dissenting).

90. Charles L. Becton, "The Drug Courier Profile: 'All Seems Infected That Th' Infected Spy, As All Looks Yellow to the Jaundic'd Eye,'" *North Carolina Law Review* 65, no. 3 (1987):423–25.

91. Ibid., 417.

92. *United States v. Elmore*, 595 F.2d 1036, 1039 n.3 (5th Cir. 1979), *cert. denied*, 447 U.S. 910 (1980).

93. 490 U.S. 1 (1989).

94. 490 U.S. at 10.

95. 490 U.S. at 13 (Marshall, J., dissenting).

96. Morgan Cloud, "Search and Seizure by the Numbers: The Drug Courier Profile and Judicial Review of Investigative Formulas," *Boston University Law Review* 65, no. 5 (1985):873.

97. 831 F.2d 1413, 1418 (9th Cir. 1987), *rev'd*, 490 U.S. 1 (1989).

98. *Grant v. State*, 461 A.2d 524, 526 (Md. App. 1983).

99. *Reid v. Georgia*, 448 U.S. 438, 441 (1980).

100. Admittedly, the court's application of this distinction was not without difficulties. The *Sokolow* majority questioned, for example, whether the lower court's illustrations of "ongoing criminal activity" factors, traveling with an alias or taking an evasive path through the airport, had "the sort of ironclad significance attributed to them by the Court of Appeals" (490 U.S. at 8).

101. 471 U.S. 1 (1985).

102. 471 U.S. at 18–19.

103. Steven L. Winter, "*Tennessee v. Garner* and the Democratic Practice of Judicial Review," *New York University Review of Law and Social Change* 14, no. 3 (1986):683.

104. Ibid., 684.

105. Ibid., 684–85.

106. 471 U.S. at 19.

107. 471 U.S. at 19.

108. 471 U.S. at 19–20.

109. 414 U.S. 218 (1973).

110. 414 U.S. 260 (1973).

111. 414 U.S. at 223 n.2.

112. 414 U.S. at 235.

113. 453 U.S. 454, 460 (1981).

114. 414 U.S. at 248.

115. *Robbins v. California,* 453 U.S. 420, 450 n.11 (1981) (Stevens, J., dissenting).

116. Amsterdam, "Perspectives on the Fourth Amendment" (see note 13), 417.

117. Amsterdam, "Perspectives on the Fourth Amendment," 416.

118. *Massachusetts v. Painten*, 389 U.S. 560, 565 (1968) (White, J., dissenting).

119. 436 U.S. 128 (1978). In accepting the government's contention that "subjective intent alone...does not make otherwise lawful conduct illegal or unconstitutional," the Court noted that "almost without exception in evaluating alleged violations of the Fourth Amendment the Court has first undertaken an objective assessment of an officer's actions in light of the facts and circumstances then known to him."

120. *Diggs v. State,* 345 So.2d 815, 816 (Fla. Dist. Ct. App. 1977).

121. *Harding v. State*, 301 So.2d 513 (Fla. Dist. Ct. App. 1974).

122. *State v. Volk*, 291 So.2d 643, 644 (Fla. Dist. Ct. App. 1974).

123. *Abel v. United States*, 362 U.S. 217, 226 (1960).

124. 864 F.2d 1512 (10th Cir. 1988).

125. 864 F.2d at 1518.

126. LaFave, *Arrest* (see note 9), 512, 495.

127. Ibid., 494.

128. *Panama Refining Co. v. Ryan,* 293 U.S. 388 (1935) (Cardozo, J., dissenting).

129. Gerald M. Caplan, "The Case for Rulemaking by Law Enforcement Agencies," *Law and Contemporary Problems* 36, no. 4 (1971):506.

130. *Florida v. Wells*, 495 U.S. 1, 4 (1990).

131. McGowan, "Rule-Making" (see note 12), 686.

132. 457 U.S. 307, 323 n.30 (1982).

133. 463 U.S. 29 (1983).

134. Ibid., 43 and note 9 (quoting *Burlington Truck Lines, Inc. v. United States*, 371 U.S. 156, 168 (1962).

135. *Greater Boston Television Corp. v. F.C.C.*, 444 F.2d 841, 851 (D.C. Cir. 1970).

136. Karl N. Llewellyn, *The Common Law Tradition: Deciding Appeals* (Boston: Little, Brown, 1960), 28.

137. 480 U.S. 340 (1987).

138. 468 U.S. 897 (1984).

139. "Rethinking the Good Faith Exception to the Exclusionary Rule," *University of Pennsylvania Law Review* 130, no. 6 (1982):1618.

140. John Kaplan, "The Limits of the Exclusionary Rule," *Stanford Law Review* 26 (1974):1050.

141. "Rethinking the Good Faith," 1619.

142. *Johnson v. United States*, 333 U.S. 10, 14 (1948).

143. *Illinois v. Krull*, 480 U.S. 340, 366 (1987) (O'Connor, J., dissenting).

144. 428 U.S. 465, 492 (1976).

145. 457 U.S. 537, 561 (1982).

146. *United States v. Peltier*, 422 U.S. 531, 558 n.18 (1975) (Brennan, J. dissenting).

147. Ibid.

148. 440 U.S. 741 (1979).

149. 440 U.S. at 755–56.

150. McGowan, "Rule-Making' (see note 12), 684.

151. Amsterdam, "Perspectives on the Fourth Amendment" (see note 13), 416.

152. McGowan, "Rule-Making," 678.

153. President's Commission on Law Enforcement, *Task Force Report: The Police* (see note 18), 18–19.

154. McGowan, "Rule-Making," 686.

155. President's Commission on Law Enforcement, *Task Force Report: The Police*, 189.

156. McGowan, "Rule-Making," 681.

157. Amsterdam, "Perspectives on the Fourth Amendment," 419.

158. Llewellyn, *Common Law Tradition* (see note 136), 263.

159. McGowan, "Rule-Making," 678.

160. President's Commission on Law Enforcement, *Task Force Report: The Police*, 20.

161. Goldstein, *Policing a Free Society* (see note 14), 118.

162. Harold E. Pepinsky, "Better Living Through Police Discretion," *Law and Contemporary Problems* 47, no. 4 (1984):253.

163. Llewellyn, *Common Law Tradition,* 217.

164. H. Richard Uviller, "The Unworthy Victim: Police Discretion in the Credibility Call," *Law and Contemporary Problems* 47, no. 4 (1984):32.

165. Goldstein, *Policing a Free Society*, 111–12.

166. 388 U.S. 293, 302 (1967).

167. *Simmons v. United States,* 390 U.S. 377, 385 (1968).

168. Caplan, "Case for Rulemaking" (see note 129), 507.

169. Jerry V. Wilson and Geoffrey M. Alprin, "Controlling Police Conduct: Alternatives to the Exclusionary Rule," *Law and Contemporary Problems* 36, no. 4 (1971):496.

170. Caplan, "Case for Rulemaking," 507–8.

171. Wilson and Alprin, "Controlling Police Conduct," 497.

172. H. Richard Uviller, *Tempered Zeal* (Chicago: Contemporary Books, 1988), 107–9.

173. Ronald J. Allen, "The Nature of Discretion," *Law and Contemporary Problems* 47, no. 4 (1984):3.

174. Goldstein, *Policing a Free Society*, 112.

175. See, e.g., *New York v. Belton*, 453 U.S. 454 (1981).

176. Caplan, "Case for Rulemaking," 503–4.

177. Consider the Blackmun interpretation of *Bertine* in the later *Wells* case, quoted in note 48 above.

178. LaFave, *Arrest* (see note 9), 513.

CHAPTER 7

The American Bar Foundation Survey and the Development of Criminal Justice Higher Education

Donald J. Newman

The focus of the American Bar Foundation Survey of Criminal Justice on decision making and the exercise of discretion by criminal justice agencies provided a new and fresh perspective on the implementation of the criminal law in action. It documented in great detail hitherto largely ignored contextual features of the decision-making process, such as the complexity and low visibility of many of these decisions and their systemic interrelationships. Many of the effects of this research on the organization and practices of criminal justice agencies have been explored in previous chapters. In this chapter I shift the focus to provide a historical account of the impact of the survey on the development of criminal justice education at the graduate level, drawing on my own observations and personal involvement in this development.

An important major consequence of the Bar Foundation research, ancillary to its research objectives, was the move into our colleges and universities of serious concern for criminal justice. Certainly the domestic problem of crime control was a field worthy of study and analysis by university scholars. But the problem of crime control had been largely ignored in higher education, although universities have typically responded well to other major domestic problems, from food to transportation. It seemed to many scholars that the research results of the Bar Foundation were certainly worthy of sustained, continuing study and analysis. Indeed the books produced from the survey data created a beginning literature about the reality of daily criminal justice processing. Many of the persons connected with the ABF project were professors from law schools and other academic disciplines. Given this, it was inevitable that universities (law schools, at first) were looked to as appropriate centers for continuing the thrust begun by the ABF field survey.

With many byroads, universities eventually did become involved in criminal justice education and research. In a real sense, the widespread presence of criminal justice academic programs on American college and university campuses today may be the *major* contribution of the American Bar Foundation survey. This chapter will briefly relate the major events in the history of this educational development, certainly a complex story in its own right, yet one directly related to the ABF experience and the people involved with it.

The structure, the placement, and the definitions of schools of criminal justice are only part of the story, though an important one. The follow-up question is whether the creation of these schools, the spread of this academic field, has advanced our understanding of the complex system of crime control and whether the academic programs did or did not build on the contributions of the American Bar Foundation survey research.

This chapter will deal with these issues: the difficulty of creating a new university academic field and whether, having been created, it has contributed in significant ways to the understanding and effectiveness of our crime control efforts. It also raises the question of the likely future of this academic enterprise, so much a product of the ABF research begun more than thirty-five years ago.

CRIMINAL JUSTICE EDUCATION

The field survey findings eventually were published in five books under the direction of Frank J. Remington of the University of Wisconsin Law School, who was field director of the ABF survey. A historical account of the process and authorship of these five books is set forth in the introductory chapter of this book.

Development of Educational Materials

As the field survey reports were being studied and the resulting five books were being prepared, Frank Remington and Donald Newman put together in 1960 a mimeographed collection called "Criminal Justice Administration: Materials and Cases." This collection was revised annually and grew as the massive supply of data from the ABF survey was analyzed and organized. Edward L. Kimball, who joined the University of Wisconsin law faculty in the early 1960s, became involved and assumed a major responsibility for updating and revising the materials. Also, Marygold Melli, a law professor, introduced a section on juvenile justice administration. Finally, Herman Goldstein moved to the University of Wisconsin Law School, where he joined the project, and the resulting work, published in 1969, had the same title as the 1960 collection, but it now had five authors.[1]

This casebook was intended primarily for use in law schools and, to the extent that criminal justice became an academic offering, the law school was a logical setting for such a course. After all, our crime control system rests on, indeed is created and enabled by, both substantive and procedural law. True, the ABF survey stressed the actual daily operation of the criminal process by focusing on the law in action rather than in statutes, low-visibility decisions, puzzling complexity, and broad discretion exercised by all on-line actors from police to parole boards. But this is not simply a system of informal social behavior, of values and norms shared and shifting without formal controls. The whole significance of the Bar Foundation study was to counterpoint the law in action with formal legal mandates, expectations, and controls and, while describing low-visibility discretionary decisions, to suggest dealing with criminal behavior by governmental processes.

The decade of the sixties, when this material was being put together, was the beginning of the Supreme Court's active involvement in matters of criminal law and procedure. After many years of virtually ignoring crime-control matters, of a "hands-off" doctrine in regard to many issues in criminal justice, the Court suddenly and persistently began to intervene at many major stages in crime-control processing. Some of the Court decisions attempted to control discretion by placing standard due process restrictions on system actors. For instance, both *Mapp v. Ohio*[2] and *Miranda v. Arizona*[3] were attempts to control police behavior. However, in other cases the Court seemed to recognize the complexity of street and prosecution decision making and reflected this in its decisions. Certainly *Terry v. Ohio*,[4] *Santobello v. New York*,[5] and later *Tennessee v. Garner*[6] reflected more accurately the Bar Foundation approach to discretionary behavior. In any event, court involvement in criminal justice issues proliferated, altering the dimensions of criminal justice in very profound ways. What was more sensible, then, than to introduce law students and, of course, others interested in crime control to educational materials highlighting both everyday practice and emerging court intervention?

Summer Seminars for Legal and Social Science Scholars

Early versions of the "Pilot Project Reports"[7] and, later, of the criminal justice materials and cases were used as educational devices in three summer seminars for professors with an interest in these developments. The first, in 1958, brought together a group of lawyers and social and behavioral scientists, all of whom had an interest in some aspects of crime control. It was directed by Frank Remington and Lloyd Ohlin and was funded by the Ford Foundation. It involved such well-known scholars as Frank Allen of the University of Michigan Law School and Joseph Goldstein of Yale University Law School. The second seminar, in 1960, again assembling criminal law professors and social scientists, was funded by the Social Science Research Council and was directed by Remington and Victor Rosenblum, a prominent political scientist from Northwestern University. A number of nationally recognized scholars attended, including Sanford Kadish, Gilbert Geis, Edward Kimball, and Hans Toch. The third seminar, in 1963, was directed by Remington and Donald Newman and was supported by the Ford Foundation. This third summer program brought together young criminal law professors, including such participants as Joel Handler and Fred Cohen, and was designed to interest them in criminal justice administration rather than formal substantive criminal law and procedure.

If the question is whether these summer seminars made any long-range difference in the career work of the participants, the answer is somewhat disappointing. With some exceptions, both the criminologists and the law professors remained traditional in their disciplines. Perhaps some legal literature was reflected more commonly in criminology articles and texts and other social science monographs. And some of the Bar Foundation terminology—police discretion, plea bargaining—appeared in both legal and sociological treatises. But certainly no immediate educational revolution occurred from these seminar groups being exposed to the criminal justice materials.

Eventually a credit course, Criminal Justice Administration, was developed and offered in the curriculum of the University of Wisconsin Law School. And a group of other Bar Foundation participants—Frank W. Miller, Robert O. Dawson, George E. Dix, and Raymond I. Parnas—published a work, entitled *Criminal Justice Administration: Cases and Materials*,[8] that was similar to the Wisconsin treatise and offered courses in their own law schools.

Law Student Summer Field Placements in Criminal Justice Agencies

Another educational experiment was tried at the Wisconsin Law School, one that has worked consistently well for many years. Second-year law students were selected for summer placement in correctional settings, ranging from the prisons and juvenile training schools to probation and parole. Students were supported by a grant from the National Council on Legal Clinics (Ford Foundation funds) and, in general, were *not* those who desired a professional career in the practice of criminal law. The idea instead was to give them a unique field experience working with criminal offenders to catch and hopefully hold their interest in correctional concerns long after they became members of the practicing bar. This idea was suggested by Lloyd Ohlin, who had noticed that young persons often entered the field of criminology having had some sort of summer experience with delinquent youth or in other correctional settings. At any rate, it was hoped that this correctional experience, so atypical for law students, would influence their later careers whether they became involved in criminal justice as defense attorneys, prosecutors, or judges or simply as members of the bar serving on committees having to do with sentencing or corrections.

Summer field experiences were preceded by a preparatory course and followed by a post-field seminar. At first law students served as correctional interns, doing some counseling in the prisons, conducting presentence investigations in the field, or supervising reduced caseloads of probationers and parolees. After some experience, the students began counseling offenders on civil matters ancillary to their convictions and sentences. Offenders, particularly prison inmates, have many civil problems ranging from family matters such as divorce or guardianship of children to the ownership and distribution of property. None of these issues can be addressed personally by inmates while under sentence. The law students helped them deal with some of these matters and aided them in their legal and administrative concerns (obtaining a driver's license, etc.) as they neared release.

The summer experience at Wisconsin, limited in numbers, proved successful; and a similar program, but involving placement in police agencies, was developed when Herman Goldstein joined the Wisconsin faculty.

At about the same time, similar programs involving law students were initiated with continuing success at other law schools. For example, the Prison Law Project was introduced at Harvard Law School by James Vorenberg and Lloyd Ohlin in the late 1960s. However, in this chapter I have confined myself to a historical account of those developments in which I was directly engaged and that appeared to be inspired by the survey research findings. Many law school and criminology programs, for example, were stimulated to address criminal justice issues in greater depth as a result of the publication of the work of the President's Commission on Law Enforcement and Administration of Justice in 1967,[9] which in turn was influenced by the survey findings and its chief participants. It would be a very large and difficult task to trace these various influences on the development of graduate-level criminal justice education. I have therefore concentrated on what I know best, 'that is, those lines of influence that flowed most directly from the survey findings and its chief participants.

These experiences certainly appeared worthwhile. Some evidence suggests that they had a continuing effect on the participants in sustaining their interest and concern about corrections and policing after they graduated. Begun in the 1960s, they are continuing in somewhat modified and more sophisticated form today.

Problems with Teaching and Researching
Criminal Justice in Law School Settings

The same growth and development cannot be said for the law school criminal justice courses based on the survey findings. After the Remington, Newman, Kimball, Melli, and Goldstein book came out in hard cover in 1969, Edward Kimball prepared annual supplements for a number of years. In 1982 a second edition of the text, somewhat abbreviated, was published. The juvenile justice materials by Marygold Melli were dropped, and Walter Dickey, a law professor who was later to become director of Wisconsin's Division of Corrections, became an active participant on the team. The new publication, same title, now had as its authors Remington, Newman, Kimball, Goldstein, and Dickey.[10]

Despite the start at Wisconsin, at Washington University in St. Louis with Frank Miller, and elsewhere, criminal justice courses did not flourish in law schools. Why the administrative aspects of criminal justice have not been given greater emphasis is unclear. One apparent reason is that administrative material is more difficult to teach than more formal appellate case decisions. Knowledge of actual street practices, of trial courts, and of correctional practices is commonly not possessed by the law professor whose own legal education focused primarily on formal sources of law. Most law professors do not ride in police cars, watch prosecutors bargain in hallways, tour prisons, or sit with parole boards. Without these experiences, it is difficult to be comfortable teaching the administrative aspects of criminal justice.

In any event, emphasis on criminal justice has been limited to a few schools like Wisconsin, where the law-in-action and law and society research commitments have made it possible to emphasize day-to-day criminal justice practices.[11]

Most law school research has not involved field studies or statistical measurements of social phenomena. Instead, traditional research has involved case analysis and the assessment of legal concepts and appellate court decisions relating to current and usually controversial legal issues. But behavioral research— field measurements of the conduct of agents or practitioners or the daily consequence of court or legislative mandates on operating agencies—is comparatively rare. Law schools have simply not been structured to do operational on-line research in criminal justice or, for that matter, in other fields. This may change, however, as concern about crime continues to increase and as the judiciary plays a less and less significant role in the development of criminal justice policy. The consequence is that important decisions will be legislative and administrative in nature, and law practice, legal research, and teaching will have to reflect these changes.

Although criminal justice has not yet really flowered in American law schools, by the late sixties and early seventies it had penetrated more broadly into the university system and was beginning to spread as a new type of social or political science education across the campuses of the nation.

CREATION OF THE STATE UNIVERSITY OF NEW YORK AND THE FIRST SCHOOL OF CRIMINAL JUSTICE

Governor Nelson Rockefeller and the State University of New York

The development of the School of Criminal Justice at the State University of New York at Albany is important because it created a model of graduate criminal justice education that has had a profound influence on such programs throughout the country. I have, therefore, gone to some lengths to detail the process through which this model emerged and, for historical purposes, the contributions of those who contributed most significantly to this development.

In his first term as governor (1958–62), Nelson Rockefeller created, with legislative support, the large, multicampus State University of New York (SUNY). Ten years earlier, Thomas Dewey, who was then governor, had linked together existing teachers' colleges into an administrative whole called the "State University of New York," but Rockefeller made a quantum leap by building new university centers and four-year campuses, which moved the state university into big-league higher education. Some specialized university programs were located on campuses of private universities, the College of Agriculture at Cornell and Forestry at Syracuse, for example. And a number of teachers colleges (formerly "normal schools") were scattered across the state. Two major state medical centers also existed. But in part because of the numerous private colleges and universities in New York and the willingness of other states to accept New York undergraduates, until Rockefeller's time no large, comprehensive, statewide, state-funded, complete higher educational system existed.

Responding to the need for public higher education for thousands of New York residents who could not afford private universities and who were finding greater difficulty being accepted by other state systems (increasingly other states were placing quotas on out-of-state undergraduate students as their own resident demands increased), Rockefeller pushed the development of SUNY. This was accomplished over the opposition of private colleges and universities who saw cheaper state tuition as a form of unfair competition. Resistance was overcome by a proposal (made by McGeorge Bundy and still known as Bundy Aid) to provide unrestricted state tax funds to the private institutions in amounts varying by degree level but given to all on the basis of the number of students graduated from these schools each year. Presumably this money would be used for scholarships to make private education available to poorer but able students.

When something is done by the state of New York, it is generally large and usually of high quality. The university that Rockefeller, the legislature, and the New York Board of Regents envisioned became the largest in the nation, with some 350,000 students. Its structure and administration were, and are, extremely complex. There are four university centers, each awarding doctoral degrees in all core sciences, social sciences, and humanities, but none a complete university. Specialized schools and departments—engineering, law, and the like—are located at one center or, like agriculture at Cornell, at essentially private universities. The basic idea was, and to some extent still is, that the centers would differ in some emphases and that any new programs, consistent with the basic objectives of the campus, would be located at the appropriate site. Stony Brook on Long Island was defined as the center primarily for physical sciences, Buffalo for biological sciences, Binghamton for the humanities, and Albany for social sciences.

In addition to the four university centers, each of which granted baccalaureate, master's, and doctor's degrees, there were ten four-year colleges (some awarding master's degrees in a few fields), some specializing colleges (maritime, dance, fine arts), and about fifty two-year community colleges. All told, the SUNY system had sixty-eight campuses and some others free-standing, like the medical centers or, in private universities, like agriculture and industrial relations at Cornell.[12]

In this complex system, the School of Criminal Justice (the first in the nation with this title) granting doctoral degrees was established at the university center at Albany in 1966 and admitted its first students in 1968.

Origins of the School of Criminal Justice at Albany

No doubt the most direct and most important educational offshoot of the ABF survey was the School of Criminal Justice at Albany. It was the first of its kind, though earlier there were some police science and correctional administration programs elsewhere. But Albany was unique and indeed, in its formation, was literally a reflection of the whole Bar Foundation approach. Its program focused on the total system of crime control, not just policing or postsentencing processing. In courses it stressed street practices as well as formal controls, very much the criminal law in action. Its curriculum dealt, above all, with the complexity of our crime control system, the difficult tasks it has, and the lack of easy answers to virtually *any* issue in this system. It offered graduate level courses and stressed field research.[13]

A high proportion of the persons who recommended the school, who planned it, and who first staffed it were connected in some way to the Bar Foundation project. The text used in its basic Criminal Justice Process course was the book prepared by Remington, Newman, Kimball, Melli, and Goldstein at Wisconsin. Indeed, in the first year of student operations this text was still in mimeographed form; hardcover publication came a year later.

Why New York? Why Albany? And how did the ABF project shape this school? The conditions were just right. A new university was being created and, for a variety of reasons, detailed later, criminal justice flourished on new or secondary campuses. For the first time, crime was appearing in public opinion polls as a major domestic concern. When the polls showed it to be *the* primary domestic problem, President Johnson in 1964 announced his War on Crime, promising to banish it from our nation. Of course New York had its share of this serious problem, and Governor Rockefeller, like President Johnson, was very much a responsive political figure.

The Role of Eliot Lumbard

Rockefeller, like all New York governors, maintained an office of the counsel to the governor in his executive chamber. Rockefeller's first-term counsel was Robert MacCrate, who had a number of attorney assistants. His special assistant for law enforcement was Eliot Lumbard, a New York City attorney. Among his other tasks, Lumbard was charged with responding to the furor that arose when the state police inadvertently discovered a secret meeting of the heads of organized crime families in the small town of Apalachin, New York. In response, Lumbard held a series of organized crime conferences at Oyster Bay on Long Island at which state police from around the country, the F.B.I., and other police agencies, including the NYPD, shared information on organized crime. Six Oyster Bay conferences were held over a period of years.

Lumbard was also instrumental in creating the New York State Intelligence and Information System (NYSIIS), comparable on a state level to the national F.B.I. fingerprint and crime data files in Washington.

In setting up this intelligence service and in generally responding to New York's crime problems, Lumbard contacted a number of well-known criminal law authorities. Among them was Arthur Sherry, of the University of California Law School, who had served as overall project director of the Bar Foundation survey and was connected with the School of Criminology at Berkeley. Sherry suggested to Lumbard the creation of a New York "center" for the analysis of crime control problems, and Lumbard passed this proposal along to MacCrate, the governor's counsel, in a memorandum dated September 26, 1961.[14]

About this time, Lumbard also visited the University of Wisconsin and met with Remington, Newman, Wayne LaFave, and others from the ABF study group who were working on the Bar Foundation volumes. Lumbard brought a film about the New York State intelligence system, but also stayed to talk about the Bar Foundation project, the forthcoming volumes, and the new materials and cases we planned to use in law school teaching.

Lumbard sent another memorandum to MacCrate (just a month after his first one) describing a "school" that would "provide intellectual leadership and drive to the entire spectrum of the administration of criminal justice for training and education and research." Lumbard said it should be staffed by "top people from various disciplines" and "provide a level of continuing analysis, research and comment that is now missing."[15]

MacCrate apparently passed these memorandums on to the

governor, for in March 1962 Governor Rockefeller, in a special message to the state legislature, asked their favorable consideration in taking "a first step toward a New York State School of Criminology in the State University that will serve all those engaged in the vital tasks of maintaining law and order in our communities."[16]

Having received the gubernatorial blessing, the school was in the hopper. But what, how, and where remained to be decided.

Meeting the Personnel Needs of Criminal Justice Agencies

A number of other developments were occurring at the same time. The heads of various correctional agencies in New York, including the Department of Correctional Services, the Office of Probation, the Division for Youth, and the Parole Board, were requesting graduate-level educational programs relevant to corrections to train their field agents and mid- and top-level managerial staff. Neither public nor private universities had corrections-oriented graduate programs. In general, social work in New York State (unlike Wisconsin) was not particularly committed to educating social workers for correctional positions, yet this remained on civil service lists as a desideratum.

The State University of New York (the regents, actually a paper university without a campus) had created the free-standing Graduate School of Public Affairs, headed by a dean, located in Albany, and with three departments: public administration, political science, and political economics. GSPA, as it was known, was designed to provide graduate-level education in these fields primarily for professionals already in service in some of the massive New York state government agencies. It provided both educational and credentialing advancement for professional bureaucrats, mostly those already working in the agencies of the capital, Albany.[17]

As with many such graduate programs in public administration and political science, GSPA ignored correctional agencies. There were neither directly relevant courses nor faculty competent to offer graduate work or do research in anything like correctional administration. The correctional agency heads pressured state government and GSPA to respond more directly to their needs, and eventually a faculty line was created in GSPA for a correctional specialist. They began looking for a professor academically qualified and familiar with New York's correctional system.

I apparently fit this bill, having appropriate academic qualifications and having become very familiar with the New York corrections system in my six years at St. Lawrence University, during which I was involved with the annual correctional conferences called the Moran Institute (after a former parole board chairman), before I joined the ABF team and moved back to the University of Wisconsin. Anyway, early in 1962 I responded to a call from O. B. Conaway, dean of GSPA, came to Albany, and met with correctional agency heads, but having no desire at this point to return to New York I declined the position.[18] I was sympathetic with the agency's needs but somewhat skeptical when Conaway, showing me the Albany Country Club golf course, told me a new university would rise on this site within five years. He was correct, and the new SUNY-Albany campus was constructed over the next few years.

William Brown, with a Ph.D. in public administration from New York University and a twenty-two year successful career on the New York City Police Department (he retired as an inspector), did take the job with GSPA, although corrections was not his major academic interest. However, as the only professor in the school familiar with criminal justice, Bill did develop a curriculum for correctional administrators. Bill was also in an excellent insider's position to rally to the governor's call and support the Lumbard proposal. He did this in a series of memorandums,[19] and when GSPA was eventually absorbed by the State University and the School of Criminal Justice was created, Bill moved laterally from GSPA into the school as its first professor—representing his field of experience in policing, rather than correctional administration.

The point of this discussion of GSPA is to highlight two major issues of the time that had to be resolved before the School of Criminal Justice could become a reality. One was a turf battle, an issue that no doubt plagues all new academic programs. GSPA saw the school as its natural offspring, perhaps as a new department or center. And as Lumbard and others soon discovered, there was no assurance that the new school would be placed in the Albany university center.

The second issue, more important than turf, had to do with

expectations about the school. Whether called the "School of Criminology," the governor's title, or the "School of Criminal Justice," the eventual name, very large questions remained about what it should be, what purposes it would serve, who would staff it, who would attend it, and what degrees it would offer. Agency heads saw it as personnel credentialing; some in state government saw it as information gathering, a center of research and planning; and the university itself, on which it was literally imposed by the governor and legislature, was yet to be heard from.

Early Consultants to the Albany School

Thomas H. Hamilton, then chancellor of the state university, responding to the governor's message and at a request from Counsel MacCrate, met with Eliot Lumbard to begin the planning process. The SUNY Board of Trustees asked that a feasibility study be made, and the state legislature made funds available for this purpose. Hamilton designated Conaway, the dean of GSPA, as the university's representative, and eventually it was decided that some consultants would be hired to give advice in this matter.[20]

The first consultant was Frank Remington, who, in 1962, supported the need for academic attention to criminal justice administration, pointing out the current lack of any "professional group which sees the control of deviant social behavior by governmental processes as its main interest." Remington called for an interdisciplinary faculty of "outstanding competence" and regular "visiting faculty" to allow flexibility and give the core faculty opportunity to concentrate "research and training on particular problems of importance to the state of New York." His basic faculty model was one of public administration, with "perhaps a young lawyer with interest in administrative law" along with sociologists, psychologists, social workers, and a "lawyer with a broad interest in the field of criminal justice."[21]

Both Bill Brown and Dean Conaway responded to the Remington proposal, and eventually Conaway submitted to Chancellor Hamilton a recommendation for a center for criminal justice to be located in Albany, devoted to pre- and in-service training needs, research, and "eventually" undergraduate and graduate degree programs.[22]

At about this point Chancellor Hamilton left the university and was replaced by acting chief administrative officer J.

Lawrence Murray, who in 1964 was in turn replaced by a new chancellor, Samuel B. Gould. And MacCrate left the Rockefeller team to be replaced by Sol N. Corbin as counsel to the governor. But Eliot Lumbard stayed on and fought vigorously for the location of the school in Albany when the university trustees questioned this particular location, primarily because the only law school in the state system was located in Buffalo.

In 1963 Frank Remington returned once more to Albany as a consultant to the university, and the idea of a school of criminal justice, solely graduate level, was hardened. After the second Remington visit, Conaway wrote to the acting chancellor that undergraduate degrees should be offered by two- and four-year colleges with the "assistance of the Albany Center."[23] Eventually, Chancellor Gould decided that the school in Albany would stress doctoral education, not undergraduate or master's degrees, somewhat to the disappointment of correctional agency heads who saw the school as an alternative to social work for agency professional training.[24]

In 1963 the SUNY Board of Trustees adopted a resolution which read, in part:

> *Resolved* that the proposed establishment of a School of Criminal Justice in the State University of New York be, and hereby is approved in principle, and that the president be, and hereby is authorized to request additional funds to be made available to State University to undertake further studies leading to development of such a school.[25]

Governor Rockefeller addressed the legislature again under the heading "The School of Criminal Justice" in his annual message in January 1964.[26]

At the same time a group of planners in New York City, headed by Charles Breitel and with the advice of Sir Leon Radzinowicz, Wolfson Professor of Criminology at Cambridge, England, introduced a bill called "An Act Creating a New York State Criminological Research Foundation,"[27] which was passed by the state legislature. Rockefeller vetoed the bill, saying: "My executive budget [called for] a School of Criminal Justice within the State University which would make searching inquiries into crime causation, juvenile delinquency, law enforcement procedures, [and] criminal rehabilitation."[28]

At this point the new university chancellor, Samuel Gould, a supporter of the school proposal, invited Lloyd Ohlin, then at the Columbia School of Social Work, to advise the university about the "conceptual basis or theoretical framework of such a School."[29] Ohlin did this, recommending a strong basis of both basic and applied research, graduate-level education, basic policy studies, and greater professional development. Ohlin, using the title, "School of Criminology and Criminal Justice," recommended it be located in Albany, at first, perhaps, in GSPA, but eventually becoming a separate academic school. He called for the appointment of a dean and key faculty members to plan the curriculum.[30]

Chancellor Gould wanted Ohlin to become the dean, but at this point President Johnson's Commission on Law Enforcement and the Administration of Justice was created, and Ohlin accepted an appointment as associate director of the commission staff. The president of the university center at Albany, brought up to date by Chancellor Gould, appointed a committee to search for a dean.

The first dean was Prof. Richard A. Myren, a lawyer who was then involved in a law enforcement program at Indiana University. Myren joined the Albany faculty in 1966 and together with Bill Brown, who had transferred to the newly created school from GSPA, began a search for other faculty to help plan the school program.[31]

The Planning Year: Creation of the Albany Model

Dean Myren contacted the consultants to the school, and Frank Remington thought I might be interested. Myren contacted me in July 1966, and I agreed to come to Albany on leave from Wisconsin for a year to work on school planning.[32] I arrived in Albany in the summer of 1967.

During the intervening year Dean Myren and I were in close contact. In particular he asked for my suggestions for other faculty who might, under the same conditions of leave from their own institutions, come to Albany for the planning process. We both felt the desirability of an interdisciplinary group, for there was no academic field of criminal justice as such. I suggested a number of persons who had been involved with or knew about the ABF survey and the literature from it, which was just beginning to appear.

Two of the persons I named agreed to spend a year with us. Fred Cohen, a lawyer then on the faculty of the Texas Law

School in Austin, was a participant in the Wisconsin summer seminar where young criminal law teachers were introduced to the teaching materials developed from the Bar Foundation. I knew Fred personally, since I was a codirector of this seminar with Frank Remington. The second professor, Hans Toch, a social psychologist then with the Department of Psychology at Michigan State University, also agreed to come for a year. I did not know Toch personally at the time, but was aware that he was involved in the second summer program at Wisconsin, where the ABF criminal justice material was shared with social and behavioral scientists.[33]

The five of us, Myren, Brown, Cohen, Toch, and I, spent a planning year dealing with three major issues: (1) defining criminal justice as a degree-granting academic field at the graduate level, (2) working out a doctoral level curriculum, and (3) planning both the conceptual and the practical structure of the School of Criminal Justice. In this year we created what has come to be called the "Albany Model," which, in the main, still exists and has spread widely to other universities around the nation. Interestingly, the Albany Model is one of general definition of criminal justice and curriculum, not of research. We reached some consensus on courses, but proposals for systematic common theme research were generally opposed. It was felt to be a matter of academic freedom, research interests being in the sole province of each individual professor.

Criminal Justice Education Defined

We knew that if we were to be successful at all, questions of just what academic criminal justice is and is not would be central issues for a long while. The title alone creates expectations outside the university and confusion within. We had no problem at all explaining crime as a serious domestic issue and pointing to the lack of university involvement in systematically dealing with this problem in teaching and in sustained research.

We started by defining criminal justice as a field of study focused on the control of crime in a democratic society. True, other forms of political structures also attempt crime control, but we ducked the question of comparative, worldwide control systems, believing we had plenty to do dealing with our own social order. We stressed two major things: (1) criminal justice was not the same as criminology and (2) the entire spectrum of crime control efforts from legislation through all of the on-line enforcement, adjudication, and correctional agencies must be treated as a whole interlocking system. Criminology was and is a field of study concerned with causes of lawbreaking and the most accurate measures of crime rates. Certainly it is relevant to and indeed part of criminal justice, but the major focus in criminal justice is on the ways we attempt to control crime in our society. It may be sophistry to say that control will fail unless causes are addressed, but consensus about causes is lacking, and crime is immediate and pressing. It was crime control, not criminology, the universities failed to address.

Saying all this failed to be persuasive. Don't universities educate and train, albeit somewhat indirectly, those involved in crime control—legislators (from many fields), lawyers, judges, prosecutors in law schools, administrators in public administration programs, police in police science, and correctional personnel in other fields? What about training academies? Is this a college program for police and wardens? Is criminal justice a *professional* school?

We argued that education for crime control was as fragmented as the system itself and that the problem was important enough to be addressed by both teaching and research, in a central place, by a separate discipline. And we were clear that we were *not* a professional school, though hardly anyone else within and without the university accepted this then and some do not now. Universities tend to roughly divide their parts into hard sciences, arts and humanities, social sciences, and professional schools like law, medicine, pharmacy, social work, and nursing. Indeed the first meeting of our planning group with one of the associate chancellors of the university was with an educator responsible for nursing programs.

But we defined ourselves as an academic social science, built around the problem of crime control rather than a traditional discipline, but much like the other social sciences of sociology and psychology. We saw ourselves much closer to political science than public administration, and we distanced ourselves from professional schools like social work and library science. We saw the preparation of teaching materials, from interdisciplinary sources to be sure, and the conducting of sophisticated research on crime control to be little different in our field than in sociology or economics or similar fields. We were training not police or wardens, but scholars.[34]

Regardless of our self-conception, we did not fit well into the university table of organization. And because we were small, having no large undergraduate classes for many years, when the university roster of professional schools was called, we were among those named.

Graduate Curriculum in Criminal Justice: The Albany Model

The Albany Model rests less on our definition of academic criminal justice than on the graduate curriculum worked out over the planning year. The five of us met daily to translate our conceptions of criminal justice into a workable, doctoral-level academic list of courses and seminars. As with any group of five professors there was not always consensus, and occasionally some debates grew vigorous. At one point I suggested that all incoming graduate students be required to enroll in a "proseminar," a title I remembered from such a course in a sociology department. This involved each graduate professor meeting seriatim with the student, explaining his or her own field of emphasis and current research. The idea did not fly, but the title "proseminar" stuck and became the basic building block of our curriculum.[35]

We eventually agreed to divide the field of criminal justice into four major areas, each headed by a four-credit required survey course called (in each area) a "proseminar." The first was Nature of Crime, which was essentially a doctoral-level course in criminology dealing with theories of crime causation and crime measurement but not called "criminology" because this was the turf of the sociology department. The second was Criminal Justice Administration, a proseminar that dealt with the total crime control system as in the ABF survey, using as a text the materials and cases put together at Wisconsin. The third area, Law and Social Control, dealt with the legal process used to deprive a variety of persons (delinquents, mentally ill, etc.) of their liberty. The fourth proseminar, Planned Change, dealt with techniques for changing persons (rehabilitation), communities, and organizations such as the police or prison systems.

These four survey courses were the basic foundation of the Albany Model. The proseminars defined an area, a subfield, as well as being a required, graduate level, introductory course. Each proseminar had a list of graded courses dealing in greater detail with some aspect of the area. For instance, in the administration area one course was Prosecution and Adjudication and another was The Incarceration Process. And more specialized than the courses were seminars, of variable credit, listed in each area. So, for instance, a seminar on Prison Disciplinary Procedures or Long Term Inmates might be offered under the administration area.

In this manner, a substantive field of academic criminal justice was created. Whether the Albany Model has really dominated the field and spread throughout the country is subject to debate. Albany faculty and alumni tend to think so; others see variations on these four areas as significantly different.[36] In my opinion, variations are minor, sort of like saying that Auburn was not the prototype congregate maximum security prison because of minor architectural variations as prisons were built from state to state. The variations in criminal justice curricula commonly mentioned occurred most frequently in police science and correctional administration programs trying to catch up.

Of course, doctoral-level education is not simply class work and comprehensive examinations. It was agreed by the university and by our planning group that we would offer the Ph.D. but no other doctoral degree such as the D. Crim. from Berkeley. And above all a Ph.D. is a *research* degree, requiring the conducting of original research and defense of a doctoral dissertation.

Therefore, it was really necessary for us to create a fifth area, research methodology. Two types of research were considered appropriate: legal research and statistical measurement. Later historical research and some other nonquantitative methods were allowed for dissertation work. This was in direct contradiction to the American Bar Foundation survey techniques, which were essentially observational and descriptive. At the time it was felt more important to understand than to measure. But by the time the school was opened, qualitative research was denigrated as unscientific, and the now-ubiquitous computer was beginning to take over the land. This decision, stressing quantitative research techniques, had very serious consequences for the whole field of criminal justice, not just for academia.

Legal research required the assembly of at least a minimum law collection, and the university library sought to do this under the guidance of Fred Cohen and a legal librarian hired for this purpose. The Albany Law School and the New York State Library were also available.

Quantitative methodology meant high priority in hiring faculty competent in this area, for none of us were. I remembered Robert Hardt from years earlier in the Eastern Sociological Society and suggested his name. Bob was then at Syracuse University and did indeed join our faculty to provide competence in statistics and research design. Many additional quantitative methodologists followed so that we were able to offer advanced statistics, advanced research design, and computer competence. All doctoral candidates eventually had to pass tests demonstrating "research tool" abilities.[37]

Structure of the School: Faculty and Student Criteria

After a curriculum satisfactory to the planners was on paper and moving through the complex layers of approval necessary in New York State, we turned our attention to conceptual and policy matters necessary to make the school operational. We made some very important decisions at this stage and took some hard stands that, though softened somewhat over the years, at the time and in the decade following contributed greatly to the success of the school. These decisions included the following.

The school would be free-standing, headed by a dean. Original emphasis would be on doctoral-level education, both teaching and research. Faculty would be full-time members of the school; there would be no adjunct or joint-appointment professors. Entering graduate students would also be full time to produce graduates as soon as possible.

At the time, these were hard line decisions. Among other things, the full-time student requirement eliminated most fully employed criminal justice personnel who were used to taking one course at a time (in evenings) working toward a twenty-year doctoral degree. Until much later when some agencies, such as the New York State police, began sending troopers on full-time academic leave, we were not serving the state bureaucracy, as was the original intent of GSPA.

Because criminal justice was a new field, there were no undergraduate prerequisites except good grades and high Graduate Record Examination scores. Likewise, the cadre faculty had no specific academic requirements, including advanced degrees. Interest in some aspect of criminal justice and a national reputation as a scholar constituted the test. We needed a mixture of lawyers and social scientists, but otherwise no specific field of education was required.

The cadre faculty was required to cut itself adrift from more traditional university homes and cast their fates with this new field. Those of us who did so wondered if students would really enter this new graduate program and, if so, what they would be like and what expectations they would have.

Students did come and have continued to come over the past twenty years. At first they all wondered what they would do if indeed they received a master's or Ph.D. degree. Would there be jobs? What kind? Where? But the questioning ended after a few years, among the faculty, too. The discipline became established and seemed likely to continue. So far it has provided field employment opportunities for all graduates, master's and Ph.D. alike.

The Albany School After Twenty Years

The School of Criminal Justice at Albany has been operating continuously for more than twenty years. A large alumni group has been produced. More than 125 Ph.D. graduates and 500 master's degree graduates are in academia or field agencies. Today the full-time faculty numbers fifteen, including a dean.

In general the Albany Model of a criminal justice curriculum still exists very much as it was drafted that planning year. Changes have been made, of course, in the curriculum and original structure of the school. In general, the faculty remains full time, without adjuncts or joint appointments, and over the years prominent visiting professors have come and gone almost every year, contributing greatly to the program and to the reputation of the school.

The full-time student stance has been softened a little, but in general practitioners enter our student body more frequently on paid leave from their agencies as full-time graduate students rather than part-time students taking only single courses. Many active police officers and correctional workers have received master's degrees, and some police officers have earned doctorates.

An undergraduate major has been added to the school, growing out of courses first taught solely by graduate teaching fellows but now a full-fledged program involving some of the senior faculty as well. On paper, at least, the school has lost some of its autonomy, having been merged into the Rockefeller College of Public Affairs and Policy, with a provost now standing between the school's dean and the higher university administration.

In general, however, after twenty years the school is much the same as it was in its opening days. Changes in curriculum and structure have been largely cosmetic, sort of like calling an old prison a correctional facility.

Overall, the curriculum of the school—the Albany Model— has been very successful and widely imitated. The quality of faculty and students has remained high. As a legacy of the Bar Foundation survey, the school itself and the spread of the concept of higher education in criminal justice are truly remarkable and certainly major contributions.

But there is trouble in paradise, and its seeds were planted in the planning year at Albany twenty years ago.[38] This has to do with the research component of criminal justice higher education, left in those years, and now, to the whim of individual professors, chosen for faculty status by some demonstrated yet vague interest in studying almost any aspect of crime, criminal behavior, or crime control. There was then, and there is now, no consensus on the range of interests, focuses, or methodology of criminal justice research. Perhaps this is as it should be, indeed as it must be in American universities. But note that the Albany Model is limited to course work, to curriculum spread and coverage, at all degree levels, and not to research directions or methods.

The results of supporting eclectic research, of defining criminal justice solely in curriculum development but not at all in its research interests, will be detailed later. First it is necessary to look at the spread of this new academic field, whatever its limits, from Albany and some other centers throughout American higher education.

THE SPREAD OF CRIMINAL JUSTICE HIGHER EDUCATION

The spread of degree-granting schools and departments of criminal justice has been called a "quiet revolution" in American higher education. The proliferation of these programs at all aca-

demic levels—graduate, undergraduate, and two-year community colleges—has been truly remarkable and, given the traditional nature of college curricula, a real revolution.[39]

Within a decade of the creation of the Albany school, by the
mid-1970s, there were 729 associate degree programs, 376 bachelor's degree majors, 121 master's degree curricula, and about 5
doctorate-level criminal justice major fields in American colleges
and universities.[40] In another ten years, by the mid-1980s, the
numbers had grown to 871 bachelor's degree programs, 349
master's, and 7 doctoral granting schools. All this is despite
major reductions in federal funding with the abolition of the
Law Enforcement Assistance Administration (LEAA) and the
Law Enforcement Education Program (LEEP), which supported
college education for police officers, during the presidency of
Jimmy Carter.[41]

This spread of criminal justice programs was not due to sud-
den insight into their intrinsic worth. Quite the contrary. Academic criminal justice, as represented by the Albany school, was
vigorously opposed by various academic groups with a long tradition in police science and correctional administration. And it
was opposed by a number of sociological criminologists as turf
invasion.[42] Two major developments, quite different in nature,
helped spur the growth. The first involved education and training
grants from the Law Enforcement Assistance Administration,
and the second, proselytizing by some prominent criminal justice
educators, notably Dean Richard Myren of Albany and Donald
Riddle, the president of John Jay College in New York City.

The Federal Office of Manpower and Training

In addition to block grants for manpower, equipment, and
demonstration projects, LEAA provided funds for criminal justice education. LEEP gave funds directly to in-service and preser-
vice police students and some correctional students as well,
although many fewer of these. In response to federal money, a
number of colleges, particularly junior and two-year community
colleges, added police science courses, often taught by adjunct
professors from the community, usually police officers themselves. Nearly half of all LEEP-funded students were in these
programs, which, in general, were technical, vocational offerings,
not really academic in a traditional sense. In effect, a number of

police departments were using community colleges much like training academies.

As the concept of 'criminal justice'—meaning total system focus, understanding of the complexity of issues and responses, quality interdisciplinary education, and meaningful research on significant crime control problems—came to dominate "respectable" academic programs and professional organizations of educators, the federal granting agencies set similar standards for support of academic programs. At first, the federal program for police education (LEEP) was primarily vocational, but this changed with new organization of the agency in 1976 when J. Price Foster became director of manpower and training in LEAA. He was a strong believer in high-quality criminal justice education that covered the entire criminal justice system, not simply agencies in it. He sought to get rid of "cop shops" and vocational education in colleges.[43] Proposals from single colleges and from entire state systems of higher education requesting LEAA funds were evaluated by outside consultants to his office. Unless these programs were truly total system in scope and unless the course descriptions reflected academic rather than vocational materials, federal funds would be denied. The dean and faculty from Albany were frequently asked to make such evaluations.

University systems themselves, seeing the mushrooming of criminal justice programs on multiple campuses, viewed this growth with wonder and some suspicion. For instance, I was asked to evaluate all criminal justice programs, those operating and those proposed, in the Wisconsin higher educational system. Programs existed on many campuses, from the university in Milwaukee to the college in Superior. Platteville, in the western part of the state, had a large undergraduate program; Oshkosh wished to open one. The regents put a moratorium on programs until after my evaluation, during which I recommended closing some and changing others to create a more complete, higher-quality criminal justice approach.[44] Similar reviews were done by others around the nation and, in the main, the Bar Foundation theme of treating criminal justice as a total system, focusing on practice and legal controls, won the day.

By and large, because of the federal thrust toward criminal justice and a modicum of quality education (even the Police Professors Association no longer held it necessary for one who taught police to have been a policeman),[45] the program title of "criminal justice" replaced police science and correctional administration everywhere. Even the most prominent police administration programs, like the one at Michigan State, and correctional administration in places like Maryland and Florida became known as schools of criminal justice.

Some of the changes were cosmetic. A number of police administration programs simply changed names, perhaps added a course in corrections, and went merrily ahead. Outside evaluations exposed many such flimflams and they were denied funding. The result was that some high-quality programs in criminal justice were developed in many four-year colleges and some community colleges, too.

It was reasonably easy for many of these places to improve quality in teaching at both ends of the criminal justice process, policing and postsentencing. The most difficult part was to have adequate coverage of the middle stages, from bail through prosecution, adjudication, and sentencing. Nonetheless, serious attempts were made in many places to give full-scope coverage, sometimes with adjunct prosecutors and judges, but in general the federal mandate was met in the funded schools.

Criminal Justice Education Proselytizers

The prototype police administration school was the one founded by August Vollmer in California at Berkeley. Vollmer himself talked of bringing many fields together (standard sociological criminology, legal relations, criminal psychology, and so forth), but the Berkeley school curriculum was highly vocational, though not as much a training school as the one begun in San Jose by William Wiltberger, a Vollmer protege. Wiltberger wanted to "divorce police training from collegiate red tape," and his school had the frank mission of "training people to go out and do police work."[46] Vollmer sought to *educate* police leaders and, in this sense, was more open to other standard academic disciplines that would make his programs more acceptable in the university scholarly community. His faculty and staff did police surveys and wrote texts. Vollmer himself wrote *The Police and Modern Society* in 1936,[47] and one of his students (eventually his replacement as head of the Berkeley school), Orlando W. Wilson, wrote *Police Administration*, first published in 1950 and still in print with the aid of coauthors after Wilson's death.[48]

A number of police science or police administration programs developed, many of them by proteges of Vollmer. Some
were located in universities: the University of Washington, San
Jose State, Michigan State, and the like. Others were in four-year
colleges, but most were in what at the time were called "junior
colleges," now better known as "community colleges," offering
two-year programs, many in vocational subjects.

In 1946 an organization, formed before World War II by
Vollmer and called the "National Association of College Police
Training Officials," changed its name to the Society for the
Advancement of Criminology, but not without some opposition.
Wiltberger from San Jose called the new name "bunk," saying
that his interest was "turning out expert police officers not crimi-
nologists."[49]

The new title was unfortunate in other ways. For many sociologists, criminology meant the study of crime causation, but to
these police professors, criminology largely meant crime detection and enforcement, and indeed the new organization limited
membership to those who instructed in "professional and vocational training programs in criminology."[50] Eventually the Society for the Advancement of Criminology ran head-on into the
American Society of Criminology (ASC), an organization dominated by prominent sociological scholars. Increasingly the police
science professors felt the ASC was inhospitable to them, and in
1963 they formed a new association of their own, the International Association of Police Professors (IAPP).

But trouble was not over for the IAPP. Richard Myren had
spent ten years in a law enforcement program at Indiana before
becoming dean at Albany, where he became convinced that police
training, as practiced by most members of IAPP (of which he was
a member), was too vocational, too narrow to survive in academia. The same feeling was shared by Don Riddle, also an IAPP
member, who became president of John Jay College in New York,
a police school largely for officers of the NYPD. Myren and Riddle (both of whom became presidents of IAPP), along with some
other colleagues, joined together in an informal retreat at Hard
Labor Creek State Park outside Atlanta, Georgia, after the 1969
meeting of the IAPP in that city. At the instigation of Bill Mathias
from the University of South Carolina, six or seven professors
attended, and this small informal gathering has been named the

"Hard Labor Creek Group" by historian Frank Morn.[51] It met together annually for at least a decade to discuss police education. In general, the group agreed that the future lay in criminal justice education, not police vocational training, and eventually they came to dominate IAPP. Six of the next presidents of the organization came from the Hard Labor Creek Group.

The Creation of the Academy of Criminal Justice Sciences

Eventually Myren and Riddle were active in changing the name of IAPP to the Academy of Criminal Justice Sciences (ACJS) and vigorously advocated adding criminology, law and legal practices, courts, and correctional interventions to policing studies to make a criminal justice package an academic discipline. The older police training professors found themselves back to square one in ACJS as criminologists and correctional researchers, and those interested in court processes from bail to sentencing joined the society.[52]

Most police professors in the older programs were not academics but policemen themselves or police administrators, teaching police techniques, but not pursuing scholarly activities. Increasingly their credentials were being examined by their own colleges. Even Berkeley, after strong internal criticism during O. W. Wilson's tenure, struggled for academic acceptance, succeeded for a while, but became radicalized during the Vietnam years and was abolished.[53] Other programs sought to survive internal attack by more traditional academics but received no help from the national organization, ACJS. Quite the contrary, ACJS fought for accreditation of academic programs, and, although this itself did not succeed, the pronouncements of Myren, Riddle, and other Hard Labor Creek Group members effectively removed police training programs from college campuses.

Survival After the Demise of LEAA

Lyndon Johnson was an unfortunate wartime president. He lost the war in Vietnam, the War on Poverty, and the War on Crime. After the Omnibus Crime Control and Safe Streets Act and the creation of LEAA poured a great deal of federal money into crime control, the very nature of the war itself became a political liability. Instead of declining, crime seemed to grow worse. The money spent on law enforcement was used largely for hardware, refurbishing police armaments, and bringing the computer to many criminal justice agencies. Better crime data are often embarrassing, for the more accurate the picture of lawbreaking that we have, the more inefficient our enforcement measures appear.[54]

The war in Vietnam led to widespread civil disobedience at home, while the assassination of Martin Luther King brought street rioting across the country. Campus riots were also common in antiwar protest days. In the domestic melee the police and other criminal justice agencies were seen as repressive and brutal. The poor, objects of another war, were often the major targets of law enforcement. Police became compared to an army of occupation in minority neighborhoods. Indeed "law enforcement" and "War on Crime" came to be viewed as code words for racism.

In short, the War on Crime became a political embarrassment, and, although it lingered through the Nixon presidency (in fact, a new president's crime commission was created),[55] by the time of President Carter, the War on Crime could no longer be openly expressed. LEAA was abolished, and, except for a small research bureau, the federal War on Crime was over, ignominiously lost.[56] Today we are moving into a federal war on the epidemic growth of drug use, but this war has yet to be clearly defined. Already it has generated racial and ethnic overtones on the domestic front, and it raises some tough political issues on the control of drug trafficking from the South and Central American fronts.[57]

In theory, the end of significant federal funding for crime control, particularly the ending of LEEP funds, should have seriously reduced, if not ended, the spread of criminal justice education. After all, the influx of federal money was a major factor in its spread and, indeed, in its acceptance on some money-short campuses. But this did not happen, at least to a significant extent. A few totally LEEP-funded programs failed, generally those in small community colleges. In general, however, criminal justice education remained widespread in United States colleges and universities and has expanded.

The most serious aspect of the end of federal funding was a drying up of widespread research grants. The National Institute of Justice (NIJ) still funds some criminal justice research, as do other federal agencies. But the golden days of lots of federal research money are gone. In general, private funding sources have not moved back into this field since being replaced by federal agencies some years ago.

Location and Identity in Universities and Colleges

The academic revolution of criminal justice was quiet, more like an epidemic than a revolt. It caught by surprise many college administrators, trustees, regents, and faculty in traditional fields. New disciplines in college curricula tend to grow slowly, in response to outside pressures and needs, and tend to be added reluctantly by educators jealous of traditional fields and suspicious of change that might threaten academic standards or create imbalance in teaching loads and research opportunities.

Generally the response to demands for university involvement with nontraditional problems or fields can be handled by the creation of research centers and institutes. They are temporary in duration, funded by "soft" money (grants and awards from external funding sources), and staffed by consultants and released-time professors not part of the permanent line-staff tenure-track professoriate of the college or university. Or new programs can be housed in the "extension division" common in some land grant universities. Here shadow faculty, not part of the heart of the college, can offer short-term training institutes or engage in "practical" research or consultation to meet specific needs not considered to be of mainline academic concern.

Overall, however, criminal justice did not follow these attached-but-not-in routes. True, there were some law school research centers—at Chicago and Harvard, among others—but generally criminal justice became a free-standing academic discipline, a major in undergraduate programs, and a separate graduate offering in many colleges and universities. The really revolutionary aspect of this development was that criminal justice became an academic offering built around a problem, crime control, rather than a traditional academic discipline like sociology, psychology, history, biology, and other core physical or social sciences, or the humanities. Although not unique—somewhat similar developments have occurred in computer science, labor and industrial relations, forestry, and the like—the rise and growth of criminal justice has been startling enough to give pause to accrediting bodies, trustees, university councils, and other academic governance units.

Location on New and Secondary Campuses

In general, older and prestigious universities in the United States are organized as tightly as panzer divisions. The addition of new degree granting programs is inevitably slow and reluctant, and, if created at all, new programs must follow a long pathway of academic debate, suspicion of theoretical soundness and necessity, challenges to academic standards of faculty and curriculum, and, less noble perhaps, fights for turf and resources.[58] Specialized professional schools may be added to large universities that tolerate some off-line programs—pharmacy, veterinary schools, atmospheric sciences, and even nursing. But, with some exceptions, criminal justice did not claim professional school status. Instead it sought and won placement among the social sciences in undergraduate curricula and a status comparable to political science, sociology, or public administration in graduate programs.

What made it possible, and certainly speeded the revolution, was the great national expansion of colleges and universities in the three decades following the years of World War II. New colleges and universities, and major branches of old ones, were created, built, and staffed with the rapidity and universality with which we build prisons today. And for approximately the same age cohort. Young people, returning veterans (not only of World War II but later of Korea and Vietnam), baby boomers, echo boomers, and the great desire for postsecondary education among almost ever-increasing proportions of our youth, fueled the necessity for college expansion. This expansion, primarily in public, state-funded higher education, swept our nation.

The older, prestigious colleges and universities, from Colgate to Harvard, held their own but became more selective. State-funded higher educational systems became just this, *systems* of complex levels of education, from two-year community colleges to doctorate-granting universities. Mega-universities were created, governed, and evaluated by various accrediting bodies. These new and expanded state universities, as well as their private counterparts, responded to the great social movements sweeping our nation. The attack on poverty with a promise of educational mobility, the civil rights movement, women's liberation, and the other vast changes in our culture, each in its own way, contributed to the incredible growth of colleges and universities.

It was in this context of great social change, vast educational entrepreneurship, and the zeitgeist that stressed both the worth of college education and the corresponding demand that colleges meet our societal needs, that criminal justice entered the academic marketplace.

No old, established, and highly prestigious private university or college—Princeton, Yale, Harvard, Pennsylvania, Hamilton, Colgate, Union, and all the rest—adopted a criminal justice program. Nor did the great state universities—Michigan, Wisconsin, Ohio State, Illinois, and others. Instead, criminal justice programs originated, grew, and flourished in *new* state universities (e.g., State University of New York) and, in the main, on the secondary campuses of state university systems.[59] University of Wisconsin, not in Madison, but in Milwaukee. Not University of Michigan, but Michigan State. Not Illinois at Champaign-Urbana, but Illinois in Chicago Circle. Not Rutgers at New Brunswick, but Rutgers in Newark. Not Florida in Gainesville, but Florida State in Tallahassee, International University in Miami, and Florida Southern in Tampa. The new wine simply did not fit in the old bottles, was not acceptable to established universities and colleges. But new universities and recently opened secondary campuses accepted, though rarely welcomed, criminal justice in their structures and their catalogues.

Why Survival and Growth?

Academic criminal justice is still alive, well, and expanding. New doctoral programs, often frankly based on the Albany Model, have opened in recent years. The number of master's degree programs has increased almost 200 percent in the past few years. And everywhere baccalaureate majors are booming. Why should this be so?

There are probably numerous reasons, but it seems likely that four major factors account for the continuity and the growth of this field:

1. Despite the decline of federal support, crime remains a domestic problem of the highest priority.

2. Criminal justice is an intrinsically interesting subject. Cops and robbers is standard American folk fare, and academic concentration in this field is ever fascinating, changing,

and current. Put another way, it is simply more interesting as a discipline than many of the traditional social sciences, including the big two: sociology and psychology.

3. Literature in this field has mushroomed over the past twenty years. Scholarly journals, textbooks, monographs, and all-in-all a solid scholarly literature are available at all academic levels.

4. Employment in field-related positions is still available. Graduates with bachelor's degrees have no worse chance of field employment than sociologists or psychologists or historians with only a baccalaureate. And, with some prior agency experience, probably a better chance. Master's degree graduates are filling research positions in crime control agencies and planning commissions and are working on-line in police and correctional functions. Doctoral graduates mostly become professors, but some find top-level research and planning jobs. Employment opportunities are by no means saturated.[60]

In the expansion of criminal justice programs, at all academic levels, the Albany Model has played an extremely important role; in part because this model appears to have worked well for twenty years, and in part because Albany doctoral alumni increasingly spread throughout higher education. They bring to their new academic posts the germs of the Albany Model and a solid grounding in criminal justice education.

To the extent that the Albany experience is an outgrowth of the Bar Foundation survey, and I think this case has been made, then its implications extend far beyond the Albany school and, indeed, have spread through the higher education institutions of our nation.

THE AMERICAN BAR FOUNDATION SURVEY
AND CRIMINAL JUSTICE EDUCATION TODAY

The ABF survey was, in itself, a modest study. It took a long time, nearly seventeen years, from start to completion, but only two years were spent in gathering data through field observations. It engaged a lot of people, a number of whom became prominent scholars and leaders in criminal justice education. Yet it was intended as a pilot study, involving only three states with roughly similar legal systems (no grand jury indictments in common felony cases), and, except for Detroit, did not deal with crime control in our major metropolitan centers.

Although one of its major contributions was the focus placed on the entire criminal process, from police investigation to parole, as a complex, interlocking decision system, it did not actually fully cover all decision stages. For instance, little emphasis was placed on the bail decision point, and prison processes were untouched. First appearance before a magistrate was treated primarily as an end to police control over suspects. The complexity of pretrial release was analyzed and dealt with later by the Vera Foundation in the Manhattan Bail Project.[61] Prisons and, to a lesser extent, jails had been much studied by sociologists, though not in the Bar Foundation style of decision stages through the correctional process. They were omitted from the field research, however, because they were perceived as being at an already well-researched stage.[62] Except for sentencing, probation, and release from correctional facilities on parole, study of the correctional process was abbreviated.

Yet despite limited settings and incomplete coverage, the survey had a significant impact on many aspects of criminal justice practices, particularly policing, and of course led directly to the development of academic programs in this field. "Criminal justice" became a much more widely used, if not uniquely new, term in our social lexicon. And other phrases, too—"police discretion," "plea bargaining"—comparatively new then, are widely used and understood today.

As I think has been demonstrated, the contributions to the development of academic criminal justice by the ABF survey and the personnel involved in it are profound. Indeed, the creation of this new university field as it now exists may be the Bar Foundation's most important legacy. How well this has all turned out is another question, difficult to assess with certainty after twenty years of academic experience, but with some indications that the results are mixed. No surprise, perhaps. Most experiments in education (or otherwise for that matter) take turns unanticipated by and often unwelcome to their founders.

Major Contributions of the ABF Survey
to Criminal Justice Higher Education

Conceptual Development The most important contribution of the ABF to higher education is the conceptual development of criminal justice itself. This has been translated into an important academic field focused on societal response to a major domestic problem. If nothing else, sustained university involvement in its study is clearly necessary.

Emphasis on the Total System Emphasis on the total system of crime control, including all the operating agencies from police to parole boards, is characteristic of criminal justice programs today. Set against legislation and appellate court decisions, the daily decision choices of police, prosecutors, trial judges and juries, probation officers, correctional administrators, and parole officials become the scope of coverage. No single agency or decision stage dominates academic interest. No longer are the police and policing or corrections and prisons the sole focus of academic teaching and research. Instead, the entire system is treated as an interlocking series of related decisions. This, of course, is a major change from the cop shops and penology programs of prior academic involvement.

Study of Daily Operations Academic criminal justice stresses the actual daily operations in the criminal justice process, highlighting ordinarily low-visibility decisions and informal practices in processing cases. In this way, it makes discretionary choices visible and perhaps possible to review, contain, or control.

Stress on Complexity Criminal justice emphasizes the complexity of situations, decision choices, and consequences in field responses to a wide variety of conventional crimes. The absurdity of quick-fix panaceas from full enforcement to harsh sentencing becomes apparent when day-by-day crime control situations are understood. And simplistic answers to *any* crime control problem fall when the complex balance between values of individual freedom, due process, and the objectives of effectively and efficiently controlling crimes, from skid-row inebriation to robberies, is seen in operational context. If nothing else, higher education in criminal justice should shatter the myth of system tinkering as a quick panacea for any type crime control.

Continuing Need for Research   Academic criminal justice, more than anything else, emphasizes the need for sustained and sophisticated research in all aspects of criminal justice administration. The Bar Foundation survey claimed no final answers to controlling crime but did highlight the need to carefully examine daily practices of the crime control agencies. The ABF survey involved field research and, to this extent, was a harbinger of the need to look beyond appellate court decisions or the official summary data of agencies to understand the realities of criminal justice in our world.

Policing in University Studies   The ABF survey brought police and policing into the mainline arena of university teaching and research. Police had always been the least professionalized of criminal justice agencies, with officers viewed more as automatons, as gatekeepers carrying out legislative and court mandates, than as decision makers in their own right. The ABF survey vastly increased knowledge of the police role, probably more than all others. Far from simple gatekeepers, police came to be seen as much more important and policing as the most complex, most difficult, and perhaps most controversial role in our system of crime control. No longer was it appropriate for the academic focus to be on police structure and administration in a separate university corner called "police science." Police officer judgment and discretion became a main theme in criminal justice programs, and policing came to be viewed not only as the first point of citizen contact with the system, but also as serving the most important role in the entire system.

Increased Scholarly Literature in the Field   The ABF survey both created and stimulated a large amount of scholarly literature in the field of criminal justice. In addition to the five final monographs, from the early publication of the pilot project volumes on, increasingly sophisticated articles and research papers traceable to ABF work began appearing in journals, in both law and social science. Today, a large amount of respected literature in this field exists, certainly not all derived from the ABF work. But a good deal of it started there, and the Bar Foundation deserves its share of credit for stimulating modern scholarly analysis of criminal justice issues.

Contrary Developments and Unanticipated Consequences in the Academic Field of Criminal Justice

As with all academic programs, criminal justice had two major missions: educating students about all dimensions of crime control in a democracy and conducting research to advance knowledge of the field. The didactic mission was accomplished best, producing successive waves of graduates with sophisticated awareness of the complexities of on-line crime control and the delicate balance between individual freedom and efficient and effective law enforcement and court and correctional processing. It produced manpower for the agencies of crime control, offering higher educational credentials for those already working in the field and first-time employment for newcomers. There was, and continues to be, a need for this. Field-related employment and promotions up the managerial ladders of crime control agencies have been the common, even usual, result of graduation from academic programs in this new field.

The second mission, research, has gone on from day one. A large, research-based literature in the field has grown. But the impact of this research, the serendipitous paths it has followed, has only partially met the hopes and dreams of those who started this venture.

Many of the myth-destroying results of the ABF study—the folly of full enforcement, the futility of mandatory procedures for control of extremely complex behaviors, the lack of easy solutions to intrinsically variable law violation situations—have not carried over. Indeed much of the research, and the advocacy flowing from it, has done the opposite. Particularly in the area of sentencing and corrections, major research thrusts have sought to demonstrate the feasibility of quick-fix, sure-fire, simple solutions to extremely complex issues.

On balance, some hopes were realized, some were dimmed. An assessment of the negative or, at best, mixed results of this academic venture would include the following.

Primary Concern for Academic Acceptance   As the new kid on the block, criminal justice tended to see its first task as winning recognition and acceptance in the world of academia. This is understandable, perhaps, for faulty had to be wooed from traditional fields and potential students had to be convinced of its

worth. And the fate of police science and correctional administration programs, often considered by the uninformed as parents
of criminal justice, was well known. If not actually abolished,
many teetered on the rim of being cut or shunned for the academic heresy of not being sufficiently scholarly for full university
membership. They were considered too vocational, too training
oriented.

So, as with all new fields, criminal justice faculty spent a
great deal of time defining the field, putting in place checks and
balances to avoid the fate of older cop shops, and, in general,
seeking respectability in college and university corridors. All of
this is time consuming and diversionary from the more fundamental tasks of researching and understanding the crime control
system of our society. In short, the first few years—perhaps
nationally as long as a decade—were involved in self-preening
and academic aggrandizement.

Among other things, criminal justice professors sought to
build new national societies and regional associations. The
American Society of Criminology experienced a period of rapid
growth over the past twenty years. It attracted persons from
many academic disciplines and operating research agencies. It
became the major multidisciplinary outlet for the reporting of
research at annual meetings and publication in the ASC journal
Criminology. However, the principal organization for teachers in
criminal justice programs still is the Academy of Criminal Justice
Sciences discussed earlier. ACJS grew primarily out of police
organizations (the International Association of Police Professors)
and attracted to membership mostly community college and
undergraduate professors and administrators.[63] The organization
actively debated curriculum, faculty standards, and for a while,
the possibility of becoming a criminal justice accrediting body.[64]
The bottom line, however, is that the association's major contribution was not to criminal justice education but to professional
politicking.[65] It became a vehicle for professors in third-tier programs to achieve office in a national organization. It gave annual
awards to prominent scholars, most of whom were nonmembers,
thereby borrowing some academic prestige.[66] And, almost despite
its early limitations in scholarship, it has grown, and it holds an
annual conference where papers are delivered by recent waves of
well-educated young criminal justice professors.

From the perspective of outside impact on the daily operations of the criminal justice system, the beginnings of academic criminal justice were wheel spinning. But inside academia it worked well. Criminal justice won acceptance on most campuses and a good deal of respect on some.

The early Albany Model—or comparable models by any other name—had four parts that aided in this university acceptance:

1. Sound curriculum development through the doctoral level took a total system approach and set rigorous academic performance standards.

2. It called for staffing by an interdisciplinary faculty each meeting traditional academic standards for appointment and tenure.

3. It required full-time faculty and full-time students during the developmental years. This eliminated heavy adjunct professor staffing, the bane of earlier police and correctional programs. Adjuncts have no continuing responsibility for the development of the field and no real continuity beyond teaching classes. It also avoided the joint-appointment techniques, involving part-time academics with primary loyalty to their basic discipline. Joint-appointment faculty tend to run home when it rains. And full-time students increased production of alumni at the cost, of course, of denying one-step credentialing to persons already working in the field who labored toward degrees over many years.

4. Criminal justice was located in the university as a relatively independent school or department, not merely a branch of some other academic unit. It wanted as much academic and budgeting autonomy as possible. It sought a position of no loyalty except to the field, no budget but its own, no recruitment or promotion of faculty except as self-determined, subject only to overall university standards of academic excellence. Attempts to gain such status were rarely successsful. Criminal justice often found itself a part of some broader university unit, usually a school of urban affairs or one with a similar title. But enough autonomy was won to make the field not only visible but largely self-contained.

Adherence to these four principles during the developmental years was essential to survival in the university. But just doing this involved endless internal committee work, many skirmishes with cognate fields and university administrators, and what, to many waiting to evaluate the field, must have seemed to be little more than busy work. They asked: When will criminal justice get on with it? When will it address the major crime control problems of our world?

Lack of Central Research Themes   In the development and spread of the field there was some consensus about commonality of curriculum. There were variations from place to place, including a few differences in program names—"Justice Studies," "Public Justice"—but most were called "Criminal Justice," and the courses covered the total system, from police to prisons and release. The weakest points in curriculum, except for law school programs, were in the middle stages from charging to sentencing. Nonetheless, agency-specific curricula, police studies or correctional administration, fell by the wayside, and, by and large, students educated at one level in one place could transfer credits and knowledge to another with a good deal of comfort and continuity.

Although curriculum themes of total system and the complexity of choices and alternatives have carried through course work, criminal justice research has followed no such common pattern. A total lack of consensus about the nature, range, focus, and methodology of criminal justice research continues. Perhaps this is inevitable, and quite proper, in a university setting.

In general, the strongest fiber of academic freedom is attached to the research interests of any professor. An agreed-upon curriculum must be offered for proper program accreditation. Almost everywhere courses have the same or similar titles, although there is certainly wide freedom given to professors in text selection, course content, and teaching techniques. But the research thrust of any department or school is simply the cumulative interests of the professors and their graduate students. Faculty hiring practices in any given program ultimately determine the research contributions of this department.

Although there is much rhetoric about interdisciplinary staffing, in most places faculty structure was one or two lawyers joining with a large group of sociologists. Occasionally there is a psychologist, a police science graduate, or a political scientist, but on the whole, sociologists along with a few lawyers have come to dominate the field.

Faculty are selected, in part, by necessary curriculum coverage, and, in most programs, survey and follow-up courses reflect more or less traditional sociological or law school offerings. Criminology, constitutional law, delinquency, community and institutional corrections, organizational change, and the like are by no means unique to criminal justice. A traditionally educated sociologist or lawyer can find plenty to teach in standard criminal justice curricula.

Faculty are also selected by demonstrated interest in some, indeed any, aspect of crime or delinquency (and this is often more important than teaching competence). The standard academic test of research and publication—publish or perish—is rigorously applied in criminal justice programs as part of the need to be seen as appropriately scholarly to belong in the university. The focus of any professor's work is largely irrelevant as long as there are sufficient books, monographs, refereed articles, and other academic equivalents having some reference to crime or delinquency. Any topic remote from or close to crime control— women in prison, self-concepts of delinquents, subcultures of violence, deterrence, inmate tattooing, terrorism, homosexuality, homicide rates, delinquent cohorts, victim studies, battered women, sentence disparity—is generally considered appropriate, as long as sufficient publications accompany the applicant's resume. The result, of course, is that the collective research of any program is the result of chance, drift, and the foibles of staffing patterns.

The research of some professors reflects the Bar Foundation's interests in on-line enforcement decision making; others are far remote. Collectively, research products from the field have turned out to be eclectic, almost random, with only a distant relevance to the origins of the field of criminal justice.

Quantitative Research Methodology and Identity with Criminology   As the field of criminal justice aged and faculty rosters expanded, quantitative research came to dominate annual programs and publications. Not only was observational research, as in the Bar Foundation survey, denigrated, it was virtually outlawed. Competence in the use of computers and statistical techniques of a great deal of sophistication came to be required of graduate students. Numbers crunching came to dominate criminal justice, a situation not unlike the one in most social sciences, where precision of measurement was held necessary to convert these fields into "real" sciences. Truth was to be found in regression analysis. Few articles for publication would be accepted without appropriate tables, graphs, charts, and extremely careful methodical analyses.

After a few years of growth and expansion, most curricula of criminal justice programs came to be dominated by two developments that have had a profound effect on the field. The first was the duplication of essentially criminology courses and the second was an exclusive stress on quantitative measurement.

With some exceptions, most of the funded and published research of early years could well have been done by criminologists in sociology departments. For instance, a great deal of effort was spent on the measurement of the incidence of crime in our society, a traditional criminological concern. Victimology studies, as a contrast to officially reported crimes, occupied a number of faculty and graduate student assistants for some time. Likewise, self-report studies, primarily of delinquents, became a major research focus.

In addition to crime rate measurements, a lot of research dealt with causal theories of delinquent, not criminal, behavior. Some studies were of adult crimes, robberies for instance, but in the main, delinquency dominated causal research, as it has in conventional criminology. Longitudinal studies of youth cohorts by sociologists at the University of Pennsylvania have resonated throughout the country and currently are a major research interest. Deterrence studies, particularly of the death penalty, a standard sociological research topic, also became a continuing research focus. Compliance with gun laws, the effect of stricter punishments for driving while intoxicated, and the like were also commonly dealt with by criminal justice scholars using careful methodology and clever statistical analysis. The basic question these illustrations give rise to is whether departments of criminal justice are merely new sites for standard criminological research. A second question is how much high powered statistical analysis really contributes to our understanding of crime control.

Simplistic Answers: Just Deserts, Determinant Sentences, and Guidelines   One of the major contributions of the Bar Foundation was the demonstrated complexity of crime control responses.

There clearly were no easy answers, no simple formula responses, to any issue from police choices to parole decision making. Moreover any attempt to mandate responses, to eliminate judgment at any point in the system, simply diverted discretion elsewhere. Yet with the advent of computers and line-of-best-fit statistics there was concerted effort to quantify and to mandate decision making, particularly in the later stages of the process.

In the early and mid-1970s a major sentencing change, a "reform," swept the nation like a plague. In response to a number of perceived inequities in the indeterminate sentence structures found in all states, proposals were made to return criminal sentences to flat, definite terms with no spread between minimum and maximum prison terms. Parole would be unnecessary in a determinate sentencing structure, and parole boards could be abolished. A number of criminal justice professors, Andrew Von Hirsch, first at Albany now at Rutgers, and David Fogel, at Illinois, led this trend.[67]

The movement to abolish parole and indeterminacy, which were so hard won in our system of criminal justice, was supported by both liberal and conservative factions in and outside criminal justice. A number of prison inmates argued for determinacy, feeling that commonly imposed indeterminate sentences left them anxious and unsure of their release dates and that discretionary parole board decisions cloaked racial and political discrimination. When they went in, they wanted to know when they would get out. No discretion, under the guise of rehabilitation, should decide prison terms. Instead, all who were convicted of the same crime should do the same time; they wanted definite sentences and certainty of release. Many assumed that the time they would do under such a system, based solely on convicted criminal behavior, would be shorter than if they had to convince a parole board of their readiness to return to the community.

Conservatives also resonated to the determinate sentence, particularly its parole abolition thesis. Parole was long viewed as an usurpation of legislative and judicial sentencing power, a form of leniency that returned high-risk prisoners too early to community living. A get-tough-with-criminals sentiment was growing in America at the same time prisoners themselves were calling for parole abolition and flat sentences. Indeed, the death penalty, thought outlawed in 1972, was on the way back and is now bigger (in terms of death row inmates) than ever in our history. For once both liberals and conservatives agreed, and the result was the overturn of indeterminate sentences and abolition of parole in about ten states.

The shorter, definite sentences hoped for by the inmates did not come about. Uncertainty and disparity among those convicted of the same crime could be addressed by long as well as short definite sentences, and long definite sentences, without chance of parole, became the order of the day. It was during this movement that prison populations began growing to the overcrowded state in which they now exist.[68]

The definite sentencing movement rested on two general views of imprisonment. The first was that rehabilitative efforts common in prisons were ineffective. "Nothing works" was demonstrated by some follow-up studies of inmates who returned to crime and imprisonment.[69] It mattered little that many rehabilitative measures in prison were largely functional in removing some of the pains and drabness of incarceration. David Rothman had called rehabilitation the "noble lie" because many prison keepers knew they could not change their sinners to saints, yet offered rehabilitative programs to soften the prison existence and perhaps improve some of the life chances of their charges.[70] They did not expect miracles, but rehabilitation critics did.

The second string on the definite sentencing bow was "just deserts," the imposition of punishment resting solely on the crime committed. Punishing criminals became a theme of the 1970s, one as common as was rehabilitation in the preceding decades. Just deserts distributed punishment in proportion to the criminal act, not to any circumstances surrounding the offense or differences in conditions in offenders' backgrounds. It sought to end sentence disparity by incarcerating all criminal offenders for the same term, based on the act. And indeed this does end one form of disparity, namely persons convicted of the same crime sentenced differently. But another disparity exists if two dissimilar persons, convicted of the same crime, are sentenced alike.

Just deserts and the move to definite sentencing were opening shots in the attack on the sophisticated analysis of decision making in criminal justice exemplified by the Bar Foundation material. More attacks would follow, as the methodologists with their computers sought to quantify criminal justice decisions.

One of the major research contributions of criminal justice professors was the development, implementation, and spread of parole guidelines. And after parole guidelines came sentencing guidelines, which are now dominating the sentencing structures of many jurisdictions. Professor Leslie Wilkins at Albany was in the forefront of the parole guideline movement.[71] Wilkins hit on the idea of quantifying parole release decision making by extracting and weighing factors that affected the release decision. Once this was done, he could build a guideline table of these variables in an "experience table," one axis of which indicated the seriousness of the offense and the other the risk of reviolation. A line of "best fit" was drawn among experience variables that, if read correctly, would result in the time of parole release (or denial) in any given case. Such tables could be prepared and given to parole boards, and the proper and consistent release or denial decision could simply be read from the intersecting variables. It was a paint-by-numbers approach that, it was claimed, would make parole fair, consistent, and automatic unless the board members could explain, in writing, why they deviated from the guideline choice.

Once appropriately researched and developed, Wilkins convinced the federal parole board to try his guidelines. Eventually they adopted these, and federal law was altered to accommodate this technique. Wilkins was proud that his basic approach moved from preliminary research to actual legal implementation in about four years. Indeed few research projects in this field can come anywhere near the translation of a research topic to mandatory implementation in this time frame.

If factors in parole release could be quantified, tabled, and mandated, why not sentencing choices? Why not indeed. Sentencing guidelines were the next step. Following Wilkins's pioneering work, many academicians and practitioners got into the act, and sentencing guidelines now exist in the federal system and in many states.[72]

It is interesting to speculate on the long-term consequence of the use of "hard data" methodology and computer technology to quantify sentencing and parole decision making. In addition to the Bar Foundation evidence of the complexity of *any* decision choice in crime control processing, there has been a long history of parole and sentencing institutes during which board members and judges dealt with all the variations in objectives and relevant factors in release and sentencing decisions. Federal judges met together by circuits in sentencing institutes for years. Many states followed the federal lead for their criminal court judges. And parole decision-making institutes were active for these same years under the sponsorship of the National Council on Crime and Delinquency.

One thing that was clear from these training conferences was that neither parole release nor sentencing choice was a simple matter. Disparity was and is an issue, but it is neither easy nor simple to define, given equally valid objectives for decisions with different results. Saying that sentencing offenders convicted of the same crime to different terms is disparate or that sentencing offenders with vastly different backgrounds convicted of the same crime to the same sentence is also disparate is easy. But the word *disparity* is pejorative; it implies a wrongful decision, one not justified by the facts or the purpose of the law. The difficulty is that many different objectives are appropriate in making a sentencing or release decision but often lead to different, not necessarily disparate, results. One judge may sentence an offender to prison primarily to restrain or incapacitate him, an appropriate sentencing goal. Another judge, in a similar case, may sentence the offender to a different term as an example to others, a deterrent objective that is also appropriate. A third judge might select a different sentence believing prison programs could rehabilitate the violator. And so it goes. And parole board members consider many factors other than risk of reviolation in making release decisions. A parole commissioner may properly take into account the inmate's institutional adjustment that, if bad, involving chronic troublemaking, may lead to parole denial because the board does not wish to encourage institutional disruption.

Sentencing, release, and revocation decisions are as complex in their own way as police investigation and arrest decisions. All call for a sophisticated knowledge of the consequence of decisions on other parts of the system. Arrest practices clearly affect correctional intake down the line, and sentencing choices reverberate back to police arrest procedures. Likewise parole decisions affect police work because known criminals are sent back to the community.

Sentencing is not just a judicial choice, nor is it easily controlled by legislative desires to mandate punishment. The entire prosecution process, including prevalent plea bargaining practices, is as much a part of sentencing as judicial decisions from the bench. To attempt to quantify these stages and to mandate the results is actually a disservice to honest, thoughtful judgments by the actors. Moreover, since only certain decisions are guidelined and mandated, the homeostatic balance of the complex criminal process is ignored. To create sentencing guidelines without corresponding prosecution guidelines and, for that matter, without police arrest guidelines is to force discretion, necessarily exercised, to other stages in the process.[73]

Could *all* decisions be guidelined and mandated? Perhaps, but like the myth of full enforcement, if it ever came about, it would likely be, in the words of Judge Charles Breitel, "ordered but intolerable."[74] Oversimplification of complex decisions is contrary to everything the Bar Foundation study demonstrated. To the extent this study influenced American higher education in criminal justice, and it certainly did, it lost its impact in the computer revolution that led to sentencing guidelines and the punitive philosophy of just deserts. Yet both developments came out of criminal justice education.

And it might be noted that crime measurement studies themselves, quite apart from the guideline development, have not really addressed the complexity of labeling pointed out in Bar Foundation research. Because of the near universality of plea bargaining, conviction labels of prison inmates by no means necessarily reflect their actual criminal conduct. Yet conviction labels are often taken as "hard data" in follow-up recidivism studies of released inmates. And caseloads of probationers are often analyzed as if they were selected from carefully prepared presentence reports. It is nearly as likely that the prosecutor made a probation promise, without any presentence report, in exchange for a guilty plea. Yet probationers, too, are "hard data" for computer analysis.

Of course, sophisticated statistical measurements of social and criminal data have value. Evaluation studies of criminal justice programs would be virtually impossible without accurate follow-up measures. But garbage in, garbage out is a common designation of computer research. Oversimplification of operational complexity is anathema to really understanding the criminal justice process. Needed most are sophisticated designs or models of whole-system decision making that, perhaps, can be translated into computer language. To seize one or two decision points and simplistically quantify the decision is bad enough. To mandate the quantification is ludicrous.

The School of Criminal Justice at SUNY at Albany is the oldest graduate program in the field and, according to a wide variety of outside rankings, possibly the best. Over the past twenty years, Albany has granted some 125 Ph.D. degrees and more than 500 master's degrees.

A question can be fairly put about the quality as well as the quantity of the doctoral dissertations completed under Albany faculty sponsorship. In this regard, I examined the first 101 doctoral dissertations completed in the school and classified them according to whether they were products likely to be unique to a school of criminal justice or could just as well have been done in other, more traditional departments. I am fully aware that my (or any) classification system can be questioned and, indeed, that some folks would say that any research done in a criminal justice setting is criminal justice as long as it has something to do with crime or delinquency.

At any rate, admitting all biases, my classification of the first 101 dissertations is as follows:

Twenty-eight focused on criminal justice issues (eleven on policing, two on bail, three on prosecution, five on sentencing [all on guideline research], four on corrections, and only three on the total system or at least more than one decision stage in it).

Forty-one dissertations were essentially standard criminology research and could well have been done in a sociology department (of these forty-one, eight dealt exclusively with delinquency).

Twelve dissertations were essentially social-psychological in content, dealing with such matters as stress among criminal justice personnel, inmate coping in confinement, and classification of delinquents by maturity levels.

Five dissertations were essentially legal and could have appeared in standard law reviews.

Six were historical studies of programs, agencies, or prison systems.

Nine were sort of traditional police or correctional administration work, having to do with agency organizational structure, recruitment standards for personnel, manpower selection testing, or other bread-and-butter matters.

All told, from the point of view of a purist in criminal justice and a veteran of the American Bar Foundation wars, the research results are somewhat disappointing. The Albany Model, to the extent it exists at all, begins and ends with curriculum and educational standards. It clearly does not extend to any sort of systematic research. Indeed, if the school were looked at backwards, inferring what it was from its doctoral research products, one would be hard put to describe it. The research output is fragmented and eclectic and casts little shadow, except for individual efforts here and there.

Problems in Teaching and System Research   Perhaps criminal justice became much like older sociological programs in both teaching and research because it is difficult to teach and to research, at least by professors trained in more traditional academic fields. Knowledge of the real world of policing, prosecution, sentencing, corrections, and beyond requires intimate familiarity with field practices by persons who have been there, either in employment or in observational research. A sense of the complexity of the police task or of parole decision making cannot be learned from studying charts of police organizational structure or reading about parole. Just as law professors, used to teaching from casebooks, had little knowledge of street practices, so criminologists, though perhaps very familiar with some part of the criminal justice system (usually prisons, juvenile training schools, or community corrections), were lost dealing with other parts. The very existence of criminal justice as a new discipline meant that it was not covered in more traditional curricula or research. The easiest thing to do, maybe the only thing at first, was to carry old discipline issues and techniques into the new field. At any rate, both the courses and the research products of criminal justice have been almost indistinguishable from criminology with some standard legal research thrown in.

Virtually no attention has been given to the total system of criminal justice except in single, broad introductory survey courses. And here it is a rare professor who has had the knowledge to move comfortably from police issues to prosecution and adjudication, sentencing, and beyond. And research that has focused on one stage in the process usually has failed to address the effect of change on other points in the system flow. As has been noted, sentencing guideline research almost totally ignored the discretion of prosecutors to actually control sentencing outcome. An awareness that discretion denied one place balloons in another has been missing in much of criminal justice research.

How this could go on in a new academic field that grew out of the Bar Foundation work is inexplicable. Instead of carrying forward with analysis of the overall process, instead of focusing on the complexity of street, court, and correctional situations, the trend has been to ignore system issues and to search for simple answers in controlling crime.

Not all is gloom and doom. Some excellent research has been done in policing, and one of the contributions of the new field has been to bring realistic policing issues to scholarly consideration.[75] But the middle stages of the process, particularly charging and adjudication, have not had the same kind of attention. And, of course, the end of the system, from sentencing to parole, has fallen into the computer trap.

It may be that more sophisticated policing research developed because it was *not* in the ken of traditional sociologists. And for the same reason, prosecution and adjudication were avoided because they were not of standard criminological interest, it being commonly assumed that only lawyers could deal with middle-stage issues. But corrections and parole were standard criminological fare, and adding only sentencing (an "input" decision) meant that most of the work (and the greatest distortion of reality) was done in these areas.

At any rate, a rather strange skewed curricula and research emphasis has characterized the new field. Policing has been left to a few well-known researchers, but the result is that much more is known about policing today than ever before. Low-visibility decisions have been explored and police discretion analyzed and evaluated so that policing issues are much better understood. In fact, one major contribution of the new field is the growth and spread of police professionalism.

The middle stages of the process, with the exception of alternatives to bail, have been largely untouched since Bar Foundation days. And sentencing and beyond have become so oversimplified and computerized that the end game of the criminal justice process is in worse shape today than it has ever been.

Academic Pundits and Lack of Professional Responsibility   Perhaps one of the most unfortunate consequences of the new field of criminal justice has been a lack of professional responsibility among some researchers and scholars who, clothed in the gowns of academia, promulgate simple panaceas to what are really extremely complex issues. A case in point is just deserts as an attempt to address the complicated problem of sentence disparity by suggesting elimination of indeterminate sentences and abolition of discretionary release. This is linked with overstated criticisms of correctional rehabilitation efforts by limited "nothing works" research. The result of a few theoretical monographs and a couple of evaluative articles has been an epidemic sweeping away of individualized sentencing and the end or weakening of parole. One of the consequences of this has been extensive prison overcrowding. And perhaps as serious has been the widespread belief that our system can be made fairer, more just, by mandating sentencing provisions. Charging disparity was literally ignored; the role of plea bargaining, so important in the Bar Foundation research, has been virtually unmentioned in the widely touted just-deserts movement, with its methodological partner, sentencing guidelines.

Just deserts are not really just, and guidelines result in simply different forms of disparity. Yet scholars in criminal justice programs, in theory aware of the homeostatic balance of the system and the common consequence of discretion denied one place appearing elsewhere, not only reported but actively sought political acceptance of their tenets.

There are plenty of other examples. Selective incarceration, transfer of violent delinquents to criminal courts, arrest of one partner in domestic disputes, "scared straight," genetic causes of criminal behavior, sentences of life without parole, and myriad other single dimension solutions to multidimensional problems have been touted at one time or another. In part this is the result of insufficient replication of research projects before results are publicized. In another part, quick-fix answers are the result of professors speaking or writing ex cathedra without sufficient evidence or thought about the consequences of their proposals. In any event, the new field of criminal justice has often been guilty of lack of restraint and lack of professional responsibility among its members in proposing crime control solutions that not only do not accomplish what is claimed but often make matters worse.[76]

Insufficient Attention to the Changing Nature of Criminal Populations   The poor, uneducated, and culturally deprived always have been the major population dealt with by the police and other agencies in our traditional crime control system. Indeed the common criminal codes of all jurisdictions outlaw behavior usually only relevant to our lower classes. Anatole France once said, "The law, in its majestic equality, forbids both the rich and the poor to steal bread and sleep under bridges at night." True, sometimes less impoverished, more highly educated middle- and upper-class suspects are caught in the ordinary crime net, usually for offenses driven less by poverty than by addiction or psychological twists. Sex offenses, drunk driving, and some violent crimes cross class lines. In the main, however, our conventional criminal justice system deals with the inhabitants of urban ghettos and rural slums.

Historically our poorest classes were made up disproportionally of successive waves of immigrants. Prison populations of any state, then and now, reflect newcomers to our slums. German immigrants, Polish, Irish, Italian, middle European, and succeeding waves each have had major experiences in our crime control system. Today the bulk of urban slums are filled with racial and ethnic minorities, primarily African Americans and Puerto Rican and Mexican immigrants, but also pockets of Vietnamese, Cubans, Thais, and other minorities. Our rural slums hold native Americans (Indians) and the residue of poor and uneducated from earlier European immigrations.

In brief, over the years the characteristics of populations dealt with by our criminal justice system have changed. And these changes are not only in skin color and language. There are today quite different family patterns, religions, motivations, expectations, and all the other differences that arise with significant movement of different populations into a common locale, our ghettos and slums.

A question can be put as to whether our criminal justice system can and does accommodate well to such cultural changes and, more relevant here, whether criminal justice evaluation, in books, journals, courses, and research, can and does reflect the new nature of populations from which come our ordinary criminals.

The answer to the first is that the system found it very difficult to adapt to the new lifestyles of the modern poor. There are literally hundreds of illustrations from the acceptance of the Muslim religion in prisons to affirmative action in agency hiring practices. And many similar issues have affected and continue to affect criminal justice education. Textbooks, for instance, are little different in content or illustrations from when Irish immigrants made up a disproportionate part of prison populations (and of police forces). Except for a table or two, it is hard to discover that 80 percent of our prison populations today are Black or Spanish speaking. And our texts and research blandly deal with "family visits" to correctional facilities with little reference to the real household structures of urban slum dwellers.[77] The same affirmative action issues that faced, and continue to face, crime control agencies also exist in academia. There are few Black or Spanish-speaking professors and proportionately fewer minority students at all degree levels.

In short, a good deal of criminal justice education, in classroom and research, goes on as if Jimmy Cagney were the typical criminal and Pat O'Brien the understanding Catholic chaplain. Offender-producing subcultural environments have changed, but criminal justice education only weakly reflects our new world.

Areas Rarely Researched or Taught   Despite the Bar Foundation's focus on the total crime control system, most criminal justice research today remains specific to single agencies. And except for a survey course or two, so does criminal justice teaching.

In part, this no doubt results from the inherent difficulty of following data through successive stages in criminal processing. In spite of computer capabilities, most data gathered by criminal justice agencies are for in-house use, summary information about single agency functions. Flow data, that is, tracking cases from arrest through charging, adjudication, sentencing, corrections, and release, are almost nonexistent and hard to generate. The system is not structured or budgeted as a whole; the total process exists in reality only for those who have gone all the way through it or for scholars who conceive of it in its entirety. Measuring it systematically is something else again, and despite such efforts as project SEARCH,[78] flow data are uncommon.

Put another way, the actual effect of any changes in police arrest practices on correctional programs is not easily measurable, nor, in reverse, is there any real knowledge about the consequences of parole release practices on police enforcement. Instead, most research, operational as well as academic, is agency specific. Criminal justice scholars study the police or prisons or community corrections, yet rarely link them into any kind of system decision network.

Certain parts of the system, certain decision stages, have been relatively neglected in criminal justice research. Both ends of the process, policing and sentencing and corrections, have been the sites of most academic research. The middle stages—the functions of prosecutors, the role of grand juries, preliminary hearing decisions, and pleadings or trials—have been relatively neglected. Likewise, in criminal justice curricula, many fewer courses are found in the middle areas than on either end.

Overemphasis on Serious but Small Proportion of Problems Dealt with by the Criminal Justice System   Most criminal justice activity in academic programs reflects disproportionate, though not necessarily wrong, emphasis on the most serious problems dealt with by the criminal justice system, from policing to prisons. The use of lethal force by the police, the death penalty, rape and violent sexual crimes, youth gangs, and life in maximum security prisons are common fare. Although all of these issues and more like them are obviously important, they represent a distorted view of the daily activities of most crime control agencies. The bulk of enforcement, court processing, and correctional energies are spent on controlling much more prosaic, less threatening, behavior. Police responses to broken windows; lower court processing of drunks, the homeless, and the disoriented; and incarceration in lockups and county jails rather than prisons are more the bread and butter of the system than shootings and executions.

The Bar Foundation research focused not only on low-visibility decisions of on-line personnel, but also on low-visibility handling of routine, day-by-day processing of essentially nuisance behavior. "Golden-rule" processing of inebriates, break-it-up-and-move-along orders of the police, lower court bullpen plea bargaining, and the like all gave a street flavor to crime control that is missing from emphasis on rarer but more dramatic crime control situations.

The consequence of the focus of research and teaching on more serious crimes and harsher interventions is to perpetuate a war model of crime control. It reinforces certain practices, such as using arrest to measure police effectiveness, rather than more-difficult-to-measure indexes, such as keeping the streets cool and orderly. It suggests controls on enforcement excesses that may, in their zeal, sweep away sensible discretionary judgments exercised by on-line actors. In everyday practice, the full force of enforcement power is used rarely and only in extremely aggravated cases. Rules imposed to control important but rare phenomena may choke off sensible and effective street practices in less serious but more routine cases. In short, the heavy crime focus of courses and research studies distorts the reality of everyday crime control efforts, presenting a picture of our system as a battle rather than an order-keeping effort at domestic tranquillity. It may be that given the link of ordinary crime to poverty, a plan for reconstruction of our urban and rural slums would be more effective than war.[79]

THE FUTURE OF CRIMINAL JUSTICE EDUCATION

Solidifying the Field

Despite some vagaries in the quality and focus of research, criminal justice as an academic program has been very successful. It has weathered the loss of extensive federal funding that first goaded its growth. After some initial hesitancy and suspicion, it has won a favored place on many of those campuses on which it exists. Its imposition on colleges at first elicited responses similar to those of communities when new prisons are proposed. Strong initial opposition but, once built, nearly impossible to move or close. University administrators have come to see criminal justice as a popular drawing card for students, a favored major in undergraduate studies, and a high quality and attractive graduate program. It has won the hearts and minds of administrators who budget on the basis of student load and, in spite of jealousies here and there, has earned the respect of scholars in more traditional fields.

All the evidence so far indicates that academic criminal justice programs will continue to grow and spread. Courses in the field are current and interesting, and field related employment opportunities continue to exist. And, of course, crime control remains a domestic problem of the first order.

Location on Prestigious Campuses

Criminal justice programs, at all degree levels, probably will move into first tier universities from their present second tier locations. Indeed a good deal of high quality research and publication on criminal justice mainline topics is now done by academics in some of the most prestigious universities, who are presently housed in more traditional settings. If the field continues to develop in areas not represented in a standard criminology sequence, then its separate identity will become more attractive to scholars interested in control issues. In turn, these academics may find, as many have, a more comfortable home in a discrete field. Eventually, I believe, full-scale graduate programs in criminal justice will exist on such campuses.

New Student Populations

Already, significant changes have occurred in the types of students entering criminal justice graduate schools. Although they still come from diverse bachelor's degree backgrounds, many more have had field experience in criminal justice agencies prior to enrollment. The most remarkable increase has been in police officers, at least at Albany, who are allowed to attend for a full year while still on salary from their agencies. This means they receive a master's degree and then generally return to their employment. Some, having fulfilled residency requirements, begin work on a doctorate. And we have awarded some doctorates to working police.

The growth in the number of police in the program, in fact the growth in the number of all high-quality students, has been due in part to alumni, now in the field or in academia, who send their best and brightest. And increasingly bright students come as the reputation of good criminal justice programs spreads across campuses, particularly if high-quality undergraduate courses exist.

Most master's degree graduates return to or join criminal justice agencies. Many who return take their old on-line positions, and newcomers find themselves in research and planning. Ph.D. graduates in criminal justice, as in *all* fields, mostly become professors and increasingly have come to dominate papers and panels at national association meetings. Many criminal justice graduates have published books, monographs, and texts. Some are simply dissertations in print, but others rest on later research.

One of the greatest changes in academic criminal justice, larger even than general changes in the field, is the proportion of female graduate students. Criminal justice in all aspects has traditionally been a male field, but this has changed markedly. At present, graduate student populations are nearly half of each sex and so are the undergraduate majors. From token enrollment in early years the growth has been steady. As with graduate police being used primarily in planning or academy training, it would be disappointing if all research by female students were focused solely on women's issues in crime control. Although some tend to focus on such issues, a good deal of research by female graduate students has been mainline. Women master's students have become involved in general research and planning and in federal and state crime control agencies and commissions. Increasingly also female graduate students, at the master's level at least, are on-line police officers or come from the uniformed or administrative staffs of correctional agencies. Some also come to criminal justice after earning a law degree.

Undergraduate students, in good programs at least, are first rate. Criminal justice courses by no means offer a "gut" program, but are in general as tough as any social science offering. In many places it is more difficult to major in criminal justice than in other fields. Indeed it is difficult to be admitted to classes. Many are large, enrollment is limited by classroom size, and there are always waiting lists. Most undergraduates have no intention of following a criminal justice career, though many believe it is good preparation for law school. They simply find the topic interesting, current, and full of plenty of controversial issues.

All in all, academic criminal justice seems healthy. It is growing more commonplace in more colleges and universities. I believe it will spread in all directions and at all degree levels to be found nearly as frequently in curricula as older social sciences. A solid body of scholarly literature is growing. "Vocationalism" is rarely raised as a criticism today.

The recruitment of minority students has been difficult, but some growth has occurred. Minority faculty are still far underrepresented on college and university criminal justice faculties. The minority graduate students who have enrolled, mostly Blacks, have been competent and occasionally outstanding. However, their research interests are nearly exclusively on Black or other minority issues across the system. This is understandable, perhaps, for although race has always been a research variable, adequate literature about the Black experience in managing the system, or being processed by it, is far from complete.

Increasingly, criminal justice programs are attracting a number of foreign graduate students, many from the Far East. It may seem strange for such students to study the American crime control system, for often their home systems are quite different. Yet they seem to make the transition well, and, of course, in recent years a number of criminal justice professors have become interested in cross-cultural comparisons. The presence of significant numbers of foreign students in criminal justice programs adds a good deal to department and school environments. New perspectives, new issues, and different ways of responding to crime not only are interesting and challenging but perhaps will add an important dimension to the field.

Curriculum Standardization

Fairly early in the growth of the field, the Academy of Criminal Justice Sciences attempted to accredit curricula. This movement never reached full flower, but simultaneous pressure by the federal Office of Manpower and Training did lead to total system coverage in programs seeking federal funds. The Albany Model of four substantive areas and a research component probably became the most common departmental structure, but variations continue around the "planned change" section of the Albany structure. In general, however, most current curricula are more alike than different. Most, like Albany, combine criminology, criminal justice administration, and some law courses with a research methodology sequence. The purpose of the Albany Model and its followers was and is to produce graduates broadly knowledgeable about the criminal justice system, generalists rather than practitioners. Presumably all graduates are knowledgeable about crime control issues and are capable of producing and consuming research in this area.

Although critics of the four-area model correctly point out that, except for the criminal justice area, the other parts could well be located in sociology or political science departments or law schools, together they seem to make a cohesive whole. It is oversimplification to say, as some critics do, that the Albany

Model is simply the result of common sense.[80] At best this is Monday morning quarterbacking. The model was thought through, and worked through, by a handful of people at a particular point in time before *any* model existed. The Albany curriculum model is not the only choice, but it has been the most imitated. It certainly contains problems, detailed above, but it is likely to remain the most common core course structure in criminal justice programs for some time.

The major areas of emphasis may continue to follow .the Albany start, but new courses and new research emphasis on drug law enforcement, organized crime, terrorism responses, and systems for enforcing corporate compliance will probably be added. And the research methodology sequence will continue as more sophisticated hardware and more refined computer programs are developed. In general, however, curricula of the future will likely be much like those of the past. After all, if it is not broken, why fix it?

Research Trends

Criminal justice research will have to focus more directly on crime control issues if it is to survive as a distinct academic field. Traditional criminological research on crime rate measurement and causal-theory building may, indeed should, return to criminology faculties in sociology and psychology departments. Naturally, some criminological research will be centered in criminal justice departments. But, in the main, issues more commonly addressed elsewhere in the university should not dominate the new field.

If criminal justice is to fulfill its potential, focus, at a minimum, should be directed toward the development of conceptual frameworks for understanding, measuring, and evaluating crime control efforts. Quantitative computer research, as valuable and important as it is, should not be used, as it has been, to mask complexity, attempting to simplify dimly understood processes. Observation and description still have an important place in understanding the dimensions of our system. And so do other techniques—experiments, demonstration projects, and cross-jurisdictional comparisons. The inherent danger in all research is that techniques come to dominate substance and conceptual development. What is observed and what is measured are fully as important as how. Exquisite methodology applied to trivia results in no more than exquisitely measured trivia.

It is unlikely and no doubt undesirable that any common approach to research will be developed. The range of topics included in crime control are immense, and the methods for studying them are bountiful. There probably is a need for approximately similar curricula across programs, but research should remain unfettered as long as it is generally directed to field relevant problems.

Research needs to move up a few steps, to frankly face the complex nature of crime control in the context in which it occurs and to address it in these terms. This is a difficult charge, for the criminal justice system exists in a complex multiracial, multiclass society and is only one of an interlocking set of legal and economic systems that affect all aspects of our social order. From the public school to various health and welfare systems, government resources at all levels are allocated by policies forged in a very complex political and economic arena. Certainly such factors as population growth and distribution of available resources affect all criminal justice efforts (as well as those of other systems) and relate directly to both research and system change. The field does not exist in a vacuum, and dimensions of its political and economic setting are as important in understanding crime control and evaluating its effectiveness as studying on-the-street decision making.

Perhaps we need to toss the net wider and deal with criminal justice at macro levels of change. Leslie Wilkins comments:

> [Crime] may be studied by macro as well as by micro models but these approaches should never be confused. I find it interesting that if we have problems with excessive use of credit, we do not pick out a few debtors and discuss their early childhood....Rather, we alter the interest rate. But if we wish to study gambling, somehow it seems more reasonable to select a sample of gamblers and talk to them about their habit. Is it because credit is legal we use macro methods of analysis, gambling is not legal so we turn to micro methods? This is a very weird way of deciding the kind of model to use....
>
>   It is my view that criminal justice should emphasize and develop its function as part of the managerial machinery of society....If we wish to change penal structure because it is too costly, too severe or too inefficient it is to the sociopolitical

structure of society that we must direct our attention. Further studies focused on offenders will not be useful. The offender is not a problem for society but a problem of society.[81]

Jay Albanese agrees. He says:

Criminal justice programs in general have shown little effective interest in the law and policy that guide the system. For better or worse, the criminal justice system is a political system in which politicians make the laws, and direct the policy, which guide its operation. It can be argued that the efforts of graduate programs in criminal justice testify to this failure by not targeting those skills required to produce better managers of criminal justice administration.[82]

There are problems with this call for macro analysis and its action component, which attempts to change the political-economic process to reduce crime. A basic question is whether academics should become activists in what, in effect, would be a public policy science. Some feel that the field should remain an ivory tower research enterprise, not a crime-reducing political coalition. Donald Cressey said, some years ago, "Criminologists should not abandon science to become policy advisors in this repressive war on crime."[83]

How this matter is resolved, if it ever is, will determine research directions in the future. Academic attempts to influence public policy are common today. Schools of public affairs or policy studies are widespread and, indeed, often the academic home of departments of criminal justice. Clearly micro studies of crimes and criminal justice responses have had little effect on our crime rate. It may well be that effective crime reduction, the basic charge to the field, will dictate new and wider-net research in the years to come.

Granting agencies, in particular the federal government, will no doubt continue to shape academic research as funds are designated for problems defined outside academia. But this has always been the case. So while the range of research problems will probably continue to follow the winds of political priorities, the skill and sophistication of research remain the obligation of the criminal justice professionals. The best and brightest in academia should now be able to approach criminal justice research in a manner that faces complexity, understands the workings of the process, measures as precisely as possible, and evaluates and assesses with deserved attention to the realities and limits of controlling crime in a democratic society.

Increased Professionalism of On-Line Personnel

Almost since the times of Robert Peel and Thomas Mott Osborne, police and prison personnel have sought recognition as professionals, not simply as jobholders and gatekeepers. Middle-stage practitioners, magistrates, prosecutors, and judges had this status, owing first allegiance to the profession of law and only second to their roles in the criminal justice system. In our society higher education is the route to professional status, a symbol of appropriate credentials to justify expert decision making.

Until the advent of criminal justice programs in college and university curricula, nonlawyer personnel borrowed credentialing from academic fields not their own, fields sometimes only remotely related to their tasks. Police science programs generally reiterated technical skills but, being college based, provided some access of practitioners to upper mobility in their agencies. Correctional workers in prisons, training schools, and probation and parole sought academic endorsement from a variety of curricula in social sciences and social work. These were academic areas frequently peripherally related to their work and sometimes hostile to preparing students for employment in "authoritarian settings." Criminal justice provides an academic home for on-line personnel on both ends of the system with law remaining the academic situs of lawyer practitioners.

Academic criminal justice is, or certainly should be, more than simply a credentialing device. Properly taught and adequately researched, it will prepare on-line manpower to become truly professional. Indeed it has already done so. Police and correctional employees, adequately educated in this field, are increasingly sophisticated in knowledge of their own functions and those of others at different decision stages in the process. The complexity of all issues in crime control are dealt with today not only by skilled researchers, but also by those responsible for policies and practices in the on-line agencies. The generalist nature of most criminal justice education moves all exposed to it well beyond the role vocational skills taught in the past. Sophisticated knowledge of total system issues is increasingly producing law enforcement and correctional personnel equipped to deal in more effective ways with crime control and to avoid the simplistic types of responses that have so often characterized the history of our criminal justice efforts.

CONCLUSION

As criminal justice education matures and becomes more comfortable and secure in university settings, the field may turn outward and fulfill a helpful role in dealing with our major domestic problem of crime. As with any new endeavor, there will be false starts, chicanery, promises beyond delivery, and a lot of wheel spinning. But criminal justice seems to be established as a worthy focus of university teaching and research. It may yet do for domestic tranquillity what other university-based programs have done for equally complex and difficult problems in our society.

Perhaps the greatest challenge to the field of criminal justice and its academic base now and in the future is to concentrate effort on the development of more adequate conceptual frameworks for research than has characterized criminal justice programs during the past two decades. The Bar Foundation survey generated a conceptual model that stressed attention to the complexity of criminal justice decisions, the consequences of low visibility in decision making, the means for control of discretion, the dangers of oversimplification of the bases for decision, the appropriate allocation of discretion, the definition and structure of agency roles in criminal justice as they affect decision making, and the need to take account of the systemic and interactive effects of decisions. Research and instruction without a conceptual foundation do not advance our understanding of criminal justice systems or the need and direction of developmental and reform efforts. Our understanding of crime control will not progress unless we pursue a more disciplined conceptual approach to criminal justice research and teaching.

NOTES

1. Frank J. Remington, Donald J. Newman, Edward L. Kimball, Marygold Melli, and Herman Goldstein, *Criminal Justice Administration: Materials and Cases* (Indianapolis: Bobbs-Merrill, 1969).

2. 367 U.S. 643 (1961).

3. 384 U.S. 436 (1966).

4. 392 U.S. 1 (1968).

5. 404 U.S. 257 (1970).

6. 471 U.S. 1 (1985).

7. "American Bar Foundation Survey of Criminal Justice: Pilot Project Reports," 7 vols. (Dec. 1957, Mimeo.; on file with the Criminal Justice Reference and Information Center, University of Wisconsin-Madison, Law School). For a list of early scholarly papers based on the pilot project data, see Wayne R. LaFave, preface to *Arrest: The Decision to Take a Suspect into Custody,* ed. Frank J. Remington (Boston: Little, Brown, 1965), x.

8. Frank W. Miller, Robert O. Dawson, George E. Dix, and Raymond I. Parnas, *Criminal Justice Administration: Cases and Materials* (1971; Mineola, N.Y.: Foundation Press, 1976).

9. President's Commission on Law Enforcement and Administration of Justice, *The Challenge of Crime in a Free Society* (Washington, D.C.: U.S. Government Printing Office, 1967).

10. Frank J. Remington, Donald J. Newman, Edward L. Kimball, Herman Goldstein, and Walter J. Dickey, *Criminal Justice Administration: Cases and Materials,* rev. ed. (Charlottesville, Va.: Michie Co., 1982).

11. Editor's note: Prof. Vic Rosenblum, who reviewed this paper at our request, feels that Newman has understated the impact of empirical research such as the ABF survey. Rosenblum believes that both law faculties and appellate courts have become more responsive to the issues raised by careful research into existing administrative practices.

12. Universities and colleges in the State University of New York system are listed in "Policies of the Board of Trustees" (1987).

13. Richard A. Myren, "State University of New York at Albany, School of Criminal Justice: Establishment, Initial Faculty Planning; Development and Maturation, Conclusion" (June 1976, Mimeo.).

14. Memorandum to Robert MacCrate from Eliot Lumbard regarding training and intellectual leadership for the administration of criminal justice, Sept. 26, 1961.

15. Memorandum to Robert MacCrate from Eliot Lumbard regarding criminal justice projects in New York, Oct. 13, 1961.

16. *Governor Nelson Rockefeller's Message to the New York State Legislature, Albany, New York,* March 23, 1962, 2.

17. The Graduate School of Public Affairs (GSPA) was founded by Gov. Thomas E. Dewey in 1947 "to ensure better government."

18. Correspondence between O. B. Conaway, Jr., dean of GSPA, and Donald J. Newman regarding faculty appointment in the Graduate School of Public Affairs, March 27, 1962; May 15, 1962; and June 5, 1962.

19. See, for instance, memorandum to O. B. Conaway, Jr., dean of GSPA, from Professor William P. Brown regarding the proposed school of criminology, Oct. 4, 1962.

20. Thomas H. Hamilton memorandum regarding feasibility study, school of criminology, July 13, 1962.

21. Report from Frank J. Remington to O. B. Conaway, Jr., dean of GSPA, entitled "Proposal to Establish a School of Criminology at the State University of New York at Albany," Nov. 15, 1962.

22. Memorandum to Dr. Thomas H. Hamilton, chancellor, from O. B. Conaway, Jr., dean of GSPA, regarding proposed center for criminal justice, Dec. 21, 1962.

23. Memorandum to J. Lawrence Murray, acting chancellor, from O. B. Conaway, Jr., dean of GSPA, regarding proposed establishment of a center for criminal justice in the State University of New York, Feb. 6, 1963.

24. Letter from Richard A. Myren to Eliot H. Lumbard regarding decision of Chancellor Gould to open school in 1968 with a doctoral program, rather than in 1967 with a Master of Arts, Oct. 21, 1966.

25. Minutes of the board of trustees, State University of New York, Dec. 12, 1963, 4.

26. *Governor's Message to the New York State Legislature,* Jan. 8, 1964, 17.

27. New York State Senate Bill, Intro. No. 1737, Point 1772, entitled "An Act Creating a New York State Criminal Technological Research Foundation and Prescribing Its Functions."

28. Governor's memorandum of disapproval of Senate Bill 1737, Apr. 26, 1964.

29. Letter from Chancellor Samuel B. Gould to Prof. Lloyd E. Ohlin, Nov. 12, 1964.

30. Lloyd E. Ohlin, "Report on the Establishment of a School of Criminology and Criminal Justice by the State University of New York," Apr. 1965.

31. See the discussion of "Establishment" and "Initial Faculty Planning" in "Richard A. Myren, State University of New York at Albany, School of Criminal Justice" (see note 13).

32. Letter of interest and letter of agreement from Donald J. Newman to Dean Richard A. Myren (May 23, 1966; and July 14, 1966).

33. Correspondence Newman to Myren, September 12, 1966; and Myren to Newman, September 21, 1966; Newman to Fred Cohen, February 10, 1967. All told, I recommended twelve potential faculty members to Dean Myren during this academic year.

34. School of Criminal Justice, SUNY-Albany, A Proposal for the Programs, Ph.D., M.A., M.Ph. (Master of Philosophy) in criminal justice, Sept. 1967 (tentative draft, mimeo.).

35. Memorandum to Dean Richard Myren from Donald J. Newman regarding degree programs in criminal justice, Madison, Wisconsin, March 24, 1967 (mimeo.). "Proseminar" concept discussed at p. 8 and throughout.

36. For a debate about the impact and universality of the Albany Model, see Jay S. Albanese, "A Proper Model for Criminal Justice Education?" (opposing), and Lawrence F. Travis III, "Has the 'Albany Model' Shaped Graduate Education in the Field?" (supporting) in *Northeastern Criminal Justice Report* (Spring 1989):4–6.

37. See *1989–90 Handbook for Graduate Studies, School of Criminal Justice* (Albany: State University of New York at Albany, 1989), 1–10.

38. Many memorandums were prepared the year before and during the planning year. Various organizational proposals were made, some were rejcted. In general the stance of the planners was for academic excellence of both faculty and students, self-sufficiency of the school, and quick production of graduates, consistent with academic integrity. These memorandums are kept in school files and are too numerous to fully cite here.

39. See Richard H. Ward and Vincent J. Webb, *Quest for Quality* (New York: University Publications, 1984). A report of the Joint Commission on Criminology and Criminal Justice Standards and Goals.

40. Charles W. Tenney, Jr., *Higher Education Programs in Law Enforcement and Criminal Justice* (Washington, D.C.: U.S. Government Printing Office, 1971).

41. Charles P. Nemeth, *Anderson's Directory of Criminal Justice Education* (Cincinnati: Anderson Publishing Co., 1986).

42. For a detailed and fascinating history of these conflicts, see Frank Morn, "The Academy of Criminal Justice Sciences and the Criminal Justice Education Movement" (Normal, Ill., 1984, Mimeo.).

43. For a general discussion of this, see L. J. Fry and J. Miller, "The Organizational Transformation of a Federal Education Program: Reflections on LEEP," *Social Problems* 24 (1976):259–69.

44. Donald J. Newman, "Criminal Justice Education in Wisconsin: Report and Recommendations to the University of Wisconsin System, Madison" (1974, Mimeo.), generally known as the "Newman Report I." Newman Report II was a ten-year follow-up, also mimeographed (1984).

45. A resolution by James Osterburg, himself an ex-police officer and now a professor, at the business meeting of the newly formed Academy of Criminal Justice Sciences that "practical experience in an operating agency no longer be viewed as an essential criterion for a collegiate teaching position in the field of criminal justice" passed. See "Minutes, 2nd Annual Business Meeting of the ACJS" (Omaha, Neb., Mar. 23, 1973). For a more detailed discussion of this matter, see William P. Brown, "The Police and the Academic World," *Police Chief* 32, no. 5 (1965):8; and Lee P. Brown, "The Police and Higher Education: The Challenge of the Times," *Criminology* 12, no. 1 (1974):114.

46. William Wiltberger, "A Program for Police Training in a College," master's thesis, University of California, Berkeley, 1937, 97. For a detailed discussion of the academic relationship of August Vollmer and William Wiltberger, see Morn, "Academy of Criminal Justice," chap. 1. See also Jack L. Kuykendall and Armand P. Hernandez, "Undergraduate Justice System Education and Training at San Jose State University: An Historical Perspective," *Journal of Criminal Justice* 3, no. 2 (1975):111.

47. August Vollmer, *The Police and Modern Society* (1936; reprint, Berkeley and Los Angeles: University of California Press, 1971). See also Gene E. Carte and Elaine H. Carte, *Police Reform in the United States: The Era of August Vollmer* (Berkeley and Los Angeles: University of California Press, 1975).

48. O. W. Wilson and Roy Clinton McLaren, *Police Administration*, 3d ed. (New York: McGraw-Hill, 1972).

49. Quoted in Morn, "Academy of Criminal Justice," 62. Morn's work relies extensively on archival letters, minutes of association meetings, personal interviews, and correspondence. This quote is from the

Vollmer Papers, Wiltberger Folder, Bancroft Library, University of California, Berkeley.

50. Albert Morris, "The American Society of Criminology: A History, 1941–1974," *Criminology* 13, no. 2 (1975):128.

51. See Morn, "Academy of Criminal Justice," 142 passim. Core members of the group, in addition to Mathias, Myren, and Riddle, were Gordon Misner, George Felkenes, and Richard Ward.

52. See Samuel Walker, *Popular Justice: A History of American Criminal Justice* (New York: Oxford University Press, 1980).

53. "The Rise and Fall of the School of Criminology, University of California, Berkeley" (Berkeley, n.d., Mimeo.). See also Morn, "Academy of Criminal Justice," 80 passim.

54. See James Q. Wilson, *Thinking About Crime*, 2d ed. (New York: Basic Books, 1983), 208 passim.

55. The National Advisory Commission on Criminal Justice *Standards and Goals* (Washington, D.C.: U.S. Government Printing Office, 1973).

56. Charles Weirman and William G. Archambeault, "Assessing the Effects of LEAA Demise on Criminal Justice Higher Education," *Journal of Criminal Justice* 11, no. 6 (1983):549. For a discussion of lack of a national crime control policy and the end of LEAA, see Donald J. Newman and Patrick R. Anderson, *Introduction to Criminal Justice,* 4th ed. (New York: Random House, 1989), 666–68. See also U.S. Department of Justice, "LEAA to Close April 15," *Justice Assistance News* 3, no. 1 (Feb. 1982):1; Donald J. Newman, "America Retreats on the War on Crime," *Schnectady* [N.Y.] *Gazette*, Dec. 12, 1980.

57. For a criticism of the drug war, see Patrick R. Anderson and Donald J. Newman, "Inner City Marshall Plan Could Win the Drug War," *Lakeland* [Fla.] *Ledger*, Sept. 13, 1989.

58. See Laurence R. Veysey, *The Emergence of the American University* (Chicago: University of Chicago Press, 1965).

59. Frank Morn says: "It was in the 'second tier' of higher education that criminal justice found a place. Thus relegated to the junior varsity colleges, so to speak, criminal justice had a second-string status in higher education." Morn, "Academy of Criminal Justice," 150. See also Nemeth, *Anderson's Directory* (see note 41).

60. See Howard Rothmann Bowen, with the collaboration of Peter Clecak, Jacqueline Powers Doud, and Gordon K. Douglass, *Investment*

in Learning: The Individual and Social Value of American Higher Education (San Francisco: Jossey-Bass Publishers, 1977). See also Katherine M. Jamieson and Timothy J. Flanagan, eds., *Sourcebook of Criminal Justice Statistics, 1988* (Washington, D.C.: Department of Justice, Bureau of Justice Statistics, 1989).

61. Herbert Sturz, "Experiments in the Criminal Justice System," *Legal Aid Briefcase* 25, no. 3 (1967):111; see also Vera Institute of Justice, *Programs in Criminal Justice Reform: Ten Year Report, 1961–1971* (New York: Vera Institute of Justice, 1972).

62. See, especially, Donald Clemmer, *The Prison Community*, rev. ed. (New York: Rinehart, 1958); Gresham M. Sykes, *The Society of Captives: A Study of a Maximum Security Prison* (Princeton, N.J.: Princeton University Press, 1958); Donald R. Cressey, ed., *The Prison: Studies in Institutional Organization and Change* (New York: Holt, Rinehart and Winston, 1961); and John Irwin and Donald R. Cressey, "Thieves, Convicts and the Inmate Culture," *Social Problems* 10 (1962):143.

63. Lawrence W. Sherman, *The Quality of Police Education: A Report on the National Advisory Commission on Higher Education for Police Officers* (San Francisco: Jossey-Bass Publishers, 1978), 207 passim.

64. See Larry Bassi and Ronald H. Rogers, "The Road to Accreditation," *Journal of Criminal Justice* 4, no. 3 (1976):243; George T. Felkenes, "Accreditation: Is It Necessary? Yes!" *Journal of Criminal Justice* 8, no. 2 (1980):77. See also Morn, "Academy of Criminal Justice" (see note 42), chap. 6; and Sherman, *Quality of Police Education*, 206–10.

65. Dennis E. Hoffman, Joel C. Snell, and Vincent J. Webb, "Insiders and Outsiders in Criminal Justice Education," *Journal of Criminal Justice* 4, no. 1 (1976):57. For a detailed analysis of academic politicking before, after, and during the creation of ACJS, see Morn, "Academy of Criminal Justice," esp. chaps. 5, 6, and 7.

66. See generally Morn, "Academy of Criminal Justice," 192 passim.

67. Andrew Von Hirsch, *Doing Justice: The Choice of Punishments* (New York: Hill and Wang, 1976); David Fogel, ...*We Are the Living Proof,* 2d ed. (Cincinnati: W. H. Anderson Co., 1979).

68. See Stephen P. Lagoy, Frederick A. Hussey, and John H. Kramer, "A Comparative Assessment of Determinate Sentencing in the Four Pioneer States," *Crime and Delinquency* 24, no. 4 (1978):385;

and Raymond Paternoster and Tim Bynum, "The Justice Model as Ideology: A Critical Look at Sentencing Reform," *Contemporary Crisis* 6 (1982):7.

69. See Robert Martinson, Douglass Lipton, and Judith Wilks, *The Effectiveness of Correctional Treatment* (New York: Praeger, 1975). See also Marvin Zalman, "The Rise and Fall of the Indeterminate Sentence," *Wayne Law Review* 24, no. 3 (1978):857.

70. David J. Rothman, *The Discovery of the Asylum* (Boston: Little, Brown, 1971); and David J. Rothman, *Conscience and Convenience: The Asylum and its Alternatives in Progressive America* (Boston: Little, Brown, 1980).

71. Many of Wilkins's students and collaborators wrote of this experiment and later of sentencing guidelines. See Peter B. Hoffman and James L. Beck, "Parole Decision-Making: A Salient Factor Score," *Journal of Criminal Justice* 2, no. 3 (1974):195; and Michael R. Gottfredson, "Parole Guidelines and the Reduction of Sentencing Disparity: A Preliminary Study," *Journal of Research in Crime and Delinquency* 16, no. 2 (1979):218.

72. Leslie T. Wilkins, Jack M. Kress, Don M. Gottfredson, Joseph C. Calpin, and Arthur M. Gelman, *Sentencing Guidelines: Structuring Judicial Discretion* (Albany, N.Y.: Criminal Justice Research Center, 1978); William D. Rich and Paul Sutton, *The Impact of Sentencing Guidelines on Judicial Discretion: Issues of Compliance and Disparity* (Williamsburg, Va.: National Center for State Courts, 1980); and William D. Rich, *Judicial Compliance with Sentencing Guidelines: The Decision to Incarcerate* (Williamsburg, Va.: National Center for State Courts, 1979).

73. For a brief discussion of who makes the sentencing decision, see Newman and Anderson, *Introduction to Criminal Justice*, 366–68. See also Arthur D. Little, *Determinate and Indeterminate Sentence Law Comparison: Feasibility of Adapting Law to a Sentencing Commission-Guideline Approach* (San Francisco: Arthur D. Little, 1980); and Milton Heumann and Colin Loftin, "Mandatory Sentencing and the Abolition of Plea Bargaining: The Michigan Felony Firearm Statute," *Law and Society Review* 13, no. 2 (1979):393.

74. Charles D. Breitel, "Controls in Criminal Law Enforcement," *University of Chicago Law Review* 27, no. 3 (1960):427.

75. Police literature has mushroomed in the past quarter century. The number of high quality police studies in the form of articles, monographs, and books is now too extensive to list in a single footnote. This statement could not have been made before the Bar Foundation effort.

76. To keep the peace and to be polite, pundits and panacea advocates will remain unnamed. Unfortunately, like the list of police research discussed above, the list is too long for inclusion in a single footnote.

77. In 1977, the School of Criminal Justice at Albany received a large multiphase grant from LEAA to deal with various minority issues in criminal justice education. I was project director of this grant. The Center for Minorities in Criminal Justice was established, and it operated on federal funds for four years. Part of the grant involved educational conferences between criminal justice professors in all-black colleges and the center staff. Another part was devoted to criticizing (and hopefully influencing) criminal justice literature, particularly criminology and criminal justice texts, for failure to adequately reflect minority concerns in describing persons labeled criminal and processed through the criminal justice system. Although a lot of professors were involved and a good deal of work was done, the influence on criminal justice literature has been minimal.

78. *SEARCH* is an acronym for the System for Electronic Analysis and Retrieval of Criminal Histories. SEARCH Group, Inc., *Offender Based Transaction Statistics* (Sacramento: SEARCH Group, 1978).

79. See Anderson and Newman, "Inner City Marshall Plan" (see note 57).

80. For a defense of the Albany Model against critics, see Lawrence F. Travis III, *Criminal Justice Graduate Education: An Assessment of the Albany Model,* Northeastern Criminal Justice Report (Spring 1989): 5–6.

81. Leslie T. Wilkins, "The Future of Graduate Education in Criminal Justice" (Paper delivered at the conference The Idea of Criminal Justice: The Development and Future of an Academic Field, held on the Albany School of Criminal Justice's twentieth anniversary, Apr. 13, 1989), 13–15.

82. Albanese, "Proper Model" (see note 36), 4.

83. Donald R. Cressey, "Criminological Theory, Social Science, and the Repression of Crime," *Criminology* 16, no. 2 (1978):171.

APPENDIX A:
ABOUT THE AUTHORS

Walter J. Dickey is professor of law at the University of Wisconsin, from which he received his J.D. degree in 1971. He served as administrator of the Wisconsin Division of Corrections from 1983 to 1987 and was regarded as one of the leading corrections administrators in the nation. He is director of the Legal Assistance to Institutionalized Persons Program at the University of Wisconsin Law School; coauthor with Frank J. Remington, Donald J. Newman, Edward L. Kimball, and Herman Goldstein of *Criminal Justice Administration*, rev. ed. (Charlottesville, Va.: Michie, 1982); and author of a series of published papers exploring probation and parole practices from the perspective of the agent in the field.

Herman Goldstein, Evjue-Bascom Professor of Law at the University of Wisconsin, received his master's degree in government administration in 1955 and, after serving as assistant to the city manager of Portland, Maine, joined the "American Bar Foundation Survey of Criminal Justice" and was largely responsible for the study of police in Wisconsin and Michigan. He joined the Wisconsin law faculty in 1964 after service as assistant to the superintendent of police in Chicago. His writings, including *Policing a Free Society* (Cambridge, Mass.: Ballinger, 1977) and *Problem-Oriented Policing* (New York: McGraw-Hill, 1990), have had a major impact on the development of progressive police practices throughout the nation.

Wayne R. LaFave is the David C. Baum Professor of Law and Center for Advanced Study Professor of Law at the University of Illinois. He received his LL.B. degree from the University of Wisconsin in 1959 and his S.J.D. degree in 1965. The latter degree was awarded based on his writing of the widely acclaimed book,

Arrest: The Decision to Take a Suspect into Custody, ed. Frank
J. Remington (Boston: Little, Brown, 1965), the first volume
published in the ABF series. Since then he has published extensively as the author of the four-volume *Search and Seizure,* 2d
ed. (St. Paul, Minn.: West Publishing Co., 1987); the coauthor
with Austin W. Scott Jr. of the two-volume *Substantive Criminal
Law* (St. Paul: West Publishing Co., 1986); and the coauthor
with Jerold H. Israel of the three-volume *Criminal Procedure* (St.
Paul: West Publishing Co., 1984).

Donald J. Newman was dean and a member of the faculty of the
School of Criminal Justice at the State University of New York at
Albany. No one felt more strongly than Newman the importance
of criminal justice as an academic discipline, a discipline to
which he contributed so very much through his writing, his students, and his leadership of the School of Criminal Justice. He
received his Ph.D. in sociology from the University of Wisconsin
based on his pioneering study of plea bargaining, a subject he
revisited in his ABF volume, *Conviction: The Determination of
Guilt or Innocence Without Trial,* ed. Frank J. Remington
(Boston: Little, Brown, 1966). His most recent book, *Introduction to Criminal Justice,* 4th ed. (New York: Random House,
1989), reflects his commitment to the field of criminal justice.
His friends and colleagues will find interest and comfort in this
paper completed just before his untimely death. It is vintage Don
Newman, thoughtful and blunt.

Lloyd E. Ohlin is Touroff-Glueck Professor of Criminal Justice,
emeritus, at the Harvard Law School. He received his Ph.D. in
sociology from the University of Chicago in 1954. He was the
consultant on field research for the American Bar Foundation
Survey of Criminal Justice and, as such, was primarily responsible, with Frank J. Remington, for developing the ethnographic
design of the research. He was subsequently associate director of
the President's Commission on Law Enforcement and Administration of Justice from 1965 to 1967. He is the coauthor with
Richard Cloward of *Delinquency and Opportunity* (New York:
Macmillan, 1960); editor of *Prisoners in America* (Englewood
Cliffs, N.J.: Prentice-Hall, Inc., 1973); and editor with Michael
Tonry of *Family Violence* (Chicago: University of Chicago Press,
1989).

Raymond I. Parnas is professor of law at the University of California at Davis. He received his J.D. degree in 1964 from Washington University in St. Louis and his S.J.D. from Wisconsin in 1972. He was one of the first to study the problem of domestic violence, drawing on the "American Bar Foundation Survey of Criminal Justice" findings. His publications combined these findings with the results of his own study of the response of the Chicago Police Department to incidents they called domestic disturbances. He is coauthor of *Criminal Justice Administration*, 3d ed. (Mineola, N.Y.: Foundation Press, 1986).

Frank J. Remington is Jackson Professor of Law at the University of Wisconsin from which he received his LL.B. degree in 1949. He was director of field research for the "American Bar Foundation Survey of Criminal Justice" and was editor of the five volumes published on the basis of that survey. He was draftsman of the Wisconsin Criminal Code and was reporter for the committee on the Federal Rules of Criminal Procedure. He is coauthor of *Criminal Justice Administration*, rev. ed. (Charlottesville, Va.: Michie Co., 1982).

APPENDIX B:
PROJECT PARTICIPANTS

Project Advisory Committee

Walter P. Armstrong, Jr., chairman
Grant B. Cooper
Ray Forrester
Theodore G. Garfield
Boris Kostelantez
Edward H. Levi
Whitney North Seymour
Arthur H. Sherry
James V. Bennett, special adviser

Former Members

Robert H. Jackson (1953–54)
William J. Donovan (1954–57), chairman
Gordon Dean (1953–54)
Edgar N. Eisenhower (1953–54)
John D. M. Hamilton (1959–64)
Albert J. Harno (1955–65)
Theodore Kiendl (1953–54)
Warren Olney III (1953–59)
Bolitha J. Laws (1954–58)
Harold A. Smith (1957–65)
Floyd E. Thompson (1954–55)
G. Aaron Youngquist (1954–55)
Earl Warren, adviser

Publication Staff

Frank J. Remington, director
Harry V. Ball

Robert O. Dawson
Wayne R. LaFave
Donald M. McIntyre, Jr.
Frank W. Miller
Donald J. Newman
Daniel L. Rotenberg
Lawrence P. Tiffany

Project Staff

Arthur H. Sherry, project director
John A. Pettis, Jr., assistant project director
Frank J. Remington, director of field research
Sanford Bates, consultant on sentencing, probation, and parole
Edmund F. DeVine, special consultant
Fred E. Inbau, consultant on prosecution and defense
Benjamin A. Matthews, consultant on courts
Lloyd E. Ohlin, consultant on field research
O. W. Wilson, consultant on police

Field Representatives and Research Associates

Robert W. Cassidy
Herman Goldstein
Frank J. Hodges
William L. Hungate
Donald M. McIntyre, Jr.
Roy C. McLaren
Bruce T. Olson
Donnell M. Pappenfort
Arthur W. Schumacher
Louis P. Trent
James D. Turner
John Warner

INDEX

Academy of Criminal Justice Sciences
(ACJS), 306, 316, 336
Advisory Committee on Criminal
Rules, 108
Alaska, 102–3, 105–6
Alaska's Plea Bargaining Ban Re-
evaluated, 105
Albanese, Jay, 339
Albany Model, 295, 297–301, 310,
311, 317–18, 327, 336–37
Allen, Frank, 77, 187, 200, 201, 282
Allen, Ronald, 63
Alschuler, Albert W., 114, 157–59
American Bar Association (ABA), 5,
114, 5
Standards for Criminal Justice,
100, 215
standards for urban police function, 41, 47–48, 54
"American Bar Foundation Survey of
Criminal Justice in the United
States," 15–17, 74, 240
education, today's criminal justice,
279–341
"Field Reports," 136, 149, 150,
163, 280–81
findings, 9–14, 30–39, 85–96,
101, 103–7, 112–14, 136,
146–50, 154, 155, 163–67,
176–82, 184, 193, 198–201,
211–14, 248–49, 251, 268,
280–82
methodology, 7–9, 29–30, 85–86,
298, 303, 312, 331, 332
origins, 5–7, 28–29
"Pilot Project Reports," 12–13,
30, 86, 282

post-ABF research and developments, 39–60, 76, 96–109,
151–67, 176–202, 311–33
pre-ABF research and developments, 24–28, 75, 77–85,
88–89, 136–46, 244
seminars, 12–14, 282–83
significance, 4–5, 23–24, 42, 44,
60–64, 75, 76, 110–11,
150–51, 248–49, 279–81,
311–33, 341
survey books, 13–14, 30, 178–80,
182, 280–81
American Friends Services Committee's Working Party report,
152–53
American Law Institute (ALI), 97,
215
American Society of Criminology
(ASC), 305, 316
Amsterdam, Anthony, 214–18, 245,
261
Arrest: The Decision to Take a Sus-
pect into Custody (LaFave; ed.
Remington), 13, 178–79
Arrests, 14–15, 26, 28, 46–47, 64,
324, 333
ABF research, 12, 29, 32–38, 49,
52, 62, 86, 90–93, 178–79,
193, 313
Cleveland Crime Survey and, 27,
78
decision not to arrest, 56–58
domestic violence and, 3, 11, 15,
37, 56, 60, 63, 96, 175,
177–79, 183, 185–97, 201, 329
drug use/sales and, 50–51, 60

Fourth Amendment limits on force
and custody, 240–48
Illinois Crime Survey and, 27, 78
intoxication and, 11, 33, 48–49,
60, 96
Missouri Crime Survey and, 27,
78, 80, 85, 140
Supreme Court on, 48, 54,
240–48, 254–55, 265, 266
varied uses of, 35, 47–52
Attorney General's Task Force on
Family Violence, 191

Baker, Bruce, 189–90
Bard, Morton, 45, 46, 181–82
Barrett, Edward, 108
Bates, Sanford, 137, 139, 143
Battered Wives (Martin), 185
Baumes Law (New York), 84
Beattie, Ronald, 140
Beccaria, Cesare, 136
Bennett, James, 152
Berk, Richard A., 190–91, 193
Berkowitz, Sydney, 181–82
Bittner, Egon, 40–41
"Borderland of the Criminal Law,
The: Problems of 'Socializing'
Criminal Justice" (Frank
Allen), 200
Breitel, Charles D., 97, 293, 325
Brennan, William J., Jr., 238
"Broken Windows: The Police and
Neighborhood Safety" (Wilson
and Kelling)
Brown, William, 291, 292, 294, 295
Brown v. Texas, 232, 234–36, 250
Bundy, McGeorge, 287
Burgess, Ernest, 8
Burning Bed, The (McNulty), 185
"Burning Bed, The" (TV movie), 175,
185

California, 26, 160
arrests in, 185–86, 194
domestic violence in, 182, 185–86,
194, 199–200

prosecution in, 80, 113, 186, 194,
199–200
sentencing in, 138, 153, 199–200
Camara v. Municipal Court, 226–32,
250, 262
Carter, Jimmy, 302, 307
Carter, Lief H., 113
Center for Women's Policy Studies,
185, 188
*Challenge of Crime in a Free Society,
The* (President's Commission
on Law Enforcement and
Administration of Justice),
180–81, 183
*Child Savers, The: The Invention of
Delinquency* (Platt), 201
"Chorus of Judicial Critics Assail
Sentencing Guides: 5-Year
Effort Is Called Hobgoblin of
U.S. Courts," 157
City University of New York, 181
Civil Rights Act, 57
Clark, Tom, 144
Classical model, 136–37, 139, 143,
145
Cleveland Crime Survey, 8, 27,
77–81, 139
Coalition for Battered Women, 185
Cohen, Fred, 282, 294–95, 299
Colgate University, 309, 310
Colorado, 191, 219, 222–24
Colorado v. Bertine, 218–26, 238,
250, 251, 256, 259, 261, 263,
265, 267
Columbia University, 294
Conaway, O. B., 291–93
Congress, U.S., 99, 111, 155, 157, 175
Connecticut, domestic violence in,
194
*Conviction: The Determination of
Guilt or Innocence without
Trial* (Newman; ed. Reming-
ton), 13
Corbin, Sol N., 293
Cornell University, 286, 287
Cressey, Donald, 113, 339
Crime in the United States—1986
(FBI), 196

Crime Prevention (Woods), 26–27
Criminal Justice Administration:
Cases and Materials (Miller,
Dawson, Dix, and Parnas), 283
"Criminal Justice Administration:
Materials and Cases" (1960:
Remington and Newman), 281
Criminal Justice Administration:
Materials and Cases (1969:
Remington, Newman, Kimball,
Melli, and Goldstein), 281,
285, 288
Criminal Justice Administration:
Materials and Cases (1982:
Remington, Newman, Kimball,
Goldstein, and Dickey), 285
Criminology (American Society of
Criminology), 316
"Cry for Help" (TV movie), 175
Cumming, Elaine, 41

Davis, Kenneth, 63, 100, 214, 215
Dawson, John, 73
Dawson, Robert O., 13, 283
DEA (Drug Enforcement Agency),
237–39
Delaware, stops in, 232–33
Delaware v. Prouse, 232–33
Dershowitz, Alan, 153
Detection of Crime: Stopping and
Questioning, Search and
Seizure, Encouragement and
Entrapment (Tiffany, McIntyre,
and Rotenberg; ed. Reming-
ton), 13
Dewey, Thomas, 286
Dickey, Walter, 14, 285
District of Columbia, arrests in,
242–43, 266–67
Dix, George E., 283
Doing Justice: The Choice of Punish-
ments (Von Hirsch), 153
Domestic violence, 2, 45, 47, 319
ABF research, 37, 76, 87–88,
176–82, 184, 185, 193,
198–201
arrests and, 3, 11, 15, 37, 56, 60,
63, 96, 175, 177–79, 183,
185–97, 201, 329
prosecution and, 15, 76, 87–88,
113, 175, 177–80, 183,
186–89, 194–202
statistics, 195–97
Donovan, William J., 6
Donovan v. Dewey, 229–30
Drug use/sales, 1–4, 16, 26, 41, 45, 53
arrests and, 50–51, 60

Eastern Sociological Society, 299
Education, criminal justice. *See also*
other individual colleges and
universities
ABF and today's, 311–33
defined, 295–97
future of, 333–41
overview of, 279–86
spread of, 301–11
State University of New York
(SUNY) at Albany School of
Criminal Justice, 286–303,
305, 310, 311, 317–18, 321,
323, 326–27, 336–37

Fair and Certain Punishment (Der-
showitz), 153
Family Crisis Intervention Unit pro-
ject, 181–82
Family Violence Conference
(National District Attorneys
Association), 188
Family Violence Prevention and Ser-
vices Act of 1984, 175
Family Violence Project (Center for
Women's Policy Studies), 185
Fawcett, Farrah, 185
FBI (Federal Bureau of Investigation),
196, 212, 213, 289
Federal Rules of Criminal Procedure,
Rule 11 (guilty pleas), 101,
108, 109
500 Criminal Careers and Later
Criminal Careers (Glueck and
Glueck), 139, 142

Florida, domestic violence in, 191
Florida Southern College, 310
Florida State University, 310
Fogel, David, 321
Ford Foundation, 5, 282, 283
Fosdick, Raymond, 25–26
Foster, J. Price, 303
Fourth Amendment, police rule making and
    arrests, limits on force and custody, 240–48
    Bertine requirement, 218–26
    Camara requirement, 226–31
    denouement, 268
    overview of, 211–18
    remaining problem areas, 256–67
    role of the courts to date, 248–56
    stops by plan or profile, 231–40
France, Anatole, 330

Georgia, domestic violence in, 191
Geis, Gilbert, 282
Glueck, Eleanor, 139, 142, 143
Glueck, Sheldon, 139, 142, 143
Goldstein, Herman, 12, 214, 217, 265–67, 281, 284, 285, 288
Goldstein, Joseph, 12, 97, 176–79, 184–86, 282
Gould, Samuel B., 293–94
Gustafson v. Florida, 242–45, 251, 260, 261

Hamilton, Thomas H., 292
Hamilton College, 310
Handler, Joel, 282
Hard Labor Creek Group, 305–6
Hardt, Robert, 299
Harris v. United States, 213
Harvard University, 8, 27, 284, 308, 309, 310
Hawaii, 194
Heaney, Gerald W., 157
Henry v. United States, 212
Homant, Robert J., 190–91
Hoover, J. Edgar, 139
Horton, Willie, 156
Hughes, Everett, 8

Illinois, 8, 25, 141, 160
    arrests in, 27, 50, 78
    domestic violence in, 180, 182, 194
    prosecution in, 27, 78–83, 140, 180, 194
    searches and seizures in, 262–63
Illinois Crime Survey, 8, 27, 78–81, 83, 140, 141
Illinois v. Krull, 256–57
Illinois v. Lafayette, 219, 222, 225, 262–63
Indiana, 28
Indiana University, 294
International Association of Chiefs of Police, 41, 47–48, 54
International Association of Police Professors (IAPP), 305–6, 316
International Tribunal on Crimes Against Women, 185
International University, 310
Intoxication, 2, 45, 51, 107, 320, 330, 332
    ABF research, 33, 41
    arrests and, 11, 33, 48–49, 60, 96
IRS (Internal Revenue Service), 259

Jackson, Robert H., 6, 40
John Jay College, 302, 305
Johnson, Lyndon B., 40, 44–45, 288, 294, 306
Jolin, Annette, 195
Justice, U.S. Department of, 100, 111, 191
Justice Statistics, Bureau of, 195, 196

Kadish, Sanford, 12, 282
Kansas, 42
    ABF research in, 4, 6, 7, 9, 12, 86, 176
Kansas City Patrol Experiment, 42
Kennedy, Daniel B., 190–91
Kentucky, domestic violence in, 182
Kerner Report (Report of the National Advisory Commission on Civil Disorders), 181

Kimball, Edward L., 281, 282, 285, 288
King, Martin Luther, Jr., 307
Koh, Steve Y., 158

LaFave, Wayne, 12, 13, 54, 178–80, 184, 186–87, 289
Law Enforcement Assistance Administration (LEAA), 302–3, 306–7
Law Enforcement Education Program (LEEP), 302–3, 307
Lerman, Lisa G., 199
Levi, Edward, 100
Livermore, Joseph M., 41
Llewellyn, Karl, 263–65
Loving, Nancy, 189
Lumbard, Eliot, 289, 291, 293

MacCrate, Robert, 288–90, 292, 293
McGowan, Carl, 214, 260–61
McIntyre, Donald M., Jr., 13
McNulty, Faith, 185
MADD (Mothers Against Drunk Driving), 107
Madison v. United States, 221
Maine, 153
Manhattan Bail Project, 312
Mapp v. Ohio, 215, 281
Marshall, Thurgood, 238
Marshall v. Barlow's, Inc., 226–30
Martin, Del, 185
Martinson, Robert, 152
Massachusetts, 25, 138, 142, 221
Mathias, Bill, 305
Melli, Marygold, 281, 285, 288
Michigan
    ABF research in, 4, 6, 7, 9, 12, 13, 35, 86–94, 96, 105–6, 147, 155, 156, 176, 178–80, 312
    arrests in, 35, 90–91, 178–79
    domestic violence in, 176, 178–80
    prosecution in, 35, 73–74, 80, 86–94, 96, 102, 105–6, 146, 155, 156, 178–80
    sentencing in, 89, 91–92, 94, 102, 105–6, 146, 147, 155, 156

    stops in, 234–36, 252, 253
Michigan Dept. of State Police v. Sitz, 234–36, 251–52, 261
Michigan State University, 295, 304, 305, 310
Miller, Frank W., 13, 100, 179–80, 184, 283, 285
Minneapolis Domestic Violence Experiment, 190–92, 195
Minnesota, 79, 80, 156
    arrests in, 190–91, 195, 196
    domestic violence in, 189–92, 195, 196
Minnesota Coalition for Battered Women, 196
Miranda v. Arizona, 281
Missouri, 8, 42
    arrests in, 27, 78, 80, 85, 140
    prosecution in, 27, 78–81, 85, 140–41
    sentencing in, 140–42
Missouri Crime Survey, 8, 27, 78–81, 85, 140–42
Model Penal Code (American Law Institute), 97
Moley, Raymond, 80–82, 84–85, 96
Moran Institute annual correctional conferences, 291
Morn, Frank, 306
Morse, Wayne, 140
Motor Vehicle Manufacturers Association v. State Farm Mutual Automobile Insurance Co., 253, 254, 256
Mouton, Virgie Lemond, 184
Muir, William K., Jr., 41
Murray, J. Lawrence, 292–93
Myren, Richard A., 294–95, 302, 305–6

National Advisory Commission on Civil Disorders, 181
National Advisory Commission on Criminal Justice Standards and Goals, 100, 215
National Association of College Police Training Officials, 305

National Clearing House on Domestic Violence, 185
National Coalition Against Domestic Violence, 185
National Council on Crime and Delinquency, 324
National Council on Legal Clinics, 283
National Crime Survey of 1978–82, 195
National Crime Survey Report of Criminal Victimization in the United States for 1987 (Bureau of Justice Statistics), 196
National District Attorneys Association, 188
National Highway Traffic Safety Administration (NHTSA), 253
National Institute of Justice (NIJ), 189, 191, 307
National Task Force on Battered Women and Household Violence, 185
National Woman Abuse Prevention Project, 185
Nebraska, 191–92, 195
Newman, Donald J., 12–14, 281, 282, 285, 288, 289
New Mexico, stops in, 247
New York, 26, 290, 298
    arrests in, 196, 254–55
    prosecution in, 80, 81, 84
    searches and seizures in, 254–55
New York Times, 157
New York v. Belton, 243, 254–55
New York v. Burger, 230
Nixon, Richard M., 307
North Carolina, domestic violence in, 191
Northwestern University, 282
NOW (National Organization for Women), 185

Occupational Safety and Health Act (OSHA), 226–27
Office of Manpower and Training, 336

Ohio, 8, 27, 77, 139
    arrests in, 27, 78
    prosecution in, 27, 78–81
Ohio State University, 310
Ohlin, Lloyd, 6, 8–9, 282–84, 294
Omaha Domestic Violence Police Experiment, 191–92, 195
Omnibus Crime Control and Safe Streets Act, 306–7
Oregon, 140, 189
Oregon Crime Survey, 140
Osborne, Thomas Mott, 340
Otis, James, 245

Packer, Herbert L., 10, 11, 95, 97
Park, Robert, 8
Parnas, Raymond I., 15, 54, 283
Parole, 3, 27, 84, 135–37, 143, 145–46, 152–54, 156, 159–60, 162, 283, 285, 290, 321–24, 328, 329, 331, 340
    ABF research, 7, 9–12, 38, 136, 146–51, 159, 161, 163, 164–67, 281, 313
    Illinois Crime Survey and, 141
    Missouri Crime Survey and, 140–41
    statistics, 1, 138–39, 142
    Wickersham Commission and, 141
Parole Commission, U.S., 152
Peel, Robert, 340
Pizzey, Erin, 184–85
Platt, Anthony, 201
Plea bargaining, 14–15, 84–85, 102–3, 107–8, 146, 155
    ABF research, 9, 77, 91, 94, 95, 103, 104–7, 110–12, 151, 156, 329
    Illinois Crime Survey and, 81, 83
    Missouri Crime Survey and, 81
    Wickersham Commission and, 81–82, 84
Police Administration (Orlando W. Wilson), 25, 304
Police and Law Enforcement (Homant and Kennedy), 190–91

Police and Modern Society, The (Vollmer), 26–27, 304

"Police Discretion Not to Invoke the Criminal Process: Low-Visibility Decisions in the Administration of Justice" (Joseph Goldstein), 176–79

Police Executive Research Forum (PERF), 185, 189–90

Policeman and Public (Woods), 26–27

Police Professors Association, 303

Positivist model, 137, 145–46

Pound, Roscoe, 8, 84, 139, 144

Powell, Lewis F., 219, 220, 223, 250

President's Commission on Law Enforcement and Administration of Justice, 40, 44–45, 58, 184, 215, 263, 284, 294

    Challenge of Crime in a Free Society, The, 180–81, 183

Princeton University, 310

Prison Law Project (Harvard), 284

Prisons, 5, 11, 14, 27, 60, 98, 135, 141–43, 145, 153, 154, 157, 159, 160, 162, 187–89, 197, 283–85, 290, 297, 298, 319, 321–22, 325–27, 329–33, 340

    ABF research, 90, 95, 146–47, 156, 312, 313

    statistics, 1–2

Prisons, U.S. Bureau of, 152

Probation, 3, 27, 104, 135–38, 141–43, 157, 159–62, 283, 290, 325, 340

    ABF research, 7, 12, 38, 90, 136, 146–51, 163–67, 313

    statistics, 1, 138, 142

Prosecution, 26, 43, 53, 54, 60, 64, 73–74, 96–97, 99, 100, 157, 285, 325–28, 332

    ABF research, 7, 12, 29, 35, 38, 39, 58, 75–77, 85–96, 98, 101, 103–7, 110–14, 151, 155, 156, 178–80, 313, 329

    Cleveland Crime Survey and, 27, 78–81

    dismissal of cases, 14–15, 27, 50, 78–80, 93, 95–96, 151, 178–80, 186, 188–89, 194

    domestic violence and, 15, 76, 87–88, 113, 175, 177–80, 183, 186–89, 194–202

    Federal Rules of Criminal Procedure, Rule 11 (guilty pleas), 101, 108, 109

    Illinois Crime Survey and, 27, 78, 80, 83, 140

    Missouri Crime Survey and, 27, 78–81, 85, 140–41

    plea bargaining, 9, 14–15, 77, 81–85, 91, 94, 102–8, 110–12, 146, 151, 155, 156, 329

    sex crimes and, 98, 107, 113

    victims' rights movement and, 98, 107

    Wickersham Commission and, 79–82, 84, 85

Prosecution: The Decision to Charge a Suspect with a Crime (Miller; ed. Remington), 13, 179–80

Prostitution, arrests and, 50

Punch, Maurice, 41

Radzinowicz, Leon, 293

Rehnquist, William H., 232

Remington, Frank J., 6, 7, 9, 12–15, 146, 158, 182, 280–82, 285, 288, 289, 292–95

Report of the National Advisory Commission on Civil Disorders (Kerner Report), 181

Rhode Island, probation in, 138

Riddle, Donald, 302, 305–6

Robinson, Louis N., 143

Rockefeller, Nelson, 286–90, 292, 293

Rosenblum, Victor, 282

Rosett, Arthur, 113

Ross, E. A., 8

Rotenberg, Daniel, 13

Rothman, David, 322

Rubinstein, Jonathan, 41

Rutgers—The State University, 310, 321

St. Lawrence University, 291
San Jose State University, 305
Santobello v. New York, 282
Santos v. Kolb, 109
Scott v. United States, 245–48, 250,
    260
SEARCH, project, 331
Searches and seizures
    ABF research, 32, 38
    Supreme Court on, 211–63, 265,
        267, 268
Sentencing, 1–3, 14–15, 84, 96, 100,
    101, 108, 135, 137–38, 145,
    158, 161, 162, 167, 197,
    199–201, 283–84, 319,
    321–29, 332
    ABF research, 7, 9, 10, 12, 38,
        89–95, 104–6, 110–11, 113,
        114, 147–48, 151, 154–56,
        159–60, 164–65, 313
    American Friends Services Com-
        mittee's Working Party report
        and, 152–53
    classical model, 136–37, 139, 143,
        145
    Cleveland Crime Survey and, 139
    congressional statutes and guide-
        lines, 99, 111, 157
    Illinois Crime Survey and, 140
    Missouri Crime Survey and,
        140–42
    positivist model, 137, 145–46
    Sentencing Commission guidelines,
        154–55
    statistics, 142
    Wickersham Commission and,
        144
*Sentencing: The Decision as to Type,
    Length, and Condition of Sen-
    tence* (Dawson; ed. Reming-
    ton), 13
Sentencing Commission, U.S., 154–55
Settling the Facts (Utz), 111
Sex crimes, 2, 11, 45–46, 330, 332
    prosecution and, 98, 107, 113
Sherman, Lawrence W., 190–93
Sherry, Arthur, 6, 289
Skolnick, Jerome H., 41

Small, Albion, 8
Smith, Bruce, 25–26
Smith, Harold A., 6
Social Science Research Council, 282
Society for the Advancement of Crim-
    inology, 305
South Dakota, searches and seizures
    in, 219, 250, 262–63
South Dakota v. Opperman, 219,
    220, 222, 223, 250, 251,
    261–63
State University of New York
    (SUNY) at Albany
    Graduate School of Public Affairs
        (GSPA), 290–92, 294, 299
    Rockefeller College of Public
        Affairs and Policy, 301
    School of Criminal Justice,
        286–303, 305, 310, 311,
        317–18, 321, 323, 326–27,
        336–37
State University of New York at Bing-
    hamton, 287
State University of New York at Buf-
    falo, 287
State University of New York at
    Stony Brook, 287
State University of New York system,
    286–87, 310
Stone v. Powell, 258
Stovall v. Denno, 266
Struggle for Justice (American Friends
    Services Committee), 153
Supreme Court of the United States,
    6. *See also specific cases*
    on arrests, 48, 54, 240–48,
        254–55, 265, 266
    on searches and seizures, 211–63,
        265, 267, 268
Syracuse University, 286, 299

Tennessee, arrests in, 240–41
Tennessee v. Garner, 240–42, 244,
    250, 254–55, 282
Terry v. Ohio, 212, 217, 231,
    236–37, 282
Texas, 102–3, 105, 113

Tiffany, Lawrence P., 13
Tilley, Julie, 196
Toch, Hans, 282, 295
Tonry, Michael, 154, 155

Union College, 310
United States v. Caceres, 259–61
United States v. Cortez, 231–32
United States v. Frank, 220–21
United States v. Guzman, 247
United States v. Johnson, 258
United States v. Leon, 257
United States v. Lyons, 221
United States v. Martinez-Fuerte, 233
United States v. Robinson, 242–45,
     251, 252, 260, 261
United States v. Sokolow, 238–40
University of Buffalo, 293
University of California, 6, 26, 289,
     298, 304, 306
University of Chicago, 6, 8, 9, 28, 308
University of Illinois, 310, 321
University of Florida, 304, 310
University of Maryland, 304
University of Michigan, 73, 235, 282,
     310
University of Pennsylvania, 310, 320
University of South Carolina, 305
University of Texas, 294–95
University of Washington, 305
University of Wisconsin, 6, 12–14,
     135, 280, 281, 283–85, 288,
     289, 291, 294, 297, 303, 310
Utah, probation in, 138
Utz, Pamela, 111, 113
Uviller, H. Richard, 265–67

Vera Foundation, 312
Victims' rights movement, 98, 107
Vollmer, August, 26–27, 304–5
Von Hirsch, Andrew, 153, 321
Vorenberg, James, 284

Warner, Samuel Bass, 27–28
War on Crime, 45, 288, 306–7
Washington University, 285
WEAVE (Women Escaping a Violent
     Environment), 185
Wechsler, Herbert, 97
Weninger, Robert A., 113
Westley, William, 28, 29
White, Byron R., 245
Wickersham Commission (National
     Commission on Law Obser-
     vance and Enforcement), 5, 25,
     26, 77, 79–82, 84, 85, 140,
     141, 144
Wilkins, Leslie, 323, 338–39
Wilson, James Q., 41
Wilson, Orlando W., 25–26, 304,
     306
Wiltberger, William, 304, 305
Wisconsin
     ABF research in, 4, 6, 7, 9, 12, 33,
          86, 87, 89–94, 101, 103–7,
          136, 146–50, 159–61, 163,
          166–67, 176
     arrests in, 90–91, 192–93, 195
     domestic violence in, 176, 191–93,
          195
     parole in, 135–36, 146–50,
          159–63, 167
     prisons in, 90, 135, 146–47, 159,
          160, 162
     probation in, 90, 135–36, 146–50,
          159–64, 166–67
     prosecution in, 86, 87, 89–94,
          101, 103–7, 146
     sentencing in, 89–91, 94, 104–5,
          146–48, 159–62
Woods, Arthur, 26–27
Wyoming, probation in, 138

Yale Law Journal, 158
Yale University, 12, 26, 282, 310
Youngberg v. Romeo, 252